Sephardic Genealogy

Discovering Your Sephardic Ancestors and Their World

SEPHARDIC GENEALOGY

Discovering Your Sephardic Ancestors and their World

by Jeffrey S. Malka

A
Avotaynu, Inc.
Bergenfield, New Jersey
2002

Copyright © 2002 Jeffrey S. Malka

All rights reserved. No part of this book may be reproduced or transmitted in any form or by any means, electronic or mechanical, including photocopy, recording or information retrieval systems, without prior permission from the copyright owner. Brief passages may be quoted with proper attribution.

Requests for permission to make copies of any part of this publication should be addressed to:

Avotaynu, Inc.
155 N. Washington Ave.
Bergenfield, NJ 07621

Printed in the United States of America

Library of Congress Cataloging-in-Publication Data

Malka, Jeffrey S., 1940–
Sephardic genealogy: discovering your Sephardic ancestors and their world / Jeffrey S. Malka.
  p. cm.
Includes bibliographical references and index.
ISBN 1-886223-14-9
  1. Sephardim—Genealogy—Handbooks, manuals, etc. 2. Jews—Genealogy—Handbooks, manuals, etc. 3. Spain—Genealogy—Handbooks, manuals, etc. 4. Portugal—Genealogy—Handbooks, manuals, etc. I. Title.

CS21.M35 2002
929'.1'089924046—dc21

2002026273

To my parents who taught me so much
and for my wife and children
from whom I have learned so much

Contents

List of Illustrations xiv
List of Tables xiv
Preface xv
Acknowledgments xvii
Overview xviii

PART I A LITTLE HISTORY 2
  1. Who Are the Sephardim? 3
  2. Brief History of the Jews of Spain and Portugal 11
      Early Jewish Presence in Spain 11
      Early History (to 711 C.E.) 13
      The Moors (711–1492) 13
      The Golden Age (10th–11th Centuries) 14
      Christian Spain (12th–15th Centuries) 16
      Conversos and Expulsion (12th–15th Centuries) 18
      Spanish Inquisition (15th–19th Centuries) 19
      Portugal's Expulsion 21
      After the 1492 Expulsion 21
      Suggested Reading 22
  3. Spanish Diaspora 25
      1492 Exodus 26
      New Christians or Crypto-Jews? 27
  4. Andalusian-Moroccan Jewish Universe 29
      Jewish Presence in Morocco 30
      Population Exchanges 32
      Linguistic Groups 34
      Berbers and Jews 35
      Jews of Morocco 36
      Foundation of the Golden Age of Spain 37
  5. Jews Under Islamic Rule 39
      Islamic View of the World 40
      Jews and Moslems 41
  6. Jews in The Netherlands 43
      Background 43
      Brief History 44
      Aliases 48
  7. Amazon Journey 49
      Indiana Jones Meets Tangier Moshe 49
      Migration Patterns 49

The Amazon	50
Family Names	51
Suggested Reading	52
8. Geonim	53
Babylonia	53
Geniza	54
Jewish Babylonia	54
The Exilarch	55
Babylonian Academies	55
The Gaon	56
9. Sephardic Languages	58
Hebrew	58
Arabic	60
Judeo-Spanish and Ladino	62
French	67
Berber and Judeo-Berber	68
10. Evolution of Sephardic Names	70
Biblical Era	70
Babylonian Era	72
Roman and Christian Eras	73
Spanish Names	73
Patronymics	75
Jewish Names	75
Individual Names	77
Common Sephardic Naming Conventions	77
Spelling and Acculturation	78
PART II GENEALOGY BASICS	**81**
11. How to Get Started	83
Begin With What You Know	83
Record Your Sources	84
Next Steps	85
How to Interview Effectively	87
Precautions	88
Logs	89
Learn Your History	89
Ethics	90
Suggested Reading	90
12. Sephardic Genealogy	91
Resources Common to Sephardim and Ashkenazim	91
Unique Sephardic Resources	92
13. Organizing and Documenting Records	96

Suggested Filing System for Your Documents	96
Forms and Summary Sheets	97
Documenting Sources	97
Preserving History for Posterity	99
14. Computers and the Internet	100
E-mail	100
Newslists	101
Websites	102
Limitations of the Internet	103
Internet Security and Privacy	103
15. Genealogy Software	104
16. Calendars and Date Conversions	107
Calendars	107
Conversion Tools	109
17. Periodicals	111
Genealogy Periodicals	111
Academic Periodicals on Sephardim	112
General Sephardic Periodicals	112
Avotaynu: Selected Articles	113
Etsi: Selected Articles	121
Revue du Cercle de Généalogie Juive: Selected Articles	124
PART III COUNTRY RESOURCES	**125**
18. Spain	127
Spanish Inquisition	127
Repositories with Inquisition Documents	129
Inquisition in the New World	132
Archivo General de la Nacion (AGN)	132
Archivo General de Indias	133
Notarial and Church Archives	134
Catholic Church Records	135
Ministerio de Cultura Identification	135
Church of Jesus Christ of Latter-Day Saints (Mormons) Records	136
Suggested Reading	136
19. Morocco	140
Archives	140
Other Foreign Connections	143
Vital Records	144
Jewish Community and Records	144
Ketubot	145
Cemeteries	145
Suggested Reading	145

- 20. Algeria 153
  - Archives 153
  - Naturalization Applications 155
  - Jewish Cemeteries 155
  - Place Names 156
  - Suggested Reading 158
- 21. Tunisia 159
  - Brief History 159
  - Grana Community of Tunis 160
  - Archives 161
  - Foreign Connections 161
  - Tunisia 162
  - Suggested Reading 162
- 22. Egypt 163
  - History 163
  - Jewish Records 167
  - Jewish Communities in Small Towns of Egypt 168
  - Library of Jewish Heritage in Egypt 169
  - Cemeteries 169
  - Egyptian Civil Records 170
  - Montefiore Censuses 170
  - Egyptian Diaspora 170
  - Sources Outside Egypt 171
  - Internet Resources 171
  - Suggested Reading 171
- 23. Sudan 174
  - Jewish Archives 175
  - Sudan Jewish Cemetery 176
- 24. Turkey and the Ottoman Empire 177
  - Modern Turkey 177
  - Ottoman Government 177
  - Sephardim in Turkey 178
  - Istanbul 180
  - Turkish Imperial Archives 181
  - Research Requirements 181
  - Turkish Script 182
  - Turkish Calendar 182
  - Genealogical Resources 183
  - Jewish Records 183
  - Cemeteries 185
  - Civil Records 185
  - Salname 186

Suggested Reading	186
25. The Balkans	188
Bulgaria	188
Genealogical Resources	190
Yugoslavia	191
Genealogical Resources	192
Salonica	194
Synagogues	195
Genealogical Resources	197
Suggested Reading	198
26. Italy	203
History	203
Research Strategies	205
Vital Records	206
Church of Jesus Christ of Latter-day Saints (Mormons)	207
Censuses	207
Jewish Records	208
Notarial Records	208
Other Records	209
Italian Script	209
Websites	209
Suggested Reading	209
27. The Netherlands	220
Records and Archives	220
Resources in The Netherlands	221
Civil Records	221
Jewish Records	221
Websites	224
Israel Resources	224
Suggested Reading	225
28. Iraq	226
History	226
Far-East Interlude	227
Genealogical Resources	227
Suggested Reading	228
29. Iran (Persia)	229
Genealogical Resources	232
Suggested Reading	232
30. Syria	233
History	233
Genealogy Resources	233
Suggested Reading	234

- 31. Caribbean 236
  - Curaçao, St. Eustatia and St. Maarten 236
  - Jamaica 237
  - St. Croix, St. Thomas, and Nevis 238
  - Suggested Reading 239
- 32. South America 242
  - Argentina 242
  - Brazil 243
  - Suggested Reading 245
- 33. United States 247
  - Genealogical Resources 248
  - Naturalization Records 249
  - Passenger Ship Records 250
  - Census Records 250
  - Jewish Records 251
  - Suggested Reading 252

PART IV INTERNET **253**
- Jewish Genealogy Websites 255
- Sephardic Websites 255
- Anusim or Crypto-Jews 257
- Balkans, Turkey, Greece 257
- Caribbean 258
- Egypt 259
- France 259
- The Netherlands 260
- Iraq and Syria 260
- Israel 261
- Italy 261
- Mexico 262
- Morocco 262
- North Africa 262
- South America 263
- United States 263
- Sephardic Family Pages 264
- Gazetteers 265
- People Search Pages 265

APPENDIXES **267**
- Appendix A. Etymology of Selected Sephardic Names 269
- Appendix B. Sephardic Cursive Alphabet 276
- Appendix C. Arabic Alphabet 278

Appendix D. Sephardic Documents at the Central Archives for the History of the Jewish People ... 280
Appendix E. Sephardic Register and Record Books at the Jewish National and University Library ... 281
Appendix F. Genealogy Forms ... 282
Appendix G. Jewish Names in Printed Sources ... 287
Appendix H. Moslem Calendar ... 296
Appendix I. Ottoman Records in Israel ... 297
Appendix J. Inquisition Tribunals in Spain ... 304
Appendix K. Tombstone Inscriptions from Small Egyptian Towns ... 305
Appendix L. Surnames & Synagogue Affiliations in 16th-Century Salonica ... 309
Glossary ... 317
Bibliography ... 319
Surname Index ... 334
Index ... 355

List of Illustrations

Figure 1. Spain, 711–1030 8
Figure 2. Spain at the Death of Alfonso VIII, 1214 9
Figure 3. Spain, 1212–1492 10
Figure 4. Sephardic/Ashkenazic Population Trends Through the Centuries 24
Figure 5. Sephardic Script: 20th-Century *Ketubah* 69
Figure 6. Sephardic Script. 19th-Century Letter of Introduction 69
Figure 7. Biblical Naming Pattern 80
Figure 8. Similarities between Roman and Jewish Name Constructions 80
Figure 9. Differences between Ashkenazic and Sephardic Genealogy 95
Figure 10. Resources for Sephardic Genealogy 95
Figure 11. Jewish Settlements in Morocco 148
Figure 12. Makhzen-Controlled Morocco, 19th Century 149
Figure 13. Fragment of Casablanca Cemetery List 150
Figure 14. Sephardic Family Tree 151
Figure 15. Egyptian Passport Application from 1919 172
Figure 16. Map of the Ottoman Empire in Europe, 1574 199
Figure 17. Map of the Ottoman Empire in Europe, 1813 200
Figure 18. Map of the Balkans after World War I 201
Figure 19. Modern Italy: Regions and Provincial Capital Cities 211

List of Tables

Table 1. Jewish Population Shifts 24
Table 2. Synagogues in 16th-Century Salonica 195
Table 3. Italian Provinces and Archival Addresses 212
Table 4. Selected Sephardic Surnames: Variants, Languages, Meanings 269
Table 5. Recent Sephardic Hebrew Scripts 277
Table 6. Ottoman Census and Population Records 297
Table 7. Locations and Dates of Spanish Inquisition Tribunals 304
Table 8. Surnames and Synagogue Affiliations in Salonica in the 16th Century 309

Preface

In the 1990s I helped my father edit his memoirs, an endeavor that fueled my growing interest in knowing more about my family history and its roots.[1] I soon discovered that despite the availability of abundant information and advice for researching Eastern European roots, little information and guidance existed about methods and country resources to research my Sephardic ancestry. None of the Internet's websites devoted to Sephardic topics dealt in depth with genealogy, and books on Jewish genealogy skimmed through the subject—if they mentioned it at all. In the mid-1990s, as I gained experience in researching my own Sephardic roots, I created an extensive website to share my information with others.[2]

By the late 1990s I saw interest in Sephardic genealogy increase; discourse grew about genealogy in online Sephardic newslists, the first periodical specifically for Sephardic genealogy appeared, and several other excellent websites began to develop Sephardic genealogy content.[3] Yet, in responding to readers of my website, I found myself repeatedly providing the same replies to the same basic questions concerning Sephardic ancestry. The need became clear for an English-language book that would make information on researching Sephardic families more easily available.

My hope is that this book launches many Sephardim on their search for ancestors—and thus creates incentives to develop more knowledge in the field. As more researchers become involved in the search, more resources inevitably will surface. This is not an unrealistic wish. It was not so long ago that Ashkenazic Jews were in the same position, even feeling that it would be impossible to search for their roots in the aftermath of war-devastated Europe. Now the lists of archives useful for uncovering Eastern European roots fill several books, with more information becoming available almost daily. The same will be true for genealogy in the countries where Sephardim lived, once sufficient interest is aroused.

The reader may note that there are countries for which extensive discussion of genealogical information is not presented. Despite an abundance of historical writings for these countries, including for example, Iraq and Syria, unfortunately little data exists currently about available resources for genealogical research. I

---

[1] Eli Malka, *Jacob's Children in the Land of the Mahdi: Jews of the Sudan* (New York: Syracuse University Press, 1997).
[2] Resources for Sephardic Genealogy, www.orthohelp.com/geneal/sefardim.htm.
[3] In 1998, *Etsi: Revue de Genealogie et d'Histoire Sefarades*, the first periodical on Sephardic genealogy, appeared in France, and websites such as Sephardic Studies (www.sephardicstudies.org) appeared in 2002.

hope that this book will stimulate the search for additional information about these countries that would then be included in future editions. The author welcomes contacts from readers with corrections or additions to the materials in this book.

Jeffrey S. Malka, M.D.
July 2002

Acknowledgments

First, I would like to acknowledge my 93-year-old father, Eli S. Malka, who has been both an inspiration and a source of knowledge without which writing this book would not have been possible. I am also grateful to my friend and wife, Susan, who, despite battling her own doctoral dissertation deadlines, still found time to help and advise me in writing this book. Her patience and support are greatly appreciated.

Other people who have helped with suggestions, encouragements, information, and ideas over the years are Philip and Laurence Abensur, who have taught me so much about Moroccan and Turkish genealogical resources; Mathilde Tagger, whose unselfish help and enthusiasm for Sephardic genealogy are models I attempted to follow; Laurence Feldman, who introduced me to Inquisition and Spanish archives; and Schelly Dardashti, for her help with Persian Jewish history and genealogy.

My editor, Irene Saunders Goldstein, deserves special mention. Her judicious and expert review of the manuscript has markedly improved the original's clarity and legibility and encouraged me to improve the content. My publisher, Gary Mokotoff's support and advice during the preparation of the book rendered the entire process a pleasurable event.

I was fortunate to have unlimited access to the Library of Congress and the libraries of the University of Maryland and George Mason University. I am grateful to their helpful and knowledgeable staffs. Their extensive resources supplemented my own library and were essential for both research and documentation of the book.

Overview

Researching Sephardic genealogy is similar in many ways to researching genealogy in general. But sufficient differences exist, in history, resources, and languages, to warrant compiling the special information necessary for a successful search of Sephardic ancestry. This book provides many of the necessary resources and tools for both the beginning genealogist and the more advanced researcher.

Sephardic genealogy and knowledge of resources are still in their infancy. As was true in Eastern Bloc countries until relatively recently, little is known about Sephardic Jewish material in the archives of many countries. Hints of available information sources hide buried in obscure and hard-to-find books. Isolated researchers independently discover narrow resources of value in the search for their own specific ancestry. Many resources remain to be discovered and catalogued, but much is known and available now. Yet for the person researching Sephardic ancestry, it can be a time-consuming task to determine where or what is available. This book presents most of the known resources.

Divided into four parts plus appendixes, this book serves as both a reference and a tutorial. Part I presents background and basic history necessary to underpin Sephardic genealogy research. After all, genealogy is history reflected in the lives of our ancestors. The paths of their lives reflected events large and small—from wars and migrations to economic upturns and downturns, trade routes and opportunities, and local attitudes towards Jews—as much as family feuds and love affairs.

Chapter 1 discusses the definition of Sephardim. Because of the important role Spanish Jewry played among Sephardim, a history of the Jews of Spain and Portugal is provided in chapter 2. Not all individuals known today as Sephardim had ancestors who lived in Spain. They, too, have fascinating histories of their own. Some of these histories are presented in the chapters on their resources.

Chapter 3 points out the many facets and varying histories of the Spanish and Portuguese Jews who left Spain in the centuries before or after the 1492 expulsion as they dispersed throughout the Iberian diaspora. The Andalusian-Moroccan universe, that common cultural, intellectual, and historical sphere that existed between North Africa and Moorish Spain during the Golden Age of Spain in the 10th and 11th centuries, differed greatly, both culturally and linguistically, from the world of the Jews in Christian Spain. This Spanish-North African universe is described in chapter 4. Also described are the early pre-expulsion exoduses, mostly to North Africa (see chapter 4, Andalusian-Moroccan Jewish Universe); the 1492 exodus to Portugal (see chapters 2 and 3) and throughout the Mediterranean (see chapters 20–22 and 24–25); and the later post-expulsion exodus of *conversos* (Jews who converted to Christianity) to Europe, the New

World, and elsewhere (see chapter 6, The Netherlands, for example). Sephardic Jews lived for long periods under Islamic rule; chapter 5 helps the reader understand the environment in which they lived. The Sephardic migration to the Amazon is a less-known episode of Sephardic history, described in chapter 7.

Chapter 8 describes the period of the Babylonian sages or *geonim*, whose teachings and writings formed one of the common glues that bound Sephardim together.

A researcher in Sephardic genealogy should be familiar with the languages Sephardim spoke and in which many of their records are written; chapter 9, Sephardic Languages, serves this purpose. Ancient Sephardic surnames can be useful clues in Sephardic genealogical research. An extensive discussion of the development of Sephardic and other Jewish surnames is found in chapter 10, Evolution of Sephardic Names.

Part II presents the fundamentals of good genealogical research: methodology, record organization, source documentation, and the use of computers in genealogical research. This section is aimed at the beginning genealogist and can be safely skipped by experienced genealogists, except for chapter 17 which presents information useful for advanced researchers.

Chapter 11 describes how to get started. Chapter 12 explains the similarities and differences in researching Sephardic and Ashkenazic ancestry. Chapter 13 discusses the rules of valid genealogy research; organization and documentation of records is discussed in chapter 14. Chapter 15 discusses the advantages, limits, and dangers of computers and the Internet, and chapter 16 describes software available for genealogical record keeping. The calendars used in Sephardic host countries (Julian, Gregorian, Jewish, Moslem, Ottoman civil, and other Moslem civil calendars) are explained in chapter 17, and tools for converting dates between them are presented.

A review of specialized periodicals of interest to Sephardic genealogists is presented in chapter 18 along with a list of useful articles.

Part III describes records and other resources for most countries where Sephardim have lived. Starting with chapter 19 on early Spanish records, including Inquisition and early Spanish ship passenger records, subsequent chapters describe the countries around the Mediterranean from North Africa to Italy, The Netherlands, Turkey, the Balkans, Iraq, Syria, Iran, the U.S. and beyond.

Part IV explores Internet resources and provides an extensive list of websites, categorized by country and topic. One section describes websites devoted to specific Sephardic families.

Several appendixes include lists of Sephardic surnames found in the literature and a description of origins and meanings of numerous Sephardic surnames and their most common variants. Additional appendixes provide a variety of useful genealogy forms and planning tools to organize and facilitate documenting research. There are also examples of Arabic and Sephardic Hebrew script, Moslem and Turkish calendars, a list of Spanish Inquisition tribunals and the areas they covered, and 16th-century Salonican synagogues and their member families.

At the end of the book is a glossary and an extensive bibliography intended to provide the researcher the tools and means to further his or her knowledge in specific geographical regions or periods of additional interest.

Part I
A Little History

1.
WHO ARE THE SEPHARDIM?

Sefarad is the Hebrew word for Spain. Or is it? In her study of the etymology of Sefarad Mathilde Tagger notes[1] that, as a place, Sefarad is first mentioned in the Bible by the prophet Ovadia (Obadiah) who lived around 540 B.C.E.[2] At that time, however, the area now known as Spain and Portugal was referred to as Ispamia, not Sefarad. Ovadia, therefore, was not referring to Spain when he used the word Sefarad. To this day scholars are unsure of the exact location of Ovadia's Sefarad. Studies have suggested that the biblical Sefarad may have been the town of Saparda or Sardis, located near Izmir in present-day Turkey. In contrast, *Ispamia* is described in the Talmud as being "at the end of the world," the common definition at the time for the Iberian Peninsula. Even today, the northwest coast of Spain bears the name Cape Finisterre, or cape at the end of the world.

Over time, however, Sefarad did come to mean Spain, and thus in the strict linguistic sense of the word, Sephardim (singular, Sephardi) are the Jews who came from the Iberian Peninsula. Indeed, there are some Sephardim who feel strongly that the designation Sephardim should refer solely to the descendants of Jews who lived in Spain. Even more specifically, they insist that only those whose ancestors were physically present and expelled from Spain in the year 1492 and whose descendants have continued to speak Judeo-Spanish[3] at home should be referred to as Sephardim.[4]

---

[1] Mathilde Tagger, "Sefarad: Une etymologie." *Etsi* 1, no. 1 (1998): 3.
[2] Ovadia 1:20: "the Jerusalemite exile community of Sefarad shall possess the towns of the Negev." *Tanakh: A New Translation of the Holy Scriptures according to the Traditional Hebrew Text* (Philadelphia and Jerusalem: Jewish Publication Society, 1985).
[3] The Judeo-Spanish dialect is composed of a blend of 15th-century Catalan, Castilian, Turkish, and Arabic spoken in Turkey, the Balkans, and Morocco. This language was spoken mainly by the Jews of the Eastern Mediterranean. See chapter 9, Sephardic Languages.
[4] This restrictive view is particularly prevalent among the Sephardim of Turkey and the Balkans who maintain a strong identification with Spain. Many Sephardim of Turkey and the Eastern Mediterranean descend from Jewish refugees who, when expelled from Spain in 1492, found safe haven in the Ottoman Empire. This Eastern Mediterranean group of refugees probably was third in number only to those Jews who in 1492 sought refuge in Portugal, and to the totality of Spanish Jews who went to North Africa in the centuries before and after the edict that expelled Jews from Spain in 1492. They are also those who have the most assiduously preserved old Hispanic culture and customs.

Although there may be some semantic validity to this view, considerable difficulties invalidate it. For instance, Maimonides is considered to be one of the greatest sages and philosophers to have arisen among Spanish Jewry and one whose writings defined much of Sephardic thinking. Though

But the definition is not that simple. The Jews of Spain were an integral part of the cultural and religious world of Jews who lived largely under Islamic rule and had developed customs, philosophy, and liturgy different from the Jews who lived in Christian Europe (Ashkenazim). Just like the word Sefarad, whatever its original meaning, came over time to mean Spain, the term Sephardim has taken on a much broader meaning. Today Sephardim includes Jews from communities in North Africa, Iraq (formerly Babylon), Syria, Greece, and Turkey, most of whose ancestors may never have been in Spain.

Indeed, Rabbi Marc Angel of the Sephardic-Portuguese Synagogue of New York City describes a Sephardic Jew as "almost any Jew who is not Ashkenazic."[5] The American Sephardic Federation defines the term Sephardic Jew as including "Jews whose country of origin is Syria, Morocco, Yemen, Iraq, Turkey, Greece, and Iran."[6] The rationale behind this broad definition of Sephardim is a multifactorial blend of common cultural, philosophical, and theological values, such as language, literature, cuisine, and modes of dress.

Religiously, the definition was cemented after a controversy that occurred in the 15th–16th centuries. It was then that the Sephardic mystic theologian Rabbi Yosef Caro (1488–1575) wrote the *Shulchan Arukh*, a compendium of Jewish traditions and beliefs held by Sephardim.[7] Caro intended to produce a work acceptable to Jews of all countries and traditions; therefore, he tried to be as inclusive as possible. But the influential Polish rabbi and scholar Moshe Isserles dissented. Isserles believed that many of the traditions and customs described by Caro differed from those followed by Ashkenazim. Isserles responded by writing his own commentaries, noting the differences where applicable.[8] From that time on, Jews who followed Rabbi Caro's *Shulchan Arukh* (or who descended from families that did) have been known as Sephardim, while Jews who followed Rabbi Isserles's teachings and traditions have been referred to as Ashkenazim.[9]

---

born in Cordoba (1135 C.E.), even Maimonides could not be included in the narrow definition of a Sephardic Jew because in his teens, centuries before 1492, Maimonides left Spain for Morocco and Egypt and wrote primarily in Arabic. Furthermore, Maimonides did not speak or write Ladino, a language that evolved largely in the Eastern Mediterranean area after the 1492 expulsion. Also excluded would be the large number of Spanish Jews who, when conditions deteriorated for Jews in Spain, left Spain in the three centuries preceding 1492, especially after the 1391 massacres, going mostly to the more hospitable neighboring lands of North Africa, where the conditions and culture had comforting familiarity.

[5] Sarina Roffe, "The Term Sephardic Jew." See www.jewishgen.org/sefardsig/sephardic_roffe.htm.
[6] American Sefardic Association. See www.asfonline.org/portal/ASFAbout.asp.
[7] *Shulchan Arukh* means "dressed (or prepared) table." The term symbolizes a table where all has been set in its proper place.
[8] Isserles's work is known as the *mapah*, or "table cloth," figuratively to be placed on the *shulkan arukh* of Caro.
[9] Religiously, *Sephardim* all follow the Babylonian traditions and the Babylonian Talmud, which originated in what is now Iraq, from where it spread to all the communities of the Sephardic world, both in Spain and elsewhere. Daniel Elazar noted that even the basic order of Jewish prayer, the *siddur tefila* of

For the genealogist, the broader, more inclusive definition of Sephardim makes more sense. When the Iberian Jewish exiles settled around the Mediterranean Basin from where some of their ancestors had originated, over time some families intermarried with the local Jews, who in turn were culturally influenced by and adopted Spanish traditions. Genealogically speaking, it is a rare Jew in the Mediterranean area whose family tree does not include Spanish exiles or their descendants.

Throughout the Sephardic world, including the Judeo-Spanish–speaking communities of Salonika (Greece) and Turkey, are Sephardic families with such names as Ashkenazi, Madjar (Hungarian), Russo (Russian), Tedesco (German), and Sarfati (French). These families are evidence of the integration of descendants of Ashkenazic families who had lived in Sephardic communities and adopted Sephardic traditions, and, thus acculturated, had become fully accepted Sephardim by the Sephardic communities in which they lived. Families with surnames such as Mizrachi and Hamizrachi identify Eastern (Asian) Jews absorbed into the Sephardic majority. Even surnames that suggest direct Iberian origin might in fact originally have been Ashkenazim absorbed into the Sephardic world as these families changed their names. For instance, genealogist Morris Bierbrier found evidence in the French archives that the Bianco Sephardic family originated in Vladimir, Poland, and that the original name may have been Weiss—an example of a direct translation of a surname—both Bianco and Weiss mean white.[10]

The word *Ashkenazic* also has taken on a broader meaning. Though the Hebrew *Ashkenaz* means German, the term has come to include not only German Jews, but also Jews of Eastern Europe and Russia, whether or not they had links to Germany. Here, too, Jews from areas such as Spain and North Africa settled among the Ashkenazic communities, adopted their customs, and "became" Ashkenazim. Even such classic Sephardic family names as Abrabanel have been found as family surnames in traditionally Ashkenazic countries.

When the Spanish Jewish exiles arrived in the eastern Mediterranean after 1492, they found there a Jewish population of ancient Romaniot (Greek Jews from the Byzantine Empire) and Ashkenazic Jews. Those Ashkenazic Jews were recent immigrants who had fled European pogroms to find haven under the rule

---

Rabbi Amram, reached the Jews of Barcelona in response to a query they posed the Babylonian *geonim* (Daniel Elazar, *The Other Jews: The Sephardim Today* (New York: Basic Books, 1992). Ashkenazim, the Jews who lived in Christian Europe, on the other hand, separated and largely isolated from Sephardim by geographical and political reasons, were influenced primarily by the Palestinian traditions. Until just before the exile from Spain, Babylonia, North Africa, and Spain were essentially one world with constant communication and, through most of that period, a common Arabic language. Scholars moved back and forth throughout the Sephardic sphere, and it was for all purposes a single intellectual world.

[10] Morris Bierbrier, "Tracing Ancestors in Italy and Turkey." In "Syllabus: 21st International Conference on Jewish Genealogy" (London: JGS 2001 Limited, 2001).

of the more tolerant Ottoman Empire. The Spanish exiles culturally dominated the other Jews they found in the eastern Mediterranean, and some of the local Romaniot and Ashkenazic Jews who had preceded them were absorbed into the Spanish exiles' cultural world.[11]

In contrast, the Spanish exiles who fled to the Maghreb (western North Africa) found themselves numerically overwhelmed by the greater number of local Jews whom the exiles found there. In the Maghreb it was the local Arabic-speaking Jewish populations that absorbed many of the exiles. This created a combined culture that, with the exception of small Moroccan enclaves such as those in Tetuan and Tangier, did not speak Judeo-Spanish.

Then there are the Spanish Jews who in the centuries after 1492 fled to Western Europe or to the Americas. They too did not speak Judeo-Spanish. Instead, because they maintained cultural and trading contacts with Spain, Portugal, and Holland, they spoke contemporary Portuguese, Spanish, or Dutch.

To further understand who is a Sephardic Jew, it is important to know that the Jewish population of Spain (what the Moors called "*al Andalus*") was not homogeneous. During the seven centuries of Moorish occupation, beginning in 711 C.E., the Jewish population of Spain was reinforced by large numbers of Jews from Morocco, Egypt, and elsewhere in North Africa, with whose communities contact was constantly maintained. The early grammarians and poets of the Spanish Golden Age were Jews imported from the North African Talmudic academies of Morocco and Kairouan (near the ruins of Carthage) to teach and found the Spanish academies of learning. Among these were Yehuda Hayyuj (Abu Zachariya Yahya ben Daoud el Fasi), teacher of Abulwalid Merwan ibn Janah the Jewish grammarian of Cordoba; Dunash ben Labrat, who introduced the Arabic poetry meter into Hebrew poetry; Daoud ben Abraham El Fasi El Qarai, who published a dictionary in Jerusalem in 930–950 C.E.; Dunash ben Tamim, philosopher and grammarian; Jacob bar Dunash and Adonim bar Nissim ha Levi, noted poets, and others. And these were only the early luminaries. Later came others such as Rabbi Alfasi (1013–1103 C.E.), invited, at the age of 83 to teach in Spain, where he lived for another decade.

All the famous Golden-Era Jews had Arabic or Hebrew names, spoke and wrote in Arabic and Hebrew, and had little knowledge of Spanish. In fact, Spanish did not exist yet as a language, and its dialects were then spoken by the Jews in the small, culturally backward and largely illiterate, unconquered northern Iberian rim still under Catholic control.[12] Without generalizing, because

---

[11] See for instance Vicky Tamir, *Bulgaria and Her Jews: The History of a Dubious Symbiosis* (New York: Sepher-Hermon Press, for Yeshiva University Press, 1979), pages viii, 58, and 65.

[12] Examples of some Golden-Era Jews are Hasdai ibn Shaprut, the noted physician and chief vizier of the Cordoban caliphs Abd el Rahman III and Al Hakam II; Samuel ibn Nagrila ha Nagid (the prince), poet, military commander in chief and vizier to the emirs of Granada and possibly designer of the Alhambra; Ibn Ezra, the great poet; Moshe ben Maimon (Maimonides); and others.

there are exceptions, Hispanic-sounding Jewish surnames such as Rodriguez, Henriques, Ramirez, de Soto, Dacosta, and others originated much later among the oppressed Jews of Iberia who were forced to convert to Catholicism. Notable exceptions are some surnames derived from places, such as Toledano (from Toledo) or names of plants, such as Perera and Olivera..

Today the distinctions between Sephardim and Ashkenazim have become primarily those of differing traditions, customs, and languages. In large part because of their histories, religious Sephardim follow the Babylonian Jewish customs and Caro's *Shulchan Arukh*, while Ashkenazim follow the Palestinian tradition accessed via Italy and Isserles's teachings. Differing languages (Judeo-Spanish and Judeo-Arabic on one side, and Yiddish and Polish on the other), differing religious melodies and liturgy during religious services, differences in festival traditions, and different Hebrew pronunciations are among the factors that distinguish Sephardim from Ashkenazim—although they are minimal, compared to the great similarities between these two major branches of the same Jewish family.[13]

As a final note, the researcher of Sephardic history and genealogy occasionally comes across the terms *nusach sepharad* and *minhag sepharad*. *Nusach sepharad*, which translates roughly into Sephardic version, refers to a liturgy used by Ashkenazim that incorporates certain elements from the Sephardic liturgy; *minhag sepharad* is the actual liturgy or custom used by the Sephardim. Rabbi Isaac Luria (1534–1572), who became known by the acronym ARI, was an Ashkenazic mystic who first included some Sephardic elements into Ashkenazic prayer. The *nusach sepharad*, or *nusach ARI*, as it also became known, later was adopted by the Baal Shem Tov, founder of the Hassidic movement of Ashkenazic Jewry, and his successor, the Maggid of Mezhirech. Today it is used by several Hassidic groups, which are, of course, not Sephardim.

This terminology could be a source of confusion when a researcher searches through ancestral prayer books. Some Ashkenazic prayer books might denote that they follow the *nusach sepharad* or the *nusach arizal*. That does not mean that they are Sephardic prayer books or Sephardic communities whose prayer books would indicate instead that they follow the *minhag Sepharad*. But, it obviously can be confusing. Similarly *anshei sphard* (or *sephard*, or *sfard*) synagogues are not Sephardic, but rather Ashkenazic congregations that use the *nusach sepharad* Orthodox liturgy.

In contrast, Cervantes in *Don Quixote* illustrates the sad state of literacy among Christian Spaniards. When one of his characters is asked whether he could read, the character replies in indignation, "What do you take me for? I am a Catholic gentleman."

[13] H.J. Zimmels discusses some of these differences in more detail in *Ashkenazim and Sephardim* (Farnborough, England: Gregg International Publishers, 1969).

Source: Joseph F. O'Callaghan, *A History of Medieval Spain* (Ithaca, N.Y.: Cornell University, 1975).

Figure 1. Spain, 711–1030

Source: Joseph F. O'Callaghan, *A History of Medieval Spain* (Ithaca, N.Y.: Cornell University, 1975).

Figure 2. Spain at the Death of Alfonso VIII, 1214

Source: Joseph F. O'Callaghan, *A History of Medieval Spain*. Ithaca, N.Y.: Cornell University, 1975.

Figure 3. Spain, 1212–1492

2.
BRIEF HISTORY OF THE JEWS OF SPAIN AND PORTUGAL

Meaningful genealogical research is not possible without knowing something of the history and geography of both the period and the areas researched. Knowledge of history can set in context ancestors' moves and actions; it also can suggest clues to where and how to search for additional information. Furthermore, historical knowledge is one of the best by-products of genealogical research, in that it makes the names and individuals come to life and provides a meaningful pastime while waiting for the next archival response to arrive or the next discovery breakthrough to happen!

Because the history and culture of the Jews of Spain are so central to an understanding of the Sephardic world, it is essential to be familiar with their experience. This chapter covers the history of the Jews of Spain from their earliest times to the expulsion of 1492.

EARLY JEWISH PRESENCE IN SPAIN

Most historians believe Jews first came to the Iberian Peninsula with the Roman legions between 200 B.C.E. and 200 C.E., possibly as merchants, purveyors or Roman slaves.[1] The earliest tangible evidence of a Jewish presence in Spain are the third-century C.E. grave in Abdera (today Adra in Almeria) of a young Jewish girl named Salominulla[2] and the fourth-century tombstone in Tortosa of Molliosa, daughter of R. Judah and Kyra Mirriam.[3] A second wave of Jews came to North Africa and Spain following the destruction of the second temple in Jerusalem in 70 C.E.[4]

In contrast to the view held by historians, legends passed down through generations of Spanish Jews tell of Jews who first came to Iberia (and elsewhere in the Mediterranean region) after the destruction of the first temple in Jerusalem in

---

[1] Jane Gerber, *The Jews of Spain: A History of the Sephardic Experience* (New York: Free Press, MacMillan, 1992).
[2] Jose Amador de los Rios, *Historia Social, Politica y Religiosa de los Judios de Espana y Portugal* (Social, Political and Religious History of the Jews of Spain and Portugal) (Madrid: Ediciones Turner, 1984): 68–9. See also Jewish Encyclopaedia, *Spain* (New York: Funk and Wagnalls, 1901-06).
[3] Haim Beinart, "The Jews in Castile". *The Sephardi Legacy* (Jerusalem: Magnes Press, 1992).
[4] Gerber, *Jews of Spain*.

the sixth century B.C.E.[5] Still other legends date the arrival of Jews with Phoenician merchants in the 10th century B.C.E., during the era under King Solomon when Jews spread throughout the Mediterranean coastline.[6] Some Spanish Jewish families (including Ibn Daoud, Shaltiel, and Abrabanel) claim direct descent from King David. To bolster their claims, they point to the prophecies of Ovadia, who used the name Sefarad for the land in which he prophesized Jews exiled from Jerusalem would live.[7] And some biblical scholars claim that Tarshish of the Bible was probably ancient Tartessus, a district of southern Spain whose principal city was Gades (Cadiz).[8]

Historian Norman Roth points out that at their peak, more Jews lived in Spain than in all the countries of Europe combined.[9] Historians have calculated that in the 12th century C.E., Sephardim constituted 90 percent of all the world's Jewry, though that percentage declined rapidly after that period and as the Ashkenazic population exploded in the 17th–19th centuries C.E.[10] (see Table 1 and Figure 4). Unlike Jews in Europe in the 12th century C.E., who lived mainly in large towns, Jews in Spain were found both in towns and in tiny villages among the Spanish peasants.

Chaim Raphael observes that most Jewish history until the last few centuries—starting with Abraham in Ur (Iraq), through Joseph and Moses in Egypt, the kingdoms of Israel and Judea, back to Babylon, then to Spain and the Mediterranean—has been largely the history of the Jews of Middle Eastern and Mediterranean culture, the culture associated today with Sephardic Jews.[11] Until the 15th century C.E., Sephardim constituted the bulk of Jewry and the main population and academic centers of Judaism. Beginning in the 16th and 17th centuries, though, European Jewry exploded into prominence in both culture and population; Sephardic Jews, like their host countries, entered a cultural decline that is only recently beginning to reverse itself. Similarly, in the religious sphere, most of the books central to both Ashkenazim and Sephardim were the products of Sephardic sages. Among these are such fundamental theological books as the Babylonian Talmud, *Mishnah Torah*, *Shulchan Arukh*, *Meam Loetz*, *Pele Yoetz*, *Sefer ha Halachot*, *Sefer Mitzvot*, *Sefer Zohar*, *Sefer Kuzari*, *Sefer Yesirah*, and *Sefer Merkabah*.

---

[5] Beinart, *Jews in Castile*.
[6] Gerber, *Jews of Spain*.
[7] It is by no means clear that the Sefarad of Ovadia meant Spain. See chapter 1, Who Are the Sephardim?
[8] Gerber, *Jews of Spain*.
[9] Norman Roth, *Conversos, Inquisition, and the Expulsion of the Jews from Spain* (Madison: University of Wisconsin Press, 1995).
[10] Daniel J. Elazar, *The Other Jews: The Sephardim Today* (New York: Basic Books, 1992).
[11] Chaim Raphael, *The Road from Babylon: The Story of Sephardi and Oriental Jews* (New York: Harper & Row, 1985).

Early History (to 711 C.E.)

The relatively tolerant, *laissez-faire* atmosphere prevalent in the crumbling Roman Empire's province of Hispania shattered in 409 C.E., when the Visigoths poured into Iberia from their western German homeland. The invaders, intolerant of anyone who did not adhere to their Arian Christianity (see glossary), ruthlessly killed and plundered minorities for much of the three centuries they ruled Iberia. Romans who witnessed this slaughter commented that the Iberian countryside resembled an open-air morgue.

Christianity was the central focus of the Iberian Visigoth state. Jews in particular were persecuted mercilessly for remaining true to their faith and thus denying Christ. What remained of the sciences and arts that survived from the Roman period were denounced and abolished. Trade and culture plummeted, and a dark age descended on the Iberian Peninsula.

At the end of the sixth century, Visigoth King Reccared converted to Catholicism and established his new faith as the state religion. The Church grew to become a significant political power, and its officials frequently played a major role in deciding who would ascend to the throne as king. In 638 the Visigoths declared that only Catholics could live in Spain, a statement reasserted and implemented many centuries later with the 1492 expulsion of Jews from Spain. The Catholic Visigoths outlawed the Jewish religion. Jews were sold into slavery and their properties confiscated. Large numbers of Jews fled to neighboring Morocco. Jews who stayed practiced their religion in strict secrecy.

The Moors (711–1492)

In April 711 Tariq ibn Ziyad (*el Moro*) landed at Gibraltar.[12] Commanding a small army of Berbers from Morocco, a quarter of whom were Moroccan Jews, Tariq is said to have promptly burned the fleet of ships that transported them across the straits. In a rousing speech, he told his troops that with only the waters at their rear, they had nowhere to go but forward. The Moors routed a much larger Visigoth army under King Rodrigo, and by 712, the Moors had reached the Visigoth capital of Toledo, which threw open its gates to the invading army.[13] The Moors soon ruled all but a small northern slip of the Iberian Peninsula, and *al Andalus* (Moorish Spain) came into existence.

The Moors' rapid conquest was fueled in part by the generous terms they offered the towns they besieged, which contrasted dramatically with the Visigoths' harsh

---

[12] The name Gibraltar is a corruption of the Arabic *Jebel al Tariq* (Tariq's mountain). The rock at the southern tip of the Iberian Peninsula forms one of the mythical Pillars of Hercules, the other being a mountain across the straits in Morocco.

[13] Estimates of the Moors' army vary from as few as 7,000 to as many as 120,000. However, the fact that 25 percent of the force was Jewish is consistently reported in historical accounts of the period.

rule. As he approached Toledo,[14] Tariq stated that anyone who wished to leave the city could do so, but those who elected to stay could retain their property, practice their religion freely, and be governed by their own rules and laws—but be subject to taxation.[15] To the Jews so cruelly oppressed by the Visigoths, this offer was like a promise of paradise.

There have been unsubstantiated suggestions that disgruntled members of the oppressive Visigoth kingdom may have invited the Moors into Iberia. Others suggest that the conquest was quasi-accidental, in that Tariq, on a limited expedition, unexpectedly defeated King Rodrigo. This good fortune led Tariq to change plans, call for reinforcements, and proceed further into the peninsula.

With the Moorish conquest, Spanish Judaism re-entered the cultural, linguistic, and political world of the Jewry of the Orient and North Africa. Spanish Jews renewed their knowledge of Torah and Talmud that had severely eroded during the centuries of Visigoth oppression. The Spanish Jews' relationship was particularly close with the Jews of Morocco, from where, in fact, a significant part of the Spanish Jewish population had originated.[16] The Moorish conquests in 711 meant that by the eighth century, 90 percent of all Jews lived under Islamic rule (see Table 1). Records from the Cairo *geniza* show that Jewish merchants traveled freely and widely through a huge Islamic world that extended from Baghdad and Damascus in the east to Spain in the west.[17] They traveled with little regard to what are now considered national borders. Freedom of mobility enabled Jews to travel by both land and sea from the Mediterranean to the Indian Ocean to participate in the silk and spice trade, and in the trade of Persian rugs and pearls from the Gulf of Arabia. Even more importantly, it permitted cultural exchanges throughout an immense geopolitical and scientific universe, resulting in an exceptional blossoming of the arts and sciences.

THE GOLDEN AGE (10TH–11TH CENTURIES)

The Ummayad dynasty ruled Moorish Spain for the next century. Many subsequent Moorish rulers, but not all, maintained a tolerant, multicultural atmosphere that respected and protected minorities, encouraged science and the

---

[14] Genealogists researching Toledo should be aware that the city was known to its inhabitants as *Tolitola* in both Arabic and Hebrew. The 13th-century astronomer Rabbi Ishak Aben-Zaquet Metolitola (Rabbi Isaac ben Zacot of Tolitola) is also known as Rabbi Isaac Toledano. See Don Jose Amador de los Rios, *Historia social, politica y religiosa de los Judios de Espana y Portugal* (Social, political, and religious history of the Jews of Spain and Portugal) (Madrid: Imprenta de T. Fortanet, 1875). See also Jewish Encyclopaedia, *Spain* (New York: Funk and Wagnalls, 1901–06).

[15] Islam decreed that idolaters were to be given a choice between death and conversion. The people of the Bible (Christians and Jews), however, were to be tolerated but made uncomfortable, so they would wish to see the light and convert. Special taxes were imposed on them as part of this "encouragement." See chapter 5, Jews under Islamic Rule.

[16] See chapter 4, Andalusian-Moroccan Jewish Universe, for a discussion of this close relationship.

[17] For more information about the Cairo *geniza*, see chapter 8, Geonim.

arts, and invited scholars from afar to come to Spain and serve the caliph. Flowery poetry in Arabic and Hebrew flourished, and poems were recited at languorous evening wine parties, while the other arts and sciences similarly prospered. In their desire to reproduce the elegant, cultured courts of Baghdad, Iberian caliphs far exceeded them in the end.

Moors, Christians, and Jews lived and worked together in this tolerant atmosphere. Many Christians adopted some of the Moors' culture; they became known as *mozarabs*. Spanish Jews joined the many Jews who had come to the Iberian Peninsula with the Moors and similarly adopted Moorish customs. The Jews studied Arabic and the Koran, and the Moors studied Hebrew and Jewish scriptures. In a quest for old knowledge, the Greek philosophers' original writings were eagerly sought and studied. Learned Jewish and Arab scholars translated Greek works into Arabic and Hebrew, and Jewish scholars translated them into Latin—thus setting the stage for the 14th-century European Renaissance.

Amid the fervor of intellectual curiosity and study, Jewish scholars developed the theories that created trigonometry. Moors and Jews invented algebra. Map making was a Jewish science. Arabic numbers replaced unwieldy Roman numerals.[18] The eastern Moslems learned papermaking from the Chinese, and paper was soon manufactured in Spain, for the first time in Europe. Immense libraries developed and were opened to the public. Cordoba's library in the 11th century is noted to have had a million volumes, at a time when the largest library in Europe held a mere dozen manuscripts. Eighth-century Baghdad had a street with one hundred booksellers.

Jewish philosophers studied Plato and Aristotle and developed new philosophies incorporating the Greek philosophers' theories with Jewish theology and thinking. Prominent among these Jewish philosophers was Maimonides (1135–1204),[19] who was influenced by the Arab philosopher Averroes. Maimonides' writings aroused controversy and criticism, however, from the narrowly traditional Jewish religious authorities, particularly of France and Germany. His use of reason and logic to seek deeper understanding and accommodation with the world in which he lived, rather than tradition and blind faith, was not acceptable to the orthodoxy of the northern Jews of France and Germany. Maimonides was instrumental in the use of contemporary reasoning rather than blind tradition for adhering to Jewish traditions. In his *Guide to the Perplexed*, he showed that someone exposed to Aristotelian rationality could find reason to accept ancient theological mysteries. He attempted to understand

---

[18] The inhabitants of India invented Arabic numbers, but the Arabs were the intermediaries who brought them to Europe—hence the name.
[19] Maimonides, Moshe ben Maimon, also was known by the acronym RAMBAM (Rav Moshe ben Maimon).

Chapter 2: Brief History of the Jews of Spain and Portugal • 15

ancient religious requirements in the context of his time—hence the term rational Judaism that became the hallmark of Sephardic Judaism.

Solomon ibn Gabirol, Moses ibn Ezra, and Judah ha Levi wrote exquisite poetry, and Moses ibn Ezra and many others wrote grammar and mathematical treatises. Interest in Arabic grammar sparked the development of Hebrew grammar, transforming Hebrew into a medium able to handle the new concepts and terminology of the evolving sciences and arts.

One shining personality from that golden era was Hasdai ibn Shaprut (915-970 C.E.). A famous Jewish physician, Hasdai rose to become the personal physician and chief advisor to the caliph and his chief tax collector. Hasdai used the great wealth he acquired in charitable acts: he founded rabbinical institutes, purchased Talmuds, and built synagogues. He recruited noted scholars from Morocco to Spain to expand the Hebrew language and to develop its syntax and vocabulary, a development that then permitted Hebrew to be used in science and in the wonderful Jewish poetry of Andalusia.

During this tolerant era, Jewish refugees fleeing persecution in Christian Europe flocked to Spain—much as they later did to Poland, Turkey, and in more modern times to the United States. Even educated Christian scholars seeking further erudition moved to Andalusia; some converted to Judaism. In the eighth and ninth centuries, thousands of Jews from Morocco and Egypt also migrated to Moorish Spain.

Actively engaged in trade, Spanish Jews were the main Andalusian importers and exporters of silk, leather, textiles, grain, fruit, spices, and cattle.[20] Jewish travelers such as Benjamin of Tudela left records of travels even more extensive than those of Marco Polo; traveling in 1165 to 1173, Benjamin reached China a century before Marco Polo.[21]

Communication and interchange flowed between Jewish communities throughout the Mediterranean, from North Africa to Baghdad and Damascus, to the Ashkenazic centers of Europe. Evidence for this extensive traffic in letters, goods, and travelers was clearly demonstrated by the 19th-century discovery of numerous ancient documents in the Cairo *geniza*, including a letter written in Maimonides' own hand.

CHRISTIAN SPAIN (12TH-15TH CENTURIES)

When the Catholics undertook the long reconquest of Spain, they did so under the pretext of ridding the land of the heathen Moors and their decadent

---

[20] Maimonides came from a merchant family. His brother's loss at sea on a family trading voyage forced Maimonides to resort to earning a living from medicine, since his ethical principles did not permit him to earn money from theology. Leon Roth, *The Guide for the Perplexed: Moses Maimonides* (London: Gainsborough Press, 1948).

[21] See Elkan Nathan Adler, *Jewish Travellers in the Middle Ages* (New York: Dover Publishers, 1987) for an array of first-hand accounts.

multicultural ways. After all, Christianity could not be the *one* true religion if non-Christians refused to accept it. But throughout the centuries of association with the Moors, the early Christian Spaniards had grown accustomed to intercultural exchange and had become equally tolerant of minorities. During the Christian reconquest of Spain, which took four centuries to complete, broad-minded, multicultural attitudes persisted for a while, especially among the early Christian rulers who saw value in perpetuating a system that had created so much prosperity for them. Indeed Alfonso VI of Castile, who took Toledo from the Moors in 1085, proudly named himself "emperor of the three religions."

This liberal attitude displeased the papal authorities; they frowned on the easy socialization between Christians and non-Christians. A number of 11th-century popes, from Gregory VII on, sent several edicts and bulls urging Christian monarchs to deal more harshly with their Jews and Moslems. The papal authorities sent French and other troops to assist the Spanish reconquest and deal more harshly with the enemy than the Christian Spanish troops were apt to do.

The reconquest was a lot murkier than one might think. Spanish historians rewrote history to transform their most prominent captain *el Cid* into an idealized hero fighting to restore Christianity, thereby creating a needed national rallying symbol. *El Cid* was in reality a particularly able mercenary (like many others in his day) who fought at times for the Christians and at others for the Moors. He ended by carving out for himself a personal kingdom in Valencia.[22] Even Christian kings at various times allied themselves with Moslem rulers against fellow Christian kingdoms, and vice versa, as regional power struggles played themselves out. Jewish battalions with distinctive uniforms fought in both the Christian and Moslem armies.

The continued tolerant coexistence of the religions in Spain remained abhorrent to papal authorities, especially in the 12th century, when the Christian monarchs gained control of most of Iberia. By the 14th century, events took a turn for the worse for the Jews. Periods of drought and bad crops preceded the Black Plague, which killed almost half of Spain's inhabitants and a third of the population of Europe. Christians accused the Jews of poisoning wells and blamed them for the plague. Throughout Christendom, religious fanatics whipped into murderous frenzy by traveling, self-flagellating Catholic monks and preachers massacred Jews by the thousands. At first these massacres occurred less often in Spain than in neighboring France and other parts of Europe, but gradually the old Visigoth heritage and thinking resurfaced, transforming Spain from the most tolerant nation in Europe into the country most intolerant of its minorities.

---

[22] Rodrigo Diaz de Vivar (1043–1099) was known by both Moors and Spaniards as *el Cid*. *El Cid*, Arabic for "the leader," was the name originally given to him by the Moors and immortalized in *Cantar de Mio Cid*, a 12th-century posthumous epic poem about his exploits. See O'Callaghan, *A History of Medieval Spain*.

CONVERSOS AND EXPULSION (12TH-15TH CENTURIES)

As the Catholics took over Spain and oppression of non-Christians grew, many Spanish Jews converted to Christianity. Many of these *conversos* converted voluntarily out of true conviction; these converts often became in time the most zealous persecutors of the Jews. Many more Jews converted merely as a gesture, because it was beneficial to their careers or position in court, but otherwise it meant nothing to them. Thousands of other Jews went to their deaths, condemned to burn at the stake for refusing to abandon the faith of their parents and to accept conversion. Tragic stories abound about families condemned to burn alive; mothers threw their children into the fire before jumping to follow them—to avoid the abduction and forced conversion of their children. Other Jews were the victims of forced conversions—the *anusim*—especially in 1497 in Portugal. These forced converts often clung to their Judaism in secret; they became known as crypto-Jews.

In 1391 vicious riots broke out, in Seville, Valencia, and other Spanish cities, in which thousands of Jews died. Preachers such as Ferrer roamed the country, stirring up mobs that looted and terrorized Jews. A forced debate was staged in 1431 between learned Jews and the convert Jeronimo de la Santa Fe (né Joshua Harlorki), who, two years after his conversion, had risen in stature to become chief lieutenant to Pope Boniface XIII. The debate was staged to prove conclusively that Jesus was the Messiah and was of course duly declared to have done so.

The combination of the debate, restrictive laws, and recurring persecutions resulted in great demoralization of Spanish Jewry; thousands accepted baptism. Crown and Church encouraged members of the Jewish aristocracy in particular to convert, because they needed the Jewish aristocrats to continue in their traditional roles as councilors to the government. Since the Jewish aristocracy was largely secular at the time, great numbers accepted baptism—but they continued to practice their old Jewish traditions, such as lighting Sabbath candles and not eating pork. Jewish aristocrats married extensively into the historic but impoverished Spanish nobility, to whom the Jews' wealth was a great asset. Theater and print parodies appeared calling *conversos alboracos,* from the legend of Alborak, the magic steed that transported Mohammad to heaven and was said to be "neither a horse nor a mule." The joke in the parodies was that *conversos* were called *alboracos* because they were neither Jews nor Christians.[23]

The Catholic clergy found it useful to divert their impoverished and oppressed population's attention to "the Jewish problem," and convinced themselves and others that if Jews were converted to Catholicism, Spain's problems would be over. But the over-taxed, economically deprived peasantry, envious of the Jews' economic and social success, experienced no improvement in their living conditions

---

[23] See H. Pflaum, "*Une ancienne satire espagnole contre les marranes*" (An ancient Spanish satire against the marranos), *Revue des Etudes Juives* 86 (1928): 131-150; and Haim Beinart, "The Great Conversion and the Converso Problem", *The Sephardi Legacy* (Jerusalem: Magnes, 1992).

following the conversions. Gradually the populace's anger with their monarchs, which had been deflected to their surrogates—the Jewish tax collectors—extended properly to the rulers themselves, especially following the rule of a pair of particularly ineffective monarchs and a civil war between feuding half-brothers.

SPANISH INQUISITION (15TH–19TH CENTURIES)

The interesting details of how Isabella maneuvered to become queen of Castile and chose to marry Ferdinand of Aragon in October 1469, instead of the elderly king of Portugal, are beyond the scope of this book but well worth looking up because of the insights provided into their characters. As queen of Castile, Isabella took over a lawless kingdom with a defiant nobility, widespread banditry, impoverished royal coffers, and openly debauchious clergy. Within four years of her ascension to the throne in 1474, she had established order and central authority in all of these problem areas. Her marriage to Ferdinand (the model for Machiavelli's prince) combined the states of Aragon and Castile and forged the most powerful state in 15th-century Europe.

Isabella was not initially anti-Semitic, but devout and under the influence of her confessor, Torquemada, himself of *converso* origin, Isabella learned to hate heretical behavior. When Dominican priests convinced her that many *conversos* retained their Jewish behavior or beliefs, as indeed many did, Isabella agreed to institute in 1480 the Inquisition in Seville and subsequently in other cities. That her coffers were empty and that the *conversos* were among the wealthiest and most powerful group in the land only added advantage to the decision. The war Isabella planned in order to conquer the last Moorish kingdom of Granada required large amounts of funds, which the Inquisition conveniently provided.

Although initially a primarily religious exercise, the Inquisition rapidly became racial. *Limpieza de sangre,* purity of blood, became the issue—despite the Jewish background of King Ferdinand's own *converso* grandmother. The nobility, most of whom had intermarried with *conversos,* were terrorized and impotent against the power of the Inquisition and the Crown. Little proof was needed to accuse someone of judaizing; thus one could simultaneously prove one's own piety and settle old scores.

Many *conversos* were extremely prominent, wealthy, or powerful in government. Many were intermarried with the highest nobility. The *conversos* could not at first believe that the Inquisition could affect people of their station, but they were tragically mistaken. The Inquisition, backed by the monarchy, was too powerful to stand against. Inquisitors encouraged hundreds of *conversos* to accuse others of judaizing as a way to possibly save themselves from the flames. Sometimes for reasons as trivial as wearing clean clothes on Fridays, the accused were taken during the night without warning and not seen again until the public *auto-da-fe,* during which officials imposed punishment. Under torture, confessions came readily. Property was confiscated; part going to support the Inquisition, part to the queen, and part to build churches and monasteries. The range of punishments included being burned alive, which would nominally allow the inquisitors to avoid the "shedding of blood." Others had hands severed before being burned or quartered. Mercy was shown to those who repented by strangling them before burning. The lucky ones were deprived of all their property, prohibited to hold government or other offices, and ordered to wear a *sanbenito*—a garment of penance—for the rest of their lives. After death such a person's *sanbenito* was prominently displayed in the local church as a perpetual reminder and warning. Some *sanbenitos* still hang in Spanish churches today.

Aware that many *conversos* did in fact practice Judaism in secret, the authorities ordered rabbis and other Jews to report any Jewish activities of *conversos* or suffer death themselves. If *conversos* were considered heretics, unconverted Jews were thought to be the root cause of the heresy. The Jews were to be removed to avoid contaminating good Catholics. The old blood libel—Jews murdering Christian children and using their blood in observance of Passover—was resurrected. Quotes from the gospel of John, in which he stated that Jews were the children of the devil while Christians were the children of God, were used to demonize Jews.

In 1490 a 19-year-old Jew, Yuce (Josef) Franco, his 80-year-old father, Ca (Isaac), together with a number of *conversos*, were accused by the Inquisition of having murdered a Christian boy and having used his heart in magical spells against Christianity. No crime date was given; no child had been reported missing; no one ever found a body ("it went to heaven with his soul"); and the confessions obtained under torture did not correlate. Nevertheless, the accused were burned alive in November 1491. The accusation of both Jews and *conversos* was not accidental. The case was publicized throughout Spain and used to build up momentum for expelling the Jews. Over time details and names were added to the story and a church was consecrated to the "*nino santo*" (sainted child)—who had never actually existed.

In 1492, immediately following the fall of Moslem Granada to Isabella's army, the monarchs signed the expulsion edict. Jews were to leave Spain within two months or embrace Catholicism. The expulsion edict prohibited Jews from taking gold and jewels out of Spain. Catholics were forbidden to receive Jewish property. It was, therefore, confiscated by the state. Thousands of Jews hurriedly submitted to baptism. Large numbers of others fled to Portugal, where, for the payment of 100 *cruzados* each, King Joao II allowed them temporary sanctuary for eight months. Others left for North Africa or France. Within two days of the expulsion deadline, Christopher Columbus embarked on his first journey to the New World on ships manned largely by *conversos*.[24] Jewish cemeteries in Spain were plowed under and synagogues destroyed or converted to churches or pigsties.

---

[24] Some suspect that Columbus might have been a crypto-Jew. Some clues they cite: When

The 1492 edict of expulsion remained in force and was not repealed until 1968. The *limpieza de sangre* racial laws that excluded descendants of *conversos* from jobs and academies also remained in force, some well into the 20th century. Many individuals discovered their *converso* ancestry only when they were refused certain jobs after a mandated genealogical search.

Spain's and Portugal's Inquisitions spread to their colonies, where many of the *conversos* had fled. The Inquisition continued for 350 years into the 19th century. Its last victim was a woman burned at the stake in 1821, allegedly for fornicating with the devil and producing eggs that prophesized the future.

Portugal's Expulsion

In 1497 Portugal expelled its Jews, too. Isabella and Ferdinand's only son had died, and Manuel I of Portugal, who had visions of inheriting the throne of Spain, wished to improve his chances by marrying the Spanish royal princess Isabella. To allow the marriage to proceed, the Spanish monarchs insisted that Manuel expel all his Jews. Reluctant to take this step, Manuel invited the Jews to come to Lisbon's harbor, where they would be allowed to board ships out of Portugal. Instead soldiers forcibly abducted and converted the struggling Jews. In some cases the children were forcibly abducted and converted, and their parents given the dire choice of converting or abandoning their children. Some children were abducted and given to Portuguese families who would bring them up as proper Catholics. Other children were sent away from their parents to islands on the coast of Africa. Crypto-Jews continued to exist for generations in Spain, Portugal, the Balearic Islands, South America, Mexico, New Mexico, and other places, where some can be found to this day.[25]

After the 1492 Expulsion

The travails of Spanish Jews as they sought refuge wherever they could and their identification for generations after the expulsion with the land that had so ill-treated them, but that they still considered home, is a unique and fascinating story. Deprived of their possessions, often murdered on ships for whatever little they had left, their travels took them to North Africa, Italy, the Ottoman Empire whose

---

Columbus wrote to his family, he included the Hebrew letters *bet hay* (*Bezrat HaShem*, with the help of God) in the upper corner. He never did so when writing to others or in official letters; in another letter he wrote: "David, that most prudent king, was first a shepherd and afterward chosen King of Jerusalem, *and I am a servant of that same Lord that raised him to such dignity*"; his date calculations are based on the Jewish calendar: "from the destruction of the Second Temple according to the Jews to the present day, being the year of the birth of our Lord 1481, are 1413 years"; Colombo is a common Italian Jewish name. See Howard Sachar, *Farewell España* (New York: Vintage Books, 1995).

[25] Albuquerque, New Mexico, was built by Alfonso de Albuquerque, governor of Portuguese India and a Portuguese of *converso* origin. His grandson, Luis de Carjaval y de la Cueva, gave the city its name in memory of his grandfather.

sultan welcomed them, and the frontier edges of the New World.[26] In Spain's and Portugal's New World possessions, the *conversos* and crypto-Jews moved further and further to the edges of civilization in their attempt to flee the Inquisition—which followed them wherever it could.

The story of the crypto-Jews in the New World, in Portugal and Spain, in Majorca, and elsewhere, some of whom retained the memory of their Judaism over five centuries and who only marry among other crypto-Jewish families, is another fascinating chapter in the history of Sephardic Jews, as is the history of the Inquisition in the New World. The bibliography at the end of the book lists several books that tell more of that story.

The impact of Sephardic Jews was significant wherever they settled, both in cultural and economic development. Their participation in both Spanish and Portuguese travels of exploration by Christopher Columbus, Francisco de Albuquerque, Luis Caravajal, and others, was profound. Their acknowledged preeminence in map making and navigating led to their serving as ship navigators on most Portuguese and Spanish ships, usually as new Christians. The Iberian exiles who settled in Moslem lands tended to share the cultural decline of the countries in which they resided. Others, mostly in The Netherlands and the New World, prospered and grew to new heights of prosperity and cultural development. The involvement of Moroccan Jews in the development of the Amazon and its rubber trade is another intriguing, but little known, chapter in the history of these Sephardim. The impact of Sephardic Jews in the development of Holland as a worldwide banking and sea-going world power is a similarly interesting saga.

But there is no place in this short book to do this vast story justice. The interested reader is encouraged to read some of the books listed below to learn more of this epic story.

SUGGESTED READING

Adler, Elkan Nathan. *Jewish Travellers in the Middle Ages*. New York: Dover Publishers, 1987.

Alexi, Trudi. *The Mezuzah in the Madonna's Foot: Marranos and Other Secret Jews*. New York: Simon & Schuster, 1993.

Ashtor, Eliyahu. *The Jews of Muslim Spain*. Philadelphia: Jewish Publications Society, 1993.

Baer, Yitzhak. *History of the Jews in Christian Spain*. Philadelphia: Jewish Publication Society, 1993.

Elnecave, Nissim. *Los Hijos de Ibero-Franconia* (Sons of Iberia-Franconia). Buenos Aires: Ediciones La Luz, 1981.

---

[26] The Ottoman sultan is reputed to have said, "If the Spanish sovereign is foolish enough to expel his Jews, his loss will be our gain."

Gerber, Jane. *Jewish Society in Fez 1450–1700: Studies in Communal and Economic life*. Leiden, The Netherlands: E.J. Brill, 1980.

Netanyahu, Benzion. *The Origins of the Inquisition in XIV Century Spain*. New York: Random House, 1995.

———. *The Marranos of Spain: From the late 14th to the early 16th century*. Ithaca, N.Y.: Cornell University Press, 1999.

Paris, Erna. *The End of Days*. Amherst, N.Y.: Promethius books, 1995.

Roth, Cecil. *The Spanish Inquisition*. New York: W.W. Norton & Company, 1996.

Sachar, H.M. *Farewell Espana: The World of the Sephardim Remembered*. New York: Vintage Books, 1995.

Zafrani, Haim. *Juifs d'Andalousie et du Maghreb* (Jews of Andalusia and the Maghreb). Paris: Maisonneuve & Larose, 1996.

Zimler, Richard. *The Last Kabbalist of Lisbon*. Woodstock, N.Y: Overlook Press, 1998.

Jews in Roman Empire:
  25% of Roman population in eastern Mediterranean
  10% of entire Roman Empire

48 C.E. Roman Census:
  7 million Jews (mostly in Judea, Egypt, Syria, Asia, Yemen, Ethiopia)
  8 million Jews (estimated total worldwide)

Sephardim:
  12th century C.E.   90% of world Jewish population
  1700 C.E.   50% of world Jewish population

Percentage decrease as Ashkenazim exploded in population:
  1930   10% of world Jewish population
  1990   25% of world Jewish population
          60% of Israel's population

Table 1. Jewish Population Shifts

Sources: Jane Gerber, *Jewish Society in Fez 1450–1700: Studies in Communal and Economic Life* (Leiden: E. J. Brill 1980); Israeli Central Bureau of Statistics (1982); Daniel J. Elazar, *The Other Jews: The Sephardim Today*. (New York: Basic Books, 1992); Norman Roth, *Conversos, Inquisition, and the Expulsion of the Jews from Spain* (Madison: University of Wisconsin Press 1995).

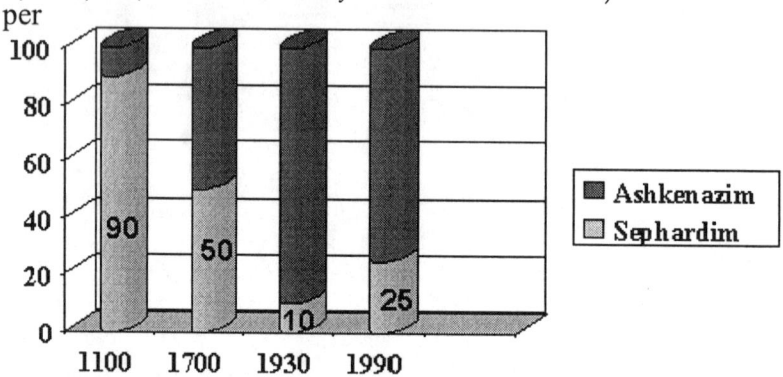

Figure 4. Sephardic/Ashkenazic Population Trends Through the Centuries

Sources: Jane Gerber, *Jewish Society in Fez 1450–1700: Studies in Communal and Economic Life* (Leiden: E. J. Brill 1980); Israeli Central Bureau of Statistics (1982); Daniel J. Elazar, *The Other Jews: The Sephardim Today*. (New York: Basic Books, 1992); Norman Roth, *Conversos, Inquisition, and the Expulsion of the Jews from Spain* (Madison: University of Wisconsin Press 1995).

3.
SPANISH DIASPORA

Because of deteriorating living conditions and increased danger, many Jews left Spain during the two centuries before the 1492 expulsion order, and, as *anusim* (forced converts) or New Christians, for centuries after that date, too. Historians have estimated that one million Jews resided in Spain in 1391.[1] But a full century before the 1492 expulsion edict, as murderous riots spread northward through Spain, Jews fled Christian Spain. Jews from as far north as Catalunya, Valencia, and Majorca fled to North Africa; most went to Algeria. Even before 1391 Jews had left Spain for safer havens—as did Maimonides, among many others—mostly to North Africa, especially nearby Morocco. Commercial and other traffic between North Africa and the Iberian Peninsula was frequent and common (chapter 4, Andalusian-Moroccan Jewish Universe).

By 1492, because so many Jews already had fled to Moslem Granada or North Africa, many Spanish towns had a much-reduced Jewish population left to expel. In 1492 the large and proud Jewish community of Gerona in northern Spain had become so depleted that only a few Jews remained in the surrounding principality of Barcelona.[2] In discussing the myths of a romanticized and idealized Spain, Benbassa and Rodrigue estimate that no more than 50,000 Jews left Spain in 1492 because so many Jews had fled earlier.[3] In his extensive study of Spanish archives, Hinajosa Montalvo notes that in the kingdom of Valencia (the present-day provinces of Castellon, Valencia, and Alicante), the 1391 riots caused such a massive flight of Jews that due to deaths, emigration, and conversions, only about a thousand Jews remained to be expelled from the kingdom in 1492. This, Hinajosa Montalvo remarks, was a tiny proportion of the previous Jewish population; the rest, including the majority of those Jews who previously had converted to Catholicism, already had fled clandestinely to either the Cordoba caliphate or to North Africa. The Jews' flight was clandestine because the authorities vigorously attempted to prevent the loss of that population. Jews in land-locked regions such as Castile fled to coastal areas such as Valencia from

---

[1] Jane Gerber, *The Jews of Spain: A History of the Sephardic Experience* (New York: Free Press, Macmillan, 1992).
[2] Haim Beinart, *The Expulsion of the Jews From Spain* (Portland, Ore.: Littman Library of Jewish Civilization, 2002). See also Vicky Tamir, *Bulgaria and Her Jews: The History of a Dubious Symbiosis* (New York: Sepher-Hermon Press, for Yeshiva University Press, 1979).
[3] Benbassa, Esther, and Aron Rodrigue, *Sephardi Jewry: A History of the Judeo-Spanish Community, 14–20th centuries* (Berkeley & Los Angelos: University of California, 2000).

which to board ships, or they went south to the Moslem-controlled regions of Iberia.[4]

A decade before the 1492 expulsion edict, there had been an earlier expulsion order. This one, issued in January 1483 by the Inquisitional fathers of Seville and the Diocese of Cordoba, gave all Jews in their area one month to leave Spain. Affecting an estimated 4,000 households (20,000 individuals), the edict was soon joined by similar edicts affecting all the cities of Christian Andalusia.

1492 EXODUS

Of the Jews expelled from Spain in 1492, the largest number, fully one third of all the exiles, went to Portugal. To obtain permission to enter Portugal and stay for a limited time, Portugal's king exacted a payment for each person crossing the border. Just five years later they were faced again with the choice of conversion or expulsion from Portugal. Instead of being allowed to leave on promised ships, they were forcibly converted *en masse* in Lisbon harbor. Some of their children were abducted and given to Catholics for a proper upbringing. Still other abducted Jewish children were sent to the desolate island of San Tome off the coast of Africa, where many of them died.

The second largest group of Spanish exiles went to North Africa, mostly to Morocco. On the journey, many passengers were tossed overboard by ship captains or stranded and left to die on Moroccan beaches. Those exiles who survived the trip settled mainly in the towns of northern Morocco, but they also filtered throughout the country, which, due to massacres and oppression, had a much-diminished Jewish population. A small number of the Spanish exiles who went to North Africa in 1492 went to Algeria and Tunisia. In contrast to the blending of segments of the two Jewish populations in Morocco, in Tunisia the local indigenous Jewish population maintained their separation from the Spanish exiles until well into the 20th century.

A third group, which settled in the Ottoman Empire, was second in numbers only to the Jews who went to Morocco. Earlier the Turkish sultan had uprooted the Jews of Salonica to populate his newly conquered Constantinople (Istanbul). Therefore many Spanish Jews were instructed to settle in the now depopulated Salonica, as well as in other Ottoman territories where they were needed. Thus Salonica, whose population ultimately became 90 percent Jewish, became essentially a Jewish city, a major Sephardic center—which perished almost entirely during the Nazi Holocaust.

Some exiles from eastern Spain sought refuge in Italy (see chapter 24 on records in Italy and how to find them). Many exiles sailed to Genoa, where they were refused permission to land. They sailed subsequently from port to port.

---

[4] Jose Hinojosa Montalvo, *The Jews of the Kingdom of Valencia: From Persecution to Expulsion, 1391–1492* (Jerusalem: Magnes Press, Hebrew University, 1993).

Some finally were allowed to land in Naples, only to be expelled again soon afterwards. Many ended up settling in the Papal States, especially in Rome, creating a large Sephardic presence in that city.

A smaller group of 1492 exiles went to Eretz Israel.[5] These Jews settled mostly in Safed, at the time a larger commercial center than Jerusalem and thus more attractive to the exiles who needed to earn a living. An even smaller number of Jews from northern Spain fled to Navarre. There a few years later, they were again forced to choose between exile and conversion; having no exile route open to them, they had no recourse but to convert.

The Inquisition was established in Spain in 1478, and later also in Portugal. The resulting constant risk of being accused of judaizing made life much more precarious for New Christians, even if they intended to be truly Christian. Many, therefore, sought to leave before having to defend themselves in an Inquisitional tribunal. New Christians gradually left during the ensuing centuries, going to places such as Antwerp and Frankfurt, and later Amsterdam, Italy (Livorno, Pisa, and Venice), and the Ottoman Empire. Others went to the New World among the *conquistadores*[6] and settlers, where they spread throughout the Caribbean and North and South America. A small number even reached Eastern Europe (the town of Zamosc in Poland is a notable example), usually arriving as traders from the Ottoman Empire.

NEW CHRISTIANS OR CRYPTO-JEWS?

Were the Jewish converts to Christianity true Christians or were they crypto-Jews? This question has raged for centuries and probably will always be a focus of debate. Some scholars, including Baruch Spinoza and the noted historian Bension Netanyahu, believed they became true Christians to the best of their abilities and soon lost all traces of Jewishness.[7] Other scholars, such as Beinart and Kamen, asserted that they were crypto-Jews holding tenaciously to their Jewishness and what fragments of their Judaism they could retain.[8] Common sense dictates that the truth lay not only between these two views, but probably along a broad spectrum, the view of most modern historians. It stands to reason that the majority of *conversos* fell among the many shades between a full embrace of Catholicism and secret, active retention of their Judaism.[9] Many must have

---

[5] *Eretz Israel* is Hebrew for the Land of Israel.
[6] *Conquistadores* were the Spanish and Portuguese adventurers conquering the New World territories.
[7] Bension Netanyahu, *The Marranos of Spain: From the Late 14th to the Early 16th Century according to Contemporary Sources* (Ithaca, N.Y.: Cornell, 1973).
[8] Haim Beinart, "The Great Conversion and the Converso Problem" *The Sephardi Legacy* (Jerusalem: Magnes, 1992); Mark R. Cohen, *Under Crescent and Cross: The Jews in the Middle Ages* (Princeton, N.J.: Princeton University Press, 1994).
[9] See Renee Levine Melammed, "Some Death and Mourning Customs of Castilian Conversos,"

even varied in these attitudes through their lives as people of all faiths vary in their attention to religion through their lives even today. The Amsterdam community (chapter 6, Jews in The Netherlands) had the experience of New Christians who adopted Judaism, only to return to Catholicism, sometimes several times in their lives.

It would be foolhardy to lump all *conversos* into one descriptive basket. No doubt some embraced their new faith fully. And no doubt many, especially among the Portuguese forced *conversos*, clung desperately to the faith of their fathers and did all they could to teach it secretly to their children. Most *conversos* probably simply tried to survive as best they could in very dangerous times.

Exile and Diaspora (Jerusalem: Ben Zvi Institute, 1991) describing findings from Inquisition trials.

4.
ANDALUSIAN-MOROCCAN JEWISH UNIVERSE

The history of the Jews of Spain is often discussed as if this Jewish community existed in isolation. Of course, that was not the case. The Moors who conquered Spain in 711 brought with them large numbers of Jews, and Jewish life in southern Spain, or Andalusia, was largely an extension and mirror of Jewish culture in Morocco. Moroccan Jews, who had accounted for 25 percent of the invading Moorish armies, flowed in large numbers into Andalusia after the conquests. Jews in Andalusia and Morocco constantly communicated not only with each other, but also with Jews throughout the Mediterranean, a vast area that lay within the Moslem world. Haim Zafrani, the foremost expert on Andalusian and Moroccan Jewry, writes that Morocco was an integral part of what he calls the "two parallel societies" and discusses the "15 centuries of a culturally and historically inseparable entity of Andalusian-Moroccan society."[1] Zafrani asserts that the Golden Age of Sephardic Jewry was a product of the symbiotically twined cities of Fez and Cordoba, Ceuta and Lucena, Tetuan and Granada; of two parallel societies with identity of situations in all the domains of social, economic, and religious life.[2]

Jews in Morocco and in Moslem-ruled Andalusia shared a common culture. Jews in both societies spoke Arabic, the international language of the sciences and the intelligentsia, although Jews often wrote the language using Hebrew letters. Maimonides wrote all his works in Arabic, using Hebrew script,[3] except for his *Mishneh Torah* (written in 1170-80 C.E.), which he wrote in Hebrew.[4] Interchanges between the two countries were frequent. Jews oppressed and expelled from the Iberian Peninsula by the Visigoth Catholic Council of Toledo in 612 C.E. flowed into Morocco. Large numbers of Jews came to Spain during the Moslem conquest of Spain in 711 and during the balance of the eighth and the ninth centuries. When local conditions suffered in Morocco, Jews moved to Andalusia. As late as the 15th century, prominent families such as the Ibn Danan and Gagin families of Morocco among many others, escaped local turmoil by moving to Moslem Granada. In the reverse direction, many Jews from Spain returned to Morocco, including the same Ibn Danan and Gagin families. These

---

[1] Liberal translation of the French text of Haim Zafrani, *Juifs d'Andalousie et du Maghreb* (Paris: Maisonneuve & Larose, 1996).
[2] Zafrani, *Juifs d'Andalousie et du Maghreb*.
[3] Leon Roth, *The Guide for the Perplexed: Moses Maimonides* (London: Gainsborough Press, 1948).
[4] *Mishneh Torah* (Commentary on the law) is Maimonides's magisterial compendium of the laws of Judaism. See Roth, *Guide for the Perplexed*.

migrations took place not only after the 1492 and 1497 expulsions from Spain and Portugal, but also much earlier, even before the Christian riots and massacres of 1391—and certainly after 1391—and then again following the expulsions of 1492 and 1497.[5]

Following the 1492 expulsion, large numbers of exiles fled to Morocco. Hirschberg cites sources that put at 20,000 those who went to the Moroccan city of Fez alone (though other sources put them as low as 4,000), with additional thousands settling in other Moroccan cities.[6] Significant Spanish exile presences developed in the Moroccan cities of Fez, Debdou, Tetuan, Meknes, Sale, Larrache, Arzilla, Rabat, and Safi.[7] The entire Jewish population of the island of Majorca fled in 1498 to North Africa and to France. Zafrani points out that the similarity of cultures is clearly evident when one compares the *takkanot* (rabbinic ordinances) of Toledo and those of Fez, or the responsas of Ben Aderet of Barcelona and of Jacob Aben Sur of Fez.[8]

JEWISH PRESENCE IN MOROCCO

The Jewish presence in Morocco is so ancient that it reaches back to the realm of legends: legends of a stone marker near Zagora bearing an inscription indicating that in the 13th century B.C.E. King David's general "Joab pursued the Philistines to Tazzarine,"[9] and "of the Berbers being descendants of Philistines who fled David's armies to this region."[10] Some believe that the Jews of the Moroccan town of Massa descend from Jonah following his whale journey; that the town of Safi was founded by Shem, a son of Noah; and that the Jews of Asfalou in the Atlas Mountains sent King Solomon a large contribution to finance the building of the Temple in Jerusalem.[11] In fact the Jews of Ifrane (Oufrane), who believe they descend from the biblical tribe of Ephraim, do not fast on the ninth of Ab (the day that commemorates the destruction of the Temple and exile); according to their tradition, they already had settled in the Maghreb by then.[12]

---

[5] Because of turmoil in Morocco, many Spanish Jews fleeing the 1391 massacres went to Algeria and Tunisia. Among them were the noted rabbis Isaac bar Sheshet Perfet and Simon ben Semah Duran.

[6] H.Z. Hirschberg. *A History of the Jews of North Africa*. (Leiden, The Netherlands: E.J. Brill, 1974).

[7] Esther Benbassa and Aron Rodrigue, *Sephardi Jewry: A History of the Judeo-Spanish Community, 14–20th Centuries* (Berkeley: University of California, 2000).

[8] Zafrani, *Juifs d'Andalousie et du Maghreb:* 17.

[9] Tazzarine is about 50 miles from the Toghra gorge in the Atlas Mountains.

[10] Andre Goldenberg, *Juifs du Maroc: Images et Textes* (Jews of Morocco: Images and texts). (Paris: Les Editions du Scribe, 1992).

[11] Massa, Safi, and Asfalou are Moroccan towns that, prior to the 20th-century exodus of Moroccan Jews to Israel, France, Canada, and elsewhere, had large Jewish populations.

[12] Maghreb is the Arabic term for western North Africa. Ifrane is a Moroccan town with an ancient Jewish population.

The Phoenicians are known to have brought in their ships Jewish merchants who settled throughout the Mediterranean. Historical accounts record Jews of Morocco trading gold with the Phoenicians in the fourth century B.C.E. The destruction of the first Temple in 586 B.C.E. brought to Morocco still more Jews, who settled in the Atlas Mountains and traded in the salt and gold that they brought in caravans from further south (see Figure 11, Jewish settlements in Morocco). Jews came with the Romans who occupied Mauritania Tangitana (northern Morocco) in the first century C.E. Visitors to the remains of Volubilis, a Roman city that historians believe may have served as the alternate capital of the Roman province, can see a carved inscription about a Jewish "*matrona bat rav Yehuda nah*" (lady, daughter of rabbi Judah of) and a bronze, seven-branched Jewish candelabra among the ruins.

Less known is that in the second century C.E., there were apparently not one but several Jewish kingdoms in southern Morocco. These kingdoms were in Oufrane (Ifrane), Zagora, Tafilalt, Telouet, and Tamgrout. In these areas some Jews converted to Christianity and fought in subsequent battles against the Jewish kingdom in which the Jews apparently ultimately prevailed.[13]

The story of the kingdom of Oufrane, based on oral testimony and Arab accounts, bears retelling. In the 1940s Pierre Flamand collected the oral history of the Jews of the south of Morocco.[14] He tells of how, after the destruction of the first Temple in 586 B.C.E., "during the times of *Nibochat Nissar*,"[15] the remnants of the Hebrew tribe of Ephraim fled to the oasis of Ifrane in the Moroccan Anti-Atlas mountain range, along the way crossing Egypt and the Sahara. In this green region of Morocco, covered with orchards of olive, almond, and fig trees, they established a powerful Jewish kingdom, which they called the "second" or "little" Jerusalem and built a wooden replica of the Jerusalem Temple. Under their first king, Abraham Ephrati (the Ephramite), and his descendants, who retained the surname Ephrati, the Jewish settlers ruled the surrounding peoples. Legend has it that following the return to Judea of the other Jewish exiles from Babylonia, these Ifrane Jewish exiles refused the invitation to return to Judea and help rebuild Israel. To that decision is attributed their subsequent gradual loss of power. The Ephrati family surname, later changed to Afriat, survives to this day in the Moroccan diaspora.

Jews from Ifrane insist still that they descend from the tribe of Ephraim.[16] This claim bears an interesting historical parallel to that of the Jews who also escaped

---

[13] Manuscript *Chott el Maghzen*, translated by Pierre Flamand, *Quelques manifestations de l'esprit populaire dans les juiveries du Sud-Marocain: Diaspora en terre d'Islam*, vol. 2 (Casablanca: Imprimeries Reunis, 1959). The manuscript was found by Rabbi Moise Jacob Toledano, who discusses it in his *Neer Hamaarab* (Light of the west), (Jerusalem, 1911).

[14] Flamand, *Quelques manifestations*.

[15] Nibochat Nissar is Nebuchadnezzar.

[16] According to local oral histories, these Jews heard of the destruction of the second Temple in one

Chapter 4: Andalusian-Moroccan Jewish Universe • 31

the destruction of the Temple to settle on Elephantine Island in the southern Nile. However, unlike in Egypt, there have been virtually no archeological digs in southern Morocco.[17]

Are these legends echoes of a lost past or the fanciful imagination of storytellers? Who can tell? But the legends are persistent and consistent. It makes sense for the southern Moroccan Jews to create a glorious past for themselves. But the local Berbers tell the same stories, and they have no self-serving reason to do so. Archeological digs in the Atlas Mountains might reveal fascinating finds when they are undertaken. Perhaps even buried ancient scrolls are preserved in the Saharan sands, *genizot*,[18] or mountain caves. Who knows what fascinating artifacts wait to be discovered there? Antiquarians already have pillaged precious documents from *genizot* and collections in Morocco and sold them to private collectors, in whose possession they remain largely unknown and unavailable to scholars.

POPULATION EXCHANGES

Moroccan Jews traded widely with Spain. Indeed, the history of the Jews of Morocco and of Spain is one of constant cultural interchange and frequent population transfers, with people moving to wherever the grass was greener at the time. When the Vandals came to coastal Morocco and were later replaced by the oppressive Greek Christians of Byzantium, Jews fled to the more hospitable and impregnable Atlas Mountains of the south.[19] In 612 C.E., Spanish Jewry fled Visigoth repression en masse to nearby Morocco following their expulsion from Iberia by the 17th Catholic Council of Toledo; later some Jews returned. Numerous accounts confirm that fully 25 percent of the Moorish army Tariq's used to conquer Iberia in 711 C.E. was made up of Jews from Morocco and large numbers of Jews from Morocco and elsewhere in North Africa settled in Spain during the long Moorish era that followed in Spain.

When conditions deteriorated for Jews in Spain, during periods of both Moslem fundamentalism and Christian oppression, Jews fled by the thousands to Morocco thus returning to the land where many of their ancestors had

---

of two ways, depending to the version told. In one version, as the refugees settled in Lisbon, Granada, and Morocco, some families settled in Ifrane bringing news of the loss of the Temple. In another version, word of the destruction was brought to them by the Prophet Eli the Galilean.

[17] Flamand reports on two graves in the cemetery of Ifrane, one of the oldest Jewish cemeteries in Morocco. One grave was that of Joseph ben Maimon from the Jewish calendar year 3756 (6 C.E.) and the other of Eli the Galilean from 3757 (5 C.E.). Flamand, *Quelques manifestations*.

[18] *Genizot* (plural of *geniza*) are places where Jewish documents and books to be disposed of are buried to obey the admonishment to not knowingly destroy pages that might include the name of God.

[19] The southern regions of Morocco have been independent throughout their recorded history, resisting all conquerors, including the kings of Morocco and even French colonial armies, until well into the 20th century.

originated. Cordoban philosopher Maimonides and his family are one example of the many who followed this route of exile. After 12 years of flight through southern Spain, Maimonides and his family fled to Fez in Morocco, where he studied medicine from 1160 to 1165 and wrote his "Letter on Apostasy." In Fez he continued his work on the *Mishneh* commentary. Like many other Spanish expatriates, he later moved on further into the Islamic world, passing briefly through Palestine, where tradition holds his father died, and finally settling in Egypt in 1165, where he spent the rest of his life and career before his death in 1204.[20]

Maimonides was not alone in his choice of destinations. Thousands of Spanish Jews crossed the nine-mile Straits of Gibraltar to Morocco. They did so throughout the linked history of the two regions, but in especially large numbers during periods of oppression, and especially after the 1391 Christian riots and massacres that started in Seville.

When Isabel and Ferdinand expelled the Jews from Spain in 1492, tens of thousands of Jews fled to Morocco, the closest non-Christian territory. But this time, the Moroccan Jews did not welcome them back into their community. The exiles' attitudes of superiority did not endear them to the local *toshabim* Jews, and their *kashrut* (rules on kosher food butchering) was suspect.

By 1492, many Spanish Jews, especially those who had lived for long periods under Christian rule, had acquired the culture and attitudes of their Christian neighbors, including haughty disdain for anything associated with the Moors or their language. While the Spanish Jews were firmly anchored in their Judaism, their many familial relationships with both *converso* and old Christian families (almost all Spanish nobility had Jewish marriages adorning their family trees) reinforced their sense of Spanish—as opposed to Moorish—identity. Furthermore their Moroccan cousins had suffered a cultural decline and loss of status.

This situation inevitably set the stage for a clash between the two groups when exiles arrived in 1492 Morocco. These Spanish exiles wished to have nothing to do with their Moroccan brethren and referred to them as *forasteros* (strangers, outsiders). Their sense of frustration was accentuated when Moroccan rulers insisted on considering them on a par with Moroccan Jews in matters of taxation and community affairs. The cultural differences between the exiles and the local Jews persisted for a long time, especially in the northern cities of Tetuan and Tangier. Over time, however, outside of Tetuan and Tangier, the two cultures

---

[20] Maimonides and his family fled a Spain governed by the fanatical Almohad Berbers of the Atlas Mountains of Algeria. In Egypt Maimonides lived first in Alexandria (1165-66) and then Fostat (old Cairo). See Leon Roth, *The Guide for the Perplexed: Moses Maimonides*. (London: Gainsborough Press, 1948).

borrowed from each other and eventually merged to form what Benbassa and Rodrigue call "a unique Sephardized Judeo-Arab civilization."[21]

After 1492, fear of the Spanish Inquisition forced many of the new *conversos* to leave Spain. The majority migrated to countries in Western Europe and the Americas, but some *conversos* went to the Balkans, the eastern Mediterranean, and North Africa, either directly or following a stay in Italy. As the most assimilated and secular of Spain's Jews, the *conversos* considered themselves Spanish or Portuguese first and Jewish or Catholic second. When these *conversos*, who were predominantly from the upper class, wealthy, and better educated than the rest, joined the early exiles in the eastern Mediterranean, as often seen throughout history, their behavior and mannerisms were inevitably emulated by the masses of both the recent exiles and the local Jews. This served to further fuel attitudes of superiority.[22] Some Spanish exiles remained in enclaves in northern Morocco, which retain to this day a Spanish look and feel, facilitated by the proximity of Spain itself. Other exiles moved further south to the relative safety of the Berber-controlled mountainous regions. Among the most prominent of the exiles who drifted south was the Perez rabbinical family. Perez family records tell of their journey and life in the Atlas Mountains.[23] Still other exiles, perhaps most of those who went to Morocco, gradually merged with the local Jewish communities. This may explain the proliferation of names of Spanish origin among the Moroccan Jewish population. The more highly educated and culturally advanced exiles soon assumed leadership positions among the local Jews.

LINGUISTIC GROUPS

Following the 1492 expulsion from Spain, there were three Jewish linguistic groups in Morocco. One group lived in the region of Spanish Jewish enclaves in northern Morocco. Here, in northern towns such as Tetuan, the exiles recreated a Spain away from Spain. In this region Ladino and Hakitia (see chapter 9, Sephardic Languages) persisted and *romancero* were sung. A more populous area of northern and central Morocco was populated by the second group, composed of a mixture of Arabic-speaking *toshabim* (indigenous Moroccan Jews) and a substantial number of exiles who had merged with them. This group, by far the

---

[21] Benbassa and Rodrigue, *Sephardi Jewry*.
[22] The sense of superiority and desire to remain separate pervaded many of the colonies of the post-expulsion exiles. It is still clearly tangible in northern Morocco. In the Grana Spanish-Portuguese community of Tunis, the communities remained divided into the 20th century and a wall divided the cemetery. In early Istanbul and Turkey, Sephardic exiles remained separate from the earlier Romaniot (Greek) Jews and refused to have a Romaniot Jew represent them as part of the Jewish *millet* (community).
[23] The Perez family settled in the Dades valley in a *mellah* (Jewish quarter) that took on the name of *Akko Perez*.

largest of the three, now predominantly speaks French, a result of the educational efforts of the *Alliance Israelite Universelle*, which came to Morocco in the late 19th century.

The third, and most ancient, group is composed of the Jews who lived in the Atlas Mountains of southern Morocco.[24] In this unconquerable region are valleys in which more than 90 percent of the local Berber population still speaks only Berber dialects (primarily Tamazight or Tachelhit). The Jews who lived among the Berbers also spoke Berber, although almost all also spoke Arabic and read Hebrew. These Jews wrote in either Judeo-Arabic or Judeo-Berber, using Hebrew script.[25] These Jews worked mostly as artisans or small merchants and farmers. Early 19th-century trading with residents of the south of Morocco required local contacts and protection agreements with the Berber chieftains. The 19th century saw a flow of Jews to the regions of Morocco controlled by the Berbers. By the late 19th century, when it became clear that better protection could be obtained from the various foreign consulates along the coast of Morocco, Jews relocated to the coastal cities.

BERBERS AND JEWS

Berbers lived in the Maghreb before the Carthaginian, Roman, or Arab conquests. The Berbers now make up about 1 percent of the population of Tunisia, 5 percent of Libya, 20 percent of Algeria, and more than 30 percent of Morocco, especially in the southern regions. Because the Jews who lived in the mountainous Berber regions spoke Berber, a raging debate arose in which some academics theorized that these Jews originally may have been Berbers who converted to Judaism in the distant past. Others vehemently deny this theory. Both arguments are based on little evidence either way.

The theory held by the scholars who contend that some North African and Spanish Jews might be of Berber origin seems to have originated from an error in the translation of words of the early Arab historian Ibn Khaldun. Khaldun wrote that certain Berbers had "perhaps" become judaized in the distant past, but that these no longer were Jewish by the time of the Arab conquest in 642 C.E.[26] The theory of Berber origin is based on the ability of Jews who lived among the Berbers to speak Berber. Such conclusions are as unwarranted as assuming that all American Jews originally must have been Anglo-Saxon tribes that converted to Judaism because all American Jews speak English, and, although some can read Hebrew very few can actually speak it. Or that French Jews must have

---

[24] Of course, not all the Jews who lived in the Berber-dominated south were connected to the ancient Jews.

[25] See chapter 9, Sephardic Languages.

[26] Talbi Mohamed, "*Un nouveau fragment de l'histoire de l'Occident musulman*" (A new fragment of the history of the Moslem West), *Cahiers de Tunisie* 19, nos. 73-74 (1971): 19-52.

originally been Gauls who converted to Judaism. Instead it is more logical to assume that because they lived for generations in a region where the majority of the population spoke only Berber, to deal and trade with the Berber majority, Jews learned to speak Berber. This is no different from Sephardic emigrants from the Balkans to America having to learn to speak English to deal with the surrounding population. The Jews of the Atlas Mountains perpetuate the legends of ancient proud kingdoms, shared history with ancient Israel, and descent from the tribe of Ephraim. Oral history this may be, but until serious digs are conducted in their regions, it appears to be more substantial evidence than linguistic abilities.

JEWS OF MOROCCO

For most of its history, Morocco was not a single country, but rather a series of disparate and warring principalities. While Jews in one city might have lived reasonably well, others during the same period might have been oppressed or massacred in a neighboring city or region. The Moroccan ruling dynasties followed each other, often with the regularity of about three generations apart reflecting the rise and fall of power among various Berber tribal groups.[27] Gerber describes how Moroccan dynasties ruled with the support of their own tribesmen, while oppressing the other tribal groups whom they viewed simply as sources of revenue and taxation.[28] The rule of the Almoravides dynasty (1062–1147) of the Sanhaja Berber tribes was followed by the fanatically fundamentalist Almohads (1147–1269) of the Masmuda tribes from the mountains of Algeria, who offered all non-Moslems a choice between conversion to Islam or death, often by burning alive.[29] The Almohad reign was a period of repression and intolerance of Jews, massive forced conversions, and massacres of Jews in their realms in both Andalusian Spain and Morocco.[30] The Almohad martyrdoms and forced conversions almost wiped out Jewry in Morocco and its intellectual centers. Yet by the 20th century, Moroccan Jewry had grown to become the largest Jewish population outside Poland and the Ashkenazic world—which raises the question of where all these Moroccan Jews came from. Despite the travails of the Almohad reign, this was also a period that saw the Moroccan

---

[27] This regularity prompted Arab historian Ibn Khaldun to describe the "cyclical nature" of Arab and Berber kingdoms. Jane Gerber, *Jewish Society in Fez 1450-1700: Studies in Communal and Economic Life* (Leiden, The Netherlands: E. J. Brill, 1980).
[28] Gerber, *Jewish Society in Fez*.
[29] Among the Jews burned alive during this period was Judah Hacohen ibn Shusan, a Jewish judge (*dayan*) in Fez. Almoravides is the Spanish name derived from their Arabic name *Al Morabitoun*.
[30] Some of the leading Moslem Moroccan families trace their origins to the forced *anusim* of this period. They are the families of Ben-Jellum, Ben-Shegran, El Kohen, Tazi, Benani, Ben Kiran, Bahri, Beldi, Berrada, Guessus, Bennis, and others.

poets Moses ben Ezra and Yehouda Halevy acclaimed in Granada and Lucena and the creations of mathematician Samuel al Maghrabi.

The Marinids (1269-1450) of the Zenata Berber tribes followed the Almohads in ruling Morocco. This period was a golden era of respite for the Jews of Morocco. During the Marinid rule, Jews served as viziers (ministers) and councilors. During this period noted kabbalists and philosophers emerged, including Judah ben Nissim ibn Malka and Nissim ibn Malka,[31] and the poets Nahum Hamarabi and Judah ben Youssef Sijilmassi. Some historians have speculated that the Marinid rulers needed the support of the kingdoms in Spain to maintain their rule and found the Moroccan Jews with their close ties to the Spanish Jews a particularly useful asset to help them achieve this aim. Others believe that this group of Berbers felt a special kinship with the Jews.

The Bannu Watta dynasty (1450-1550) followed the Marinids and then the Saadian Sharifs (1550-1650), who depended on Arab rather than Berber support.

By the 19th century Jews controlled much of Morocco's international trade. Jews also engaged in great numbers in smaller commerce, administration (especially under the French), money changing, and the rabbinical fields. Jews were the metal workers, artisans, shoemakers, shopkeepers, and expert gunsmiths. In the countryside some even occasionally farmed the land. In the urban areas of Morocco a significant poorer Jewish underclass barely survived from day to day. For more details, see the Suggested Reading section in chapter 20, Morocco.

FOUNDATION OF THE GOLDEN AGE OF SPAIN

Many of the poets, grammarians, and sages who founded and gave rise to the Jewish schools of the Spanish Golden Age (10th-11th centuries) originally came to Spain from Morocco. These luminaries include the following:

- Yehuda ibn Quraysh in the ninth century laid the foundation of Hebrew grammar, and, in his "Epistle to the Jews of Fez", wrote a comparative study of Semitic languages.
- Dunash ben Labrat was the first to use the Arabic meter in Hebrew poetry. Born and studied in Fez, he later moved to Spain.
- Yehuda Hayuj (also known as Abu Zachariah Yahya ben David Al-Fasi), also born and studied in Fez, moved to Spain and became the teacher of the Cordoban grammarian Abulwalid Merwan Ibn Janah.

---

[31] *Kabbalah* (Hebrew for received knowledge) is a movement of Jewish mysticism that produced a number of books in 13th century Spain, notably the *Zohar*. After the expulsion of Jews from Spain, leading kabbalists settled and flourished in 16th-century Safed, Palestine. The movement reached mass popularity among Jews in the 16-17th centuries and continues to influence the Eastern European Hassidic movement.

- David ben Abraham al Fasi Al Qarai, also from Fez, was the author of a noted dictionary (*Kitab jami al alfaz*) published in Jerusalem in 930–950 and again in 1936 and 1945.[32]

Still other luminaries include the philosopher and grammarian Dunash ben Tamim and the noted poets Jacob bar Dunash and Adonin bar Nissim Ha Levi. The 12th-century scholar and poet Yehuda ben Samuel ibn Abbas el Maghribi wrote a poem recited widely today during Rosh Hashana and Yom Kippur services. The poem uses Abraham's sacrifice of Isaac as a metaphor to express the lament of a Jewish father who lost his son to Islam.

Prominent among Talmudic authorities was the eminent Rabbi Isaac Alfasi (1013–1103), known by the acronym RIF, who lived in Morocco where he wrote numerous responsas and the Talmud *katan*. Alfasi attained worldwide renown that continues to this day.

The 12th-century poet Yehuda ben Samuel Ibn Abbas al-Maghribi left a lasting legacy. His poems form part of the Jewish High Holidays liturgy. In the 14th century, the noted kabbalists and philosophers Nissim ibn Malka and his son Judah ben Malka wrote numerous philosophical works, studied to this day.[33]

These and many other examples demonstrate the close symbiotic relationships and the continuous give and take between the Jews of Morocco and those of Moslem Spain and indeed with Jews throughout the Islamic world, as one sees when Shlomo ben Yehuda from Fez (Morocco) was chosen in 1087 to become the head (*Gaon*) of the distant Talmudic Academies of Babylonia.

---

[32] Zafrani, *Juifs d'Andalousie et du Maghreb*, 49-51.
[33] See Georges Vajda, *Juda ben Nissim ibn Malka: Philosophe Juif Morocain*. (Paris: Larose, 1954).

5.
JEWS UNDER ISLAMIC RULE

For a significant part of their history, Sephardic Jews lived in Moslem and Middle Eastern lands, while Ashkenazic Jews lived in Christian and Eastern European lands. Christian rulers viewed their Jews as an alien population; they often expelled the Jews—or kept them isolated from the main population. By contrast, in what later became Moslem countries, Jews often were an integral part of the populations that existed before the advent and conquests of Islam. Jews were, therefore, more integrated into both the pre-Moslem and subsequent Moslem society. As an existing part of the pre-Islamic conquered populations Jews were not considered strangers to the land, which may explain why, in sharp contrast to Christendom, they were never expelled from Islamic countries.

A discussion of Jewish life under Islam inevitably seems to lead to a comparison with Jewish life under Christianity. This is unfortunate because instead of the complicated and varied response the question deserves, it instead tends to lead to a summary answer that has been politicized over the past century.

There is no question that Sephardic Jews living in Moslem countries as a whole historically fared better than their counterparts in Christendom. Although Jews have suffered massacres and humiliations under Islam, these hardships did not compare with the virulent anti-Semitism of Christian countries, with their periodic mass expulsions, pogroms, ghettos, inquisitions, and eventually the Holocaust. Under Islam, however, Jews were always considered second-class citizens and subjected to repeated humiliation, special taxation, and occasional massacres (as during the 12th-century massacre of the Jews of Fez or the *fatwa* authorized slaughter in 1465 of the Fez Jewish mellah).[1] Mohammad himself slaughtered an entire Jewish tribe in Medina when they refused to accept his new faith.

Nineteenth-century European historians romanticized and glorified the Golden Era of Jews in Spain because it suited their purposes to do so. At the time of the French Revolution and Napoleon's emancipation of the Jews, European enlightenment tantalizingly seemed to finally promise—but then not deliver— equality for Europe's Jews. Jewish historians such as Graetz and Ashtor wrote

---

[1] A *fatwa* is an Islamic command issued by a religious authority. A *mellah* (salt) is a Jewish quarter in Morocco. Elsewhere Jewish districts were known as *hara* (lane).

glorified histories of the lot of Jews in medieval Islamic Spain.[2] European Jewry used these accounts, as Bernard Lewis writes, as a stick with which to beat the Christian nations and reproach them for their still unequal treatment of the Jews among them, in comparison with what Jews seemed to have achieved under Islam.[3] Reality was not quite that rosy, however, as Maimonides wrote in his epistle to Yemen's suffering Jews: "No nation (Islam) has ever done more harm to Israel. None has matched it in debasing and humiliating us."[4]

The establishment of the State of Israel further complicated matters. Arabs eagerly adopted the exaggerated utopian accounts of Islamic Jewry and used them to embarrass the Israelis for their treatment of the Palestinians, while perpetuating the myth that Jews and Arabs lived in perfect harmony and peace until the State of Israel came into being. In reaction, authors such as Bat Yeor created what some have called a counter-myth of the horrible conditions for Jews under Islam.[5] Historians Bernard Lewis[6] and Mark Cohen[7] both point out that things were never as utopian as the romanticized versions would have you believe—nor as bad as in Christendom—but the meaningless argument as to which Jews had suffered more or less was engaged—a meaningless argument because Jews had suffered under both Islam and Christianity.

ISLAMIC VIEW OF THE WORLD

The early founding Moslems saw the earth as divided into three spheres. On one side was the Islamic world, *darb el Islam*, the sphere of Islam, where the population was all Moslem or under Moslem rule. The Moslems believed that in time all peoples on earth should accept Islam as the true faith, and that it was the duty of the Moslems to bring this about as quickly as possible. This urgency fueled the rapid expansion of Islam in the explosive first century after the birth of Islam (622 C.E.) when the Moslem armies seemed invincible.

A second sphere was the pagan world, *darb el harb*, the sphere of war. This sphere of the world was to be forcibly conquered, and the vanquished pagan populations gave only two choices: death or conversion to Islam.

The third sphere, *darb el salah*, the sphere of peace, was composed of people whom the Moslems believed had received a distorted revelation of the true nature of God, but who needed to progress to the correct revelation provided by

---

[2] H. Graetz, *History of the Jews* (Philadelphia: Jewish Publication Society of America, 1891-98); Eliyahu Ashton, *The Jews of Moslem Spain* (Philadelphia: Jewish Publication Society, 1993).
[3] Bernard Lewis, *The Jews of Islam.* (Princeton, N.J.: Princeton University Press, 1984).
[4] Moses ben Maimon, *The Epistle in Yemen,*. in Norman A. Stillman, ed. *The Jews of Arab Lands: A History and Source Book* (Philadelphia: Jewish Publication Society of America, 1979), 241.
[5] Bat Yeor, whose name means "daughter of the Nile," was born in Egypt and wrote the French book *Les dhimmis*, published in English by Associated University Presses in 1985.
[6] Bernard Lewis, *The Jews of Islam* (Princeton, N.J.: Princeton University Press, 1984).
[7] Cohen, Mark R. *Under Crescent and Cross: The Jews in the Middle Ages* (Princeton, N.J.: Princeton University Press, 1994).

Mohammad.[8] This third sphere consisted of both Jews and Christians, also known as the people of the book, or *ahl al kitab*. Having received partial truth, Jews and Christians, collectively known as *dhimmis* (protected people),[9] were to be tolerated under Islamic rule and indeed to be protected by the rulers.[10] As *dhimmis* they were allowed full autonomy in their own internal affairs and could engage in most occupations.

Although their persons and property were somewhat protected, and they enjoyed some freedoms, to encourage them to convert to Islam, the *dhimmis* were to be made "uncomfortable" in a variety of ways. Modeled on earlier Byzantine Christian anti-Jewish laws, "conversion inducements" included special taxes (*jiziya*, poll tax, and *haradj*, produce tax), the wearing of distinctive yellow clothing, prohibitions against riding horses or wearing swords, building or repairing places of worship, holding public religious ceremonies, striking a Moslem (even if struck first), and others. Jews always were to occupy a position in society inferior to the Moslems. They could never command a Moslem, and the Jews were to be generally scorned. These inducement discomforts were codified as the Pact of Omar, based on the verse of the Koran that the Jews be made to suffer "till they pay the tribute readily, offered on the back of their hands, in a state of humiliation."[11]

JEWS AND MOSLEMS

Jews enjoyed two or three mostly good centuries in Moslem Spain. By the 12th century circumstances took a serious turn for the worse, especially when fundamentalist Moslem forces came into power and made life miserable for both Jews and Moslems living in Spain.

But just as Christian rulers did not always rule according to the precepts of their faith, neither did all Moslem rulers reflect their religious teachings in the manner they governed. There was often a wide schism between what faith taught and the actions of a ruler. Enforcement of the Pact of Omar varied greatly depending on time and place. Generally the farther the location from Arabia, the less stringently were the restrictions enforced—except for intermittent periods of Islamic fundamentalism.

When the Shi'ite Moslem sect came into power in Persia during the 16th century, the Pact of Omar was enforced to the extreme. Persian Moslem clerics labeled Jews as ritual polluters and forbade them to touch food that would be

---

[8] The Arab world into which Mohammed was born was a pagan world. Mohammed's ideas about monotheism resulted from his contacts with Jews, mostly Karaites, and the Christians he met in Arabia.
[9] Though they were both included as *dhimmi*, the Koran had a greater problem with Christians than with Jews, because the Christian Trinity seemed similar to polytheism. See Koran sura 5:116, where God asks Jesus, "Didst thou say unto men, 'Worship me and my mother as gods in derogation of Allah?'"
[10] The protected people also included the Zoroastrians.
[11] Koran, sura 9:29.

eaten by Moslems. Jews were forbidden to walk in the rain, because any water cascading off them would become polluted. Early Moslem Spain in the west and Turkey and the rest of the Ottoman Empire in the east were the most lax in this respect. But conditions for Jews varied in these areas, too, depending on the time period. When the fanatical and religious Almohad dynasty gained power in 12th-century Spain, restrictions were strictly enforced; it was not an easy time for Jews.

When the Moors conquered Spain in 711, they were a minority of the population. The tolerance shown by the Moslem rulers towards Jews and Christians in part was a pragmatic strategy; the Moorish rulers needed their subjects' help to govern the country. The Jews, a fellow Semitic people with a language similar to Arabic, and with a long-standing love for education, rose rapidly to positions of importance and influence in Moslem Spain.

In the Moslem state of Granada, Jews were so prominent in both population and government that the Arabs referred to it as *Garnatat al Yahud* (Granada of the Jews). In the 11th century, Samuel ben Joseph Halevi ibn Nagrela, a Jewish physician, was named grand vizier to King Badis of Granada and commander-in-chief of the armies, both appointments in blatant disregard of the Pact of Omar. On Samuel's death in 1056, his son Joseph succeeded him in his position.

But on December 30, 1066, Moslem factions angered by the disobedience to the rule that no Jew was to command Moslems caused Joseph to be murdered on his way to Shabbat services. Following that event, a Moslem riot ended in the deaths of 1,500 Granadian Jews. Though Jews continued to hold prominent positions in financial and cultural circles, their prominence was precarious.

Jews in Moslem Spain spoke and wrote in Arabic; often they wrote Arabic using Hebrew letters. Maimonides, Ibn Gabirol, ibn Ezra, and other Jewish writers, poets, and philosophers of the period wrote in Arabic. As Arabic grammar was developed, it prompted a revival of spoken Hebrew and the development of its grammar with a resulting flow of delightful Hebrew poetry. For many centuries, Arabic was the language of the intelligentsia and the sciences. Moslems and Jews studied the ancient Greek texts, long lost to the Europeans, and translated them into Arabic.

In summary, Jews living under Islam have had periods of ups and downs, but they were always second-class citizens. When Jews rose to positions of power in Islamic countries, it was always in disregard of Islamic *dhimmi* laws that specifically prohibited non-Moslems from commanding Moslems. Periods of Jewish prominence were followed regularly by Moslem religious reaction that punished the Jews for their effrontery and success. Under more secular Moslem rulers Jews lived under better circumstances, but the periodic rise of more religious and fundamental regimes meant hardship for both Jews and moderate Moslems.

6.
JEWS IN THE NETHERLANDS

BACKGROUND

A century or more before the Spanish expulsion edict of 1492, thousands of Jews left Spain; most went to neighboring North Africa. In 1492, the same year that the Catholic monarchs took Granada, the last remaining Moorish kingdom in Spain, they expelled all Jews from Spain, giving them just three months to decide whether to convert to Catholicism or to leave Spain forever. Symbolically, August 2, 1492, the last day Jews were allowed to remain on Spanish soil, coincided with the Hebrew calendar's ninth day of Ab, the anniversary of the destruction of both the first and second Temples in Jerusalem and of other catastrophes in Jewish history. Estimates of the numbers of Jews living in Iberia on that date vary. Excluding the Jews who already had converted to Christianity in previous centuries, approximately 400,000 Jews lived in Spain and another 80,000 in Portugal.[1] About one-third of the Spanish Jews accepted baptism, perhaps thinking they were buying themselves more time to make a final decision on leaving their homes. In so doing, they inadvertently established themselves as future victims of the Inquisition's tribunals and torture chambers.

Another third of Spain's Jews in 1492 chose to leave the peninsula, even though they were forbidden to take with them any gold, silver, or jewelry. They left with only the clothes on their backs. Jews in northern Spain departed by the northern route to Navarre, France, Italy, the Balkans, and Turkey and the rest of the Ottoman Empire. Jews in southern Spain left via the southern route to Morocco and elsewhere in North Africa, Palestine, and the Ottoman Empire. Along both exile routes, Jews settled to form new Sephardic communities.

The remaining third of Spain's Jews paid a stiff ransom to be allowed to take refuge in the neighboring kingdom of Portugal. As events unfolded, it became clear to them that their refuge was only a brief respite. Five years later, Portugal's royal family contracted a marriage alliance with a Spanish princess; a condition of the marriage was for the king of Portugal to agree to expel those Jews from his kingdom who refused to convert to Christianity. In 1497 Portugal's monarch issued an edict giving its Jews a choice between conversion and expulsion. But

---

[1] Four hundred thousand is the classically accepted number. However more recent scholarship suggests that so many Jews had fled Spain in the 1-2 centuries prior to 1492 that a mere 50,000 Jews remained to be expelled from Spain. See Chapter 3, Spanish Diaspora and Benbassa, Esther, and Aron Rodrigue, *Sephardi Jewry: A History of the Judeo-Spanish Community, 14–20th centuries* (Berkeley & Los Angelos: University of California, 2000).

Portugal's monarch had no desire to lose his valuable Jewish subjects, who, according to some estimates, numbered about a third of the population, and were a particularly industrious and important group. As the Jews gathered at Lisbon's harbor to board ships to take them into exile, they instead were rounded up and forcibly baptized.

As a consequence of the expulsion edicts and the ensuing baptisms, a large number of New Christians, or *conversos*, now populated Portugal. "New Christian" was the official designation given to the new converts to Christianity, many of whom had chosen baptism under duress, in order to distinguish them from "old Christians." The designation marked them for suspicion in the centuries to come.

Also referred to as crypto-Jews, a large percentage retained their Jewishness hidden behind a Christian façade; they endeavored to maintain Jewish traditions in secret.[2] As late as the 20th century, researchers have found pockets of crypto-Jews in parts of Portugal and Spain still secretly practicing remnants of the faith of their ancestors.

Brief History

New Christians were carefully watched and could not leave Portugal easily during the first century after the expulsion. When they were able to do so, in a process that extended over several centuries after 1492, many secret Jews gradually made their way off the Iberian Peninsula to North Africa, the Ottoman Empire, Italy, France, The Netherlands, and South America. In their safe havens, most reverted openly to the practice of Judaism. Refugees who had fled to Spanish and Portuguese colonies in the Americas, where the Inquisition cast its long shadow of torture and terror, were forced to remain in a culture of secrecy. A great number of inhabitants in the South American countries of Brazil, Argentina, and Colombia, and in the southwestern United States today recall or firmly believe that they descend from crypto-Jews.

Many of the early *conversos* traveled the northern route through Bayonne, Bordeaux, Paris, Brussels, and Antwerp before settling in southern Holland, attracted by the country's trading opportunities, as they previously had been attracted to Antwerp for the same reasons. They trickled in from both Antwerp and Iberia. Because of the early obstacles preventing their departure, this *converso* exodus began in earnest about a century after the 1492 and 1497 expulsions and continued over the next three hundred years.

Other waves of Sephardic migration to The Netherlands came from the Ottoman Empire and North Africa and from Dutch Brazil after Portugal reconquered the colony in 1654. Though cautious at first out of long habit and

---

[2] *Marrano* is a pejorative term meaning pig. Crypto-Jews or *anusim* (Hebrew word meaning a forced convert) are the preferred terms today.

concern for their *converso* relatives still living in Iberian lands, most *conversos* in Dutch-controlled areas reverted openly to Judaism. But after a century or more of publicly practicing Catholicism, most *conversos* who came to The Netherlands had little, or distorted, knowledge of Judaism. Many were quite assimilated and had adopted a secular approach to both Catholicism and Judaism.

The rabbis of the Sephardic community in The Netherlands, in response, adopted a reactionary, zealous insistence on strict adherence to Judaism for those who had reverted to its practice. Some *conversos* found this rabbinical rigidity unpleasantly reminiscent of the Catholic rigidity from which they had fled. The Dutch Sephardic rabbinate took a particularly unforgiving approach toward the few "*relapsos*," Jews who had reverted back to Catholicism.[3] Moreover, the Dutch Sephardic rabbinate imposed special hurdles and restrictions for those who elected to return to Judaism after once again relapsing into Catholicism. Free-thinking philosophers such as Baruch Spinoza provoked rabbinical wrath when his views and writings questioned or contradicted Jewish orthodox theology.

In 17th-century Protestant Holland, it was significantly easier to be a Jew than a hated Catholic. Under the leadership of Prince William of Orange, Holland had gained its independence from Spain subsequent to a Protestant rebellion against oppressive Spanish Catholicism. To quell the upstart Calvinists in the Spanish Netherlands, Spain sent the Duke of Alba, who undertook his assignment with great cruelty and resultant massacres of Protestant rebels. The Protestant forces under William of Orange ultimately succeeded in winning their freedom from Spain. In their declaration of autonomy, they specifically outlawed religious oppression, text that obviously would benefit the Jews who would later live among them even though the authors did not have them in mind.[4]

The *conversos* who settled in 17th-century Holland legitimately could claim to be Iberian, Catholic, or Jewish. Leaving aside their own, often very real, desire to return to the faith of their ancestors, being Jewish in Protestant Holland was by far the safest of the three self-identifying options. Similarly, to avoid antagonizing their Dutch hosts—who viewed Spain and Catholicism as the arch enemy—the Sephardic community in The Netherlands elected to label itself a "Portuguese" Jewish congregation rather than Spanish-Portuguese. This designation contrasts sharply with Sephardim elsewhere in the Diaspora and the sub-set of Dutch Sephardim who moved to England after Cromwell allowed Jews back into England. Because in Portugal so many Jews had been forcibly converted en masse to Catholicism, "New Christians" formed a nation within the Portuguese nation. Jews and non-Jews both openly referred to Dutch Sephardim

---

[3] The most famous *relapso* was Uriel Acosta, whose emotional and tragic life, in and out of Judaism, inspired several plays. Isaac la Peyrere, author of *Praeademitae*, is another famous *relapso*.
[4] Article XIII of the 1579 Proclamation of autonomous confederation under the Union of Utrecht.

as *homens da nacao* (men of the nation). The label "Portuguese" or "Portuguese merchant" became a euphemism for *conversos* in many parts of the world.

During the 17th century, imbued with Protestant zeal, the Dutch Protestants were quite enamored of the Old Testament. They viewed and referred to themselves as the "people of Israel" fighting the "philistine" Spaniards. Prince William of Orange was the "Maccabee" fighting the hated "Haman" (the Spanish Duke of Alba). Their pledge of allegiance was filled with references to the parting of the waters, having been saved by the God of Israel, and similar biblical metaphors.[5]

But, despite its Old Testament rhetoric and imagery, The Netherlands remained a Calvinist Christian country with a previous history of anti-Semitism during the Middle Ages, incited by the then-prevalent cult of Mary and the anti-Jewish stories of early Christianity.[6] Although by far the best haven for Jews in 17th-century Christendom, Jews lived under significant restrictions even under Dutch rule. Jews were allowed to practice only certain professions, and intermarriage with Christians was forbidden. Jews had limited access to the stock market; Jewish brokers could trade stocks only with other Jews. Dutch citizenship was conferred only to certain Jewish merchants of great importance. Dutch Jews were allowed into Dutch guilds in 1795, and they obtained full civil rights only after Napoleon conquered The Netherlands. Napoleon also brought civil registration and the adoption of surnames to The Netherlands and to many Dutch Jews. Unlike their Ashkenazic brethren, Sephardic Jews long previously had adopted surnames and registered them in early Sephardic congregational records.

Despite their difficulties, the Dutch Sephardim enjoyed great success and prominence in The Netherlands. The majority were small merchants or shopkeepers. They dealt in tobacco and fish; worked as tailors or goldsmiths, physicians, or moneychangers; and ran grocery stores. But some Sephardic families, such as the Pereira, Barrios, and Pinto families,[7] among others, rose to great wealth. Sephardic merchants dominated the lucrative trade in sugar, tobacco, silk, and precious stones. They used their knowledge of Spanish and

---

[5] H. M. Sachar, *Farewell Espana: The World of the Sephardim Remembered* (New York: Vintage Books, 1995), 277-303.

[6] The Middle Ages saw numerous anti-Jewish attitudes in Dutch books and poetry. The earliest records of Jews in Holland are of moneylenders in the 12th century, although there may have been earlier settlements, as Jews traveled with the Roman legions elsewhere in the Roman world. Jews were expelled from The Netherlands in the mid-13th century and again in the 15th century.

[7] Their Spanish names provide a clue to their *converso* origins. There were some non-*converso* Iberian Jews among the Sephardic settlers in Holland, typically from the Ottoman Empire or North Africa. They usually can be identified by names of Hebraic rather than Hispanic origins, such as the Dutch Saltiel family. In Holland the majority of Sephardim were *converso* families who reverted to Judaism, but in the Mediterranean, the Balkans, and Turkey the reverse was true and here too the surname often gives a clue of the family's history. See chapter 10, Sephardic Names.

Portuguese to great advantage when trading with South America or with Spain and Portugal where they often had the added advantage of dealing with their own kinsmen. The early *conversos* who settled in The Netherlands already were successful merchants, and it was largely their expertise and connections with Spain, Portugal, and Brazil that enabled The Netherlands to gain its 17th-century international trade and economic supremacy. Wealthy Sephardim were very important both in the founding and the running of the Dutch East India and West India companies.

Sephardim from abroad also found great success in The Netherlands, including David Mesquita, Chaim Toledano, and David Shalom from Morocco, or the Azevedo brothers, David Torres, and Isaac Sasportas, from Algeria. The favorable conditions in The Netherlands attracted Sephardim from all over the world; the Sephardic congregations grew from 100 families in 1617 to 400 families in 1650, and to 3,000 Sephardim in 1700, finally reaching 4,700 at its peak, mostly in Amsterdam.

When the Sephardim first settled in The Netherlands, they formed three small congregations (Neve Shalom, Beth Yaacov and Beth Israel), which in 1639 combined to form one congregation.[8] Ninety percent of Holland's Sephardim lived in Amsterdam, where in 1675 they built the famous Esnoga synagogue. This landmark Sephardic temple would become the model for several others, including the historic Bevis Marks synagogue in London the Mishne Torah synagogue in Curaçao and Touro synagogue in Newport, Rhode Island.

The 18th century saw a decline in Dutch fortunes worldwide. With the near bankruptcy of the Dutch East India and Dutch West India companies, Sephardic fortunes also declined. At the same time, impoverished Ashkenazim who had fled German and Eastern European pogroms inundated Western European Jewish communities, including the Jewish community in The Netherlands. Ashkenazim became the overwhelming majority of Jews in The Netherlands and the new image of Dutch Jewry.[9] The Dutch perception of Jews became increasingly one of disdain and ill will. In 1793, Napoleon's troops invaded The Netherlands, and Napoleon declared the equality of all men. In 1796 Jews finally gained full citizenship and the oppressively autocratic rabbinate lost its total authority over the Jews.[10]

---

[8] The combined Sephardic congregation's coat of arms is fascinating in its symbolism. It shows a pelican (also present in the royal crest of the kings of Portugal) dripping drops of blood from her breast, with which she feeds her three chicks.

[9] Eighteenth-century Dutch Jewry totaled 20,000 Ashkenazim, compared to about 3,000 Sephardim.

[10] Until then the Sephardim were an autonomous community in Holland, with their judges and *parnassim* able to levy taxes and fines and even excommunicate members with devastating results. These individuals were then shunned, severly limiting their ability to conduct business or trade. The Dutch rabbinate were autocratic and wielded their powers with great severity.

The Nazi era brought some peculiar developments. The Nazis pondered whether the Sephardim, who came from Iberia and who were so different from the Nazi propaganda images of stereotypical Jews, really were ethnically Jewish. In an attempt to escape the Nazi death camps, some Sephardic families produced Inquisition-era family trees proving they had never been Jewish. In the end, however that subterfuge failed, and fewer than 25 Sephardic families escaped annihilation in the concentration camps.

ALIASES

Sephardic merchants in The Netherlands, in an effort to protect their relatives in Portugal—and even themselves as they traveled through Spanish or Portuguese lands in pursuit of their lucrative trade with Spain and Portugal and their possessions—adopted aliases. These aliases can be deciphered easily using information in legal documents that include both real names and aliases. Sometimes the change was just in the first name, as in Josef Mendes da Costa (of London), who became Juan Mendes da Costa. At other times the entire name was changed, as in the following examples:

Samuel Abrabanel → Samuel de Sousa
Samuel Aboab → Antonio Sanches de Pas
Yosef Cohen → Jeronimo Henriques
Isaac Franco → Francisco Mendes de Madeiros
Isak Gaon → Philipe Diaz
Menasseh ben Israel → Manuel Diaz Soeira
Salomon Naar → Manual Ramirez de Pina
Josua Sarfati → Thomas Nunes de Pina
Jacob Semach → Antonio Hidalgo Cortissos
Aron Musafia → Manuel Nunes
Michael Nahmias → Miguel de Crasto
Josue Nehemias → Antonio Lopez

The Shaltiel family research group has posted an extensive list of names and their aliases on a web page at maxpages.com/donadeli/Aliases.htm; sources of information for these aliases is not included. An extensive list was also published in the March 2001 issue of the Sephardic genealogy periodical *Etsi*.[11]

---

[11] Vibeke Sealtiel-Olsen, "Aliases in Amsterdam", *Etsi* 4, no. 12 (March 2001): 3-7.

7.
Amazon Journey

Indiana Jones Meets Tangier Moshe

Twenty-year-old Moshe Levy brushes the bugs away from his suntanned face and thinks of his family in Morocco as he drifts down the river. He and others like him live in Jewish communities deep in the Amazon jungle, in places with names like Cameta, Obidos, Itacoatiara, Manaos, and Tefe in Brazil, or in Tarapoto, Yurimaguas, Pucallpa, and Iquitos in Peru. Moshe's boat is laden with the supply of rubber he has just bartered for with his jungle contacts. Further down-river he will meet his old childhood pal Shlomo Benoliel, who used to sit on the bench next to him in Hebrew school in Tetuan. As he has done repeatedly in the past, Moshe will transfer his rubber supplies to Shlomo and load up more pots and pans and other utensils to use for bartering up-river.

A script for a new Indiana Jones movie? Not at all. The part played by Moroccan Jewish immigrants in the development of the Amazon rubber trade is a little-known facet of Moroccan and South American Jewish history.

Moroccan Jews, like the members of many North African Jewish communities, engaged primarily in trade and commerce; typically they disdained the building trades, farming, and other similar forms of labor. Other than a few wealthy business owners, most Jews were small traders or peddlers whose activities varied from selling trinkets in the *souks* (markets) to financing caravans to sub-Saharan Africa in search of gold, ivory, ostrich feathers, and the like. These caravans were usually organized and run by branches of their families living along the caravan routes in southern Morocco. Other Moroccan Jews worked as tailors, cobblers, silversmiths, and at similar occupations.

Migration Patterns

Because of the precariousness of life during most of their history, Moroccan Jews were accustomed to packing up and moving about from town to town—or even out of the country. Sometimes Jews migrated to avoid plagues and disease (mostly cholera), to escape oppression by a sultan or danger in a war zone (for example, the 1844 migration of up to half the Jewish population of Tangier to Cadiz and Gibraltar in anticipation of a French attack), or because of marriages between families in distant towns in or outside of Morocco. The mass migration of Moroccan Jews to Israel in recent times was not an anomaly, except for its size. In pre-expulsion Spain, back-and-forth migrations and marriages between Spain and Morocco and other North African Jewish communities were not unusual. The "back and forth" nature of these migrations was also a characteristic, as seen in chapter 4, Andalusian-Moroccan Jewish Universe. By the 18th century, communities of Moroccan Jews had established themselves elsewhere—in Gibraltar, London, Manchester, among other places.

In the 19th century, the *Alliance Israelite Universelle* established schools in Morocco which encouraged the learning of building trades as a remedy to the prevailing poverty. Particularly in northern Morocco, however, young Jewish men dreamed of adventures and trading in the New World. Many did leave, a number of them to locations where they saw their chances for riches to be best: Rio de Janiero, Caracas, and Belem at the mouth of the Amazon where a synagogue was established in 1824.

The Amazon

A depressed economic climate in Morocco, an influx of Spaniards into northern Morocco who competed for scarce jobs, migrations of Jews from southern Morocco fleeing draughts, and disease conditions prompted a mass migration in the mid-19th century of Jewish teenagers. They traveled mostly from overcrowded northern Moroccan towns, to seek their fortunes in South America's Amazon Basin. Rubber trees are abundant in the Amazon forests; when Charles Goodyear invented a process to vulcanize rubber, he created a durable product that could be used in 1880 in the manufacture of rubber tires. This created a huge new market for the sap of the Amazon's rubber trees.

Moroccan Jews went to the Amazon to share in that wealth, with the intention of sending money back to their impoverished families, which they faithfully did, and to return when they could, which they also did—part of the back-and-forth migratory tradition. A Jewish cemetery was established in Belem do Para, and the Eschel Abraham and Shaar Hashamaim synagogues were founded in 1824 and 1826, respectively.

At first the young adventurers embarked on lengthy three-month voyages aboard slow-sailing ships. With the advent of steamships to Brazil, the trip shortened to a mere three weeks, and the emigration volume increased dramatically. Frequent return trips to Morocco with the accumulated wealth became practical. The wealth of the returning sons contrasted sharply with the abject poverty at home; even more sons became motivated to seek the Amazonian *eldorado*,[1] leaving largely female Jewish populations behind. Records of the *Alliance Israelite Universelle* show that many Moroccan Jewish families survived largely on the money sent home by their sons in the Amazon.[2]

In 1910 low-cost rubber from Southeast Asian plantations deflated the price of rubber worldwide; the Amazon rubber industry crashed. Amazon Jews moved on to greener pastures elsewhere in the Americas or returned to Morocco and the

---

[1] *Eldorado* is the fabled land where the streets are paved with gold.
[2] Alliance Israelite Universelle Archives, 45 Rue la Bruyere, 75009, Paris.

colorful Indiana Jones chapter of Moroccan Jewry ended. It was for many Moroccan Jews, however, the first step in their emigration to the New World.

Alone for long periods of time in the depths of the Amazon forest and bereft of the presence of Jewish women, many of these adventuresome young men took Indian wives. Though many of the traders ultimately returned home, this resulted in generations of mestizo children who to this day strongly identify with being Jewish and carry typically Jewish surnames. They practice a peculiar blend of remembered Jewish practices and elements of Catholicism and Amazon Indian beliefs. The isolated mestizo Israelite community of Iquitos in Peru and their beliefs and self-identification are well described in Segal's well-documented *Jews of the Amazon*.[3]

FAMILY NAMES

Robert Ricard lists the following names of Tangier and Tetuan families that went to Brazil or Peru: Abecassis, Abejdid, Benamor, Benelbaz, Bentes, Delmar, Farache, Gabbai, Levy, Marquez, Perez, Salgado, and Serruya.[4]

Families from Mogador, Rabat, Casablanca, and elsewhere also participated in the move to the Amazon. Among these are Abensur, Assayac, Azulay, Attias, Benayon, Benchimon, Bendelek, Benzaquen, Cohen, Edery, Fonquinos, Levi, Nahmias, Nahon, Pinto, Sarraf, and Serfaty.

Segal lists all persons buried in the Iquitos Israelite Cemetery with year of burial, ages, and birth places, where known. He also lists Jews who settled in the Peruvian Amazon obtained from Rosenzweig's records, with birth places, whether they left offspring in the Amazon, and whether they died in the Amazon or returned home.[5]

Jacques Cukierkorn, a Sao Paulo (Brazil) rabbinical student at the Hebrew Union College in Cincinnati, wrote in 1993 that "an estimated 10% of the Brazilian population is of *marrano* origin" and describes attempts by some of them to rediscover their past history.

Today, Belem has about 1,000 Jewish families and Manaus about 140 Jewish families, almost all descended from the original Moroccan emigrants. Jewish tombstones carry such names as Assayag, Athias, Auday, Azancot, Azulay, Barcessat, Becheton, Benarroch, Benayon, Bencheton, Benchimol, Bendelak, Benjo, Benoliel, Bensimon, Benzaquin, Benzecry, Cohen, Dabela, Dahan, Elaluf, Foinquincs, Franco, Gabbay, Hassan, Israel, Lancry, Laredo, Levy, Melal, Murcian, Obadia, Roffe, Sabba, Scares, Serfaty, Sicsu, Sorrulha, Sorruya, Tobelom, and Zagury.

---

[3] Ariel Segal, *Jews of the Amazon: Self Exile in Earthly Paradise*. Philadelphia: Jewish Publication Society, 1999.
[4] Robert Ricard, "*Notes sur l'immigration des Israelites marocains en Amerique espagnole et au Bresil*" (Notes on the immigration of Moroccan Jews in Spanish America and in Brazil). *Revue Africaine* (1944).
[5] Segal, *Jews of the Amazon*.

Suggested Reading

The interested reader is encouraged to seek out Susan Gilson Miller's excellent and perceptive article entitled "*Kippur* on the Amazon."[6] The title arises from her eloquent description of these intrepid Jewish explorers, almost all of whom came from Morocco, joining together for *Yom Kippur* services in huts built in the jungle, surrounded by fires to keep away the wild animals which they could hear roaring outside. In her article she quotes from Abraham Pinto's personal diary:

> Lest we forget the religion of our fathers so far away, each of us left Tangier carrying with us the book of Kippur in order to celebrate this day as it should be. Before leaving Tefe for whatever part, we fixed the date of the Holy Day to celebrate it wherever we might be ..... and planned to meet two or three days beforehand to celebrate together. [On meeting], our oarsmen built us a little hut in a place cut out of the jungle. We lit a bonfire and fed it through the night to keep away the wild animals and snakes that might come near. . . . One night of Kippur our peons killed a tiger near our little hut; but even for that we did not interrupt our prayers.[7]

The following also provide more information:

Bentes, Abraham Ramiro. *Das Ruinas de Jerusalem a Verdajante Amazonia* (From the Ruins of Jerusalem to Verdant Amazonia). Rio de Janeiro: Edicoes Bloch, 1987.

———. *Primeiros imigrantes hebreus na Amazonia* (First Jewish Immigrants to Amazonia). Rio de Janeiro, 1987.

Susan Gilson Miller, *Kippur on the Amazon* in Harvey E. Goldberg, *Sephardi and Middle Eastern Jewries: History and Culture* (New York: Jewish Theological Seminary, 1996) 190–209.

Ricard, Robert. *Notes sur l'immigration des Israelites marocains en Amerique espagnole et au Bresil* (Notes on the immigration of Moroccan Jews in Spanish America and in Brazil). *Revue Africaine* (1944).

Rosenzweig, Alfredo. *Judios en la Amazonia Peruana, 1870–1949* (Jews in the Peruvian Amazon: 1870–1949) (*Majshavot: Pensiamentos* 4, nos. 1–2. (1967): 19–30.

Segal, Ariel. *Jews of the Amazon: Self Exile in Earthly Paradise* (Philadelphia: Jewish Publication Society, 1999).

Tagger, Mathilde. "*Juifs Marocains au Bresil*" (Moroccan Jews in Brazil). Paris: *Revue du Cercle Généalogie Juive*, no 38, (Summer, 1994).

Weinstein, Barbara. *The Amazon Rubber Boom, 1850–1920*. Stanford, Cal.: Stanford University Press, 1983.

Wolff, E. & F. Wolff. *Sepulturas de Israelitas* (Jewish Tombstones). Sao Paulo: Centro de Estudos Judaicos, 1976 and 1983.

---

[6] Susan Gilson Miller, *Kippur on the Amazon* in Harvey E. Goldberg, *Sephardi and Middle Eastern Jewries: History and Culture* (New York: Jewish Theological Seminary, 1996) 190-209.
[7] Miller, *Kippur on the Amazon*.

8.
GEONIM

Two great religious traditions exist in Judaism today. The Sephardim follow the Babylonian Jewish tradition, and, for a variety of geopolitical and historical reasons, the Ashkenazim follow the Palestinian tradition brought to Europe via Italy. In order to understand the historical and religious background of Sephardic traditions, it is useful to review some of the history of the Babylonian tradition and how it developed and unified the Sephardic world. This chapter describes some interesting nuggets of information; an excellent source of additional information is *The Geonim of Babylonia*.[1]

BABYLONIA

During the first millennium of the Common Era, Jewish communities throughout the Diaspora looked to Babylonia for leadership. Scholars and others sent queries to the prestigious rabbinical academies of Sura and Pumbadita in Babylonia, requesting opinions and advice about all sorts of matters of importance related to their communities. As the replies made the long return trip to their destinations, the rabbinical academies' *responsas* (replies to rabbinical queries) were copied by Jewish communities en route and studied throughout the Jewish world. Rabbinical academies existed in Palestine, too, but the Babylonian academies prided themselves in the continuity, and thus authenticity, of their oral tradition of Judaism, as compared to the Palestinian authorities, whose oral tradition was repeatedly interrupted and troubled by local political turmoil. This continuous Jewish oral tradition subsequently became codified in the *Mishnah* and the Babylonian Talmud, used to this day to interpret the Torah. After the 10th century C.E., rabbinical leadership passed from the Babylonian Talmudic academies to the academies of North Africa and then to those of Andalusia, which by then had matured and developed sufficiently to become independent of the Babylonian authority's leadership.

At the end of the 19th century, the Cairo *geniza* was discovered. The study of its contents have provided great insight into the ongoing message traffic with the Babylonian academies in this otherwise poorly documented period of Jewish history. Because two of the *geonim* (one from Pumbadita and one from Sura) happened to carry the author's ancient surname—not that any genealogical links have been found to date—they sparked a personal interest in learning more about the *geonim*. Any excuse to learn is a good one!

---
[1] Robert Brody, *The Geonim of Babylonia and the Shaping of Medieval Jewish Culture*. (New Haven: Yale University Press, 1998).

Geniza

What exactly is a *geniza*? To observe the traditional Jewish prohibition against destroying any document that contains the name of God, when such documents have passed their useful life, they are relegated to the *geniza*—a designated repository, often a hole or cellar in a synagogue. There they lay forgotten for centuries.

Geography dictated that much of the message traffic of the first millennium passed through North Africa on its way to and from Babylonia. Copies of the original documents often were made along the way and kept for local study. When these copies became too worn for further use, these copies, which because of their nature frequently contained the name of God, were placed in the local *geniza*.

The continuous Jewish presence and ancient age of synagogues in Cairo, made the 19th-century discovery of the *geniza* there an incomparable event. Invaluable copies of ancient documents retrieved from the *geniza* represented a historian's treasure trove. The local dry, desert air ensured little deterioration of these documents with the passage of time.

Jewish Babylonia

The geonic period of Jewish Babylonia spanned the first 10 centuries of the Common Era. With continuing turmoil in the Jewish homeland, concern arose among religious leaders about the possible loss to future generations of the oral tradition that was so essential to Judaism. During first five centuries of the millennium, scholars undertook an effort to document and thus ensure the preservation of this Jewish heritage.

A careful, preparatory clarification of the teachings started the ambitious multi-century effort, followed by a meticulous redaction of the oral tradition that accompanies the Torah. The result became known as the Babylonian Talmud and the *Mishnah*. In a responsa he wrote in a reply to a question on when the Talmud was "written"—a copy of the response was found in the Cairo *geniza*—Sherira Gaon emphasizes that, because it was documentation of a traditionally oral tradition, the Talmud should not be referred to as having been written, but only as having been redacted. In fact the Babylonian Talmud is the written record of the oral discussions of the learned Babylonian rabbis as they tried to clarify and interpret the oral tradition of the *Mishnah* (*shanah* = to repeat).

Little is known of the history of the first half of the millennium. The second half of the millennium (mid-5th century to mid-10th century C.E.) is known as the geonic period.

Three Jewish power elites existed in Babylonia during the geonic period: the exilarch and the two rabbinical academies of Sura and Pumbadita.[2] A fourth, unofficial power group, which became particularly important in the 10th century, were the wealthy Jewish merchants of Baghdad. This fourth group wielded its power, especially during the 10th century, by forging alliances with the other three groups as they jostled for power.

THE EXILARCH

The exilarch was the secular member of the three power groups. A descendant of the Jewish royal family in exile, he could claim descent from King David through Jehoiachin II (Kings 25:27), the king of Judea whom Nebuchadnezzar had exiled to Babylonia. In Babylonia, the exilarch held court, moved with great pomp, and was the official representative of the Jews to the Babylonian ruler—though his exact powers and duties are not clearly known. Known to the Jews as the *nasi* (prince), succession was not necessarily linear from father to son. Instead the exilarch was selected from among possible candidates in the royal family in a process still not clearly understood, but in which the rabbinical academies played a significant role. Following his selection the exilarch was officially confirmed in his role by the ruler of Babylonia. The exilarch controlled a territory (*reshut*) that he taxed to support himself and his court.

Two geonim are highlighted here: Bustanai, the first exilarch in the Islamic era, and Anan, an exilarch removed from office because of disagreements with rabbinical authorities. Anan was an early leader of the Karaite sect, a Jewish sect who accepted only the written scriptures (*Kara* = to read) and rejected all subsequent rabbinic clarifications, including the *Talmud*.

BABYLONIAN ACADEMIES

The early Jewish academies of Babylonia coalesced into the two often-competing academies of Sura and Pumbadita. Each academy was headed by a rabbinical authority, who, after the mid-fifth century C.E., was given the title of *gaon*. Unlike hereditary exilarchs who descended from King David, the *geonim* (plural of *gaon*) did not need to arise from a specific family, but, they did come from a small number of rabbinical families. The *gaon*'s social standing and prestige apparently was equal to that of the exilarch.

Both the Sura and Pumbadita Talmudic academies were located near Baghdad, the seat of the Abbassid caliphate and the center of the Islamic world that extended from Spain to India, a world in which 90 percent of the Jews of that era lived. For the Jewish people, Babylonia was the home of the Babylonian Talmud and *Mishnah,* and the Babylonian Talmudic academies were the centers of Jewish

---

[2] There were other rabbinical academies in Babylonia, but these were the two influential ones. At times Sura may have had a sub-academy belonging to the Exilarch.

learning. The academies also served an important role of education for the best rabbinic minds of the era.

Scholars classically divide the first millennium of the Common Era into 4 rabbinical periods:
1. The period extending from the first to the third centuries is known as the era of the *tannaim* (reciters).
2. From the third to the fifth centuries was the era of the *amoraim* (sayers). The *amoraim* were the sages who produced the *Mishnah* and the Talmud.
3. The first half of the sixth century is known as the era of the *savoraim*. These scholars labored to clarify the few remaining issues not addressed by the *amoraim*.
4. Finally, from the middle of the 6th century to the mid-10th century was the era of the *geonim*, the period of greatest interest to Sephardic history.

THE GAON

The *gaon* was the head of his academy. His title is said to derive from the Hebrew *Rosh Yeshiva Gaon Yacov*, "head of the Yeshiva, pride of Jacob." The person second in command to the gaon was known as the *av bet din*.

The *gaon's* several official functions included heading the academy (*yeshiva*), educating the rabbinical students, acting as the ultimate rabbinic judge, and responding to queries from anywhere in the Jewish world. His prestige was equal to that of the Exilarch and like him, each academy had its own *reshut* (territory), similar to but often larger than that of the exilarch. Like the exilarch the *gaon* would tax his *reshut* for funds to support the academy. These funds supplemented contributions that arrived with the queries.

Each academy met twice a year for a one-month official session presided over by its *gaon*. At this official session the *gaon* would assign topics for the members to research and study during the five-month period preceding the next official session. A report by a Rabbi Nathan of Babylonia describing his visit to an academy provides a fascinating glimpse into the academy's proceedings. During the official academy sessions, Rabbi Nathan reported that the *gaon* would sit facing rows of scholars. There were seven such rows of students facing him, ten deep in the case of Sura, and thirteen in Pumbadita. The scholar's position in these rows was strictly assigned; the first scholar in each row carried the proud title of *rosh kallah* (head of the row). Additional student "auditors" which could number an additional 400 students surrounded the learned rows, known as the Sanhedrin. Besides learned discourses, the front-row scholars would exhaustively discuss queries that had come from around the Jewish world to the academy. When they finished their discussions, the *gaon* summarized, corrected, and added to the discourse. He then dictated a *responsa* to the query, signed the document, and ordered it to be sent to the inquirer.

The names and the exact chronology of the Babylonian geonim are known; they appear in a responsa written by one of the last *gaons* (Sherira), found in the Cairo *geniza* (though two earlier versions were also known). In his reply Sherira provides a detailed list of the *geonim* and their dates of service—a list reproduced in many contemporary books and other sources (see, for one, the *Jewish Encyclopedia*). Sherira's detailed *responsa* provides most of the information we have about that era—an era that provided the liturgy, theology, and traditions that became the common heritage of Sephardim throughout the world.

As noted in chapter 10, Evolution of Sephardic Names, many ancient Sephardic surnames originated in the Babylonian period. Examples include Ibn Zur (Abensur), Sasson, Ben Sushan, Malka, Gabbai and Hasdai. Common Jewish given names also come from that era, for example, Esther (from the Babylonian goddess *Ishtar*) and Mordechai (from the Babylonian god *Mordok*).

9.
SEPHARDIC LANGUAGES

Sephardim lived in many countries and spoke a variety of languages. Their records are written in as many languages. A major obstacle facing the Sephardic researcher is the need both to understand at least some of these languages and to read the scripts in which the records were written. In addition to English, languages of Sephardim include Spanish, Portuguese, Arabic, Hebrew, Turkish, Judeo-Spanish, Judeo-Arabic, French, and Dutch.

Handwritten scripts pose additional problems. Not only did writing styles change over time, but in some cases, professional scribes made special efforts to write in obscure ways that would ensure their professional "job security," not only to create the records, but also to interpret them. This problem for the genealogist is evident in the early notarial records of Spain and Portugal and also in records written in Arabic script in North Africa and Turkey. It therefore may become necessary for a researcher either to become familiar with obscure scripts before making a trip to the archives or to hire someone familiar with them to conduct the research.

Though many of the rabbinical works of Spain were written in Hebrew, a surprisingly large number were written in Arabic. The Jews' knowledge of Arabic, Hebrew, and Latin had significant historical implications. In their strivings for learning, Jewish and Moslem scholars translated the knowledge they acquired from ancient Greek texts into Arabic, their common language. These and other works were later translated into Latin, thus spreading knowledge in response to the awakening interest in Europe. The early translations of medical treatises, mathematics, philosophy, geography, and literature were the all-important spark that ignited and fed the European Renaissance.

Ottoman records were written in Osmanlica, the Turkish language written in the Arabic alphabet, until 1928. At that time the modern Turkish republic decreed an official change to the use of the Latin alphabet, with slight modifications to accommodate a few additional sounds.

HEBREW

No language is more closely associated with the Jewish people than Hebrew. Many Sephardic documents were written in Hebrew, but the language is written in many styles.[1]

---

[1] Hebrew writing style have varied with time and geographical location. Language experts

The block letters used in modern printing are the most familiar. But Sephardim printed their important nonliturgical books in what today is known as Rashi script. They also used a cursive script in everyday writing that differs greatly from modern Hebrew cursive script, the latter derived from the Eastern European Hebrew cursive. When Sephardim wrote in Judeo-Spanish or Judeo-Arabic, they used Hebrew letters in Sephardic cursive script (see Appendix B).[2]

Jews wrote Hebrew in either block letters or in one of the cursive scripts. The block letters, more often vertically rectangular than square, are of Aramaic origin brought to Judea by the returning Babylonian exiles. The scribes used this formal script when writing Torah scrolls, prayer books, and other important liturgical texts. Although the appearance may vary, depending on whether the document is Sephardic, Ashkenazic, or other, block scripts are similar enough so that if one is familiar with one block script, it usually is not difficult to read any of the variants.

The other main style of Hebrew writing is cursive script. This informal, more rapid style of writing is usually encountered in correspondence, personal notes, and even court documents. Originally derived from block letters, over time it has evolved to become different in appearance. Because of the type of records in which genealogists search for information, cursive is the script a genealogist will encounter most frequently. This cursive script is used in the Judeo-Arabic of North Africa and the Judeo-Spanish of the Balkans. In the Balkans the cursive script is also known as Solitreo, from the Portuguese word *solitrar*, which means to spell, because the writer would spell phonetically or transcribe Judeo-Spanish words into Hebrew letters. Although this Hebrew script sometimes is referred to as Rashi script, when handwritten, it is more correctly referred to as Sephardic cursive (See example in Figure 5). Aranov writes that after the Spanish expulsion, when some Jews from the Maghreb moved to Palestine, their descendants'

---

recognize Babylonian, *Maaravic* (*Maghreb*), Sephardic, *Zarfatic* (central and northern France), *Parsic* (Iran), *Itallik* (Italian), and *Levanic* (Greek) types of writing. Among these are some recognizable groupings of interest to the reader.

The style of Hebrew writing used in the Maghreb is called *Maaravic*, derived from the Babylonian style of Hebrew writing, which itself arose from the Aramaic letters adopted by the Babylonian Empire and the Jews who lived there. From the Maghreb the *Maaravic* style was introduced into Spain and Portugal, where it became known as Sephardic style, but remained essentially identical to the Magrebian *Maaravic* style. From Spain the Sephardic style spread into Provence, Languedoc, and the Comtat Venaissin. The Ashkenazic Hebrew writing style, on the other hand, is derived from the *Zarfatic* style of central and northern France and is part of a different script group.

[2] Spanish written in Hebrew script is known as *aljamiado*. Few examples of *aljamiado* are still preserved in Spain. One, part of the *Puerta de Reinosa* in the Spanish town of Aguilar de Campóo (Palencia), records that "Don Çag ben Maleke and his wife, Doña Bellida, paid for the construction of the turret entrance built in 1381." See Jose Luis Lacave, "Material Remains," in Haim Beinart, *The Sephardi Legacy* (Jerusalem: Magnes, 1992).

cursive script took on an affected appearance, creating a variant that became known as Holy Land or Western Palestinian cursive.

The *mashait* style is a third script and is derived from the cursive script. Before the advent of printing, scribes and copyists needed to produce large numbers of books of a philosophical, kabbalistic and rabbinic *halakhic* nature. These books were not held at quite of the same level of respect as the Torah and prayer books, but were felt to deserve more than the common everyday cursive script. The scribes needed to use something faster to write than the slow and tediously penned formal square block letters but yet showing more respect and care than the plain and rough everyday cursive script. The *mashait* script evolved, therefore; it consists of a more elaborate and decorative form of cursive script that the scribes used for writing such texts.

When the printing press came along, the Sephardic *mashait* script was used as the model characters for these types of printed books and these print characters became known as the Rashi or rabbinic script because books containing Rashi's commentaries and other rabbinic books were printed in it. However, as Birnbaum points out, the name is a misnomer because even though printed in this Sephardic type of script, Rabbi Rashi, who was French, would have actually written in Zarfatic script, not the Sephardic script referred to here

Arabic

Arabic was spoken in Andalusia not only during the eight hundred years of Moslem occupation, but in southern Spain long after the Christian reconquest was completed in 1492.[3] Arabic had long been the language of the intelligentsia throughout Spain. Moreover, most Sephardic Jews outside Spain lived in Moslem countries where Arabic continued to be written and spoken. In his study of the languages spoken by Jews in the Kingdom of Sicily, Rocco reports that Sicilian Jews used three primary languages, Sicilian, Arabic, and Hebrew, with Hebrew reserved primarily for liturgical use.[4,5] As a result, records and books written by Sephardim in Spain, North Africa, and elsewhere were frequently written in Arabic. The great scholars Maimonides, Saadiya Gaon, and Ibn

---

[3] Arabic was spoken throughout the Iberian Peninsula. Many documents issued by Christian monarchs show their signatures in Arabic. Modern Spanish is riddled with words derived from Arabic. After 1250 C.E., Jews in northern Spain spoke mainly Romance-Castilian and Romance-Catalan. The Jews of Andalusia, however, continued to speak Arabic until 1492. See David Romano, "The Jews' Contribution to Medicine and General Learning" in Beinart, *Sephardi Legacy*.

[4] There was no common Italian language until much later. See chapter 26, Italy.

[5] Benedetto Rocco, "Le tre lingue usate dagli ebrei in Sicilia dal sec. XII al sec. XV" (Three languages used by Jews in Sicily of the 12th to 15th centuries), in *Italia judaica: Gli ebrei in, Sicilia sino all'espulsione del 1492: atti del convegno internazionale, Palermo, 15-19 guigno 1992*. Rome: Ministero per I beni culturali e ambientali, Ufficio centrale per I beni archivisti, 1995.

Pakuda all wrote in Arabic; their works were only later translated into Hebrew and other languages to make them more accessible.

When Moslem armies spread Islam to Andalusia in the West, they also spread the Arabic language and alphabet. Even people in Moslem countries who spoke languages other than Arabic wrote using the Arabic alphabet. Examples include Persian and pre-1928 Turkish languages. A genealogist researching documents in the archives of Moslem countries or Jewish documents created during the almost eight hundred years of Moslem Spain will usually find them written in Arabic script, if not in the Arabic language.

In 1492 Arabic was still spoken in Christian Spain. The first person from Columbus' crew to set foot in the New World is believed to have been Luis de Torres, whom Columbus described as "one who had been a Jew and knows Hebrew and some Arabic." Arabic continued to be spoken in Christian Spain, especially the area around Valencia, for at least a hundred years after the expulsion. Several laws outlawing its use were enacted a century after 1492. In 1492 many Jews in Spain either still spoke Arabic or had parents who did.

Because Arabic today is a spoken language whose alphabet has changed little, it is not difficult to find individuals who can translate documents written in Arabic. Difficulties occur when the language is *not* Arabic, but it is written in Arabic characters. Until 1928 for example, official documents in the Ottoman Empire were written in the Turkish language—but in Arabic script, the so-called Osmanlica script. In 1928 the Turkish republic by decree changed the Turkish language from Arabic to Latin characters, with the result that most Turks today cannot read the old documents. A researcher in Ottoman archives must both read Arabic and understand Turkish, a difficult and unusual combination of skills.

The Moslems learned about paper making from the Mongols, and the skill spread rapidly throughout their world. Eighth-century Baghdad had a street with a hundred bookseller shops, and tenth-century Granada boasted a library of a million volumes, at a time when the largest collections of manuscripts in Europe contained fewer than a dozen books each.

The explosive expansion of Moslem conquests in the first century created an empire that necessitated knowledge and sophistication the Arabs did not possess—if the empire were to be governed at all. This spurred a quest for knowledge from wherever it could be found, a quest in which all populations within the Moslem world participated, including Jewish scholars. Throughout the Moslem world, newly acquired knowledge was feverishly debated and then published in books that circulated, thus fostering a rapid spread of new knowledge throughout the Moslem world. Throughout the 8th to 11th centuries, the so-called Golden Era of Sephardic Jewry in Spain, Arabic was the language that both Jewish and Moslem scholars used to communicate. Since the overwhelming majority of Jews lived in Moslem-controlled areas at that time, this was the language most Jews spoke. Most scholarly books of the time, including those by such Jewish authors as Maimonides, ibn Pakuda, and Saadiya Gaon, among numerous others, were written originally in Arabic and only later translated into Hebrew.

After Latin, Arabic is the language that had the most impact and left the most words in the languages of Spain. Examples are *aceite* (oil), *aceituna* (olive), *alcalde* (mayor or judge), *alquimia* (chemistry), *algebra, alcali, tarifa* (tariff), *alcazar* (castle), *aduanas* (customs), *asasinos* (assassin), *cenit* (zenith), *cero* (zero), *naranjas* (oranges), *almíbar* (syrup), *alfalfa, alcachofas* (artichoke), *albaricoques* (apricots), *algarrobos* (carob beans), *arroz* (rice), *azúcar* (sugar), *algodón* (cotton), and *ojala* (God willing), to mention just a few.

Arabic also was spoken throughout the countries of North Africa, so many documents in these countries of interest to genealogists are in Arabic or Judeo-Arabic.[6] Although Arabic dialects vary from country to country, classical Arabic, in which most documents are written, is essentially the same everywhere.

A table of the Arabic alphabet that may be helpful in deciphering some archival documents appears in appendix C. The Arabic language is similar in many ways to Hebrew. Many words have the same roots, and many names of the letters of the alphabet are similar. Knowledge of one language greatly facilitates learning the other. In fact, similarities exist among all the languages that arose in that part of the world. For example, it might surprise the reader to know that *Cohen* and *Cohanim* also mean priest in Punic, the language spoken by the ancient Phoenicians and their descendants in Carthage.[7]

JUDEO-SPANISH AND LADINO

Moshe Lazar, writing about Ladino and Spanish Jewish literature, points out, as have others, that the Spanish-speaking Jews of Christian Spain expelled in 1492 tended to resettle not only according to their towns of origin in Spain, but also according to their social rank and cultural heritage. Jews who were more religious and traditional settled in the Ottoman Empire. Aristocratic, upper-middle-class, and more assimilated Jews settled in the Christian West.[8] Lazar explains that this created two distinct cultures and literary styles in exile, the oriental and the occidental. The split, which occurred centuries before the expulsion, was given great impetus following the 1391 riots, when many Jews in Christian Spain were either killed or forced to convert to Christianity. A third

---

[6] Judeo-Arabic is a mixture of Arabic, Hebrew, and Aramaic written in the Hebrew alphabet. In Morocco after the Spanish exile of 1492, Judeo-Arabic also included many words derived from Spanish languages, especially concerning commerce.

[7] The Phoenicians had several settlements in Spain, hence the Spanish towns with Hebraic-sounding names such as Barchilona (our coast) and Malaca (Malaga).

[8] See chapter 6, The Netherlands.

group is composed of Arabic-speaking Jews from Moslem Spain, many of whom had left Iberia even earlier.[9]

Many (though not all) scholars believe that Ladino (from *enladinar*, to translate into Latin/Spanish) should refer only to the liturgical language, the literal word-for-word translation of Hebrew prayer text into Judeo-Spanish. These scholars insist that Ladino should not be used to refer to the Judeo-Spanish vernacular. Judith Cohen describes the liturgical Ladino with the following example: "*la noche la esta*" (the night that is) for the Hebrew "*ha-laila ha zeh*" of the Passover Haggadah instead of the vernacular *esta noche* (this night). Because a specific Hebrew or Aramaic word, unless circumstances dictated otherwise, always was translated into a specific Spanish word, some have called liturgical Ladino "Hebrew clothed in Spanish," exemplified by the 1553 Bible of Ferarra.[10]

As the term Ladino has come to be used today, it means the more corrupt Judeo-Spanish vernacular spoken by some exiles from Spain. Until recently native speakers of Judeo-Spanish did not use the term Ladino to refer to the language they spoke; they referred to their spoken language as Djidio, Spaniol, Spaniolit, Hakitia (in Morocco), or Djudezmo (Jewish). Today, however, except for some academic purists, most speakers have adopted the terms Ladino or Judeo-Spanish for the vernacular as well.

Ladino is essentially 14th- and 15th-century Castilian, with contributions from Gallego-Portuguese, Catalan-Valencian, Aragonese, Hebrew, Turkish, Arabic, and other languages.[11] Like many Jewish languages, Judeo-Spanish originally was written using the Hebrew alphabet. It incorporated words and expressions from the languages of the many countries in which the Jews lived following their exile from Spain, including Turkish, Arabic, Italian, and Greek and uniquely colorful expressions. The characteristics of spoken Ladino varied among Sephardim who lived in different communities.

It is a common misconception to assume that Ladino was the language of all Sephardim, or even of all Sephardic exiles. Ladino was the traditional language of the Spanish exiles who settled in the eastern Mediterranean and the neighboring Balkans. The Jews of Spain fled the Iberian Peninsula in several waves. Those who fled Spain before 1492 did not necessarily speak the amalgam

---

[9] Moshe Lazar, *The Sephardic Tradition: Ladino and Spanish Jewish Literature* (New York: Norton, 1972).

[10] The Spanish-language Bible of Ferrara (1553) was published by two *conversos:* Yom Tob Atias (alias Alvaro Vargas) and Abraham Usque (alias Duarte Pinel). See Aron di Leone Leoni, "New information on Yom Tob Atias (alias Alvaro Vargas), co-publisher of the Ferrara Bible," *Sefarad* 57 (1997):1.

[11] These Spanish languages are mostly from northern (Christian) Spain. There was no "Spanish" language at that time; instead, a variety of Romance (Latin-based) languages were spoken in the different regions or kingdoms of the Iberian Peninsula. One of these languages, Castilian, spoken in Castile, later became dominant and served as the basis of what is now called Spanish. Spanish speakers in South America still often refer to their language as "*castellano*" or Castilian.

of Iberic languages that in exile became Ladino. The Spanish Jews who left long after 1492, the *marranos,* or *anusim,* spoke mainstream contemporary Hispanic languages and wrote using the Latin alphabet. Those who went to the Americas spoke Castilian, which remained contemporary. Those who left prior to 1492, especially very early, often spoke Arabic, especially if they had fled Moslem Spain.

Because the Sephardim of the eastern Mediterranean and Balkans wrote their 14th–15th century (pre-Cervantes) oral language phonetically using Hebrew letters (Solitreo), they soon lost familiarity with the Latin alphabet and the subsequent language evolution in Spain.[12] Isolated in an unfamiliar Turkish or Greek environment, Ladino (or, more correctly, Judeo-Spanish) developed as a lingua franca among the Sephardim of the eastern Mediterranean linking the communities of Salonica, Istanbul, Rhodes, including settlements in Ottoman Palestine. Even among these groups significant regional variations existed, with adoption of various local words and phrases, or differing pronunciations that caused the vernacular to diverge increasingly over time among the various communities, as well as from the liturgical Ladino, to the point that many Judeo-Spanish speakers needed the biblical Ladino interpreted for them to understand it. Speakers of Judeo-Spanish in Salonica, Macedonia, Bosnia, Serbia, and Romania spoke what has been called Western Ladino, derived largely from the dialects of northern Spain and Portugal. In Constantinople, Adrianopole, Izmir (Smyrna), and Rhodes, the Oriental Ladino spoken is said to reflect the Castilian dialect of central Spain.[13] Speakers of Judeo-Spanish in Morocco who were in closer contact with Spain and had added their own set of phrases to their Judeo-Spanish could understand, but often only with difficulty, the oral Judeo-Spanish of the Balkans.

In The Netherlands, England, and South America, the situation was different. In The Netherlands the Sephardim quickly began speaking Dutch. Reinforced by new *converso* immigrants from Portugal and familiar with the Latin alphabet, the Sephardim of Antwerp and Amsterdam had access to the linguistic and cultural changes in the Iberian Peninsula, so their Portuguese and Castilian languages did

---

[12] Prior to the 20th century, except for an educated elite, the majority of Sephardim of the eastern Mediterranean could not read the Latin alphabet or afford books from Spain. Several authors (Harris, Pulido, Luria) have noted that because of their cultural isolation from the mother language and culture, by the 19th century many Judeo-Spanish speakers were unaware that the language they spoke was a form of Spanish and some expressed surprise at being told so. They believed they were speaking a "Jewish" language. A story is told that when a Spanish ship docked in Istanbul, the local Sephardim thought the sailors to be Jewish because they recognized their language as being similar to their own Djudio. See Tracy Harris, "The Prognosis for Judeo-Spanish: Its Description, Present Status, Survival and Decline, with Implications for the Study of Language Death in General." Ph.D. diss., Georgetown University, 1979.

[13] *Encyclopaedia Judaica,* c.f. Ladino.

not remain isolated. The same applied to the Sephardim in North Africa and in England.

While the early Sephardic settlers in North America retained their Hispanic names and their Judaism, as well as their self-image as Sephardim, they rapidly assimilated and soon lost their Spanish language and culture.[14] Those who came to the Americas later (except for the Ladino-speaking 20th-century immigrants from the eastern Mediterranean) spoke the Spanish or Portuguese of the countries they lived in.

The Spanish Jews who went to North Africa found a large population of local Jews who spoke Arabic, and, except for a small area in northern Morocco, they were numerically overwhelmed by the local Jews. The Arabic culture in North Africa was familiar to the exiles. After all, the Moslem caliphate of Granada in southern Spain still existed just months before the expulsion date. Moslem Andalusia and North Africa were culturally and linguistically a single entity.[15] Particularly for the Jews of Andalusia, the transition to Arabic-speaking North Africa, especially close-by Morocco, was not as great a dislocation as that into distant Turkey or Greece. Exiles to North Africa spoke either a form of Judeo-Spanish that came to be called Hakitia (Jaketia) or Arabic, possibly depending on from which part of Spain they originated and whether or not they had settled in a region of North Africa that already had a large population of speakers of Judeo-Arabic.[16] For those who spoke Hakitia, Spain was close enough to Morocco that the language and culture of the exiles could keep up with those of the mother country; their Judeo-Spanish progressively diverged from that of the Balkan Jews.

Pre-1492 expulsion exiles from Spain found it much easier to blend into the familiar Arabic language and culture of North Africa than later exiles, many of whom settled into the unfamiliar Turkish or Greek language and culture of the eastern Ottoman Empire. In northern Morocco, many Jews spoke both Hakitia and Spanish. They spoke Hakitia, with its many Hebrew words and expressions, at home or among themselves, and Spanish to their Christian neighbors. Hakitia likely never was used as a liturgical language, but always as a means of verbal communication. When Moroccan Jewish scholars wrote in Spanish they did not use Hakitia.

---

[14] Dinah Lida, "Language of the Sephardim in Anglo-America." In *Sephardim in the Americas: Studies in Culture and History,*" Martin Cohen and Abraham J. Peck, eds. (Tuscaloosa: American Jewish Archives and University of Alabama Press, 1993).

[15] Haim Zafrani, *Juifs d'Andalousie et du Maghreb* (Jews of Andalusia and the Maghreb) (Paris: Maisonneuve & Larose, 1996).

[16] Hakitia, Haketia, or Hakatia (sometimes written Haquetia because there is no *k* in Spanish), comes from the Arabic word *haka*, which means narration, and translates into "the language they narrate or speak in."

In the eastern Mediterranean and the Balkans, Judeo-Spanish served as a unifying force closely associated with the Sephardim's identity as Jews in a foreign land. The language underscored their differences from the surrounding Turks, Greeks, and Armenians, all of whom spoke their own separate languages.

Using Judeo-Spanish for all activities and businesses in Ottoman Sephardic communities was facilitated by the Ottoman *millet* system, which allowed non-Moslem populations to self-govern in most matters and to run their own affairs under their own religious leadership. The Ottoman Empire allowed its non-Moslem nationalities, including the Jews, to govern themselves as separate *millets* (nationalities or religions). Each *millet* was self-governing in matters such as education, religious law, and justice within the community. The leader of the community, the *hahambashi* or chief rabbi, represented the community to the Ottoman government.

Eastern Mediterranean Ladino persisted for a number of reasons: a sense of identity, the Ottoman *millet* system, nostalgia for Spain, and the exiles' desire to retain as much of their Spanish culture as possible. Sephardic women played a major role in preserving the vernacular language. Living in a Middle-Eastern world, they largely stayed at home or within the Jewish community. Unlike their men, having little need to interact with the local culture beyond the community, many women did not speak or learn even rudimentary Turkish, Greek, or Arabic. They preserved Judeo-Spanish as a language of the home and community. Nostalgia for Spain and its traditions is most evident in northern Morocco, Turkey, and Greece, countries where Judeo-Spanish in its several forms retained its fiercest adherents.

The Ashkenazic parallel to Judeo-Spanish is Yiddish, 11th-century German written in Hebrew letters, which incorporates words from Hebrew and the Eastern European countries where Ashkenazim lived. Despite a large literature and theater in Yiddish, it has largely come into widespread disuse as a spoken language among current Ashkenazic generations.

Judeo-Spanish is threatened with a similar fate in the modern world, despite its historical and identity values. It has ceased to be the dominant language spoken at home, replaced by French, Hebrew, English, and other modern languages. Sephardim whose parents may have spoken Judeo-Spanish or Judeo-Arabic often marry spouses whose parents may have spoken Yiddish—or, more likely today, Hebrew, English, or French—and may have little interest in the language for everyday communication.

The late 19th and early 20th centuries saw the flowering of a body of new Yiddish literature and theater. During the same period, Judeo-Spanish in the eastern Mediterranean faced successive adverse events. *Alliance Israelite Universelle* schools introduced modern European culture through the medium of the French language.[17] The French language, identified with modern European thought and culture, was adopted avidly by educated, upwardly mobile Sephardim. Consequently, spoken Judeo-Spanish became stigmatized as backward, and its use bespoke a lack of education. Sephardic authors and playwrights began writing in French and other languages. Some used Judeo-Spanish in comic situations as a means of ridicule.[18]

Ataturk's modernization reforms of the 1920s forced all children in Turkey to attend elementary schools where they were taught in Turkish—exposing children of Ladino speakers to Turkish at an early age.[19] Nationalist reforms in other Balkan countries did likewise for their own languages, exposing more Judeo-Spanish speakers to the languages of their adopted countries. In 1928 all citizens in Turkey were ordered to use exclusively the Latin alphabet; that decree applied to Judeo-Spanish too. Still later, the Nazis dealt Judeo-Spanish a final blow by destroying many of the Jewish communities, including Salonika, that still had significant numbers of Judeo-Spanish speakers.

Despite efforts to teach Judeo-Spanish and keep it alive, the existence of a number of periodicals still written in Judeo-Spanish, and recent recordings of Ladino songs, resuscitating the language appears to be an uphill battle.[20] Like their Ashkenazic cousins, the younger generations are rapidly losing fluency in the language, and its survival as a spoken language is at severe risk.

FRENCH

In the late 19th century, the *Alliance Israelite Universelle* established schools throughout North Africa, Turkey, and elsewhere in the Jewish world. Through these schools the *Alliance* was instrumental in teaching the French language and propagating it as the "intellectual language of Europe." French was rapidly adopted and soon began to replace Judeo-Spanish and Judeo-Arabic as the language of the Sephardim, especially throughout North Africa. Even the Sephardim of the Balkans, noted for having most fiercely held close their Spanish exile culture, found that many of their educated younger elite were speaking French (or Italian if they went to Italian schools), in preference to Judeo-Spanish. Judeo-Spanish, after having long been a language of prestige and commerce, was relegated to a language spoken mostly by the uneducated and poor. It began to be referred to as jargon, and those who spoke it interspersed it with more and more French, or other foreign words, in an attempt to show their erudition.

---

[17] The *Alliance* opened schools in Salonika and Izmir/Smyrna (1873), Haskoy (1874), Istanbul (1865), Sofia (1887), and Monastir/Bitola (1895).
[18] By contrast, in earlier centuries authors produced liturgical works in Judeo-Spanish such as Jacob Culi's 1730 encyclopedic work *Meam Loez*.
[19] Prior to the 1920s Jewish children went to Jewish *millet* schools, where instruction was in Ladino.
[20] A newslist for Ladino speakers is available at www.sephardichouse.org/komunita.html.

Throughout North Africa, French became the language of educated Jews. Except for some enclaves that, for historical reasons, spoke Italian,[21] French became the defacto language of the North African Sephardim. It did not hurt that the French Napoleonic edicts emancipated the Jews and promised them full civil equality, even though reality often belied that promise and anti-Semitism flourished in France.

BERBER AND JUDEO-BERBER

No document of value to a genealogist exists in Berber, which, except for rare Hebrew documents, was not a written language. The close historical association with Jews in North Africa and Spain makes it a topic of interest to the genealogist.

The origin of the Berber (*Imazigh*) people is not known with certainty, but they appear to have originated from a merging of indigenous African inhabitants and invaders from Europe. Many tribal groups now called Berbers have little in common other than linguistics. Even the various languages they speak have similarities only in the same manner as do French and Italian. In Morocco, three main Berber dialects are spoken, which experts believe diverged from each other a thousand to two thousand years ago.[22]

To trade with the Berbers, the Jews who lived among them needed to learn their language. For several centuries at least, the Berber languages existed mainly as spoken dialects. Typically the languages were not written, but some rock inscriptions in the Berber script date back to 139 B.C.E.

Jews who lived in Berber regions wrote oral Berber using Hebrew script, in the same manner that Jews elsewhere wrote their Arabic, Ladino, or Yiddish in Hebrew characters. The Berber written in Hebrew that incorporates Hebrew and Aramaic words is known as Judeo-Berber.

---

[21] The Spanish and Portuguese community of Tunis, known as the *Grana*, was an offshoot of the Sephardic Jews of Tuscan Livorno (Leghorn). They retained a long-time allegiance to Italy. See chapter 22, Tunisia.

[22] The three Berber dialects spoken in Morocco are *tachelhit* (spoken from the town of Essaouira to the south), *tamazight* (spoken in the middle Atlas region), and *dhamazight* (spoken in the Rif mountain area).

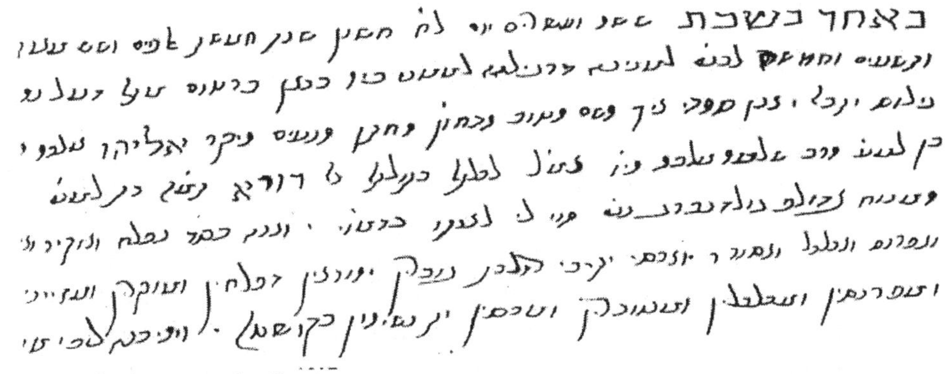

Source: Author's personal collection.

Figure 5. Sephardic Script: 20th-Century *Ketubah*

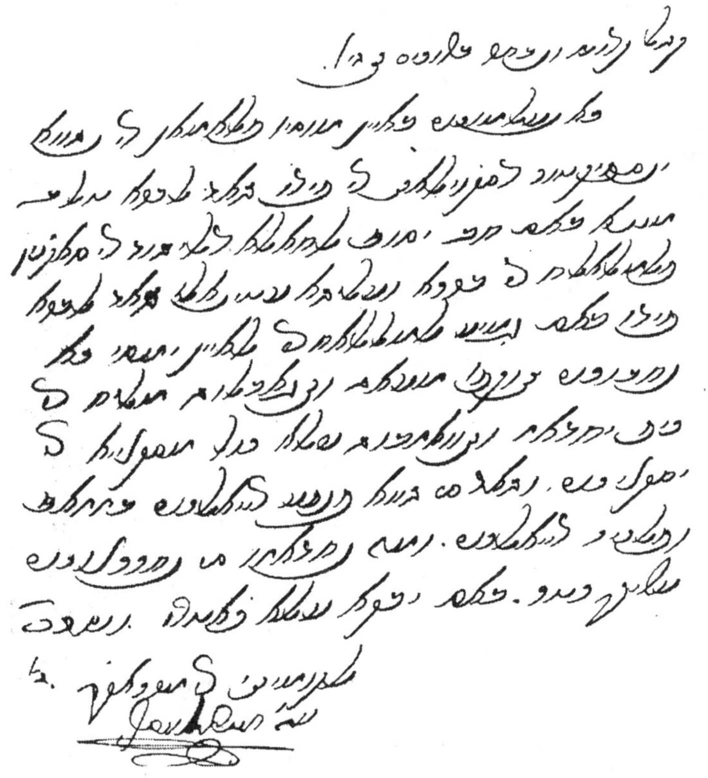

Source: Pierre Flamand, *Les communautes israelites du Sud-Marocain* (Jewish communities of southern Morocco) (Casablanca, Morocco: Imprimeries reunies, 1959).

Figure 6. Sephardic Script. 19th-Century Letter of Introduction

Chapter 9: Sephardic Languages • 69

10.
EVOLUTION OF SEPHARDIC NAMES

To Jews a name has great importance and meaning. Among no other people does traceable genealogy go as far back into history as it does among Jews. The Jewish family tree extending back to Adam and Eve has been adopted even by non-Jewish peoples as their own universal, ancient family tree.[1]

Because Sephardic Jewish names are ancient, they serve as the best link to a distant past. This chapter describes how Sephardic Jewish names have evolved over the centuries and presents a discussion of major factors that have contributed to their structure, reflecting Biblical, Babylonian, Roman, Christian, Arab, and Spanish influences.

The study of names and their origins (onomastics) offers considerable insight into the history of some ancient Sephardic families. The Ben David family of Spain, for example, was accepted by Andalusian poet-philosopher Abraham ibn Ezra, Rabbi Benjamin of Tudela, and Isaac Abrabanel as having descended from the royal family of King David.[2] The same is true of the Abrabanel family of Seville and several other Sephardic families. Some present-day Sephardic surnames, for example, Shaltiel, Obadiah, Perez, and Barzilai, appear in the lists of Babylonian exiles who returned to Jerusalem found in the Biblical books of Ezra and Nehemiah.[3]

BIBLICAL ERA

Patronymic names that reveal ancestry appear in the Bible only after Abraham is introduced. Before Abraham the Bible does not identify individual lineages.[4] From Abraham on, the Bible carefully maintains lineages until Talmudic times, after

---

[1] Ernest Renan, *Histoire generale des langues semitiques* (General history of Semitic languages), 4th ed. (Paris: Michel Levy Freres, 1863). See Genesis 5:1: "This is the book of the generations of Adam."

[2] Abraham Laredo, *Les Noms des Juifs du Maroc* (Names of the Jews of Morocco) (Madrid: Institut Montano, 1978).

[3] Ezra and Nehemiah identify the exiles in their lists as members of the tribes of Judah, Benjamin, and Levy who had been taken as prisoners from the southern kingdom of Judah and exiled to Babylonia—thus providing a link to past genealogies in *sefer yohasin* (see later in chapter). The northern kingdom of Israel, populated by the other 10 tribes of Israel, had been defeated by the Assyrian king Tiglith-Pileser and dispersed into exile in 733 B.C.E., long before the southern kingdom of Judah's defeat by the Babylonians. These Israelites essentially had disappeared from the scene by the time the Babylonian Jews returned from exile, except for remnants living in the kingdom of Judah and perhaps in distant places such as Morocco (see chapter 4, Andalusian-Moroccan Jewish Universe).

[4] The name Abraham means father of the multitude.

which the records of lineage were disrupted by the dispersal of Jews into the Diaspora.[5]

Ancient Jewish society, known collectively as *bene Israel* (children of Israel) or *am Israel* (people of Israel), was structured into three societal groups. The broadest social level was that of the tribe, followed by the clan or extended family, and finally the family unit (see Figure 7). The tribe (*mateh* or *shebet*) was ruled jointly by a patriarchal ancestor and the priesthood. The patriarch (later the *nasi* or *nagid*) dealt with temporal matters and the priesthood with matters that fell under its religious purview. As Jewish history evolved, the role of the top secular ruler was taken over by the judges and still later, when the monarchy developed, by an elected or anointed king.

Below the level of the tribe came that of the extended family or clan (*mishpacha* or *aloof*). The *mishpacha* was governed by the elders (*zekenim*) or leaders (*aloofim*). This level was composed of related families within the tribe. The third and most intimate level was that of the group living within the same tent (*ohel*) or house (*bayit*)—what we would call today the family unit—governed by the family patriarch or father (*ab* or *ba'al ha bayit*).

Proof of membership in a tribe, and thus eligibility for sharing its assets and enjoying its protection, lay in carefully maintained lists of generations.[6] These official lists, kept by the priesthood, were called *sefer toledot* (book of generations). Later in history, after the Babylonian exile, the lists were referred to as *sefer yohasin* (from *yachas*, to enroll).[7] These lists were of utmost importance in determining one's identity and place in society. For example, when the exiles returned to Jerusalem from their Babylonian exile, individuals whose names were not found in the genealogy lists were excluded from the reconstituted Jewish community.[8]

---

[5] Chronicles I:9: "All Israel was registered by genealogies."
[6] Numbers 26:53-4: "'Unto these the land shall be divided for an inheritance according to the number or names. To the more shalt you give the more inheritance, and to the fewer thou shalt give the lesser inheritance; to each one according to those that were numbered of it shall its inheritance be given;" a list of names follows.
[7] Numbers 1:1-2. "And the Lord spoke unto Moses in the wilderness of Sinai, in the tent of the meeting, on the first day of the second month, in the second year after they were come out of the land of Egypt, saying: 'Take ye the sum of all the congregation of the children of Israel, by their families, by their fathers' houses, according to the number of names, every male, by their polls," Numbers 1:18: "And they assembled all the congregation together on the first day of the second month, and they declared their pedigrees after their families, by their fathers' houses, according to the number of names, from twenty years old and upward, by their polls;" Numbers 1:20: "And the children of Reuben, Israel's first born, their generations, by their families, by their fathers' houses, according to the number of names, by their polls, every male from twenty old upward, all that were able to go forth to war."
[8] See Ezra and Nehemiah.

BABYLONIAN ERA

After Nebuchadnezzar defeated the kingdom of Judah and destroyed the Temple in Jerusalem in 586 B.C.E., the Judean nobility and priestly hierarchy were taken as captives to Babylonia, where they were allowed to settle and live freely.[9] From that population sprang the Babylonian exilarchs and the Babylonian Talmudic academies with their *geonim* (see chapter 8, Geonim), and, on their return to Judea, the nucleus of the restored Jewish nation in Jerusalem. The Babylonian exile and destruction of the Temple constituted a disruptive period for the Israelites. They suffered the loss of some of their carefully maintained lists of generations, resulting in efforts to reconstruct and maintain the *sepher yohasin*.

During the stay in Babylonia it had become customary, especially for the leaders of the exiled Jews, to acquire Aramaic names. Aramaic, the language adopted by the Babylonian kingdom, was the lingua franca used throughout that region. The change was made in some cases by adding the Hebrew suffixes *alef-yod* (implies "connected with"), as in Barzelai (*barzel* means iron) or an *alef*, as in Malka, supposedly derived from the Hebrew *melekh*.[10] Others during the Babylonian period took on names that incorporated non-Jewish deities. Examples are Esther (from *ishtar*) or Mordechai (from *mordok*).[11] Still others used the names of Babylonian angels or months of the Babylonian year, while a number simply made their names sound more Aramaic, as in the change of Hananyah to Hanina.

When Jews were dispersed into the Diaspora following the Roman destruction of the second Temple in Jerusalem (70 C.E.), the loss of continuity in the carefully maintained genealogies left gaps that precluded for most the ability to identify officially with one of the 12 tribes of Israel, except for the Levites and Cohens, who retained their surnames for religious functions. Over time it then became more prevalent to take on the name of a notable ancestor as the family name, sometimes even when the genealogy was known. One example is the Ben Maimon family, which in this manner declared its identification with Rabbi Mosheh ben Maimon (Maimonides), even though Maimonides's genealogy could be traced back to Ovadia.

During the Golden Era in Spain, Jewish names were mainly patronyms, as in Moshe ben Maimon, Hasdai ibn Shaprut, Moshe ibn Ezra , and Shlomo ibn Judah

---

[9] Recent DNA markers for the "Cohen gene" (Cohen is the surname of Jewish families who were priests) have been found to be present in greater concentration among Jews from Babylonia (present-day Iraq) than among any other group of Jews.

[10] Malka means king in Aramaic and in Punic. Although Barzelai is found in the lists of returnees from Babylonia to Jerusalem, Malka is not. One might assume then that members of that Malka family did not return with the first waves of returnees. It is thus not surprising that two of the later Babylonian geonim (Rab Malka bar Aha, gaon of Pumbadita [771–75 C.E], and Mar Rab Malka, gaon of Sura [885 C.E.]) , were bearers of that name.

[11] Queen Esther's Hebrew name was Hadassah; Esther was her Babylonian name.

ibn Gabirol.[12] Ancient hereditary family names such as Sasson, Cohen, and Levi also are found. Over time many patronyms became hereditary surnames in their own right.

ROMAN AND CHRISTIAN ERAS

Romans bore three names (see Figure 8). The Roman naming system was based on the cult of the ancestor and maintenance of family hearth fires. Roman names consisted of the *agnomen* (individual's given name), *cognomen* (usually the father's name) and ancestral *nomen* (common ancestor or guild name).

Intent on breaking the hold of the clan on the individual and wishing to transfer individual loyalty from the pagan clan and family to the new family of Christians, Christianity placed emphasis on the individual as a member of a universal family. The baptismal, or "Christian," name became the only name of importance, and surnames essentially disappeared in the early Christian world, except for those of noble families, who retained their surnames because they based their power on their ancestral land ties. Adhering to local customs, most Jews in the Christian world ceased to use their family or tribal names. Except for surnames necessary for religious reasons, such as Levy or Cohen, Jews in these lands regularly used single names such as Isaac the Jew or nonhereditary patronymic names extending back one generation, such Moses, son of Isaac.

Around the 12th century, trade, taxation, and larger populations created the need for a two-name system to identify individuals. Surnames began to reappear in Europe, but they were now related to land (de Valois, de Bergerac) or descriptive, such as of occupations (Carpenter, Butler, Smith). Descriptive names did not necessarily continue to the next generation. For instance John Carpenter's son might have been Andrew Smith.

Because of the long-standing Christian naming tradition, the individual's name remained "the name" and the other the "surname." In Spain, where Arab-Jewish influence was significant, the name structures retained their old original designations; they were called *nombre* (first name) and *appelido* (family name).

SPANISH NAMES

Surnames came to Spain with the Romans at the beginning of the first millenium. When the Visigoths conquered the Iberian Peninsula, however, they abolished the use of surnames, and the Iberians once again used just one given name. Following the Arab conquest of Spain in 711, the Arabs introduced patronymics. By the 12th century, Spain had adopted the Arab custom of using patronymic surnames, and in the 13th century surnames became hereditary.[13]

---

[12] Ibn Gabirol was known to the Latin world as Aviceron.
[13] By contrast, Jews in the Austro-Hungarian Empire did not adopt surnames until the end of the 18th century, followed soon thereafter by Napoleon's decree to do so in his domains. Sweden did not adopt surnames until

Spanish secular names differ in structure from names commonly used elsewhere. For the last millennium, women in Spain traditionally kept their surnames throughout their lives and did not adopt their husbands' surnames when they married; therefore, wife and husband usually had different surnames. The child of such a union would thus inherit two surnames and use them both, listing the father's surname first and mother's second. In this manner Pedro, son of Alicia Hernandez (mother) and Carlos Menendez (father), would be named Pedro Menendez Hernandez. This convention persists, a source of confusion for strangers to Spanish names because of the mistaken assumption that the last listed name is the surname. But it would be incorrect to refer to Pedro as Mr. Hernandez (actually his mother's father's name). He should be referred to correctly as Mr. Menendez Hernandez or as Mr. Menendez.[14]

To confuse matters further, one or both of the parents' surnames may be a composite, consisting of two surnames connected by a hyphen and passed to the next generation as a single hyphenated surname from either parent. Sometimes this is done to differentiate a common surname. This pattern is reflected among Sephardic Jews with such hyphenated names as Cohen-Bensussan, Cohen-Scali, and Cohen-Alfasi, or Levi-Hasdai, Levi-Susan, and Levi-Abulafia.

Spanish surnames in 19th-century and earlier documents can be even more confusing to the genealogist. In some families, sons and daughters could choose their surnames from among all the parents', or grandparents', surnames. One can easily visualize bequests being designated on condition of the use and perpetuation of one's surname. This pattern could create the confusing situation of two brothers having different surnames.

To complicate matters further, one's given name (*nombre*) often consisted of several names.

Many Sephardic families with surnames of Spanish or Portuguese origin adopted the surnames when their ancestors converted to Christianity. Examples include Henriquez, Rodriguez, Gomez, and many others.[15] Because *conversos* often adopted the surnames of their Catholic godfathers, a researcher may find brothers who converted at different times with different godfathers and different surnames. If *conversos* later returned to Judaism, they usually retained the Spanish Catholic surnames they had acquired when they were baptized, but they resumed using their Hebrew given names. Thus we find the numerous Rodriquez, Henriquez,

---

the 19th century. Italy was a hybrid; northern Italy was part of the Holy Roman Empire, and its Jews followed Ashkenazic naming patterns. Jews in central and southern Italy followed Sephardic naming patterns.

[14] Because of this problem, and in an attempt to conform with practice in the non-Hispanic world, Spain passed a law permitting the order of the surnames to be reversed so that the father's surname comes last, but only if the requesting individual is over age 18. Prior to that age, both parents must consent to the change.

[15] Rodriguez is the most common Christian surname in Spain.

Gonzalez and similar surnames among Sephardim today. These were names adopted at the time of baptism.

Spanish surnames originating from place names, such as Toledano or Sevillano, give no indication as to whether or not the family had at one time converted to Christianity. Overtly religious names, such as "de la Santa Cruz," or "de San Jose" usually indicated a New Christian family eager to prove adherence to their new faith. Names taken from plants or trees, such as Perera (pear tree) and Olivera (olive tree), or animals such as Ovejas (sheep) apparently were adopted by forcibly converted Jews in Portugal. Converts related or allied to families of Spanish nobility frequently adopted the names of those families—and also adopted their coats of arms for good measure.

PATRONYMICS

Patronymic names exist in most Western cultures, especially among Jewish, Christian, and Moslem populations. Such names may incorporate the Hebrew prefix *ben* (son of); the Arabic *ibn* (son of), *abu* (father of), or *um* (mother of); the Germanic-Anglo-Saxon suffix *son* (son of, as in Johanson), the Scandinavian *sen* (son of, as in Johansen), and the Russian *vitch* (son of). The Spanish equivalents are *ez, az, iz, oz,* and *uz,* with *as, is, os,* and *us* more commonly found in Portugal. Hernandez originally meant son of Hernando.[16] In Portugal the equivalent surname was Hernandes.

These structural factors may serve as helpful clues in evaluating some Sephardic surnames. Sephardic Jews lived among many cultures, and they adopted many of the prevailing patronymic conventions. It always has been part of the Sephardic culture to participate fully in the surrounding mainstream culture in sharp contrast to the isolationism traditional in many Hassidic and other eastern European Jewish groups. Jews who lived in Moslem-dominated areas of Spain could have surnames that included the Arabic *ibn* (as in ibn Ezra, the great Sephardic poet of Moslem Andalusia). *Conversos* would take on the surnames of their Catholic godfathers and follow Iberian name patterns. Ashkenazic Jews when taking on surnames would similarly take on the Germanic or Russian patronymic constructions of where they lived.

JEWISH NAMES

Beginning with the rising power of the rabbis in the Babylonian period and continuing into the Sephardic world outside Christian influence, knowledge of law

---

[16] Other examples are Alvarez (son of Alvaro), Diaz/Diez (son of Diego), Gonzalez (son of Gonzalo), Guttierrez (son of Gutier, form of Wotier), Fernandez (son of Fernando), Lopez (son of Lope), Marquez (son of Marco), Martinez (son of Martin), Mendez (son of Mendo), Nunez (son of Nuno), Perez (son of Pero or Pedro), Rodriguez (son of Rodrigo), Ruiz (son of Ruy), Sanchez (son of Sancho), and Suarez (son of Suero).

and science conferred prestige and status among Jews, and even came to be considered of greater social importance than descent, whether from royalty or other lineage. The rabbis stated in the Talmud that "a bastard educated in the law is nobler than an ignorant high priest." Some families adopted surnames based on notable learned ancestors.

In biblical times, an individual's Jewish identity was tied closely to the individual's name and his genealogy as recorded in the *sepherim toledot* or *yohasin*. The family surname denoted the individual's belonging to one or the other families, clans or tribes. Here is how this played out in that ancient world. Members of the nation of Israel were *bene Israel* (sons of Israel); those of the Gad tribe *bene Gad* (sons of Gad) or *ha Gadi* (the Gadian); those of the Obadiah or Zakai families were ben Obadiah or ben Zakai, or just Obadiah or Zakai, and so on.

Surnames could specify the individual's father, as in Shlomo ben Maimon ben Hasdai. The second *ben* means son of the family Hasdai, meaning belonging to or descended from. If the ancestor were a notable person, that person's name would become the new family name, as in Ben David (ibn Daoud), one of several Sephardic families that claims descent from King David.

The Sephardic naming patterns described below were followed most strictly by the Sephardic Jews of Spain, Morocco, the eastern Mediterranean, the Balkans, and South America. Elsewhere greater variations occurred.

In Spain and Provence (France) during the Middle Ages, many Jewish names were translated into Latin versions. For instance, the Hebrew Hayyim became Vital or Vidas (life); Shemtob became Bonhom, Santob, or Santon (good name); Yom Tob became Bondia or Bondion (good day); Tob Elam became Bonenfant, Bonfils, or Bofill (good child); Serfati became Al Frangi or Frances (French person); and Zennah became Crescas or Berdugo (branch).

In Iraq and Syria many, but not all, Jews who were not descendants of Spanish exiles did not use hereditary family names as late as the early 20th century. Instead they used the patronymic tradition of using the name of the father as the second name. Shlomo son of Shaoul, for instance, would become known as Shlomo Shaoul. Following Sephardic tradition, Shlomo's eldest son would be named Shaoul after his grandfather, to be known as Shaoul Shlomo. This naming pattern repeated itself over generations.

In the 20th century, the most recent father's name used in this way became a hereditary surname. A hereditary surname was borne by future generations of the family. In some families *ben* was added, creating, for instance the Ben David family name.

Like Spanish Jews, the Jews of Morocco bore names arising from Hebrew, Arabic, Aramaic, or Spanish roots. About 10 percent of Moroccan Jews carried surnames of Berber origin. Berber names are recognizable in that they usually begin with *O* (son of), *Wa* or *A* (O'hanna, Oiknine, Wahnon, Waknin, Aknin, or Assouline, for example).

INDIVIDUAL NAMES

Jewish first names are religiously linked to an individual's spiritual identity, not only throughout life, but also after death. Sephardim imbued by mysticism and Kabbalah were careful to choose names that would not portend bad destinies.[17] Babies were often named after living relatives. In Ashkenazic tradition, however, naming a child after a living relative was avoided, allegedly for superstitious fear that the angel of death might mistakenly take the child instead of his or her older namesake.

Both Sephardic and Ashkenazic traditions linked the name to an individual's fate. Name changes were infrequent in both traditions, undertaken only in cases of grave illness or threat to life, following specific rituals known in Hebrew as *shinui hashem*. Even an error in the spelling of a name in a religious divorce document would render that divorce religiously invalid.

In the Bible, individual names were often bestowed to describe an individual's hoped-for destiny or characteristics. King David named his son Shlomo (from *shalom*, peace) because he hoped he would transmit to him a kingdom in peace. Adam named his wife Hava (life) because she was to be the mother of all living people. Other biblical names incorporated the name of God, as in Eliahu or Adoniram, or were based on animal names, as in Deborah (bee), Yonah (pigeon), and Yael (mountain goat).

The importance of the individual's Hebrew name in Jewish tradition is repeatedly illustrated in the Bible. The reader will note the importance that observant Jews give to the name of God, which is not to be taken in vain, and in fact is not even to be said aloud. In the Bible, when Abraham is given the covenant his name changes from Abram to Abraham to mark the change in him. Jacob dreams that he wrestles with an angel. He is transformed by that struggle and, to mark that transformation and new destiny, his name is changed from Jacob to Israel. A clear link is evident between the individual's name and his destiny.

COMMON SEPHARDIC NAMING CONVENTIONS

As noted above, unlike Ashkenazic Jews, Sephardim name their children after living relatives. Sephardim traditionally name their children using the following convention:
1. First-born son named after paternal grandfather
2. Second son named after maternal grandfather
3. First daughter named after paternal grandmother
4. Second daughter named after maternal grandmother
5. Next child named after paternal uncle or aunt

---

[17] Kabbalah (received knowledge in Hebrew) was a mystical Jewish religious movement. With origins in the first century C.E., it came into prominence during 13th–century Spain and reached its greatest influence during the 16th–17th centuries and in the Ashkenazic Hassidic movement.

6. Next child named after maternal uncle/aunt
7. And so forth

If a grandparent (paternal or maternal) or sibling were deceased, his or her name often would take precedence over the living relative. Although this practice was followed generally, many exceptions were made to this naming convention. Some Spanish exiles named children after their own parents. Some families preferred to name their children after the prophets, judges, or famous individuals. After Cyrus of Persia conquered Babylonia and allowed the Jewish exiles to return to their homeland, many Jewish parents named their children Cyrus in his honor.

Sons born after the death of their fathers usually were given the father's name followed by Hayyim (life). Daughters born after the recent death of a sister were often called Bienvenida (welcome). Seriously ill persons would change their names to Hayyim or Raphael in the case of men, or Vida or Aisha (life) in the case of women.[18]

Spelling and Acculturation

Spelling was a pre-occupation of the 20th century. In earlier times, numerous spellings were used for the same name. Among Sephardic names, common variations of the same name include:

Aben, Ibn, Aven, Avin, Ben—all meaning "son of"
Abram, Abraham, Ibrahim, Abrahim
Aaron, Aron, Aharon
Cavalleria, Caballeria, Cabellera, Cavallera
Elazar, Alazar, Alacar
Esther, Ester, Azter, Ezter
Hasdai, Chasdai, Azday, Açday[19]
Isaac, Isach, Azach, Açach
Jacob, Jaco, Iacob, Iaco
Reyna, Reina, Avenreina, Avireina
Sahadia, Çahadia, Sadia
Salamon, Solomon, Çulema, Salamo, Shlomo
Sasson, Çaçon
Shaprut, Saprut, Çaprut, Xaprut

Sephardic Jews who lived in Arab, Spanish, Italian, French, Dutch, or other countries often modified their names to conform to the local culture. The name Shlomo would appear, for example, as Suleiman (Arab or Turkish), Solomon (English), Salomon (French), and Salomone (Italian), with equally varied nicknames

---

[18] Laredo, *Les Noms des Juifs du Maroc.*
[19] The Spanish ç (cedilla under a c) sounds similar to s.

(Mony, Solly, Sol). During the Babylonian, Hellenic, Roman, Arab, and other periods, Sephardic Jews adopted Babylonian, Greek, Roman and Arab names respectively. Some examples include:

    Habib (beloved, in Arabic) → Caro or Querido (Spanish)
    Zemach (branch, in Hebrew) → Crescas (in Spanish)
    Asher (Hebrew) → Maimon (fortunate, in Arabic)
    Malka (king, Aramaic) → AbenRey, Soberano (king, in Spanish)
    Shalom (peace or greeting, in Hebrew) → Benveniste (welcome, in Spanish) or Berfet/Barfat in Provence (from Perfetto)
    Shoshan (lily, in Hebrew) → Ibn Shoshan (ibn, son in Arabic), later Sasson

Sephardim also adopted geographical names as surnames. Examples include Belmonte (in Spain), Cordovero (from Cordoba), Toledano (from Toledo), Medina, Malka/Malqui (from Malaga), Cardozo, and Ashkenazic (from Germany).

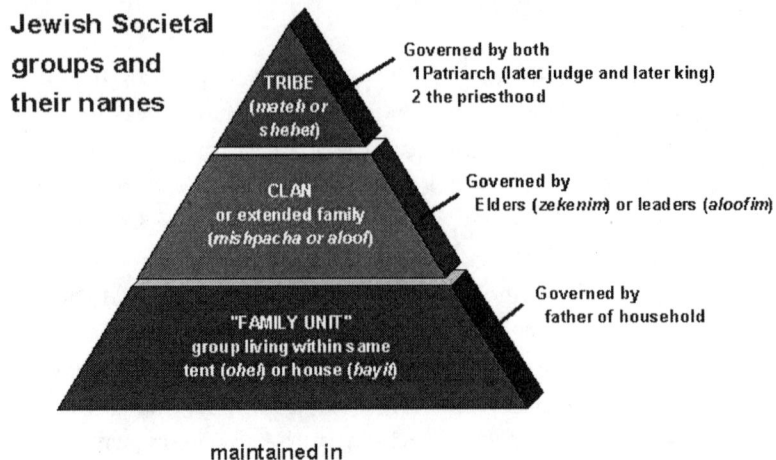

Jewish Societal groups and their names

- **TRIBE** (*mateh* or *shebet*) — Governed by both 1 Patriarch (later judge and later king) 2 the priesthood
- **CLAN** or extended family (*mishpacha* or *aloof*) — Governed by Elders (*zekenim*) or leaders (*aloofim*)
- **"FAMILY UNIT"** group living within same tent (*ohel*) or house (*bayit*) — Governed by father of household

maintained in Sepher Toledot and (after exile) Sepher Yohasin

Figure 7. Biblical Naming Pattern

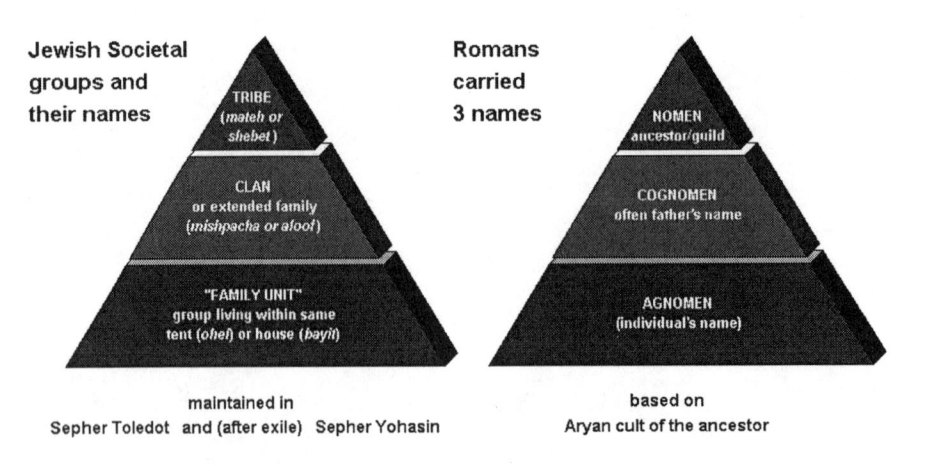

Jewish Societal groups and their names

- **TRIBE** (*mateh* or *shebet*)
- **CLAN** or extended family (*mishpacha* or *aloof*)
- **"FAMILY UNIT"** group living within same tent (*ohel*) or house (*bayit*)

maintained in Sepher Toledot and (after exile) Sepher Yohasin

Romans carried 3 names

- **NOMEN** ancestor/guild
- **COGNOMEN** often father's name
- **AGNOMEN** (individual's name)

based on Aryan cult of the ancestor

Figure 8. Similarities between Roman and Jewish Name Constructions

80 • *Sephardic Genealogy: Discovering Your Sephardic Ancestors and Their World*

Part II
Genealogy Basics

11.
How to Get Started

Genealogy novices share a common misconception: Their family trees are out there, all ready to print out, if only they knew where to look. Reality is different. Unless your family is famous enough to have had research conducted and a book written about it, or if a relative has already compiled the family history, it is necessary for you to build your family tree. Starting from scratch permits you to experience the joys of search and discovery that make genealogy such an addictive and popular hobby. Doing genealogy is like being in a mystery novel in which the genealogist is the chief detective. Clues sometimes lead to dead ends, but at other times they lead in unsuspected and fascinating directions. As the voyage of discovery proceeds, your horizons broaden as you learn more about history, culture, Judaism, and other subject areas that you might not otherwise have discovered or deemed interesting.

Begin With What You Know

Start with what you already know and then develop the unknown one step at a time. Start by systematically writing down what you know about your family. Use a pedigree form or family group sheet (see Appendix F, Genealogy forms) and fill in your name, your parent's names, and (if known) your grandparents' names.[1] To family sheets add your siblings' names and the names of your parents' siblings and their spouses. Add their children's names. If you are married, enter your spouse's name and your children's names, if any. Use women's maiden names on genealogy forms.

If you have completed all the above, you will have filled in the names of four generations—grandparents' generation, parents' generation, your own generation, and your children's generation. If that were all there were to genealogy, it would be quite boring. But you will learn how to flesh it out and make it interesting.

Let's add some dates. For each person listed, enter a birth date and (if applicable) a date of death. You may already know some of these dates, but for others it will be necessary to do some research, but not yet! More information will be needed, and it is best to ask others for all their information once, rather than one question at a time.

Organization pays off. Make a list of persons for whom information is needed, and list under each name the specific information items you will seek. If you are

---

[1] A good source of pedigree and other genealogy forms can be found in Sharon DeBartolo Carmack *Organizing Your Family History Research* (Cincinnati, Oh.: Betterway Books, 1999).

using a computer software program to record your data (see chapter 16, Genealogy Software), your program may have a report for "missing data."

Other necessary information includes place of birth, place of death, and, if known, where buried (town and cemetery), for each individual. The places of birth and death are important because they permit you to search efficiently for birth and death records. Get as much *specific* information as possible. Names of countries alone are not enough; names of towns or villages are needed, but if country is all that can be determined at present, record it and consider it a clue to be built on.

RECORD YOUR SOURCES

Always record your sources for every item of data to avoid creating genealogically useless information. From whom or where did you obtain that name, date, place name, or other piece of information? Be specific and include the date the information was obtained; that information might differ from what you might learn at a later date. Recording sources is discussed in chapter 13, but it is important to do it right from the start and to develop the habit of adhering to this important rule. Do not depend on memory. The source description should be sufficiently detailed that someone else can locate the data later just from the information you recorded.

Review the list of information you still need, and determine which person would be the best source for that information. Start with your parents if they are living. Encourage them to talk freely while you take notes. Without interrupting the flow of information, try to pin down specific names and places. Parents are also a good source for finding out which of the older or other relatives would know most about the family history. Before doing any interviews, read the section below on interviewing and oral history. Consider taping all your interviews; the stories that accompany the dates and places may be wonderful!

Next, look through old photo albums. Notice unknown faces. Notice backgrounds that could hint at different localities, especially overseas. Vacation photos might yield valuable clues, because a trip may have been to see relatives. Locate old letters, old postcards, maybe *ketubot* (Jewish marriage certificates), and plan to ask family members about them.

Members of the older generations are the best sources of information about deceased relatives and towns of origin, but they will not always be available to ask. A common lament of genealogists researching their own family trees is having lost the opportunity to interview a deceased relative before that person had died. Frequently older relatives are best interviewed face to face. Arrange to visit them in person, if possible. If a face-to-face interview is not possible, a phone call or letter with a questionnaire might suffice.

Interview, write, or phone other relatives. Keep a log of people to whom you wrote, what information you asked for, and when you made the request. Cross-check each piece of information you receive with several sources. Memories are fallible, and as any good reporter knows, it is necessary to confirm information from more than one source whenever possible.

This is a good start! Do not worry if you have not obtained all the information right away. Like a good detective story, your family's "mysteries" will not be solved in the first chapter of the book. But you already may have enough information to create an impressive family tree that not only will give you a sense of achievement, but can also serve as a tool to obtain still more information from others. If you include a copy of the family tree with requests for information from relatives, it tends to create increased interest and may encourage remembering long-forgotten events and details.

Genealogy software can speed creation of family trees, but if it is not available, sketch the family tree on a piece of paper, as genealogists have done for centuries. A genealogy software package is strongly recommended, however, because of its numerous advantages (see chapter 15, Computer Software).

NEXT STEPS

Next steps are difficult to describe because the possibilities are endless. You must tailor your research to fit the information you need about your particular family. Not all families have the same history or have lived in the same countries. For a family that came to the United States during the massive immigration waves of the early 20th century, for example, you will probably find valuable information in U.S. ship passenger records and naturalization records. If a family had lived in Salonica, the sources of information would be different from those for a family that had lived in The Netherlands or North Africa. It is important to determine the history of the family, and of the region in which they lived, before embarking on a plan of research.

When determining the travel history of your family, pay attention to branches other than yours. A branch of the family may have emigrated to Israel or South America. Although you might not start with them, researching the side (or collateral) branches often yields productive breakthroughs.

No detective concludes his or her case by interviewing witnesses of an event. After your initial interviews, analyze each interview to find clues among persons or documents that may have been overlooked. Part I of this book presents chapters on historical trends, but you should attempt to learn even more about the countries involved in your research. The suggested reading sections in the chapters in Part III should help. Visit the websites listed in Part IV, and familiarize yourself with maps of the countries you are researching. The bibliography may offer additional guidelines.

Individualized research is the most interesting part of genealogy, but many people initially feel stumped or lost. The following are concrete steps to help get you started. But remember that these are only first steps; diverge as you need to.

1. **JewishGen Family Finder.** Discover if other genealogists are researching the same families you are, and make yourself known to them. One easy way to do this is to list in JewishGen's Family Finder your name, the families, and the relevant geography you are researching.[2] In this important database, researchers of Jewish families list their own names and the families and towns they are researching, allowing them to make contact with each other and share information.
2. **Family Tree of the Jewish People.** Peruse the listings in this database, also maintained by JewishGen, which currently includes a reported two million individuals.[3] Most of the families currently listed in both JewishGen's Family Finder and the Family Tree of the Jewish People are Ashkenazic; but the best way to change this proportion is by listing your own Sephardic interests and names.
3. **Newslists.** Join the newslists mentioned in chapter 14, Computers and the Internet, and ask questions on their forums. Information abounds that is unpublished but known to individuals who have traced families with circumstances similar to yours.

   When you sign your messages to these newslists, list the families and towns you are researching under your signature. See the relevant newslists for examples. Another correspondent on the newslist might unexpectedly contact you to tell you he or she is researching the same family you are—or is your previously unknown second cousin. Such events happen more frequently than one would guess.
4. **Genealogy newslist archives.** Most newslists maintain archives of their past messages. Search genealogy newslist archives for keywords, such as family names, towns, and countries. Your efforts may produce a wealth of information. The Internet has allowed amateur genealogists to ask questions and share information with unprecedented ease. Fellow genealogists are eager to help and share what they know.
5. **Family websites.** Look for websites on the Internet about specific families. Sometimes family websites have useful information, but their main value may be in facilitating contact with others who have an interest in that family name. To find family websites, search for the family name using Internet search engines (some good ones are listed in Part IV, Internet), or look through the list of Sephardic family pages in Part IV.
6. **Literature Search.** Search for your family name in the *Jewish Encyclopedia* or books such as Laredo's *Les Noms des Juifs du Maroc*.[4]

---

[2] JewishGen's Family Finder may be accessed on the Internet at www.jewishgen.org/jgff.
[3] Family Tree of the Jewish People may be accessed on the Internet at www.jewishgen.org/gedcom.
[4] Abraham Laredo, *Les Noms des Juifs du Maroc* (Names of the Jews of Morocco) (Madrid: Institut Montano, 1978).

7. **Genealogy periodicals.** Subscribe to genealogy periodicals, especially *Etsi* and *Avotaynu*, to learn about resources and others' research methods. Eventually discover additional new resources yourself and share your findings with others whether by writing an article, giving a talk, or simply sharing them on a newslist or at a genealogy society meeting.
8. **Jewish education.** Continue your education in the history of the Jewish people. Join a local Jewish genealogy society to gain practical advice and help.

HOW TO INTERVIEW EFFECTIVELY

Prepare

Preparation has a great impact on the quality of your interview. Review your list of missing information and determine who might best be able to provide answers. Whenever possible, list several names as potential sources of information for each item. It is wise to ask for the same information from more than one source.

Compile a questionnaire for each potential interviewee that lists the specific questions to ask that person. Review the list to determine whether it suggests additional or follow-up questions that you might ask that person. A good question to ask any interviewee is, Who else should I speak to?

Set Priorities

Interview living persons first. Archives and documents almost always will be available to research, but persons have a limited life span. For the same reason, interview the eldest or those in frailest health first.

Do not limit yourself to interviewing just parents and grandparents. Uncles, aunts, and even more distantly related or unrelated persons can be important sources of information. In fact often one person in the family is known to "know about these things." You yourself are in the process of becoming just such a person.

Conduct the Interview

Ask open-ended questions. "Tell me about your home town," "tell me about your father," "what was it like living in that town?" are more likely to be informative than closed-end questions such as "what was the name of your home town?" or questions that require yes-and-no answers. Do not interrupt; appear interested by nodding or smiling. Particularly if you are taping the interview, keep the spotlight on the interviewee.

Schedule the interview at a time when the interviewee is relaxed and has the time to talk to you uninterruptedly. Always call ahead or write.

Bring a family tree with you. It will add interest, refresh memories, and permit the person interviewed to notice possible errors.

Be relaxed and make the interview a fun conversation. Encourage musing and reminiscing by the interviewee. An occasional joke or exclamation of surprise can be helpful.

Avoid interrupting the interviewee's train of thought. If what he or she says suggests a question to you, make a note of it on a sheet of paper, but do not interrupt at that moment. Ask it later during the interview. Be sure to nail down place names, dates (as close as possible), maiden names,[5] and places of marriage, birth, and death. Places of marriage may even permit finding and retrieving lost *ketubot*[6] (see specific country chapters).

Ask to see photographs or bring some with you. Viewing photographs together can send you into areas you might not have thought of and can provide invaluable information. They also raise the excitement level and often suggest questions you might not otherwise have thought to ask.

Ask your interviewee if he or she has old documents such as *ketubot*, letters, or postcards. He or she may not be willing to share such private documents; leave this question for the end to avoid casting a shadow on the interview.

Before finishing, review your list of questions to see if you have covered them all. At the end of the interview, be sure to tell the interviewee how helpful he or she has been and how grateful you are for the information. Ask for permission to ask additional questions later. Offer to share the information you collect. You may gain an ally.

Document the interview carefully. Despite its appearance as a conversation, you have created a source document. Take notes during the interview, and add to them and polish them as soon as possible after the interview, especially if you had not taped it. Memory is surprisingly tricky, especially over time. Mark the time, date, and place of the interview, along with the full name of the subject.

PRECAUTIONS

Although it is wise to gather information about others who share common family names (you may find a connection later), do not add them to your family tree until you have found a verifiable direct link. Avoid the urge to try to link your family with a famous individual, a common error made by beginners—not valid genealogy. Read about that notable person if he or she interests you, expand your knowledge, but do not assume links until you can prove them.

---

[5] Sometimes a person may not remember a relative's maiden name but will remember the name of that woman's brother.

[6] A *ketubah* is a Jewish marriage certificate. It is an excellent source of dates, names, and places. *Ketubot* always lists names of parents, and often several generations on each side.

Be Wary of Family Legends

Most families, especially Sephardic ones, have passed down to them legends about their ancestry; there may even be some truth to them! Stories of descent from King David, for example, are common among Sephardim, and because of their history, they may be true. As a genealogist, though, you must take family legends with a grain of salt. Record them because they add color to the picture you are creating—and they *may* have some validity and offer research leads. But mark them clearly as legends, and do not accept them as fact unless you find documentary proof of their veracity.

LOGS

Maintain two types of logs. In a research log, list what you need to do and where. The research log allows you to organize and group together tasks you need to accomplish. This tool is similar to a shopping list on which you group together all the items you need from the grocery store, the pharmacy, and the cleaners. In genealogy you group together all the information you need to look for at this library or that archive, or all the questions you need to include in a letter, or, even more importantly, when traveling to another city or country, all the places you need to visit for your research.

The research log also is useful as a reminder of what remains to be done. When a brilliant idea comes to mind as you read an article or speak to someone, jot it down in your research log. Rereading a research log often reminds you of things you once meant to do and prevents the loss of leads and clues.

A results log lists what you have done and the results achieved. It documents whether you have done a specific piece of research or visited a source—and, most importantly, what you found there. Documenting negative results is of paramount importance because it avoids repeating searches that have no useful results.

A hand-held computer or organizer is an excellent tool in which to keep these logs; the electronic tool can be with you wherever you go, allowing you to both record and review. Paper will also do fine.

LEARN YOUR HISTORY

Learning the history of the period and place you are researching is essential. This activity brings your ancestors to life and explains many of their actions. In addition history directs you where to look for information. For example, if your ancestor lived in an area of Morocco under Spanish rule, relevant records are likely to be in Spanish archives. Later this same area may have come under French rule; the archives might be in France.

History may explain certain population migrations. It is easy to conclude that a relative left Spain in 1492 because of the expulsion decree, but lesser events may have prompted the move at another time. History may tell you of a famine or riots that occurred at a certain time. Inquisition records may tell you of the trial of a family relative or another threat prompting flight. A dry list of names of dead relatives makes for boring reading. An important part of genealogy is to flesh out names and bring them to life. You can do this by incorporating stories about the individuals or facts about the period they lived in. This is particularly easy for recent relatives; record their stories. What may seem to be commonplace stories to you will be invaluable, fascinating information to future generations who later find your genealogy documents.

Ethics

Privacy concerns are important. You may collect data, but do not publish information about living persons without their expressed permission to do so. Some family relatives may not wish to share information they have with you. Most genealogical researchers have encountered this problem. Remember that honey gathers flies. Try to interest them in other ways. Ask them simply to correct errors in names and dates, and then see if they become more receptive. A family tree with information you have already gathered is a wonderful tool to use in this manner. So is a genealogy scrapbook that displays family trees, photographs, copies of documents, and the like. Sometimes even this tool may backfire; some people may be aghast at all the information collected about them—even though it is openly available and retrievable from public sources.

When you write for information and advice from others, enclose a stamped, self-addressed envelope. If you write to someone overseas, include one or more international postal coupons to cover return postage. When writing, remember that you are asking a favor that will take time and effort for the other party. Remember that non-answers to queries on newslists are often the result of lack of knowledge.

Suggested Reading

Epstein, Ellen Robinson, and Jane Lewit. *Record and remember : tracing your roots through oral history.* Lanham, Md.: Scarborough House, 1994.

Freedman-Morris, Mona. *Scattered Seeds: A Guide to Jewish Genealogy.* Boca Raton, Fla.: RJ Press, 1998.

Krasner-Khait, Barbara. *Discovering Your Jewish Ancestors.* Bountiful, Ut.: HeritageQuest, 2001.

Kurzweil, Arthur. *From Generation to Generation: How to Trace Your Jewish Genealogy and Family History.* Northvale, N.J.: Jason Aronson, 1994.

Lackey, Richard S. *A Manual for Documenting Family Histories and Genealogical Records.* New Orleans: Polyanthos, 1980.

Mokotoff, Gary, and Warren Blatt. *Getting Started in Jewish Genealogy.* Bergenfield, N.J.: Avotaynu, 1999.

12.
SEPHARDIC GENEALOGY

The basic principles of good genealogy research, Jewish or otherwise, include researching from known to unknown and carefully documenting sources. Though similar in methodology to all genealogy work, differences in the sources of information specific to Jewish genealogy warrant the need for the numerous specialized books that guide for Jewish genealogy. Books also exist for the specialized resources of Scottish, Irish, German, Ukrainian, and other ancestral research. Although great similarities exist in researching Ashkenazic and Sephardic ancestry, sufficient differences between the two have prompted publication of this book (see Figure 9). This chapter describes some of the most significant resources in common and some uniquely Sephardic resources.

RESOURCES COMMON TO SEPHARDIM AND ASHKENAZIM

Many sources useful to Ashkenazic genealogical research are also useful in Sephardic research. In both cases interviewing elders and other family members is the single most important starting point, the technique that provides the most useful early information as well as important clues for further research. This is the common starting point for any family research, irrespective of nationality. The universal mistake discovered by every researcher is not having started early enough while elder family members are still around to share their knowledge and memories.

Both Sephardic and Ashkenazic synagogues and *mohels* kept **marriage, divorce, and circumcision records**. These are obviously of tremendous value in both cases. Differences appear in this category because of family names. Sephardic hereditary family surnames go further back in time, which renders older records of greater value to researchers of Sephardic families than to those of Ashkenazic families.

Holocaust records are another common research area. Though it tends to be under-emphasized, Sephardic Jews were also victims of the Holocaust. Many Sephardic communities, notably those of Salonica and The Netherlands, were almost totally annihilated. Researching Holocaust records, especially for Jews from Salonica, The Netherlands, and some North African countries can yield valuable information not otherwise available elsewhere.

Although Sephardim came to the United States at times other than the turn of the last century migrations, this massive migration included significant numbers of Sephardim from eastern Mediterranean and Balkan countries. For these **20th-century immigrants** to the United States, many information sources are the same for both Ashkenazic and Sephardic Jews. These include such items as passenger ship records, naturalization papers, and census records. During the periods the Sephardim have lived in the United States, the National Archives are an equally fertile source of information.

UNIQUE SEPHARDIC RESOURCES

Whereas Ashkenazim lived primarily in Christian Europe, Sephardim lived primarily around the Mediterranean, in countries of the Ottoman Empire, in The Netherlands, and in South America. Geography alone creates many differences in Sephardic genealogy research (see Figure 10). To begin with, the **languages** are different. Sephardic languages include Ladino, Arabic, Turkish, French, Greek, Dutch, and Spanish as compared to Yiddish and several European languages among the Ashkenazim.

Countries in which the majority of Sephardim lived maintained **records different from** those commonly seen in the Christian and European world. Some countries were culturally backward compared to the European countries; they did not start keeping records until quite late. Others, such as Spain, have records that go back a thousand years. A few, such as The Netherlands have superbly organized records that permit a descendant to reconstruct rapidly a family tree spanning three hundred to four hundred years. For others, creating the tree proves to be a stimulating undertaking that takes years. Whereas most available records for Ashkenazic research are found in archives of recent centuries, Sephardic documents can be found in both recent archives and in archives as old as 12th century or earlier.[1]

Family surnames play a role as well. Whereas most Ashkenazic family names are of relatively recent origin, which renders records older than a century or two difficult if not impossible to use, Sephardic family names frequently go back a thousand years, as noted above, and sometimes more.[2] Not only does this make ancient documents of great use to the Sephardic researcher, it also accords greater value to onomastic studies; the study of names becomes a useful tool for Sephardic families in tracing their ancestry (see chapter 10, Evolution of Sephardic surnames and Appendix A). Books on Sephardic onomastic research and even name entries in *Encyclopaedia Judaica* are among the most useful sources of information available to Sephardic family researchers.[3]

---

[1] Examples of early records are the 12th-century notarial archives of Spanish towns or the later Inquisition records of Spain, Portugal, and South America.
[2] The Shealtiel and Charlap families claim descent from sons of the exilarch Chizkiya executed in 1056 C.E. by the caliph of Baghdad.
[3] Abraham Laredo, *Les Noms des Juifs du Maroc* (Names of the Jews of Morocco) (Madrid: Institut Montano, 1978), has extensive biographical lists of more than a thousand families with detailed sources cited. It is possibly the most useful book for Sephardic genealogists because of the sources and information it provides, even for Jews who did not live in Morocco.

Sephardic **naming conventions** differ from those of their Ashkenazic brethren and these too have significance to the genealogist. Sephardim name children after persons who may be living or dead, whereas Ashkenazim typically name their children after deceased relatives. Among Sephardim, the convention is to name the eldest son after the paternal grandfather and the eldest daughter after the paternal grandmother in order to honor that person.[4] Therefore, whereas in Ashkenazic family research the date of birth of a child can sometimes be used to guess at the approximate year of death of the namesake, in Sephardic genealogy the name of the eldest son gives a clue to the name of the paternal grandfather. This can be helpful in differentiating between cousins having the same first names or branches of a family tree.

Sephardic *ketubot* sometimes list several generations on both sides of the wedding couple. Many Sephardic elders, though by no means all, can rattle off the names of eight or nine previous generations from memory.

Christian sources play a role in Sephardic research. Following the 1392 riots in Spain (see chapter 2, Brief History of the Jews in Spain and Portugal), many Jews fled to neighboring countries such as North Africa. Nevertheless, large numbers of Jews in Spain, and later in Portugal, were forced to convert to Catholicism. Some converted sincerely or because it opened opportunities for them, but a great many did so under great duress or, as was the case for the majority in Portugal, by having priests forcibly pour water over them en masse, thereby declaring them baptized and converted. For the years before these *conversos* could return openly to Judaism, records for these families will be found among traditional Christian sources, including church records.

An interesting tradition in some crypto-Jewish families was for a son to enter the church as a priest. Some rose to great power within the Church hierarchy. In this manner crypto-Jewish families would have someone to go to for protection or for "confessions" in which they would not betray their true faith.

Similarly Inquisition records often include details about the families and acquaintances of the accused. These records can yield valuable information, including the Jewish names of the families of the accused, their immediate history, and occasionally family trees. Inquisition records exist in both the Old World and the Americas (see chapter 18, Spain).

The expulsions from Spain and Portugal and their Inquisitions caused many crypto-Jews to flee to the Americas where in their attempt to stay a step ahead of the Inquisition they often tried to move to the edges of Inquisition reach. Whereas twentieth-century immigrants to the United States search through ship passenger records of ships arriving from places like Hamburg and Rotterdam, Sephardim have another older resource. The *Archivo General de Indias* (**General archive of the Indies**) museum in Seville has records of passenger lists for every ship that sailed

---

[4] See chapter 18, Evolution of Sephardic Names.

from Seville to the Americas from 1509 to 1790 (see chapter 18, Spain). These records are detailed lists of who the passenger was, where he or she was traveling and where they went after that, who they were going to meet, what their job was, plus a lot more. If it is known when an ancestor came to the Americas during this period, this archives may be a useful source of information. Of course all persons listed in these records were officially Catholic; therefore, these archives are especially useful for *converso* families who were Catholic at least for a time.

Certain archival repositories are particularly valuable for Sephardim. The **notarial archives** of Spain, which hold a thousand to three thousand entries for some towns each year, are one example. These voluminous notarial records give details of property and tax transactions. In the documents, Jews are usually clearly identified as such. Sometimes when a property sale or rental transaction appeared in several entries, as the matter worked its way through the bureaucracy, name variations of the same individual appear. These name variations may be mere translations from Hebrew to Spanish or Arabic, but they are often of great interest to the researcher.

Some Differences:

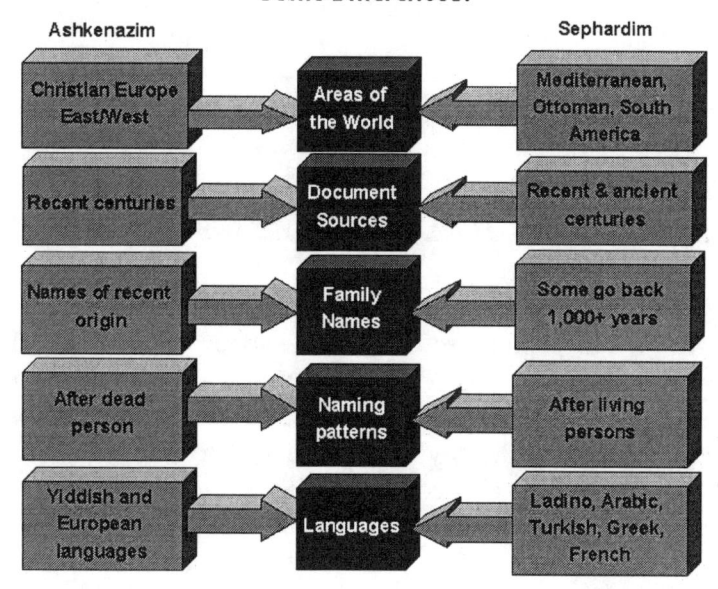

Ashkenazim		Sephardim
Christian Europe East/West	Areas of the World	Mediterranean, Ottoman, South America
Recent centuries	Document Sources	Recent & ancient centuries
Names of recent origin	Family Names	Some go back 1,000+ years
After dead person	Naming patterns	After living persons
Yiddish and European languages	Languages	Ladino, Arabic, Turkish, Greek, French

Figure 9. Differences between Ashkenazic and Sephardic Genealogy

Document Sources

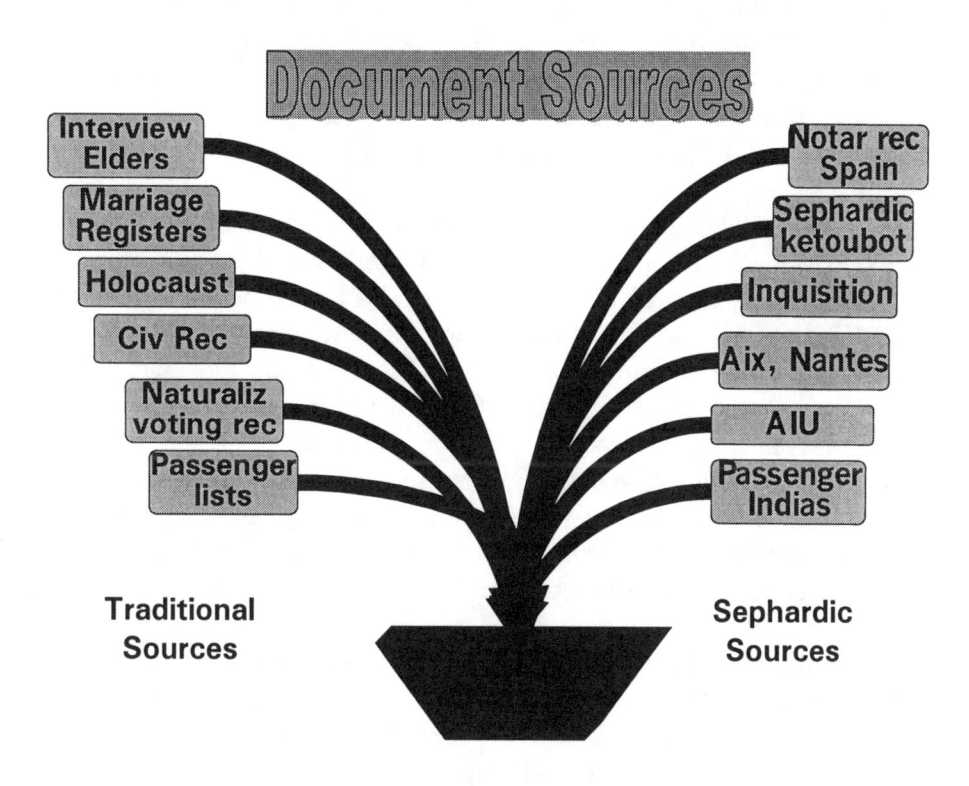

Traditional Sources:
- Interview Elders
- Marriage Registers
- Holocaust
- Civ Rec
- Naturaliz voting rec
- Passenger lists

Sephardic Sources:
- Notar rec Spain
- Sephardic ketoubot
- Inquisition
- Aix, Nantes
- AIU
- Passenger Indias

Figure 10. Resources for Sephardic Genealogy

Chapter 12: Sephardic Genealogy • 95

13.
ORGANIZING AND DOCUMENTING RECORDS

Because you have so few records when you begin to work on your family tree, it may seem a bit premature to worry about organizing them. But this circumstance changes rapidly as you collect more and more data. In time your pile of papers will grow and become more difficult to search through to find a specific bit of information. At first it may seem sufficient to put all your records in one manila folder, but the time will come soon when you will need a better system. There are many possible ways to organize your records; choose the one that works best for you.

SUGGESTED FILING SYSTEM FOR YOUR DOCUMENTS

Purchase several large file folders called file pockets in a variety of colors and a selection of matching file folders. The file pockets open up two or three inches when fully expanded. Label one folder for each family you are researching. Start with a minimum of four pocket folders, and label one for each of your grandparents' families. Later you may need to increase the number of these family folders.

Inside the file pockets, place file folders labeled for each smaller family group: for instance, one for each of your uncle's or aunt's families, and so on. Color coding the file folders by family may be helpful. As you collect documents, such as birth and death certificates, archival documents, letters, and photos, put them in the appropriate file folder within the correct pocket file or files so that you can find them easily when you need to refer to them again. If a document refers to more than one family, place a duplicate in each appropriate file.

As you do your research, you will gather information about people with similar names who might be related to your family. You will want to keep this type of information in case it becomes pertinent later—but putting it in your family folders might be confusing. Put hypothetical family information either in a separate folder within the appropriate family pocket folder or in a separate pocket folder.

Use additional pocket folders for background information. In these keep general notes or copies of articles about the history of the countries you are researching or the archives you do research in, tips on genealogy research, and copies of maps.

There always will be letters and papers that you are working on or have "recently" collected and have not yet filed in their proper places. Keep these papers together in a special open area on a bookshelf (you could use a box), and from time to time sort through them and file them properly. Realize that this is a very dangerous collection strategy, though, because unless you keep a close eye on this collection, it can grow enormously in volume! Much useful information that you intend to "look at later" can be buried and lost here. Unfortunately, experience has shown that there is no good way around amassing piles of paper other than sifting through the pile from time to time and filing the papers appropriately.

FORMS AND SUMMARY SHEETS

In time your research will expand in many directions, and you will no doubt find it difficult to remember what information is missing that you still need to look for. Individual and family forms can be helpful here. Make photocopies of the blank family record sheets and individual work sheets provided in appendix F and fill in as much information as you can. The forms allow you to see rapidly what you have already collected and what you still need to find out. File these forms in three-ring binders for easy portability on your research trips, or, alternatively, create electronic versions kept in your palmtop computer.

It is also extremely helpful to maintain research and correspondence logs. See the examples provided in the appendix F. This practice will help you avoid duplication of effort—and is especially important for negative findings. Positive findings and successful searches usually are easy to remember; the unsuccessful ones are forgotten. It is not uncommon to go to an archive or library to look for a particular item and, while there, search in many additional directions. Often these searches yield no useful information. It is important to record which information was searched for and not found, and when and where. Much time can be wasted in following tips or ideas about a research source and traveling to the archive or library, only to find out that you had already searched this source.

DOCUMENTING SOURCES

It is important to reiterate the necessity to document all the sources of the information you collect. This practice is essential and the point cannot be emphasized enough. As you review your research, you will inevitably find conflicting information. Someone's given name will be found to be different in another source, or the dates that Uncle Sam or Cousin Joseph gave you are not the same as those you recorded elsewhere for David's birth and death. If you did not record where you got the conflicting data, you will be unable to decide which information is more likely to be accurate, or even to return to the original source to try to find out if the information was recorded erroneously. You cannot rely on memory. Anticipate that you will collect data from many sources years apart; memory is not adequate to the task.

Document not just some, but *all* the information you gather. Not to do so is a common error of beginning genealogists—and even those who should know better. Sources of names and dates are obvious candidates for documentation, but they are not the only data elements to document. Who told you or where did you find out that Uncle Isaac left Italy because of such and such an incident? From whom did you find out that the family lived in this or that town or had a brother who died in this or that war or incident? Who told you that your grandfather's brother's name was Solomon? Document as much as you can about all information that you gather.

Documenting sources provides validity to your data and also allows you and others to recheck possible errors in your information and correct it. As new family history becomes available, it becomes necessary to review and verify what a source had previously told you and if there might possibly be some additional information that you did not think was important at the time. Computers shine in documenting information. Genealogy software programs make it easy to document and cross-reference separate nuggets of information—this is a major reason to use one to record your genealogy data and family tree.

Software usually prompts you step by step to document the source. Many of the source details may be the same, and the software usually permits you to reinsert common information without having to retype. But proofread your work carefully to avoid perpetuating an initial error!

The format in which you record sources is important. A discussion of this topic is beyond the scope of this book, and the reader is referred to any of a number of excellent sources, especially Lackey's *A Manual for Documenting Family Histories and Genealogical Records*, which covers the topic in great detail.[1] The following are some basics:

- When dealing with persons who provided the information, record their full names (and addresses, if possible) and the date. Note whether you kept notes of the interview and who is the repository of these notes (usually yourself).
- For information obtained from books, carefully record the author, title, city, state, publisher and the year of publication, edition, and page numbers. If possible, make photocopies to keep in your records. For rare or out-of-print books, record where you located the book.
- Record where a document was found (archive, call number, microfilm number, page number, and identifying code) and the date you saw it. Record whether you viewed an original, copy, transcript, extract, or photograph. Try to make a copy (or more than one copy) of the document for your files. You likely will need to look at it again.
- For all sources recorded, note your assessment of whether the information is reliable, probable, possible, doubtful, or untrue. Persons reading your files after you are gone will find this assessment useful. When referring to the data at a later date, when precise details of the interview or research have faded from memory, you might be glad you took this step.

---

[1] Richard S. Lackey, *A Manual for Documenting Family Histories and Genealogical Records* (New Orleans: Polyanthos, 1980).

The primary reason to document the source is to permit someone other than you to independently locate that book or document. Is the information you provide sufficient to permit that person to do so? If not, you have not properly documented your source.

Preserving History for Posterity

What should you do with all the accumulated material your research has produced? Would it not be a shame if it were irretrievably lost when you are no longer there to talk about it? Over time you will have discovered facts not only from records, but also from interviews of elderly relatives—information no longer rediscoverable once these elderly people have died and you, too, are no longer there to relay their words.

It is essential that you preserve your findings for posterity. There are many ways to accomplish that task. Some researchers write and publish books; if you feel up to the task, that is the most permanent way to preserve the information and make it available to other researchers. Others choose to preserve the information they gather simply in their genealogy or other computer software. That method is less than optimal, because the data can be lost easily, or, with technological advances, become unusable to future generations. CDs are more permanent but also suffer the risk of being thrown out with old music CDs or become unreadable with new technologies. Posting the information on Internet websites is the least permanent record of all, because websites come and go with bewildering rapidity.

An easy way to make material readily available to others is through the use of so-called "show-off scrapbooks." These scrapbooks can be as simple as a three-ring binder in which you insert pages of information. The pages might include a detailed family tree, copies of pertinent maps, and pages that present vignettes and narratives in which you describe what you know of this or that relative's life and achievements, along with copies of photographs of persons, homes, and meaningful objects. Pages describing the history of the region or period in question, as well as bibliographies, can help the reader understand the context of the family history you detail. With a simple scanner you can scan photographs and maps into the computer, and almost any word processor will create professional-looking pages that include both text and images. Once these pages have been saved in the computer, they can be produced in any number of copies and can be updated easily as you discover new information. With the ability to produce numerous copies, it is possible to provide complete binders to many members of your family at very low cost. Just imagine how a future descendant will feel when he or she comes across one of your binders with the wealth of family information it contains.

14.
COMPUTERS AND THE INTERNET

For most of us, computers have changed many aspects of our lives. Few people still use typewriters. More and more people use word processors and e-mail, and they exchange e-mail addresses almost as frequently as they do phone numbers. Even my 93-year-old father surfs the web and uses e-mail to communicate with his family and friends.

Virtually nowhere has the Internet had more impact than in the field of genealogy. Computers and the Internet have revolutionized how genealogy research is done: in research, in how records are kept, and even in how researchers communicate with each other. Numerous websites disseminate information on available archives and useful books about countries you might be researching. Other websites provide instruction on ways to conduct valid genealogical research and where to find needed resources. Some offer vehicles for researchers to communicate with large numbers of other researchers. Of the many tools useful to genealogists that the Internet provides, highest on any list are e-mail, newslists, and websites. A compendium of Internet resources is presented in Part IV.

E-MAIL

E-mail allows researchers to communicate rapidly with others whom they believe might have information about their families or towns of origin, for example. Letter writing is more time consuming than sending e-mail; e-mail messages typically result in rapid responses. Instead of waiting days and weeks for a letter to get to its destination and for the addressee to reply, e-mail can be instantaneous; frequently a reply to a message may arrive on the same day resulting in an entire new clan of relations in another country. The reply often contains a copy of the message sent originally. This feature can be useful if, as is often the case, you had written e-mails to several parties and may not recall exactly what you wrote or asked a particular respondent.

E-mail also permits exchanges with persons whom otherwise one might never have known. Most people with whom the author exchanges e-mails are people he has never met in person and whose existence he would never have known about were it not for the Internet. Some correspondents have become very close friends, and many have provided the author with information otherwise unavailable. Requests to look up information in archives or libraries in distant countries are frequently honored and provide otherwise difficult-to-obtain information.

Sometimes you may know the name of the persons with whom you wish to correspond but may not know their e-mail address. How would you find e-mail addresses? Some websites allow searching for e-mail addresses (or phone numbers). These sites are less complete and comprehensive than many phonebooks, and they frequently give old and no longer valid information, but they can be very helpful. Some Internet sites useful for finding U.S. phone numbers or addresses are:

- Lycos's "Whowhere" at www.whowhere.lycos.com
- Anywho at www.anywho.com
- Infospace at www.infospace.com
- Yahoo's "people search" at people.yahoo.com
- Switchboard at switchboard.com

Reverse directories can be used when you know the person's address or telephone number, but not their names:

- reversedirectory.langenberg.com
- www.thinkdirectmarketing.com/freesearch

If you know their e-mail addresses but not names:

- my.email.address.is/efreverse.htm

Search for birth, death, and marriage records:

- vitalrec.com
- www.knowx.com

Peruse the U.S. Social Security Death Index at

- www.ancestry.com

NEWSLISTS

Newslists are discussion groups on the Internet. Newslists are created by and for persons who wish to share information and news about a specific common interest. They provide a forum where questions may be asked. A question sent to a newslist is received by all the members of that newslist and often elicits more than one reply. The replies may provide not only answers, but also often a discussion of the responses that can provide additional information or corrections. Some replies come from experts in the field, others by fellow members sharing experiences or information they discovered in their own searches.

One of the first activities recommended to a budding genealogist tracing a Jewish family is to find and join a nearby local Jewish genealogy society. Though very useful, a local genealogy society has a limited number of members and even fewer who are focused on your particular area of research. Newslists resemble genealogy societies with very large memberships whose members are often from several different countries and have a correspondingly large and diverse knowledge base.

Newslists exist for every imaginable subject, and genealogy is just one of thousands. Some newslists deal with general genealogy. Others specialize in topics such as computers in genealogy or Jewish genealogy. Some lists share information about specific ancestral towns or countries. Some newslists are for and about particular Jewish families, such as the Abrabanel and Shaltiel newslists, whose members operate the newslists to share information.

To join a newslist it is necessary first to subscribe.

The main newslists dealing with Sephardic genealogy are:

♦ SefardForum, www.jewishgen.org/sefardsig/sefardforum.htm, the oldest newslist for Sephardic genealogy
♦ International Sephardic Newslist, groups.yahoo.com/group/sephardic_list, deals with Sephardic topics in general and some genealogy topics. It tends to focus on Turkish and Salonican topics.
♦ Historical Society of Jews from Egypt, egyjews-subscribe@eGroups.com, a newslist for and about Jews who came from Egypt

Interest has grown among descendants of *conversos* or *anusim* to explore their Jewish roots; many descendants of *anusim* have expressed the desire to return openly to Judaism.[1] The author regularly receives e-mails asking for advice from persons who either have always known that their families were descendants of crypto-Jews or wonder if that may have been the case because peculiar family traditions suggest it.[2] Descendants of *conversos* are so numerous that the *anusim* newslist where aspects of the search are discussed is quite active. To subscribe to the *anusim* newslist, access www.yahoogroups.com/arcindex.cgi?listname=anusim.

Also of interest are some more general Jewish newslists on which Sephardic topics are discussed. The largest and best known is the JewishGen discussion group, www.jewishgen.org/JewishGen/DiscussionGroup.htm.

A newslist in which all messages are in Judeo-Spanish is at groups.yahoo.com/group/Ladinokomunita.

WEBSITES

Websites are the places on the Internet that you visit when you "surf the web." When the author first started researching his own Sephardic roots, few websites posted Sephardic genealogy topics, so he started the Sephardic genealogy

---

[1] *Converso* is the general term used for Jews who had converted to Christianity. *Anusim* is the name used for forced conversions. Crypto-Jews are Jews who are outwardly of another religion while secretly remaining Jewish.
[2] Such customs include always bathing on Fridays, not eating pork at home, avoiding Christian religious art in the home, and even sometimes etching a Star of David on the tombstone.

resources website, www.orthohelp.com/geneal/sefardim.htm, to share the information accumulated and to encourage others to research their Sephardic roots, thereby uncovering more resources to the benefit of all. A list of additional websites of interest to the Sephardic researcher is presented in Part IV, Internet.

LIMITATIONS OF THE INTERNET

Although the Internet has been a boon to genealogists because of its opportunities for wide networking and rapid dissemination of information, the Internet can do only so much. The location of archives or useful books may be discovered through the Internet, but in most cases you still must travel to the archive or library, or at least use interlibrary loan. Many repositories are working to put archival materials on the web, but these efforts are still in their infancy. Most such successful efforts consist of museum art collections, encyclopedias, and of genealogical interest, lists of names, the recently inaugurated Ellis Island records database, and census lists.

The web surfer must keep in mind that genealogical information on the Internet is suspect. No one reviews the accuracy of information on websites or the qualifications of persons posting the information.

INTERNET SECURITY AND PRIVACY

Unethical individuals looking to prey on the unsuspecting have discovered the Internet. Individuals bent on mischief can access anything you write in a newslist as easily as can your intended audience. It is essential to realize that using e-mail is like sending an open postcard in the mail; its message can be read by individuals other that those for whom it is intended. Be careful to avoid posting personal information about yourself or others on the web. Remember that banks frequently use mother's maiden name for identity checking (a terrible idea today), and that piece of information is easily obtainable from a family tree. Never ever send your Social Security (or any other official identity) number in an open e-mail or to a newslist.

Another risk inherent in using the Internet is the possibility of receiving a computer virus as part of a download or as an attachment to e-mail. Make sure you have up-to-date virus protection software installed on your computer. Know also that it is not wise to open e-mail attachments from people unknown to you, because attachments may be carriers of computer viruses. Even friends may inadvertently send you a virus if their own computers are infected. Be sure you use subject lines that clearly indicate the content of the message so that others will not delete your e-mails.

15.
GENEALOGY SOFTWARE

Imagine if phone books did not list names in alphabetical order. How would you find someone's phone number? Not easily. Now imagine that the pages of a phone book were not in one book, but instead were sheets of paper filed in various disorganized folders. Some manual genealogy organization "systems" are as difficult to use.

A computer genealogy software program uses a database to organize your data to make information easy to find. What is a database, and what is so special about it? By way of example, the phone directory is a type of database—a very limited one. The phonebook organizes its name information in alphabetical order, which allows you to locate a name easily. But it does not permit you to find a person's name if all you know is an address or phone number. And it does not permit you to determine who is related to that individual, or who the individual's neighbors are, or whether that person is younger or older than the next person listed, or which people came from which towns. A computer database records information in such a way that you can determine all these things and more. Instead of searching just alphabetically by last name, you can search by age, year, place, or any other category of information supported by the software.

A genealogy computer program is a specialized type of database designed to facilitate entry and retrieval of information of use to a genealogist. Data elements such as names and relationships; dates of birth, marriage, and death; locations where these and other events occurred; travel patterns; personal information; phone numbers and addresses can be recorded and then easily found. Most important of all, the software documents the sources from which the information was obtained. This and a lot more information can be collected easily; some programs even permit inclusion of photos and scanned images of documents. This information is organized automatically and easily retrievable.

Genealogy software programs permit users to check rapidly for errors (this person could not have been his father; he was born too late for that) and missing data (need the maiden name of, etc.). The programs also enable users to print out effortlessly beautiful family trees in a variety of forms and types, a feature not only pleasing to the genealogist but also a superb tool to inspire interest in others you are attempting to involve in your research.

Genealogy software programs are worth using, especially since most cost relatively little when bought in stores or as shareware. Shareware refers to programs that are provided at no charge, usually over the Internet, to try before purchase. If you like the program, you can register it and pay its price, usually US$30-50.

Which genealogy software program is best for you is a personal choice. Usually they all do the job, but they differ in their ease of use and capabilities. Some features are critical in a genealogy software program:

- GEDCOM. The software should be able to support exchanging family trees or parts of trees with other genealogists, without having to re-enter data by hand. A GEDCOM file is a standard file format that permits genealogy programs to import and export genealogy data seamlessly. The program you choose should be able to export (create for you) or import GEDCOM files; most do so.
- Documentation. A program should provide a systematic, easy method to document sources.
- Extensive report formats
- Provision for multiple names or name changes
- Screens for missing or erroneous information

SOFTWARE PROGRAMS

A reasonably comprehensive list of genealogy software programs can be found on the Internet at Cyndi's huge genealogy website, www.cyndislist.com/software.htm#Software. Most people prefer not to switch from programs in which they have already entered a lot of data or invested time learning; take your time selecting yours. Often it is a matter of liking or disliking the interface you are presented with for data entry or the format of reports and graphics. Below are listed just a few of the most commonly used programs, without recommending any in particular.

Family Tree Maker (www.familytreemaker.com)

This popular commercial program runs on Windows 95/98/NT. Able to import and export GEDCOM and PAF (see below) files, Family Tree Maker supports excellent source identification, multiple name variants, notes, and reporting capability. It serves the needs of most amateur genealogists.

Personal Ancestral File (PAF) (www.familysearch.org)

A classic, PAF runs under Windows 95/98/NT. Available free from the website listed, it provides all the required functions to satisfy the serious genealogist who needs sources identification, notes, secure data entry, and reporting capability. The PAF Companion, a related software program, supports printing reports in a variety of additional formats.

DoroTree (www.dorotree.com)

DoroTree, a commercial program that runs on Windows 95/98/NT, is designed especially for Jewish genealogists. It features the unique ability to enter data in any combination of Hebrew on one side of the screen and English, French, German, Spanish, or Portuguese on the other. The program permits date conversions between the Hebrew and Gregorian calendars, and prints reports in both Latin and Hebrew characters. A demonstration program can be downloaded from the website to try it before purchasing the program.

Ilanot (www.bh.org.il/Ilanot/ilanot.asp)

Produced by Jerusalem's Beth Hatefutsoth, Ilanot is another Windows 98 commercial program aimed at the needs of Jewish genealogists. Available in either Hebrew or English versions, it provides Hebrew/Gregorian calendar conversions and a bar mitzvah entry field, as well as GEDCOM export.

Ultimate Family Tree (UFT) (www.ultimatefamilytree.com)

Ultimate Family Tree is a Fox-Pro©[1] commercial program that runs on Windows 95/98/NT. With screens reminiscent of classic database programs, this powerful program allows extensive search and report capability; the novice computer user might be overwhelmed. Data can be exported to GEDCOM files and to .rtf files that can be imported and edited in spreadsheets and word processors.

Brother's Keeper (ourworld.compuserve.com/homepages/Brothers_Keeper)

A commercial program that runs under Windows 95/98/NT/2000/XP, Brother's Keeper has all the usual features and a loyal following. An older version is available for free download to try the program before purchasing the latest version.

Family ScrapBook (www.orthohelp.com/geneal/fsb.zip)

Besides having all the needed capabilities, this comprehensive genealogy program has the advantage of working under DOS. The program has accurate and easy-to-use entry screens, extensive reporting capability, and GEDCOM capability. It will run not only under any version of Windows, but also on a HP palmtop pocket computer.

Its significant disadvantage is that its author no longer supports it; for those who do not need its DOS capability, the other choices might be better. The program can be downloaded free.

TreeDraw (www.spansoft.org)

TreeDraw creates and prints complex custom family trees to supplement those another software might produce automatically. You import from other genealogy programs into TreeDraw the GEDCOM files that contain your family tree data.

---

[1] Fox-Pro© is a commercial database program similar to Microsoft Access©

16.
CALENDARS AND DATE CONVERSIONS

Because of the historical periods and countries involved, the Sephardic genealogist inevitably must deal with dates according to several calendars that appear in documents. Some, including the Hebrew and the Moslem (*Hijra*) calendars, are lunar calendars. Others, including the current Gregorian, Arab civil, and Turkish civil calendars, are based on the earth's movement around the sun. But even calendars based on the solar year use a variety of different dating systems that require conversion into the Gregorian calendar.

This is a complex topic that is dealt with only briefly here. Practically speaking, genealogists only need to find a simple tool that converts one calendar date into another. Fortunately these tools exist and many are free and easily downloaded from the Internet. Some are described below.

For the purposes of Sephardic genealogy, the most important calendars the researcher needs to be aware of are the Julian, Gregorian, *Hijra* (Moslem), Ottoman civil, and several other Islamic calendars, described below.

CALENDARS

JULIAN CALENDAR

So named because it was instituted by Julius Caesar in 46 B.C.E., the Julian calendar underwent several changes before being finalized in 6 C.E. Before 46 B.C.E. the Romans used a 304-day calendar year borrowed from the Greeks. This ancient year, which legend held was started by Romulus at the birth of Rome, had 10 months (*Martius, Aprilis, Maius, Junius, Quintilis, Sextilis, September, October, November, December*) but left 60 days of the solar year unaccounted for.[1] A later Roman ruler added the months January and February as well as a short month named *Mercedinus*, inserted in alternate years, to make the calendar conform better with the seasons. Over time, this inherently inaccurate year inevitably fell further and further behind.

In 46 B.C.E., the Julian solar-based calendar was established with 12 months and the familiar alternating 30–31 days. *Quintilis* and *Sixtilis* were renamed July and August to honor Julius Caesar and Augustus Caesar respectively. Unlike the current February, the Julian February originally had 29 days that increased to 30 days every fourth year—but Emperor Augustus Caesar, subsequently moved one of its days to enlarge his own month, August.

---

[1] The Roman names for the months *Quintilis* through *December* were derived from the Roman numbers 5 to 10.

The Julian calendar was 11 minutes longer than the true solar year, accurate enough to remain in use for 15 centuries—but it, too, gradually accumulated errors over time.

Gregorian Calendar

Because of the increasing seasonal discrepancy of the Julian calendar, Pope Gregory XIII followed the advice of his astronomers and in 1582 removed 10 days from that year's October and ordered the use of a new, more accurate, calendar. It came to be known as the Gregorian calendar, the calendar the Western world uses today. Despite its greater accuracy, this new calendar year still has a 26-second error each year and, therefore, will require correction in centuries to come.

Roman Catholic countries, obedient to Pope Gregory's order, rapidly adopted the new Gregorian calendar. Unfortunately for genealogists and historians, however, other countries only did so at varying times: England adopted the Gregorian calendar in 1700, Russia in 1918, and Turkey in 1927.

Hebrew Calendar

The Hebrew calendar is based on the moon's revolution around the Earth and thus accumulates discrepancies relative to the seasons, despite an attempt at synchronizing the months with the seasons. The Jewish year, which starts in the fall, contains 12 lunar months: *tishri, heshwan, kislev, tebet, shebat, adar (adar I), nisan, iyar, sivan, tammuz, ab* and *elul* and a 13th month, *ve-adar (adar II)*, is added every seven years. Year 1—the year of creation in the Hebrew calendar—corresponds to 3,760 B.C.E. in the Gregorian calendar.

Hijra (Moslem) Calendar

The Moslem *Hijra* (or *Hegira*) year is also lunar. Used throughout the Islamic world, it appears frequently in documents a Sephardic genealogist is likely to encounter. The calendar starts on Friday, July 16, 622 C.E (the date Mohammad made the *hegira* [flight] from Mecca to Medina).

Like the Jewish year, it contains 12 lunar months of 29 and 30 days: *muharram, safar, rabi awal (rabi I), rabi thani (rabi II), jumada awal (jumada I), jumada thani (jumadi II), rajab, shaban, ramadan, shawwal, zulkadah, and zulhijah*. The genealogist typically encounters these months written in Arabic script. The months of the *Hijra* and the other Islamic years are reproduced in Arabic script in appendix H, Moslem Calendar.

Ottoman Civil Calendar

As an Islamic country, Turkey for centuries used the traditional Islamic *Hijra* calendar, but in 1789 Turkey adopted a civil calendar for official use. The civil calendar, based on the Julian calendar, was known as *sene i maliye* (or just *maliye* or *mali*, for short) or sometimes *sene i rumiye*.² Like the Julian calendar, the *maliye* contained 12 months but with different names: *maret, nisan, mayiis, haziran, temouz, agoustos, eylul, tishrin-ievvel (tishrin-ewel), tishrin-thani, kanun-ievvel, kanun-thani, shubatt*. See appendix H, Moslem Calendar.

As part of the Ataturk modernization efforts, the Turks adopted the Gregorian calendar in 1926; conversion problems ceased from that date on for modern historians and genealogists.

OTHER ISLAMIC CIVIL CALENDARS

Other Islamic countries adopted the Gregorian year to conform to prevailing 20th-century usage. The month's names varied depending on the country. In Egypt, with its long-standing European influence, the months' names were transliterations of the Gregorian names: *yanair, fabrayir, maris, abreel, mayou, youniou, jouliou, aghustous, subtambar, oktobar, nofambar,* and *disambar*. In Syria, names of the months were associated more closely with the Islamic months' names: *kanun al thani, shubatt, azar, nissan, ayar, haziran, tamouz, ab, ayloul, tishrin al awal, tishrin al thani, kanun al awal*. See appendix H, Moslem Calendar.

The modern Persian calendar was adopted in 1925. Consisting of 12 months and a complicated leap-year provision, its recent advent allowed it to benefit from modern knowledge, making it the most accurate solar calendar in use today.

CONVERSION TOOLS

Printed calendar conversion tables may be found, but in the age of computers, many software programs convert dates effortlessly. Many are available on the Internet, some online and others downloadable, frequently without charge.

ONLINE TOOLS

- JOS Calendar Conversion program provided by JewishGen at www.jewishgen.org/jos/josdates.htm converts between Hebrew and Gregorian dates.
- Fourmilab calendar converter, www.fourmilab.ch/documents/calendar, converts between Gregorian, Julian, Hebrew, Islamic, Persian, Bahai, Indian, and French Republican dates.
- PDC live, http://pdc.ro.nu/mjd.cgi, converts between Gregorian and Julian dates.
- Institute of Oriental Studies at Zurich University, www.unizh.ch/ori/hegira.html, converts between *Hijra* and Gregorian dates.

---

² *Sene* means year; *maliye* means financial; and *rumi* refers to the Romans (*runi*) and, by extension, Europeans.

DOWNLOADABLE TOOLS

- Computus. By far the most complete downloadable calendar conversion program, Computus is available at www.lib.umich.edu/area/Near.East/computus.html. It converts, in any direction, between Gregorian, Julian, Armenian, Hebrew, *Hijra*, and Turkish calendars, as well as Persian (Yezdegerd and Malikshah), Coptic, and the French Revolutionary era.
- J_Cal, www.orthohelp.com/geneal/jcal.zip, converts between the Hebrew and Gregorian calendars.

17.
PERIODICALS

GENEALOGY PERIODICALS

Avotaynu

Avotaynu: The International Review of Jewish Genealogy is the largest and best-known Jewish genealogy journal. Having first appeared in 1985 and published quarterly in English, Avotaynu is an essential resource for the Jewish genealogist. Because its contributors are mainly Ashkenazic, most articles are about topics of interest mainly to Ashkenazic researchers. Even those articles can be helpful to Sephardic researchers, because they are instructive in the best techniques of genealogical research. A surprisingly large number of articles and information of interest to researchers of Sephardic ancestry have appeared over the years. Listed below are the most important articles of Sephardic interest. In each issue is a useful "From Our Contributing Editors" section, in which experts from Australia, Brazil, England, France, and Israel, among other countries, summarize the most important events and articles from their areas of the world.

Information on annual subscriptions to *Avotaynu* can be obtained from www.avotaynu.com or 800-AVOTAYNU. Avotaynu sells a CD that includes its 57 back issues published from 1985 to 1999 (updated every three years) with full-word indexing that allows you to search rapidly and find any of the two million words in the issues—very helpful in locating articles about any topic.

Etsi

Etsi (Revue de Généalogie et d'Histoire Séfarades) first appeared in 1998 and has the distinction of being the first quarterly publication dedicated specifically to Sephardic genealogy.[1] For that reason alone it deserves support. Articles are published in French or English, each with a summary in the other language appended. A section summarizes items of interest in a variety of other related periodicals and a discussion of books of interest. A list of the articles published in its past issues is presented below. Information on annual subscriptions to *Etsi* can be obtained from www.geocities.com/EnchantedForest/1321.

---

[1] *Etsi*, c/o L. et P. Abensur, 77 bd Richard-Lenoir, 75011 Paris, France. Website: www.geocities.com/enchanted Forst/1321.

Revue du Cercle de Généalogie Juive

The *Cercle de Généalogie Juive* is one of the genealogy societies in Paris, France;[2] the *Revue* is its quarterly journal. Articles are written in French. Though focused mainly on French Ashkenazic Jews, articles are published of interest to Sephardic researchers. Some are listed below. Information about an annual subscription is available at the website: http://www.genealoj.org/.

ACADEMIC PERIODICALS ON SEPHARDIM

Sefarad

Official publication of the Instituto Arias Montano,[3] this highly respected periodical publishes articles in several languages on Sephardic topics. Genealogy researchers can occasionally find items of interest in this publication.

Sefardica

Official publication of the *Centro De Investigación Y Difusión De La Cultura Sefaradí*.[4] *Sefardica* publishes articles in Spanish on Sephardic topics.

GENERAL SEPHARDIC PERIODICALS

Los Muestros

This is an erudite quarterly publication about Sephardic topics published by Moise Rahmani, www.sefarad.org/publication/lm.

La Lettre Sefarade

La Lettre Sefarade is a quarterly on Sephardic topics in general published in French and English editions.[5] Besides articles on Sephardic history and book reviews, a small section helps those who wish to brush up on Ladino. Published at publisher Jean Carasso's expense, there is no subscription fee for either the French or English editions; it is sent free to anyone. A donation is requested.

Image

Image is a general Sephardic periodical with a readership said to exceed 250,000 in New York, New Jersey, and Florida. See the website at www.imageusa.com.

---

[2] *Cercle de Généalogie Juive*, 14, rue Saint-Lazare - 75009, Paris, France.
[3] Instituto Arias Montano, Duque de Medinaceli 4, Madrid 14, Spain.
[4] *Centro De Investigación Y Difusión De La Cultura Sefaradí*, Salguero 758 (C1177AEN) Buenos Aires, Argentina. E-mail: cidicsef@ciudad.com.ar.
[5] French edition: La Lettre Sepharade, Jean Carasso - F - 84220 - Gordes, France. E-mail: lettre.sepharade@wanadoo.fr. English edition: La Lettre Sepharade, Rosine Nussenblatt, P.O. Box 2450, Kensington, Md. 20891-2450, USA. E-mail: lettresepharade@earthlink.net.

AVOTAYNU: SELECTED ARTICLES

Topic/Article	Volume/Issue/Page
Algeria	
Civil Records of Algeria and Morocco	VI/1/29
Jewish Community in the Touat Oases	VII/4/60
Brochures on Colonization of Algeria	VIII/3/51
Algerian Jews	VIII/3/52
About the Jews of Morocco, Algeria, and Libya	X/3/38
Algerian Records in Aix-en-Provence (France)	XI/1/45
Argentina	
History of the Jews of Argentina	II/3/21
Sources of Vital Statistic Records	III/3/18
Argentina, the Other Golden Land	V/2/16
Jewish Immigration to Argentina	VII/2/34
Inquiries to Argentina	XII/1/40
Argentinean Source for Immigrant Information	XII/1/66
Using Argentina Phone Books on the Internet	XII/4/59
How to Obtain Argentinean Vital Records, Immigration Registers, Census Records; Genealogical Resources in Buenos Aires	XIII/2/50
History of the Moise Ville Colony	XIII/4/79
Moroccan Community in Buenos Aires	XIII/4/79
Jews of Belmonte	XIV/4/69
Moises Ville Colony School Records	XIV/4/69
Spanish Jewry	XIV/4/69
Australia	
Five Regional Branches of the Australian Jewish Genealogical Society	XII/4/59
Jewish Genealogical Activity throughout Australia	XIII/1/39
Egyptian Jews in Australia	XIII/4/79
Access to Census Records	XIV/2/47
Belgium	
Antwerp as Haven for Jews after Spanish Inquisition	VII/2/23
Marranos of Antwerp	VIII/2/36
Genealogy Collections of the Jewish Museum of Belgium	XIV/1/46
Bermuda	
The Jews of Bermuda	XIV/2/31
Brazil	
History of the Jews of Brazil	IV/3/19
Books on Jewish Tombstone Inscriptions in Brazilian Cemeteries	IV/3/19
Dictionario Biografico--1500–1808	V/3/23
Crypto-Jews in the State of Par	VI/1/29

Sources of Genealogical Records	VI/3/20
Famous Jewish Brazilian Families	VI/4/50
Jews, Judaizers, and Their Slaves	VII/1/20
Additional Books by Egon and Frieda Wolff	VII/3/28
Jews in the Amazonian Rain Forest	IX/1/35
Books Available on Brazilian Jewish History	IX/3/47
Jews and Marranos in Northern Brazil	IX/4/48
"Jewish Priest" of Caico	IX/4/49
The Amzalak Family History	X/1/43
Using Inquisition Records	X/4/62
Jews in the Amazon	XI/2/47
Bentes Family of Brazil	XI/2/47
Early Jewish Presence in Brazil	XIII/3/49

Bulgaria

Bulgarian Jewish Names	XII/2/45
Projects to Document Jews of Turkey, Salonika, Bulgaria, and Belgrade	XIV/2/40

Canada

Immigration Records at Archives of the Canadian Jewish Congress	II/3/12
Book Review: *Archival Sources for Canadian Jewry*	IV/2/25
Jewish Genealogical Research in Canada	IV/3/04
Inventorying Jewish Cemeteries	VI/3/20
Some Montreal Jewish Holdings	VIII/3/50
Jewish Archives of Toronto	VIII/3/50
Cemeteries in Quebec and Maritime Provinces Computerized	VIII/3/50
Jewish Genealogical Resources in Canada	VIII/4/27
Book Review: *A Biographical Dictionary of Canadian Jewry, 1909–1914*	VIII/4/61
Vital Records of Ontario	IX/1/37
Resources at Archives of Ontario	IX/2/47
Analysis of Canadian Censuses, Montreal Synagogues	IX/4/50
Vital Statistic Indexes at the Archives of Ontario	X/1/45
Analyzing Canadian Census Records	X/4/63
Canadian Ship Arrival Records	XI/3/63
Canadian Voter Lists	XI/4/54
Canadian Naturalization Records	XII/2/42
Some Canadian Vital Records Available via Internet	XIII/1/39
Look Up Your Canadian Ancestors in the Library	XIII/3/22
Vital Statistic Records and Other Sources in Ontario	XIII/3/49
Canadian Naturalization Records	XIII/3/66
Jewish Genealogical Research in Canada	XIV/4/23
Addresses of Canadian Vital Records Offices	XIV/4/69
Jewish Genealogical Resources in Quebec Province	XIV/4/69
World War I Military Records	XIV/4/69

Canary Islands
The Jews of the Canary Islands	XIV/4/29

Caribbean
Lists of Jews in Oldambtand, Hoogeveen, and Surinam	IX/2/49
Jewish Cemetery on Nevis	X/2/48
A Visit to St. Eustatius	II/2/31
Jews in the Islands of the French West Indies	V/4/13
Jews of Exotic Surinam and Their History	VIII/2/16
The Jews of the Caribbean	XI/3/48

Computers
Computers and Genealogy	VI/1/11
Genealogy Software: Relativity	VII/3/38
A Proposed Standard in Genealogical Software Systems for Identifying Jewish Persons with No Surnames	VIII/1/40
Computer Resources for Jewish Genealogy	X/1/35
List of Internet World Wide Web Sites for Jewish Genealogy Research	XII/4/21
Ilanot: Jewish Genealogy Software	XIV/2/63

Cyprus
Documenting Cypriot Jews	V/2/26

Egypt
Reports on Egyptian Records, Group for Study of Jewish Languages	IX/3/66
History of the Jews of Egypt	X/1/30
Vital Records from Egypt Available	XIII/3/33
Egyptian Jews in Australia	XIII/4/79

England
How to Obtain Vital Statistic Records from the United Kingdom	II/1/23
Guide to British Census Records	II/2/21
Immigration Records in London	II/3/16
Jewish Cemeteries in London	II/3/23
The Value of Wills to the Genealogist	III/1/20
Hyamson and Colyer-Fergusson Collections	VII/1/15
Older London Burial Records and Sites	VII/3/24
Research Using the 1891 Census	VIII/2/42
Describes Resources Available from Court of the Chief Rabbi	VIII/2/58
Passenger Lists of British Public Records Office	IX/2/47
Additional Resources for Anglo-Jewish Genealogy	IX/3/49
Manchester Jewry	IX/4/51
Bevis Marks Records	X/2/50
Naturalization and Name Changes in the British Isles	X/3/44
Indexing of London Synagogue Records	XI/1/44
Federation of Synagogues Records	XII/3/54

Elizabethan Marranos	XIV/1/46
Untapped London Resources	XIV/3/69

Ethiopia
Jewish Life in Ethiopia and Kenya	V/2/13

France
Papal Jews, Jews of North Africa, Metz	II/1/26
Sources in Bordeaux-Bayonne Area	IV/3/20
Jews of Nice	VI/1/30
Jews of Marseille	VII/4/60
Judeo-Portuguese Communities in Southwest France	VIII/1/28
Holdings of Municipal Archives in Marseille	VIII/2/37
Book on Deportation of the Jews from the Marseille Region	IX/1/39
Records Available on Immigrants to France, Records at Diplomatic Archives	IX/3/50
County of Venaissin	IX/4/52
How to Find French Naturalization Records	X/1/46
Using French Naturalization Papers and Consular Records	XII/1/41
Use of French Naturalization Documents	XII/4/11
Selected Resources for French Genealogy	XII/4/13
Basic Genealogical Research in France	XIII/1/13

General Genealogy
Archival Publications (List of Jewish Archives Worldwide)	I/1/07
Proposed Standard Numbering System for Individuals, Generations, and Charts in Jewish Genealogy	VI/3/03
No One Can Do My Research As I Can!	VI/3/06
Genealogical Networking	VI/4/16
What's in a Date? A Study of Various Calendars	IX/3/24
Names and Their Origins	XI/1/41
Hello, Cousin: The Mathematics of Ancestry	XIII/1/34
Databases Abound on JewishGen	XIV/1/15
A Beginner's Primer in U.S. Jewish Genealogical Research	IV/3/43
A Genealogist's Guide to Discovering Your Female Ancestors	XIV/4/85

Greece
Bibliography of Greek Jewry	VIII/2/40
Greek Jewry	VIII/4/56
Greek Jewish Records in Moscow to Be Returned to Greece	IX/3/52
Greek Jewry: Sources for Genealogical Research	X/4/11
Projects to Document Jews of Turkey, Salonika, Bulgaria, and Belgrade	XIV/2/40
How to Research Families from Turkey and Salonika	XIV/1/28

The Netherlands
Origin of Dutch Surnames	III/2/30
Sources of Information in Holland	III/3/22

List of Marriages of Portuguese-Jewish Community in Amsterdam 1650–1911	IV/3/21
Jewish Archival Holdings	V/1/16
Record Keeping in Holland from 1811	V/2/17
Genealogical Research in The Netherlands	V/2/18
Genealogical Sources at the Institute for Dutch Jewry in Jerusalem	VI/1/31
Dutch Publications of Genealogical Interest	VI/3/24
Amsterdam Sources for Jewish Genealogical Research	VI/3/24
Jewish Holdings in Municipal Archives of The Hague	VII/3/29
Amsterdam: Jerusalem of the West	VII/4/17
Dutch-Jewish Cemeteries	IX/1/40
Amsterdam's Municipal Archive as Source for Genealogical Research, 1812–1945	X/1/47
Using the Index to the Jewish Marriages of Amsterdam from 1650–1911 to Create Family Trees	X/2/39
Dutch Estate Tax Registers as Sources for Genealogical Research	XI/1/46
Sephardic Fraternity *"Santa Companhia de dotar orfas e donzelas"*	XII/3/55
Dutch Holocaust Records at the General Archives	XIV/1/46
Jewish Presence in Holland for the Past 400 Years	XIV/2/47

Holocaust

Books on Fate of French Jews during Holocaust	IV/3/18
Biography of Sephardic Jews and the Holocaust	VII/2/17
Book on Deportation of the Jews from the Marseille Region	IX/1/39
Romanian Records at the Holocaust Memorial Museum; Research Strategies for Records Still Held in Romania	IX/4/18
Deportations from France	IX/4/53
Yad Vashem Archives	IX/4/71
Joint Distribution Committee Records	IX/4/71
International Tracing Service Records at Yad Vashem	X/1/22

India

Jews of India	XI/3/66
Indian Jews: Bene Israel	XII/1/43
Indian Jews	XII/4/64

Iran

Iranian-Jewish Genealogy	XIV/1/51
Jadid Al-Islam: The Jewish "New Muslims" of Meshhed	XIV/2/61

Iraq

Sources of Information	V/1/35
Iraqi Jewry	XII/4/65

Israel

Genealogical Items at Jewish National and University Library	I/2/12

A Genealogical Trip: Sources of Information	III/3/14
Montefiore Census of Jews of Palestine in 1839	III/3/22
Central Archives for the History of the Jewish People	V/1/18
Genealogical Sources at the Institute for Dutch Jewry in Jerusalem	VI/1/31
Guide to Resources in Israel: An Update	VII/2/04
More Resources in Israel	VII/2/06
Censuses from the Ottoman Empire	VII/2/27
The 19th-Century Montefiore Censuses	VIII/2/25
Two Sources for Research on British Palestine	VIII/3/35
Sources for 1906–1920 Palestine Period	IX/2/50
Three Important Archives in Israel	IX/4/11
Book Review: *A Guide to Jewish Genealogical Research in Israel*	XI/4/73
Contributing Editor: An Annotated Bibliography, Jews of Bukhara, Portuguese Jews in the Caribbean, Ashkenazic Surnames in the Sephardi Diaspora	XIII/1/39
Holdings of the Central Archives for the History of the Jewish People	XIII/4/79
Kollels of Eretz Israel as a Genealogical Treasure	XIV/1/38

Italy
Papal Jews, Jews of North Africa, Metz	II/1/26
Jewish Genealogical Research in Italy	VIII/1/20
Center for Italian Jewry	X/1/23
Jewish Livorno, Italy, 1841	XII/4/62
Italian-Jewish Genealogy on the Internet	XIV/1/46

Kenya
Jewish Life in Ethiopia and Kenya	V/2/13

LDS (Mormon) Family History Library
LDS Family History Library Publications List	XI/4/75
The LDS (Mormon) International Genealogical Index: What Is It?	XII/4/07

Libya
About the Jews of Morocco, Algeria, and Libya	X/3/38

Morocco
Jewish Surnames	III/2/23
Civil Records of Algeria and Morocco	VI/1/29
Books about Spanish Jews of Morocco	VII/2/26
Sources of Information	VIII/2/37
About the Jews of Morocco, Algeria, and Libya	X/3/38
Sephardic Genealogical Research in Morocco	X/3/40
Bibliography for Jewish Genealogy in Spanish Morocco	X/3/42
Reports Address of Moroccan Jewry Source	XI/1/67
Moroccan Rabbis	XI/4/55
Moroccan Given Names	XII/1/44

Moroccan Rabbis	XIII/3/49
Moroccan Community in Buenos Aires	XIII/4/79

North Africa (*see also* **Algeria, Egypt, Libya, Morocco, Sudan, Tunisia**)
Papal Jews, Jews of North Africa, Metz	II/1/26
North African Jewry	V/3/25
Consular Records of the Levant and North Africa	XIV/3/69

Portugal
Jews of Modern-Day Portugal	I/1/14
Marranos Living in Portugal	I/2/14
History of Jews after the Inquisition	II/3/27
Bigamy among 18th-Century Jews, the Jews of Gibraltar	III/1/25
Census of Jews of Gibraltar	VII/1/27
Historical Notes about Jews of Portugal	VIII/3/52
Portuguese Marranos	VIII/3/52
Sources for Spanish and Portuguese Genealogy	XII/2/43
Jewish Sources on the Iberian Peninsula	XIII/4/79

Romania
Selected Sources on Romania at the Central Archives of the Jewish People	VI/1/15
Romanian Holdings in the Diaspora Research Institute	VI/2/13
Romanian Records in LDS Family History Library	VII/3/44
Romanian Records at the Holocaust Memorial Museum	IX/4/18
Sources for Jewish Genealogical Research in Romania	XII/3/08
Seeking Romaniote Jews	XIII/1/67
Genealogy and History: Sources of Jewish Genealogical Research in Romania (18th–20th Centuries)	XIII/3/42
Sources of Jewish Genealogical Research in the Romanian Archival System	XIV/3/22

Sephardic
Sephardic Jewry: Recommended Readings	VI/4/52
Sources for Researching My Sephardic Ancestors	VII/1/18
Spanish Inquisition in Americas	VII/1/19
Biography of Sephardic Jews and the Holocaust	VII/2/17
Ottoman Empire Resources	VIII/1/18
The Marrano Diaspora	VIII/1/09
Additional Resources for Sephardic Genealogy	VIII/2/59
Resources for Sephardic Genealogy	VIII/3/48
Sephardic Genealogical Research in Morocco	X/3/40
Rosh-ha-shana Memories and Thoughts: Sephardic in Form, Jewish in Essence XII/3/27	
Sephardic Reference Sources	XII/3/52
Converted and Reconverted: History of the Jews Who Stayed in Portugal (1497–1997)	XIII/4/9
Jewish Sources on the Iberian Peninsula	XIII/4/79

Crypto-Jews of the U.S. Southwest	XIV/4/31

Serbia

Projects to Document Jews of Turkey, Salonika, Bulgaria, and Belgrade	XIV/2/40

South America

Travelers' Guide to South America	VII/2/39

Spain

History of the Jews of Aragon	IV/3/20
Sources for Spanish and Portuguese Genealogy	XII/2/43
Jews of Andalusia	XII/4/62
Inquisition Records	XIII/1/39
Jews of Andalusia	XIII/1/39
Jewish Sources on the Iberian Peninsula	XIII/4/79
Crypto-Jews around the World	XIV/2/47
Notarial Papers of Pre-Inquisition Spain	XIV/3/69

Sudan

Jacob's Children in the Land of the Mahdi: Jews of the Sudan	XIII/4/96

Syria

Spanish-Jewish "Nobility" of Aleppo, Syria	VII/2/17
Genealogies of 30 Families from Aleppo Documented	VII/4/61

Tunisia

Matrimonial Register of Tunis	V/4/13
Biographical Index of Tunisian Rabbis	XI/1/47

Turkey

Ottoman Empire Resources	VIII/1/18
Turkish-Jewish Cemeteries of the Ottoman Period	VIII/3/45
Jews of Smyrna	IX/1/38
Jewish Surnames	IX/1/43
Ottoman Empire Jewry	XI/3/65
Jewish Settlement in Turkish Lands	XII/3/56
Jewish Newspaper of Izmir, Turkey, as a Genealogical Resource	XIII/2/50
Sources for Jews of Izmir in Israel	XIII/3/49
How to Research Families from Turkey and Salonika	XIV/1/28
Projects to Document Jews of Turkey, Salonika, Bulgaria, and Belgrade	XIV/2/40
Jewish Names in Istanbul in the 18th and 19th Centuries	XIV/3/63
Consular Records of the Levant and North Africa	XIV/3/69
Turkish Jews	XIV/3/69

United States

Lesser-Known Resources at the U.S. National Archives	IV/1/07

Naturalization and Visa Records at U.S. Immigration and Naturalization Service	V/1/12
Map Resources.at the U.S. Library of Congress	VII/4/43
Social Security Death Index New Genealogical Resource	VIII/1/42
The Social Security Death Index	IX/1/13
Romanian Records at the Holocaust Memorial Museum; Research Strategies for Records Still Held in Romania	IX/4/18
Searching for World War I Draft Registration Records	X/1/33
Jewish Sources for Genealogy at the U.S. Library of Congress	X/3/21
U.S. Holocaust Memorial Museum as a Genealogical Resource	X/3/28
Researching Post-1906 Naturalizations in Washington, D.C.	X/3/30
Research On-line or in Person at the Library of Congress	XII/3/41
The Location of U.S. Naturalization Records	XIII/1/36
How to Find a Post-1906 U.S. Immigrant Ancestor	XIV/1/41
Crypto-Jews of the U.S. Southwest	XIV/4/31

ETSI: SELECTED ARTICLES

Vol. 1, Issue 1 (Spring-Summer 1998)
Etymology of Sefarad, by Mathilde Tagger (French, English summary)

The Jewish Cemetery of Tetuan: Yesterday, Today, Tomorrow, by Philip Abensur (French, English summary)

Judeo-Spanish *Solitreo*, by Haim-Vidal Sephiha (French, English summary)

How to Find Five Generations through the Italian Consulate Archives at Izmir: The Example of the Hazan family, by Laurence Abensur-Hazan (French, English summary)

Sephardic Genealogy on the Internet, by Jeff Malka (English, French summary)

Bibliography: The Jews of Egypt, by Laurence Abensur-Hazan

Vol. 1, Issue 2 (Autumn 1998)
Berber Matter in Onomastics of Maghreb Jews, by Jacques Taïeb (French, English summary) List of Jewish Roots of Berber origin

A Genealogical Source for Salonika: The Newspaper *La Epoca* by Claude Missistrano (French, English summary)

Using the Internet as a Tool for Sephardic Genealogy, by Jeff Malka (English, French summary)

Bibliography: The Jews of Bulgaria, by Mathilde Tagger

Vol. 1, Issue 3 (Winter 1998)
Present Condition of the Jewish Cemeteries of Algeria, from Roger Latapie (French, English summary)

Some Tombstones of Old Jewish Cemeteries in Algier in 1888, from Isaac Bloch (index by Philip Abensur)

Jews of the Sudan, by Jeff Malka (English, French summary)

The Sephardi Community of Manchester and Its Sources, by Morris L. Bierbrier (English, French summary)

Bibliography: The Jews of Venice, by Laurence Abensur-Hazan (French)

Vol. 2, Issue 4 (Spring 1999)
The Jewish Cemetery of La Tour-de-Peilz in Switzerland, by Anne-Marie Faraggi Rychner (French, English summary)
Vital Records for the Jews of Algeria, from Roland Gozland (French)
La Boz del Puevlo: A Judeo-Spanish Newspaper of Smyrna before World War I, by Henri Nahum (French, English summary)
Genealogical Data Records from *La Boz del Puevlo,* by Laurence Abensur-Hazan (French, English summary)
Os Cristaos Novos: The New Christians: The de Sola Family, by Julian Kemper (English, French summary)
Bibliography: The Jewish Community of Rhodes, by Myriam Pimienta-Benatar (French)

Vol. 2, Issue 5 (Summer 1999)
Chasing the Altaras Family: An Archival Survey, by Morris Bierbrier (English, French summary)
Some Jewish Cemeteries of Morocco, by Philip Abensur (French, English summary)
Is the Purim Sarahussa from Saragossa or Syracusa? Or How to Find a Possible Origin with the Help of a Family Tradition, by Laurence Abensur-Hazan (French, English summary)
Sephardi *Ketubot*: Bibliography and Index by Countries, by Laurence Abensur-Hazan and Philip Abensur (French, English summary)

Vol. 2, Issue 6 (October 1999)
Sephardic Genealogical Information Available from Ottoman, Balkan, and Levant Postal History, by David Sheby (English, French summary)
Sephardic Genealogical Investigations in Amsterdam, by Vibeke Sealtiel-Olsen (English, French summary)
Archives: The Move of the Jewish Cemetery of Fez, Morocco, by Philip Abensur (French)
Bibliography: The Sephardis of Romania, by Michael Halevy

Vol. 2, Issue 7 (December 1999)
Dengue Fever in Smyrna in 1889, by Laurence Abensur-Hazan (French, English summary)
A Sample of the Jewish Population of Tangier in 1955 from Isaac Pimienta's Notebook, by Sidney Pimienta (French, English summary)
Bibliography: Sephardi Families, History, and Genealogy: Books at the Jewish National and University and at the Ben Zvi Institute Libraries in Jerusalem, by Mathilde Tagger

Vol. 3, Issue 8 (April 2000)
Genealogical Data in the *Alliance Israélite Universelle* Archives: Myth and Reality, by Laurence Abensur-Hazan and Philip Abensur (French, English summary)

A Family Research at the *Alliance Israélite Universelle*, by Yves Carmona (French, English summary)

Vol. 3, Issue 9 (August 2000)
Jewish Genealogical Research in Alexandria (Egypt), by Richard Léon (French, English summary)

The Genealogical Story of the Modiano Family from 1570 to Our Days, by Mario Modiano (English, French summary)

Benefits and Damage of Internet: For a Deontology in Genealogy, by Laurence Abensur-Hazan (French, English summary)

Archives: About the Italian Nationality or Protection of the Jews of Smyrna, by Laurence Abensur-Hazan

Vol. 3, Issue 10 (October 2000)
Lists of Names in the Archives of the *Alliance Israélite Universelle*, by Laurence Abensur-Hazan and Philip Abensur (French, English summary)

Sephardic Family Names in Amsterdam, 1598–2000, by Vibeke Sealtiel-Olsen (English, French summary)

Archives: The Jews of Malta in 1891

Sephardi Subjects at the International Conference on Jewish Genealogy of London (8–13 July 2001)

Vol. 3, Issue 11 (December 2000)
Sol Hachuel (1820–1834): History and Genealogy, by Philip Abensur (French, English summary)

First Experiences of an Amateur Arboriculturist, or How to Graft a New Branch on One's Genealogical Tree, by Francis Amar (French, English summary)

Jewish Cemeteries in Algeria (continued), by Anne-Marie Faraggi Rychner (French, English summary)

Vol. 4, Issue 12 (March 2001)
Aliases in Amsterdam, by Vibeke Sealtiel-Olsen (English, French summary)

Sephardic Varons: Historical Background and Distribution, by Bension Varon (English, French summary)

Ketubot Catalogues Available on the Internet, by Philip Abensur (French and English)

Report of the London International Conference on Jewish Genealogy, by Laurence Abensur-Hazan (French, English summary)

Bibliography: The Jews of Morocco, by Philip Abensur

Vol. 4, Issue 13 (June 2001)
French Naturalization Files of Ottoman Jews, by Laurence Abensur-Hazan (French, English summary)

The Jews of Leghorn: Archival Sources, by Nardo Bonomi (French, English summary)

Bibliography: Genealogical Information about Sephardi Families in the Alliance Israélite Universelle Archives, by Laurence Abensur-Hazan and Philip Abensur

Vol. 4, Issue 14 (September 2001)
Short Stories of a Great Family: About Some Toledanos in Tangier, by Philip Abensur (French, English summary)
Marriages and Engagements Announcements Records from the Newspaper *El Tiempo* of Istanbul, by Claude Missistrano (French, English summary)
The Jewish Community of Zante in the 1890s, by Laurence Abensur-Hazan (French, English summary)

Vol. 4, Issue 15 (December 2001)
Izmir and Rhodes: Taranto Family Origins, Archives, and Links to Other Sephardim, by Leon Taranto (English, French summary)
The Jewish Community and Family Names of Sephardic Jews in Ruschuk (Russe), Bulgaria, by Joseph Covo (English, French summary)
Genealogical Records of the Alliance Israélite Universelle about Smyrna (Turkey), by Laurence Abensur-Hazan (French, English summary)

REVUE DU CERCLE DE GÉNÉALOGIE JUIVE: SELECTED ARTICLES

Melanges: Relevés d'état civil en Algérie	N° 64, Hiver 2001
Mariages juifs à Constantine en 1836	N° 60, Hiver 1999
Les Juifs protégés de la France dans les échelles du Levant et de Barbarie	N° 53, Printemps 1998
Melanges: Juifs natifs de Turquie parmi les déportés de France	N° 53, Printemps 1998
Histoire et généalogie. Nossas Familhas: Itinéraires portugais	N° 54, Eté 1998
Melanges: Un voyage généalogique à Malte	N° 55, Automne 1998
Relevés d'état civil en Algérie, 1830–1890	N°57, Printemps 1999
Les dossiers de naturalisation française	N°57, Printemps 1999
Un document inhabituel: la présence d'une marraine dans un Mohelbuch alsacien	N° 58, Eté 1999
Notes: La communauté juive de Livourne	N° 58, Eté 1999
Notes: Les noms de famille juifs en Afrique du Nord	N° 58, Eté 1999
Actualities: Un annuaire des juifs d'Egypte en 1942–1943	N° 59, Automne 1999
Documents: Mariages Juifs à Constantine en 1847 et 1848	N° 61, Printemps 2000
Notes: les marranes de Toulouse	N° 61, Printemps 2000
Notes: Histoire des Juifs de Lorraine : bibliographie mise à jour jusqu'en 1990	N° 61, Printemps 2000
Familles: Daniel Morali (Medieval Spain and Maghreb)	N° 62, Eté 2000
Généalogie à Corfou	N° 63, Automne 2000

Part III
Country Resources

18.
Spain

Spain maintains separate archives for each of the ancient Spanish kingdoms. The Archivo General de Simancas holds records for the Kingdom of Castile. Another archives in Barcelona holds records for the Kingdom of Aragon. Still other archives hold records for Portugal and Navarre. When the Archivo General de Indias was founded in the 18th century in Seville, much, but not all, of the material from Spain's colonies in the Americas was collected in it, but this archive holds almost no documents from the Inquisition. The primary repositories for Inquisition records are the 19th-century Archivo Historico Nacional and the surviving local archives; the Archivo General de Simancas is the main secondary repository. The 18th and 19th centuries also saw the establishment of a Spanish Foreign Ministry archive, two naval archives (one in Madrid and the other ultimately in Viso de Marquez), and two military archives (one in Madrid and the other in Segovia). Prior to the 18th century, and continuing beyond, various special-purpose archives were established elsewhere. All these repositories may hold items of interest to the genealogist.

Spain's records go back at least to the 1200s. Spanish archives hold notarial records, Inquisition records, the ship passenger records of the Archivo General de Indias in Seville, and Catholic Church records.

Almost all available documents are from Christian-ruled Spain and, therefore, offer an incomplete record of Jewish life before the 1492 expulsion. Moslem Spain also kept extensive records, but conquering Christian armies destroyed most of them; names and stories of Spanish Jewry under Islam have largely been lost. This includes records for a great number of Jews, particularly from the "Golden Age," who lived in Moslem Spain.

Spanish Inquisition

The 15th-century Spanish Inquisition had precedents in 13th-century France and Rome, where the Vatican had installed tribunals to root out heresy. However the Spanish inquisition differed in many ways from these earlier church tribunals. Although all inquisitional tribunals in Spain, as well as elsewhere, were run by Church clerics and all were authorized by Papal authority and specific order, the Spanish Inquisition had marked differences important to note.

Earlier inquisitions were run by bishops who reported directly to the Pope. The Spanish Inquisition, though also run by Dominican clerics and instituted in 1478 by authority of Pope Sixtus IV, reported directly to the Spanish monarchs. The Crown, not the Pope, confirmed the inquisitors. Whereas earlier tribunals had been aimed at heresies and witchcraft,[1] the aim of the Spanish Inquisition was primarily to root out Jewish influence and judaizers in Spain. The property of the accused was confiscated by the Crown, which divided the spoils among themselves, the Catholic Church, and the inquisitors. This financial incentive was a major factor in expanding the work of the Inquisition, especially given the great financial needs of the Spanish war of reconquest and the enticing great wealth of many Spanish Jewish families. Pope Sixtus IV even found it necessary to issue an unusual papal bull deploring the fact that the Majorcan inquisitors were "moved not by zeal for the faith and salvation of souls, but by the lust for wealth."[2] Anonymously denouncing enemies to inquisitors was also an easy way to settle old scores.

As early as 1232, Pope Gregory IX issued a bull directing the archbishop of Tarragona to investigate and punish heretics in the lands under his jurisdiction. But, the Spanish Inquisition truly began when the Spanish Catholic monarchs asked Pope Sixtus IV to authorize the creation of a "modern" inquisition in Castile. After intense negotiations in which the Catholic monarchs wrested for themselves the authority to direct it, Sixtus IV issued his November 1, 1478, bull *exigit sincerae devotionis affectus* which created the Spanish Inquisition.

The first Spanish Inquisition tribunal was instituted in 1480 in the Castilian diocese of Seville. Two Dominican clerics, Miguel de Morillo and Juan de San Martin, have the distinction of being the first two Inquisitors named to head the Seville tribunal. This tribunal covered major areas of Andalusia with its large numbers of potential judaizers. It was soon followed by tribunals in other dioceses in Andalusia—in Jaen in 1484 (its tribunal moved in 1526 to Granada) and in Cordoba in 1482, as well as in Castile proper in Ciudad Real in 1483, and Toledo in 1485 (see appendix J).

King Ferdinand established a similar inquisition in his own kingdom of Aragon, and the tribunals in both countries were unified under one grand inquisitor, Tomas de Torquemada. It is a sad historical note that this unified Inquisition was the first government agency to officially span both Aragon and Castile as a single entity. In his years as grand inquisitor, Torquemada, Queen Isabel's confessor and of *converso* origin himself, was personally responsible for two thousand burnings and 37,000 victims who, after torture, were "reconciled" by some other form of punishment. Historian Blazquez Miguel counts 114,350 trials in Spain, of which 3,786 victims were burned at the stake.[3] In the 43 years between 1481 and 1524, the Seville tribunal alone condemned approximately

---

[1] Albigensians, Waldensians, and similar movements that the Vatican considered the heresies of the time.
[2] Baruch Bernstein, *The Chuettas of Majorca* (New York: Ktav, 1972).
[3] Juan Blazques Miguel, *La Inquisición*. (Madrid: Ediciones Penthalon, 1988).

20,000 individuals to various punishments; approximately 1,000 persons were burnt at the stake.

More information about the Inquisition can be found in books listed in the Suggested Reading section at the end of this chapter. Of particular interest are the works by Juan Blazquez Miguel, whose *"La Inquisición"* presents an excellent detailed summary. Appendix J lists the localities of several inquisitional tribunals in Spain and the dates they were instituted. Pere Bonnín extracted from Inquisition records a long list of surnames of those whom the Inquisitional tribunals had found to be judaizers; The list is published in his book *Sangre Judia*.[4]

REPOSITORIES WITH INQUISITION DOCUMENTS[5]

ARCHIVO HISTORICO NACIONAL[6]
Address: Concepcion Contel Calle Serrano 115 28006 Madrid, Spain
Telephone: 91/ 563 59 23
Website: www.mcu.es/lab/archivos/AHN.html

The Archivo Historico Nacional (AHN) in Madrid, along with the surviving local archives, is the main repository for documents of the Spanish Inquisition. Published catalogues for the documents for the tribunals of Toledo and Murcia exist but omit some documents. Inquisition records at the AHN consist of 5,344 manuscript bundles and 1,463 manuscript books, divided into sections:
- Papers of the Supreme Council of the Inquisition
- Correspondence of the Supreme Council with other tribunals in Spain
- Correspondence of the Supreme Council with tribunals in the Americas
- Correspondence of the Supreme Council with tribunals in Italy
- Records of tribunals in Spain brought to Madrid. Holdings include records of court cases from the tribunals of Cordoba, Cuenca, Granada, Logrono, Llerena, Santiago, Sevilla, Toledo, Valencia, Valladolid, and Zaragoza.

Though named for specific towns, each tribunal was responsible for a large surrounding area that included many other communities. The holdings for the

---

[4] Pere Bonnín, *Sangre judia: Espanoles de ascendencia hebrea y antisemitismo cristiano* (Jewish blood: Spaniards of Jewish ancestry and Christian anti-Semitism), 2d ed. (Barcelona: Flor del Viento Ediciones, 1998), 353–74.
[5] See also www.mcu.es/lab/archivos/arp12a.html, www.geocities.com/Paris/Metro/7857/ links espana.html and Library of Congress website, corc.oclc.org/WebZ/XpathfinderQuery? sessionid= 0:term=3252:xid=LCP for links to many Spanish archives.
[6] One of 4 national archives in Spain. The other three are Archivo de La Corona de Aragon, Archivo de Simancas, and Archivo de Indias.

tribunals for Toledo and Murcia have been catalogued, but not all holdings are listed.

- *Catálogo de las causas contra la fe seguidas ante el Tribunal del Santo Oficial de la Inquisición de Toledo y de las informationes genealógicas de los pretendientes a oficios del mismo* (Catalogue of Cases Against the Faith before the Inquisitional Holy Office Tribunal of Toledo and of Genealogical Information of Claimants). Madrid: Tip. de la Revista de archivos, bibliotecas y museos, 1903.
- Blazquez Miguel, Juan. *Catálogo de los procesos inquisitoriales del Tribunal de Santo Oficio de Murcia* (Catalogue of Inquisition Trials of the Murcia Tribunal of the Holy Office). Murgetana, 74, 7–109, 1987.

N.Moreno Garbayo provides a summary of proceedings of the various Inquisition tribunals, including some otherwise lost proceedings from the 18th century.[7]

Archivo Diocesano de Cuenca

Archivo Diocesano de Cuenca is an important repository for the Cuenca tribunal and holds a large part of the documents generated by this tribunal. See the catalogue in D. Perez Ramirez, *Catalogo del Archivo de la Inquisición de Cuenca*.[8] Address: C/Obispo Valero 2; Palacio Episcopal; 16001 Cuenca, Spain
Telephone: 96-621-2461

Archivo General de Simancas

Address: Carretera de Salamanca - Simancas Valladolid, Spain
Website: www.mcu.es/lab/archivos/AGS.html

This archive's holdings include military, judicial, tax and royal records from 1545 to the present. The holdings do not include records of the Inquisition itself but those of government and financial actions resulting from Inquisition activities. The material is divided into the following sections:

- *Contaduría Mayor de Cuentas*
- *Contaduría de Mercedes*
- *Gracia y Justicia*
- *Patronato Real*
- *Registro del Sello de Corte*
- *Secretaria de Estado*

---

[7] N.Moreno Garbayo, *Catalogo de alegaciones fiscales* (Catalog of fiscal allegations). (Madrid 1977).
[8] D. Perez Ramirez, *Catalogo del Archivo de la Inquisición de Cuenca* (Catalogue of the Archive of the Inquisition in Cuenca). Madrid in 1982.

The best available guide is the *"Guia del Investigador, Archivo General de Simancas."*[9]

ARCHIVO DE LA REAL AUDIENCIA DE ZARAGOZA
Address: Archivo Histórico Provincial, Villalpando, 7, 49071, Zaragoza, Spain
Telephone: 976/ 39 75 66

This archive holds important documents for the Kingdom of Aragon. Some material is accessible in the book by A. Ubieto Arteta, *Procesos de la Inquisición de Aragon."*[10]

ARCHIVO DE MUSEO CANARIO IN LAS PALMAS
Address: Plaza de Santa Ana, 4, 35071 - Las Palmas
Telephone: 928/32 30 20
Fax. 928/32 21 34
Website: www.mcu.es/lab/archivos/arp12a.html#6a

The Las Palmas archive in Majorca has Inquisition records for the Canary Islands, as well as records for some others that have found their way to Las Palmas. A useful book about this collection is A. Rodriguez Galindo's *El Museo Canario: Catalogo y extractos de la Inquisición de Canarias.*[11]

OTHER ARCHIVES
Archivo de Real Corona de Aragon
Address: Calle Condes de Barcelona 2 Barcelona, Spain
Telephone: 93/ 315 02 11
Website: www.mcu.es/lab/archivos/ACA.html

The *Archivo de Real Corona de Aragon,* whose holdings include some of the oldest legal, royal and ecclesiastical records in Europe, also holds documents for the areas of Barcelona and Catalonia.

The *archivos historicos provinciales* (provincial archives), website, www.mcu.es/lab/archivos/arp12a.html, hold some Inquisition documents that for some reason didn't end up in the major repositories.

---

[9] Angel de la Plaza Bores, *"Guia del Investigador, Archivo General de Simancas"* (Researcher's Guide: General Archive of Simancas). (Madrid: Ministerio de Cultura, 1992).
[10] A. Ubieto Arteta, *Procesos de la Inquisición de Aragon"* (Trials of the Inquisition of Aragon). *Rev. Archivos, Bibliotecas y Museos,* 67 no. 2 (1959): 549-99.
[11] A. Rodriguez Galindo, *El Museo Canario: Catalogo y extractos de la Inquisición de Canarias.* Museo Canario, nos. 89-103 (1966-69): 129-243; and vols. 31-32, (1970-71): 135-68.

INQUISITION IN THE NEW WORLD

The regions under Spanish control in the New World were divided into viceroyalties. In the 16th century the viceroyalties of New Spain and Peru established capitals in the cities of Mexico and Lima, respectively. Peru, by far the larger, included almost all of non-Portuguese South America (Brazil). In 1610, it was divided into the vice royalty of New Granada (Nueva Granada), which included today's Venezuela, Colombia, Panama, and part of Ecuador, and the vice royalty of Rio de la Plata, composed of today's Argentina, Uruguay, and Paraguay. The capitals of the two vice royalties were Cartagena (now in Colombia) and Buenos Aires, respectively.

In the earliest years of the Spanish colonies, the bishops ran the New World Inquisition. They concentrated primarily on misbehaving clerics and Indian victims. Their Inquisition files would, therefore, originally have been in the Episcopal (Bishop's) archives and, in some places, probably can still to be found in those repositories.

A second era, of much greater danger for Jewish converts to Christianity, began with the arrival in the New World in the late 16th century of the organization colloquially known as the *La Inquisición Espanola* and officially as the *Santo Oficio de la Inquisición* (Holy Office of the Inquisition). This government-run Spanish Inquisition organization, headquartered in Madrid, maintained tribunals in various localities in Spain to detect and destroy certain crimes associated with religious issues. The Inquisition in the New World reached peaks of Jewish persecution in 1596 in Mexico and in 1639 in Lima, Peru.[12]

Three inquisitional tribunals were established in the New World. The Mexico City tribunal covered the North American mainland, extending south to Panama and the Philippines. The Lima tribunal dealt with most of South America. The tribunal in Cartagena (then known as Nueva Granada or the Audiencia de Santa Fe) covered the northern coast of South America and the Caribbean islands. The archives in Mexico City and Lima have survived. The records from Mexico City's tribunal are in the *Archivo General de la Nacion* in Mexico City.

ARCHIVO GENERAL DE LA NACION (AGN)

Eduardo Molina y Albaniles s/n,
Col. Penitenciaria Ampliacion,
Deleg. Venustiano Carranza, 15350, Mexico, D.F.
Website: www.agn.gob.mx/indice.html

Archivo General de la Nacion's holdings consist of 1,555 bound volumes dating from 1522 to 1819. They include the records of the Inquisition of the bishops and

---

[12] *Auto-da-fe* or "act of faith" is the official name given to the public events in which victims of the Inquisition were burned at the stake.

of the *Santo Oficio de la Inquisición* that was established in Mexico in 1569. Most of the bishops Inquisition concerns trials of Indians.

The *Archivo General de la Nacion* also holds well-organized colonial records. A comprehensive guide to these records has been in process of being placed on a CD-ROM. As of about six years ago the guide to about half the holdings was searchable on this CD-ROM. Each bound volume of Inquisition records at the AGN includes a brief abstract of each file in the volume, permitting rapid searches.

The records of the Inquisition in Cartagena disappeared many years ago. However, correspondence between each of the three New World tribunals and the Supreme headquarters of the Inquisition in Madrid is kept at the AHN in Madrid. This correspondence is held in 175 manuscript bundles and 78 manuscript books. Among them are the few remaining references to cases tried by the Cartagena tribunal.

For information on Inquisition trials held in the New World, see Liebman, "*The Inquisitors and the Jews in the New World: Summaries of Procecesos, 1500–1810, and Bibliographical Guide.*"[13] Following the introduction, the book lists Inquisition records in the New World. It is also a good source for *converso* names in the New World. Its appendix includes dates of autos-da-fe in America, lists of documents of interest, and an excellent selected bibliography.

ARCHIVO GENERAL DE INDIAS

Archivo General de Indias, Avda Constitucion s/n, Seville, Spain
Telephone: +34-95-4500530
Fax: +34-95-4219485
Websites: www.mcu.es/lab/archivos/AGI.html and http://cvc.cervantes.es/obref/arnac/indias/indias.htm

Passenger lists of Spaniards who left for the Americas from 1509 to 1790 are preserved in the Archivo General de Indias (AGI) in Seville. During this period Seville was the only Spanish port from which ships were authorized to sail to the Americas. Besides listing all passengers who sailed to the Americas through 1790, the records note place of birth, name of parents and their birthplaces, and the job and destination of the passenger upon arrival. All passengers were at least nominally Christian but a significant number were New Christians or crypto-Jews going to new lands to escape close Spanish scrutiny.[14]

---

[13] Seymour B. Liebman, *The Inquisitors and the Jews in the New World* (Miami: University of Miami Press, 1975).

[14] Crypto-Jews fled to the most distant reaches of Spanish and Portuguese control hoping that the frontier regions would be safer. That is why there is now evidence of crypto-Jews in peripheral areas such as New Mexico, Texas, Colombia, Chile, and Peru.

Except for ship crews and servants of authorized passengers, a license to sail for the Spanish New World was needed. These licenses, issued by the *Casa de la Contratacion* (Chamber of Commerce) were available only for Spaniards with certificates verifying *limpieza de sangre*—pure Christian blood. New Christians, who by definition were of "impure blood," were not allowed to leave Spain for the New World. But, since they were permitted to serve as ship captains and to sign on as crew, many New Christians became captains—and then filled their ships with other New Christians, sailing away to relative safety and bringing many others as "servants." In addition passengers to the Americas could have sailed illegally on ships from England or France, or even from other ports in Spain. By including other sources, authors have estimated that the AGI-held lists may include as few as 20 percent or as many as 80 percent of the real number of passengers who sailed to the Americas during the 16th century.

Passenger information in AGI is found in two groups: *listas* (lists) or *libros de passajeros* (books of passengers), passenger lists 1509 to 1701, and *informaciones y licencias* (information and licenses), licenses and petitions for permission to travel to the Americas, 1534 to 1790. The information in the two groups provides for largely the same persons different items of information. Boyd-Bowman's 1985 book gives information for 1493 to 1539 on nearly all the 15,000 passengers (from the AGI lists and other sources) who sailed for the Americas.[15]

Archivists can search the information in this archive electronically. Requests for information should include passenger name and the approximate date of the trip to America. The Archive has published a partial list of passengers (12 volumes), but not yet in searchable electronic format.

The majority of records concerning the Spanish colonies and the Spanish colonial government are held in three repositories. The Spanish colonies were divided into 14 regions called *audiencas,* of which one was the Philippines (where a few Sephardim also fled) and the rest in the Americas. Most of these colonial records are in the Archivo General de Indias and the rest at Archivo Historico National in Madrid and the Archivo de Simancas in the province of Valladolid.

NOTARIAL AND CHURCH ARCHIVES

The best genealogical records in Spain are the notarial and church archives. They exist for every town in Spain and have survived (with exceptions) for centuries. Records commonly go back to the 1200s, and even earlier in some cases. Notarial records documented sales of land, loans of money, and other transactions. As exciting as it might be for a genealogist to access these records, the problematic reality is that for any one year, 3,000 or more unindexed, difficult-to-read pages of data exist for even small towns. The records identify

---

[15] Peter Boyd-Bowman, *Indice geobiografico de 56 mil pobladores de America* (Geo-niographical index of 56,000 American villagers) 2 vols. (Mexico City: Fondo de Cultura Economica, 1985).

the religion of the individuals recorded and their backgrounds, but for success, the researcher must know exactly when and where to look for records, and allow plenty of time for the search.

Notarial records are found in the local Archivo Historico Provinciales or, for really small towns, sometimes in the mayor's office. It is necessary to be able to read the handwriting of the period. Spanish has not changed much since the early Middle Ages, but the penmanship can look very strange, even to a native speaker who isn't familiar with the script. To add to the difficulty, scribes made their notarial records intentionally difficult to read to ensure their financial security; after all, they earned money by being able to read what no one else could understand.

Excerpts of some notarial records have been translated and printed in books such as Leon Tello's *Judios de Toledo* and Regne's *Jews of Aragon*.[16]

CATHOLIC CHURCH RECORDS

Catholic Church records go back centuries and are found in diocesan archives. Baptismal, matrimonial, and *defunciones* (death) records are relatively easy to scan quickly and, in theory, are kept for the entire community. To view and search church records requires the permission of the local bishop. When requested in writing or in person, permission is usually granted with no problem, but the decision rests with the individual cleric.

MINISTERIO DE CULTURA IDENTIFICATION

All records in the government archives discussed above are government records and should involve no special difficulties to access. Researchers should bring an ID (passport), letter of recommendation (from the researcher's embassy), and two passport photos to any of the national government archives (e.g., Simancas, Archivo General de Indias in Seville or AHN in Madrid), which will issue a Ministerio de Cultura Identification card (*tarjeta nacional de investigator*) that will open most doors. The Ministerio de Cultura ID card is also valid for the Archivo Historico Provinciales.

In summary, for *converso* searches, the notarial and church archives will reflect the everyday existence of everyone. Since the records go back for centuries, the notarial records will cover the Jewish, pre-*converso*, days of ancestors. But because they are so abundant, and because they are written in an antique script, notarial records take time to use. The researcher should become familiar with the antique script by studying examples before going to the archive and proceed with a highly focused query—know exactly what years and what places are to be

---

[16] Pilar Leon Tello, *Judios de Toledo* (Madrid: Institut Arias Montano, 1979); Jean Regne, *History of Jews in Aragon: Collection of Regesta and Court Documents 1213–1327* (Jerusalem: Magnes Press, 1978).

checked. To familiarize researchers with early Spanish scripts, three books can be helpful:

- George, R. Ryskamp, *Finding Your Hispanic Roots*. (Baltimore: Genealogical Publishing, 1997).
- Church of Jesus Christ of Latter-day Saints. *Spanish Handwriting*. Salt Lake City: Genealogical Department of LDS, 1978.
- Jorge A. Garces, *Paleografia espanola y sus peculiaridades en America* (Spanish Paleographics and its peculiarities in America). Quito, Ecuador: 1949.

Larry Feldman's *Anglo-Americans in Spanish Archives: Lists of Anglo-American Settlers in the Spanish Colonies of America, A Finding Aid* also offers useful comments on working in Spanish archives.[17]

CHURCH OF JESUS CHRIST OF LATTER-DAY SAINTS (MORMONS) RECORDS

Address: 35 North West Temple Street, Salt Lake City, Utah, 84150-3400
Telephone: 801-240-2331 or 800-453-3860 ext 22331
FAX: 801-240-1584
E-mail: fhl@ldschurch.org
Website: www.familysearch.org
See also www.jewishgen.org/databases/FHLC for database of Jewish items.

The Mormons hold the most extensive collection of genealogical records copied from archives all over the world. Their "Vital records for western Europe" CD lists 8 CDs containing Spanish records with a few dating to the 14th century.

SUGGESTED READING

Abecassis, Jose Maria. *Genealogia Hebraica: Portugal e Gibraltar, Secs. XVII a XX* (Jewish genealogy: Portugal and Gibraltar, 17th to the 20th centuries). Lisbon: Author, 1990. Five volumes of documented family trees.

Ashton, Eliyahu. *The Jews of Moslem Spain*. Philadelphia: Jewish Publication Society, 1993.

Assis, Y.T. *The Jews of Santa Coloma de Queralt: An Economic and Demographic Case Study of a Community at the End of the Thirteenth Century*. Jerusalem: Magnes Press, 1988.

———. *Jews in the Crown of Aragon, 1213–1327*. Jerusalem: Central Archives for the History of the Jewish People, 1995. Thorough study of Jews in northeast Spain.

---

[17] Larry Feldman, *Anglo-Americans in Spanish Archives: Lists of Anglo-American Settlers in the Spanish Colonies of America: A Finding Aid*. (Baltimore Md.: Genealogical Publishing Co., 1991).

———. *Jewish Economy in the Medieval Crown of Aragon, 1213–1327*. Leiden, The Netherlands: E.J. Brill, 1997. Companion volume providing the Jewish economy information on the Jews of Aragon.
Baer, Yitzhak. *History of the Jews in Christian Spain*. Philadelphia: Jewish Publication Society, 1993. A "classic."
Beinart, Haim *"The Great Conversion and the Converso Problem."* Haim Beinart, ed. *The Sephardi Legacy*. Jerusalem: Magnes, 1992.
———. *The Expulsion of the Jews from Spain*. English translation of *Gerush Sefarad*. Portland, Ore.: Littman Library of Jewish Civilization, 2002.
———. *Conversos on Trial: The Inquisition in Ciudad Real*. Jerusalem: Magnes Press, 1981.
———. *"The Jews in Castile." The Sephardi Legacy*. Haim Beinart, ed. Jerusalem: Magnes Press, 1992.
Benbassa, Esther and Aron Rodrigue. *Sephardi Jewry: A History of the Judeo-Spanish Community, 14–20th centuries*. Berkeley: University of California, 2000.
Blazquez Miguel, Juan. *La Inquisición* (The Inquisition). Madrid: Ediciones Penthalon, 1988.
———. *Ciudad Real y la Inquisición, 1483–1820* (Ciudad Real and the Inquisition). Ciudad Real: Comision Municipal de Cultura, 1987.
———. *Toledot: Historia del Toledo judio* (Generations: History of Jewish Toledo). Toledo, Spain: Editorial Arcano 1989.
———. *La Inquisición en Cataluña: el tribunal del Santo Oficio de Barcelona, 1487–1820* (Inquisition in Catalonia: Holy Office tribunal of Barcelona, 1487–1820). Toledo, Spain: Editorial Arcano, 1990.
———. *Madrid-judios, herejes y brujas: El Tribunal de Corte (1650–1820)* (Jews of Madrid, heretics, and witches: The Royal Tribunal (1650–1820)). Toledo, Spain: Editorial Arcano, 1990.
———. *La Inquisición en Castilla-La Mancha* (Inquisition in Castile-La Mancha). Cordoba, Spain: Universidad de Cordoba, 1986.
Bonnín, Pere. *Sangre judia: Espanoles de ascendencia hebrea y antisemitismo cristiano*. (Jewish blood: Spaniards of Jewish ancestry and Christian anti-Semitism). 2d ed. Barcelona: Flor del Viento Ediciones, 1998.
Cortes i Cortes, Gabriel. *Historia de los Judios Mallorquines y sus descendientes cristianos* (History of the Majorcan Jews and their Christian descendants). Palma de Mallorca: Imagen, 1985. Posthumous two-volume book by a right-wing (Falangist) Catholic author descendant. Name lists and some family trees.
Donate Sebastia, J. and J.R. Magdalena Nom de Deu. *Jewish Communities in Valencia*. Jerusalem: Magnes Press, 1990.
———. *Three Jewish Communities in Medieval Valencia: Castellon de la Plana, Burriana, Villareal*. Jerusalem: Magnes Press, Hebrew University, 1990.

Extensive study that includes multiple documents referring to Jews from the archives.

Elnecave, Nissim. *Los Hijos de Ibero-Franconia* (Sons of Iberia-Franconia). Buenos Aires: Ediciones La Luz, 1981.

Epstein, Isidore. *The Responsa of Rabbi Solomon ben Adret of Barcelona (1235–1310) as a Source of the History of Spain.* London: Ktav, 1968.

Gerber, Jane. *The Jews of Spain: A History of the Sephardic Experience.* New York: Free Press Macmillan, 1992.

Greenleaf, Richard. *The Mexican Inquisition of the Sixteenth Century.* Albuquerque: University of New Mexico Press.

Hinojosa Montalvo, Jose. *The Jews of the Kingdom of Valencia: From Persecution to Expulsion, 1391–1492.* Jerusalem: Magnes Press, Hebrew University, 1993. The most complete study of the Jews of Valencia (present-day provinces of Castellon, Valencia, and Alicante). Includes translations of archival documents, extensive name lists, and related bibliography.

Hordes, Stanley. *The Crypto-Jewish Community of New Spain, 1620–1649: A Collective Biography.* PhD diss. Tulane University, 1980.

Isaacs, Abraham Lionel. *The Jews of Majorca.* London: Methuen, 1936.

Leon Tello, Pilar. *Judios de Toledo* (Jews of Toledo). Madrid: Institut Arias Montano, 1979. Lists Jews who lived in Toledo and court documents about them.

Leroy, Beatrice. *The Jews of Navarre in the Late Middle Ages.* Jerusalem: Magnes Press, Hebrew University, 1985.

Liebman, Seymour B. *The Inquisitors and the Jews in the New World: Summaries of Procecesos, 1500–1810, and Bibliographical Guide.* Miami: University of Miami Press, 1975. Following a brief introduction, lists Inquisition Records in the New World.

de Molina, Rafael, Conde y Delgado. *La Expulsion de Los Judios de la Corona de Aragon* (The expulsion of the Jews of the Aragon Crown). Zaragoza, Spain: Institucion Fernando el Catolico, 1991.

Netanyahu, B. *The Origins of the Inquisition in XIV Century Spain.* New York: Random House, 1995.

O'Callaghan, Joseph F. *A History of Medieval Spain.* Ithaca, N.Y.: Cornell University Press, 1975.

Ortiz, Dominguez. *Judeoconversos en la espana y America* (Jewish *conversos* in Spain and America). Madrid: Ediciones Istmo, 1971.

Ortiz, Dominguez. *Judeoconversos en la espana moderna* (Jewish *conversos* in modern Spain). Madrid: Editorial Mapfre Paseo de Recoletos, 1992.

Pflaum, H. "*Une ancienne satire espagnole contre les marranes*" (An ancient Spanish satire against the marranos). *Revue des Etudes Juives* 86 (1928): 131–50.

Raphael, David. *The Expulsion 1492 Chronicles*. North Hollywood, Calif.: Carmi House Press; New York: Sephardic House. Translations of contemporary writings about Sephardim and the expulsion.

Regne, Jean. *History of Jews in Aragon: Collection of Regesta and Court Documents 1213–1327*. Jerusalem: Magnes Press, 1978.

Rodriguez Fernandez, Justiniano. *La Juderia de la Ciudad de Leon* (Jewish quarter of the city of Leon). Leon, Spain: Centro de estudios e investigacion "San Isidro," Archivo Historico Diocesano, 1969. Lists Jews and 11th- and 12th-century Jewish tombstones.

Roth, Cecil. *A History of the Marranos*. 4th ed. New York: Hermon Press, 1974.

———. *The Spanish Inquisition*. New York: W.W. Norton & Company, 1996.

Roth, Norman. *Conversos, Inquisition, and the Expulsion of the Jews from Spain*. Madison: University of Wisconsin Press, 1995. Information about *converso* families; lists *converso* names.

Sachar, H.M. *Farewell Espana: The World of the Sephardim Remembered*. New York: Vintage Books, 1995.

Singerman, Robert. *The Jews in Spain and Portugal*. New York: Garland Publishing, 1975.

Zafrani, Haim. *Juifs d'Andalousie et du Maghreb* (Jews of Andalusia and the Maghreb). Paris: Maisonneuve & Larose, 1996.

19.
Morocco

In the first half of the 20th century, Morocco was home to 250,000 Sephardic Jews, but genealogical researchers face significant difficulties in finding Jewish records. The history of the area accounts for some of these difficulties. Until very recently, government records in Morocco were less detailed than those in European countries—if they existed at all. Until well into the 20th century, the rulers of Morocco (including the French) did not control the entire country. The northern half, called the *bled el makhzen* (land of the treasury) (see map, Figure 12), was the only area the king controlled and from which he could hope to collect taxes. Until the mid-20th century, the king needed to travel regularly, accompanied by his army and entourage, to his royal cities in order to collect his revenues.

Fierce local chieftains controlled the balance of the country *(bled el siba)*. These chieftains retained their autonomy even when they nominally were under the jurisdiction of the French. These local conditions meant that until the 20th century, government birth or death registrations and census records were not kept and did not exist.

Throughout the last three or four centuries, the great majority of Moroccan Jews lived in the major cities of the *makhzen*, but they traveled to a large number of small settlements of 50–200 Jews in the *bled el siba* (see Figure 11) where they were the main traders.

Although much remains to uncover, a number of resources have been identified that can be useful to genealogists researching Jewish ancestry in Morocco.

Archives

Israel
Central Archives for the History of the Jewish People
Address: 46 Jabotinsky Street, Jerusalem
Mailing address: P.O. Box 1149, Jerusalem 91010
Telephone: (972)-2-5635716
Website: sites.huji.ac.il/archives
Email: archives@vms.huji.ac.il

The Central Archives for the History of the Jewish People holds *pinkassim* (registers) and documents from the Jewish communities of Casablanca, Fez, Meknes, Mogador, and Sefrou for the period 1710–1963. Uncatalogued and unindexed, these collections contain information at present available only to researchers onsite.

FRANCE

Archives du Ministere des Affaires Etrangeres (Archives of the Department of Foreign Affairs) has two branches. One branch is located in Paris on the quai d'Orsay and the other branch, more useful to genealogists, is in Nantes. Both are described below.

Archives du quai d'Orsay
Address: 1, rue Robert Esnault Pelterie, 75007 Paris, France
Telephone: 01 43 17 53 47
Fax: 01 43 17 52 84
Access: Monday-Friday, 9 am-6 pm; closed May 15-31

This archive holds records of diplomatic correspondence between consulates and the government in Paris. The collection is not particularly useful to genealogists unless one is researching historical events or persons of sufficient importance to be mentioned in diplomatic letters from French consulates abroad. But the quai d'Orsay Archives has a copy of the index of documents in the Nantes archives (see below), a useful research aid for Paris-based researchers planning a later trip to Nantes.

Foreigners should obtain permission to conduct research in advance by writing to the Direction des Archives du Ministere des Affaires Etrangeres, 37 quai d'Orsay, 75007 Paris, France, accompanied by a letter of introduction from their foreign embassy and two photographs. The entrance to the archives is on rue Robert Esnault Pelterie, near Les Invalides in Paris.

Archives Diplomatiques de Nantes
Address: 17 rue du Casterneau, 44000, Nantes, France
Telephone: (33) 2 51 77 25 25
Fax : (33) 2 51 77 24 60
Access: Monday-Friday, 9 am-6pm. Need Identification card and 2 photos

The Archives Diplomatiques de Nantes is one of 3 major archives located in the city of Nantes. The 3 archives are the *Archives Municipales* of the city of Nantes, the *Archives departementales de Loire Atlantique* and the Nantes branch of the *Archives du ministere des Affaires Etrangeres* (foreign affairs) also known as the *Archives Diplomatiques de Nantes*. It is this last one that is of interest to the Sephardic genealogist.

The diplomatic archives in Nantes holds overseas French embassy and consular records, as well as vital records of French citizens. The vital records include the 1925 to 1956 civil records of the city of Casablanca, as well as records of registrations made after 1956 through French consulates in Morocco.

This archives also has a collection of notarial records from the French protectorates, including Morocco, Tunisia, Syria, and Lebanon.

Records older than 100 years are available on microfilm.

If based in Paris, it may be helpful to first visit the quai d'Orsay archives in Paris to consult copies of the document indexes of the Nantes diplomatic archives there prior to coming to Nantes.[1]

Many Jews from Morocco sought French citizenship; searching for French naturalization applications and records in France can be fruitful. Similarly, for neighboring Algeria, a French protectorate. A number of these Algerian records were copied and are held at the Archives d'outre mer in Aix-en Provence, France.

ALLIANCE ISRAELITE UNIVERSELLE ARCHIVES
Address: 45 Rue la Bruyere, 75009, Paris.
Archives: by appointment
Telephone: 01 53 32 88 55
Fax : 01 48 74 51 33
Email : biblio@aiu.org
Website: www.aiu.org
Access: Monday, Tuesday, Thursday, 1–6 pm; Wednesday, 1–7:30 pm

The Alliance Israelite Universelle (AIU) established schools in many locations in Morocco during the 19th century. The AIU Archives holds information about the schools and the teachers, student statistics, and a few students' personal details or name lists. Genealogists Philip Abensur and Laurence Hazan-Abensur of Paris have spent the last two years methodically researching and documenting these archives. The records are organized into 12 alphabetically named groups of documents, of which the series E for *ecoles* (schools) offers the most genealogically useful information. From the series E group of documents, the Abensurs are creating an index of names and relevant references for the town of Izmir in Turkey, that, when finished, will be deposited at the AIU Archives. They also partially completed similar indexes for Tangier in Morocco and Alexandria in Egypt. They are working on indexes for Istanbul and Adrianople in Turkey; Tunis and Sous in Tunisia; Mogador, Tetuan, and Safi in Morocco; and Oran in Algeria.

---

[1] Philip Abensur, "*Archives du Ministere des Affaires Etrangeres,*" Revue du Cercle de Genealogies Juive 34 (Summer 1993).

OTHER FOREIGN CONNECTIONS

Records of Moroccan Jewry may also be found outside Moroccan and French archives. Melilla and Ceuta were Spanish enclaves in Morocco whose citizens registered with the Spanish authorities.[2] Registrations in those towns are part of the Archives of Spain.

Protection by foreign powers provided significant advantages, which some Moroccan Jews were able to gain by registering with consulates in Morocco of Belgium, England, France (pre-1925), Italy, Portugal, Spain, Sweden, and the United States. The consular archives of these countries would therefore be the place to look for the birth, death, and marriage records of Moroccan Jews.

BENSION COLLECTION OF SEPHARDIC MANUSCRIPTS

Address: Alberta University Library, Special Collections Section, Canada
Telephone: (780) 492-4174
Website: www.library.ualberta.ca/specialcollections/index.cfm
Access: hours change; call (780) 492-4174

This large collection of Sephardic manuscripts, most from Morocco, was originally collected by Ariel Bension of Paris. *A Descriptive Catalogue of the Bension Collection of Manuscripts* provides excellent detailed descriptions of the manuscripts, complete with English summaries.[3] Written in a Sephardic cursive script undecipherable to the uninitiated, the documents may be ordered from the information given in this catalogue. Manuscript numbers are listed, making it possible for researchers to request copies of the original documents easily by mail.

The large number of letters exchanged by various Moroccan rabbis about numerous individuals are genealogically useful; rabbis include Rabbi Jacob ibn Zur (Abensour), Rabbi Jacob ben Malka, Rabbi Serrero, Rabbi Abitbol, and others.

Although other similar repositories are not yet identified, it is likely that genealogically useful archives about Moroccan Jewry exist in other archives. Likely candidates are the Imperial Ottoman Archives in Istanbul and repositories in Morocco that might contain records of the special *jizya* tax imposed on Jews

---

[2] Melilla (from *Tamlit*: the "white" in Berber) was taken by the Spaniards in 1497 and later became a dependency of Malaga. Ceuta was named Abyla under the Phoenicians and Julia Trajecta under the Romans. In the sixth century it became the Byzantine capital Septem Fratres (from which is derived today's name). It was captured by the Portuguese in 1415 and then by Spain in 1580, remaining in Spanish hands since then.

[3] Saul I. Aranov, *A Descriptive Catalogue of the Bension Collection of Manuscripts* (Alberta: University of Alberta Press, 1979).

living in Moslem countries. Private collections of documents also probably hold much valuable material still to be uncovered.

VITAL RECORDS

As noted above, birth and death registration is a relatively recent development in Morocco. Some Jewish families registered their children's births with the French civil authorities during the French protectorate. For others the only record of a birth or death might be found in the registers of the Jewish community or synagogue (see Jewish Records section below).

Civil registration in French Morocco apparently started in 1925; these records are held at the Archives Diplomatiques de Nantes (see above). French Moroccan civil registrations before 1925 are found in French consular records (see above).

JEWISH COMMUNITY AND RECORDS

Births registered with the Jewish community are usually part of a town's Jewish community records, unless they have been moved elsewhere for safekeeping.

Jews frequently donated money to permit the publication of Jewish books. These pre-publication subscribers' names are listed in the printed book and thus provide clues about them.

Casablanca Bet Din
Address: 1 rue Adrienne Lecouvreur, Casablanca, Morocco
Telephone 2269-52 and 2228-61

Abensur described the contents of the Casablanca *beth din* (Jewish court) among other resources in Morocco.[4] Because the Casablanca *beth din* records are not indexed, exact Hebrew dates and names are essential for successful searches. Registers consist of births (but not all Jews registered their children's births here), marriage *ketubot* (but some Jews were too poor to afford a ketubah), and death records (see example, Figure 5).

Tangier
Tangier's Jewish community possesses a birth register from 1892 and a civil marriage register from 1927.

Tetuan
Tetuan has a death registry for the years 1895–1987.

Jewish community birth, death, and marriage records may also exist for other towns in Morocco in addition to the holdings itemized in this section.

Circumcision records are valuable for genealogical research, but few are in the public domain in Morocco. An 1895 circumcision register for Tetuan is held at

---

[4] Philip Abensur, "Sephardic Genealogical Research in Morocco," *Avotaynu* 10, no. 3 (Fall 1994): 40.

the Sephardic Museum of Toledo, Spain. Abensur also reports the presence of a circumcision registry from Mogador in the possession of Samuel Bandahan of London.[5]

KETUBOT

Ketubot, Jewish marriage certificates, are written at the time of a marriage and the document given to the bride for safekeeping. Noting at minimum the date and place of marriage and the names of the bride's and groom's fathers, some *ketubot* list several generations on both sides of the marriage—major genealogical finds. Several *ketubot* are in museums or archives,[6] but many surely lie gathering dust in attics or forgotten in family files.

CEMETERIES

Many ancient Jewish cemeteries exist throughout Morocco. No complete list has been identified to date. Those that are known are mostly in disarray and not well documented, if at all. Joel Zack's "The Synagogues of Morocco: An Architectural and Preservation Survey," based on a World Monuments Fund survey, lists the following Moroccan towns with Jewish cemeteries: Azemour, Casablanca, Chechaouen, El Jadida, Essaouira/Mogador, Fez, Marrakech, Meknes, Ouezzanne, Safi, Sale, Tangier, and Tetuan and some in the smaller towns of Azrou, Erfoud, Er Rachidia, Krandou, Rich, Rissani, Ait Zewrar, Tiznit, Agoim, Aoulouz, and Imzouren. But there are many more. Great need exists to list them and to record carefully the inscriptions on these tombstones, many of which have already become illegible.

SUGGESTED READING

Abecassis, Jose Maria. *Genealogia Hebraica: Portugal e Gibraltar, Secs. XVII a XX* (Jewish genealogy: Portugal and Gibraltar, 17th to 20th centuries). Lisbon: Author, 1990 (in Portuguese). 5 vols. of documented family trees Faro, Portugal: 1986 (Woodstock, Ill., U.S.A. : I. Bitton [distributor]). Though written in Portuguese, the many family trees and *ketubot* make it an invaluable resource to those searching families from those areas. Many Sephardic families from Morocco are included.

Abensur, Philip. *Archives du Ministere des Affaires Etrangeres. Revue du Cercle de Genealogie Juive* 34 (Summer 1993): 10–11.

———. "Sephardic Genealogical Research in Morocco." *Avotaynu* 10, no. 3 (Fall 1994): 40.

---

[5] Abensur, "Sephardic Genealogical Research in Morocco." *Avotaynu* 3, no. 10 (Fall 1994): 40.
[6] See Jewish National and University Library, Jerusalem, http://jnul.huji.ac.il/dl/ketubbot. *Ketubot* online are digitized, from the 1,200-manuscript collection.

Abitbol, M., ed. *Communautes Juives des marges sahariennes du Maghreb* (Jewish communities from the borders of the Sahara in the Maghreb). Jerusalem: Ben Zvi Institute, 1982.

Aranov, Saul I. *A Descriptive Catalogue of the Bension Collection of Sephardic Manuscripts and Texts.* Winnipeg, Canada: University of Alberta Press, 1979. Unique collection of primary documents, mostly from Morocco.

Ben Naim, Yosef. *Malkhei rabanan.* (Prominent Rabbis). Jerusalem: Author, 1931. Extensive Hebrew-language biographical list of rabbis of Morocco.

Bensimon, Agnes. *Hassan II et les Juifs: Histoire d'une Emigration Secrete* (Hassan II and the Jews: History of a Secret Emigration). Paris: Seuil, 1991.

Bensoussan, David and Asher Knafu. *Ketoubbot de Mogador* (Ketubot of Magador). Montreal: Éditions Du Lys, 2002.

Bruno, Louis, and Elie Malka. *Receuil de textes Judeo-Arabes de Fes* (Collection of Judeo-Arabic texts from Fez). Rabat, Morocco: Hautes Etudes Marocaines, 1939. Collection of Jewish primary documents from Fez.

de Castries, Henry. *Les Sources inedites de l'histoire du Maroc: Archives et Bibliotheques d'Angleterre, de la France, de l'Espagne, du Portugal, des Bas Pays* (Unpublished sources of the history of Morocco: Archives and libraries of England, France, Spain, Portugal, and The Netherlands). 27 vols. Paris: Ernst Leroux, 1918.

Chouraqui, André N. *Between East and West: A History of the Jews of North Africa.* Philadelphia: Jewish Publication Society, 1968.

Corcos, David. *Studies in the History of the Jews of Morocco.* Jerusalem: Rubin Mass, 1976. Part in English, part in Hebrew.

Deshen, Shlomo. *The Mellah Society.* Chicago: University of Chicago Press, 1989. Description of Jewish society in pre-colonial Morocco.

Encyclopaedia Judaica. 17 vols. Jerusalem: Encyclopaedia Judaica-Ktav, 1971. Many bearers of Sephardic surnames (e.g., Abensur, Malka, Sasson) are described in its pages. Some family trees are presented.

Flamand, Pierre. *Les communautes israelites du Sud-Marocain: essai de description et d'analyse de la vie juive en milieu berbere* (Jewish communities of Southern Morocco: Descriptive essay and analysis of Jewish life among the in Berbers). Casablanca: Imprimeries reunies, 1959. Part of series *Diaspora en terre d'Islam.*

———. *Quelques manifestations de l'esprit populaire dans les juiveries du Sud-Marocain* (Some manifestations of the popular spirit in the Jewish communities of southern Morocco). Casablanca: Imprimeries reunies, 1959. Part of series *Diaspora en terre d'Islam.*

Gerber, Jane. *Jewish Society in Fez 1450–1700: Studies in Communal and Economic Life.* Leiden, The Netherlands: E.J. Brill, 1980.

Goldenberg, Andre, ed. *Juifs du Maroc: Images et textes* (Jews of Morocco: Images and texts). Paris: Les Editions du Scribe, 1992.

Laredo, Abraham. *Les Noms des Juifs du Maroc* (Names of the Jews of Morocco). Madrid: Institut Montano, 1978. Extensive biographical list of more than a thousand families, with detailed sources. Described by the author as an onomastic study of the names of the Jews of Morocco, it is a lot more. The book includes a list of Moroccan Jewish surnames with variants and probable origins and also, under each surname, persons of note who bore that name in the past, plus the sources of that information. Furthermore, despite its title, the book is useful to Sephardic genealogists everywhere, because the names discussed here occur not only in Morocco but also throughout the Sephardic world. This is possibly the one most useful book for Sephardic genealogists.

Laskier, Michael M. *The Alliance Israelite and the Jewish Communities of Morocco 1862–1962*. Albany: State University of New York Press, 1983.

Martsiano, Eliyahu Refael. *Histoire et généalogie des Juifs de Debdou, Maroc: La généalogie de la communauté juive de Debdou et l'ascendance de toutes les familles qui la composent, à la lumière de sources et de documents inédits* (History and genealogy of the Jews or Debdou, Morocco: Genealogy of the Jewish community of Debdou and the ancestry of all the families that make it up, in the light of unpublished sources and documents). Montréal: Éditions Élysée, 2000. Describes the genealogy of the families who left Seville after 1391 to settle in Debdou at the foot of the Atlas Mountains of Morocco.

Pennell, C.R. *Morocco since 1830: A History*. New York: New York University Press, 2000.

Pimienta, S. *Indice del Libro de Actas de la Communidad Hebrea de Tanger, 1860–1875* (Index to the first Book of Acts of the Jewish community of Tangier, 1860–1875). Paris: Pamphlet, 1992.

Romanelli, Samuel. *Travail in an Arab Land*. Tuscaloosa: University of Alabama Press, 1989. Translation of travelogue of an 18th-century Italian Jew's four-year stay in Morocco.

Salafranca Ortega, J.F. *Historia de la poblacion judia de Melilla desde su reconquista por espana hasda 1936* (History of the Jewish population of Melilla from its Spanish reconquest to 1936). Málaga, Spain: Editorial Algazara, 1995. Includes census sheets, names, photos, and archival sources.

Segal, Ariel. *Jews of the Amazon: Self-Exile in Earthly Paradise*. Philadelphia: Jewish Publication Society, 1999.

Serels, Mitchell M. *A History of the Jews of Tangier in the Nineteenth and Twentieth Centuries*. New York: Sepher-Hermon Press, 1991.

Talbi, Mohamed. "*Un nouveau fragment de l'histoire de l'Occident musulman*" (A new fragment of the history of the Moslem West), *Cahiers de Tunisie* 19, nos. 73-74 (1971): 19-52.

Toledano, Joseph. *La Saga des Familles: Les Juifs du Maroc et leurs noms* (Family sagas: The Jews of Morocco and their names). Tel Aviv: Stavit, 1983. Old photos of family members.

———. *Une histoire des familles: Les noms de famille Juifs d'Afrique du Nord* (Family history: Family names of the Jews of North Africa). Jerusalem: author, 1999. (Obtain from author, P.O. Box 26308, 91262 Jerusalem, Israel). Includes biographies of past and current prominent persons.

Zafrani, Haim. *Juifs d'Andalousie et du Maghreb* (Jews of Andalusia and the Maghreb). Paris: Maisonneuve & Larose, 1996. Essential reading by the foremost living authority on the Maghreb and Jewish Andalusia.

ibn Zur, Jacob. *Et sofer*. Morocco, 16th century. In the 16th century Rabbi Jacob ibn Zur of Morocco listed the names of the Jews of his time. This list, known as *et sofer*,[7] is still used today by Jewish scribes to ensure the correct spelling of names in religious documents such as marriage and divorce certificates. Although the list does not include all known names, it is a valuable historical source of information.

---

[7] *Sofer* is Hebrew for scribe.

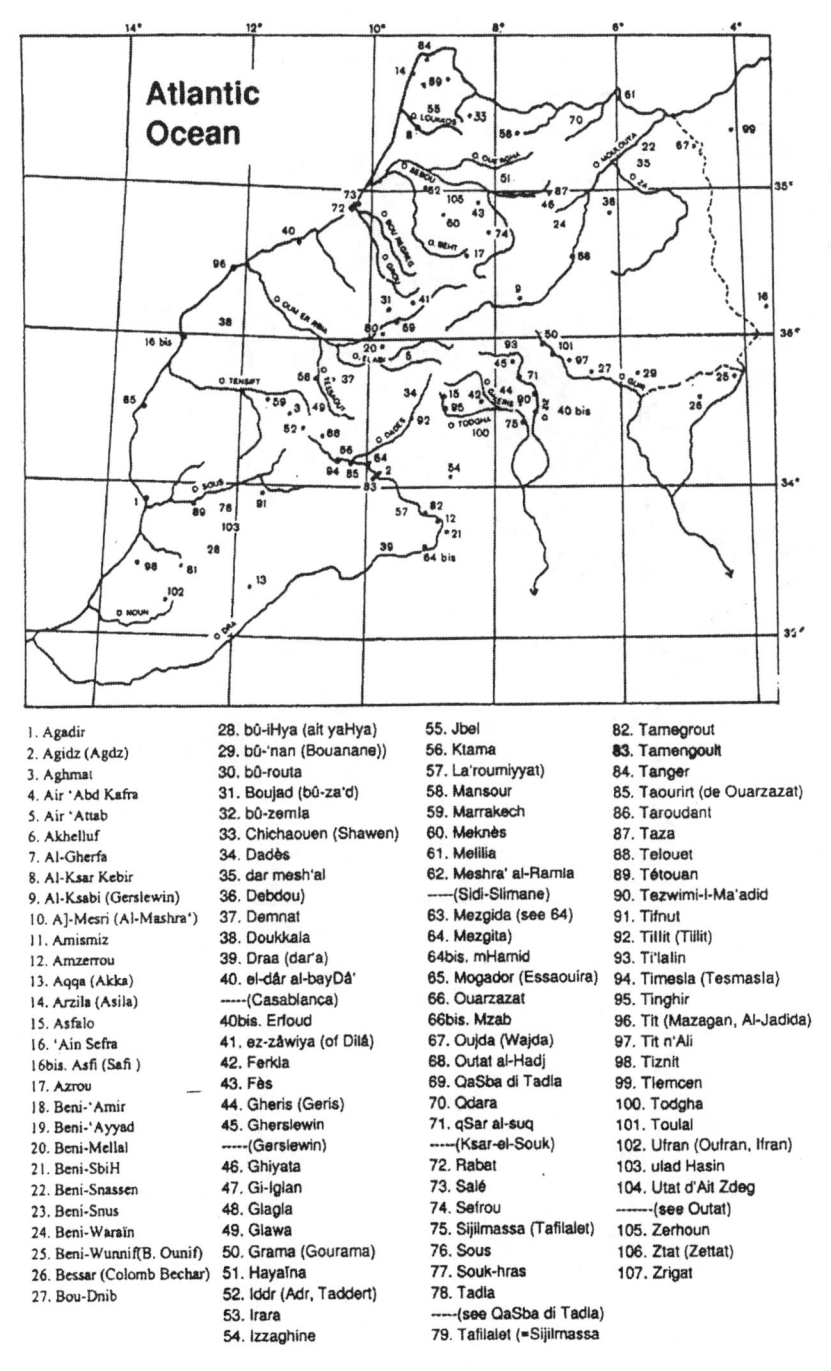

1. Agadir	28. bû-iHya (ait yaHya)	55. Jbel	82. Tamegrout
2. Agidz (Agdz)	29. bû-'nan (Bouanane))	56. Ktama	83. Tamengoult
3. Aghmat	30. bû-routa	57. La'roumiyyat)	84. Tanger
4. Air 'Abd Kafra	31. Boujad (bû-za'd)	58. Mansour	85. Taourirt (de Ouarzazat)
5. Air 'Attab	32. bû-zemla	59. Marrakech	86. Taroudant
6. Akhelluf	33. Chichaouen (Shawen)	60. Meknès	87. Taza
7. Al-Gherfa	34. Dadès	61. Melilia	88. Telouet
8. Al-Ksar Kebir	35. dar mesh'al	62. Meshra' al-Ramla	89. Tétouan
9. Al-Ksabi (Gerslewin)	36. Debdou	-----(Sidi-Slimane)	90. Tezwimi-I-Ma'adid
10. A]-Mesri (Al-Mashra')	37. Demnat	63. Mezgida (see 64)	91. Tifnut
11. Amismiz	38. Doukkala	64. Mezgita)	92. Tillit (Tillit)
12. Amzerrou	39. Draa (dar'a)	64bis. mHamid	93. Ti'lalin
13. Aqqa (Akka)	40. el-dâr al-bayDâ'	65. Mogador (Essaouira)	94. Timesla (Tesmasla)
14. Arzila (Asila)	-----(Casablanca)	66. Ouarzazat	95. Tinghir
15. Asfalo	40bis. Erfoud	66bis. Mzab	96. Tit (Mazagan, Al-Jadida)
16. 'Ain Sefra	41. ez-zâwiya (of Dilâ)	67. Oujda (Wajda)	97. Tit n'Ali
16bis. Asfi (Safi)	42. Ferkla	68. Outat al-Hadj	98. Tiznit
17. Azrou	43. Fès	69. QaSba di Tadla	99. Tlemcen
18. Beni-'Amir	44. Gheris (Geris)	70. Qdara	100. Todgha
19. Beni-'Ayyad	45. Gherslewin	71. qSar al-suq	101. Toulal
20. Beni-Mellal	-----(Gerslewin)	-----(Ksar-el-Souk)	102. Ufran (Oufran, Ifran)
21. Beni-SbiH	46. Ghiyata	72. Rabat	103. ulad Hasin
22. Beni-Snassen	47. Gi-Iglan	73. Salé	104. Utat d'Ait Zdeg
23. Beni-Snus	48. Glagla	74. Sefrou	-------(see Outat)
24. Beni-Waraïn	49. Glawa	75. Sijilmassa (Tafilalet)	105. Zerhoun
25. Beni-Wunnif(B. Ounif)	50. Grama (Gourama)	76. Sous	106. Ztat (Zettat)
26. Bessar (Colomb Bechar)	51. Hayaïna	77. Souk-hras	107. Zrigat
27. Bou-Dnib	52. Iddr (Adr, Taddert)	78. Tadla	
	53. Irara	-----(see QaSba di Tadla)	
	54. Izzaghine	79. Tafilalet (=Sijilmassa	

Source: Thomas K. Park, *The Historical Dictionary of Morocco* (Lanham, Md..: Scarecrow Press, 1996), with permission.

Figure 11. Jewish Settlements in Morocco

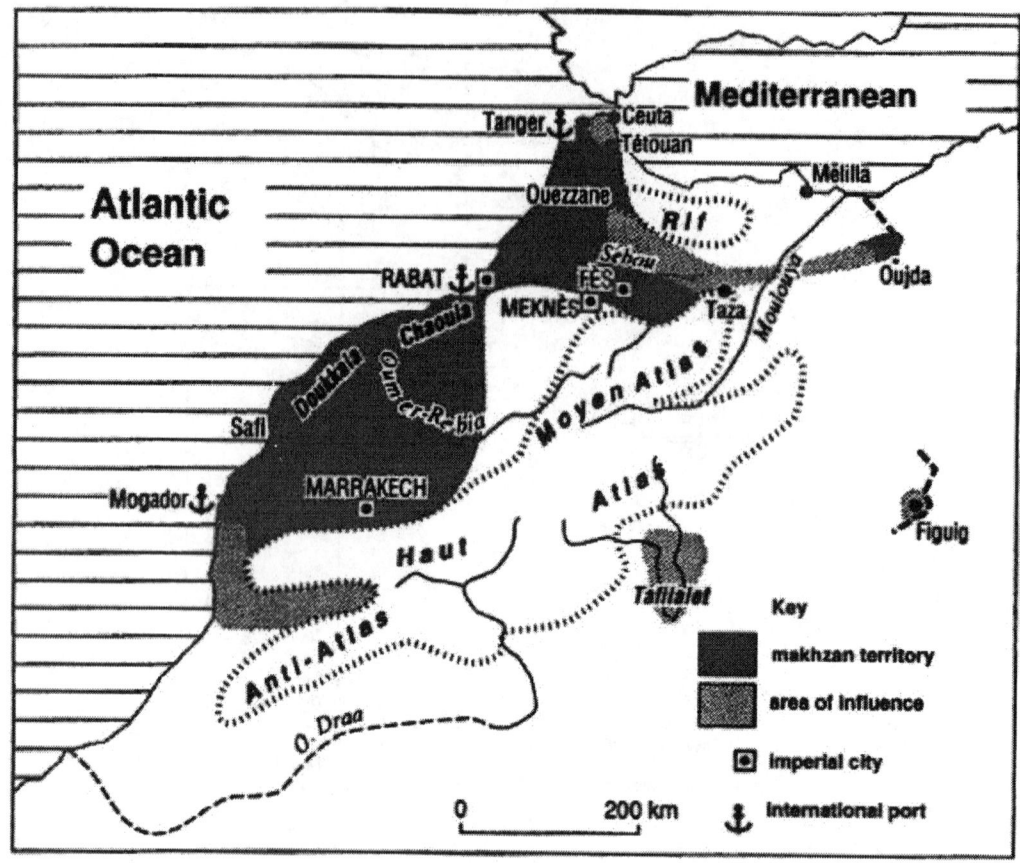

Source: Thomas K. Park, *The Historical Dictionary of Morocco*. (Scarecrow Press), with permission.

Figure 12. Makhzen-Controlled Morocco, 19th Century

150 • *Sephardic Genealogy: Discovering Your Sephardic Ancestors and Their World*

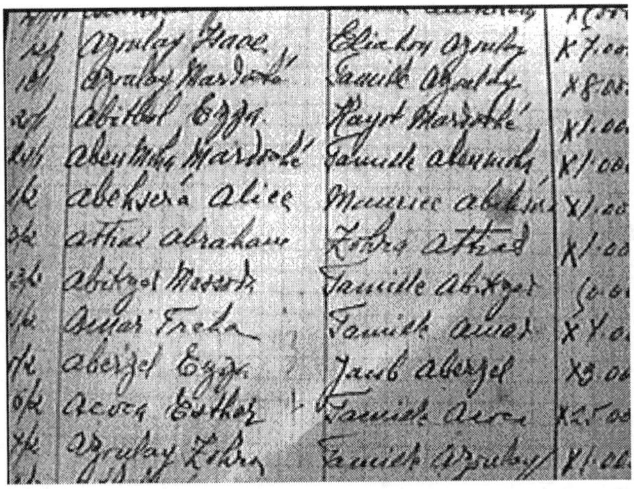

Source: Courtesy Kevin Shuster, Chicago

Figure 13. Fragment of Casablanca Cemetery List

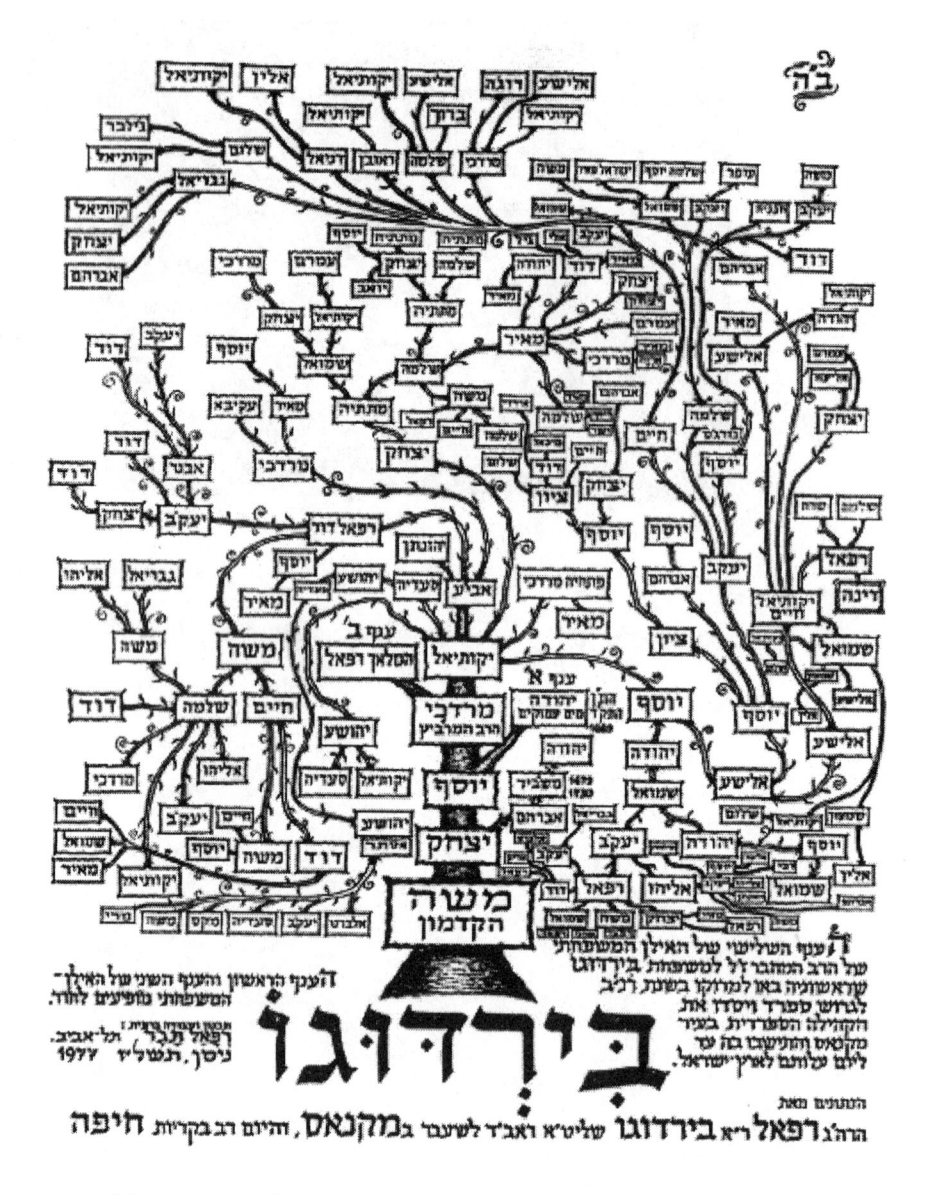

Source: www.delanet.com/~loeb, Berdugo family tree drawn by Rabbi Raphael Berdugo, with permission of Daniel Loeb

Figure 14. Sephardic Family Tree

152 • *Sephardic Genealogy: Discovering Your Sephardic Ancestors and Their World*

20.
ALGERIA

By the Cremieux decree of October 14, 1870, the Jews of Algeria who had not yet been naturalized automatically became French citizens. No special application for citizenship was required, and the process left no individual documentary traces. The law did, however, lead to the emigration of many Jews from Morocco into Algeria. Some Algerian records were copied by the French government and may be found in France (see below), but many others remain in Algeria where, for political reasons, it is difficult at present to do active research. For the history of the Jews of Algeria, the reader is referred to the suggested reading section at the end of this chapter.

ARCHIVES

ISRAEL
Central Archives for the History of the Jewish People
Address: Hebrew University Campus, Sprinzak Bldg, Givat Ram, Jerusalem, Israel.
Mailing address: P.O. Box 1149, Jerusalem 91010
Telephone at (972)-2-5635716

This repository holds the community archives of the Algerian city of Constantine from 1795 to 1960 and lists of documents concerning Jews in non-Jewish Algerian archives (17th–19th centuries). Uncatalogued and unindexed, these collections contain information that is at present available only to genealogists onsite.

FRANCE
Centre des Archives de Outre Mer
Address: 29 chemin du Moulin-de-Testa, 13090 Aix-en-Provence, France
Telephone: (33) 04 42 93 38 50
Fax: (33) 04 42 93 38 89
Website: www.archivesnationales.culture.gouv.fr/caom/fr
Access: Monday-Friday, 9am-5pm; first Thursday of each month, 1–9pm; closed 2 weeks in July.
This repository holds copies of Algerian civil records at least a hundred years old (in record group OMT/27, sub-series 109 MIOM).[1] Only about two thirds of

---
[1] France archives have privacy laws governing records less than a hundred years old.

Algerian civil records were copied by the French; some records, therefore, remain only in Algeria. Because this archive does not respond to written requests, researching these records may require a visit to Aix-en-Provence. Alternatively, because some of these records were microfilmed by the Church of Jesus Christ of Latter-day Saints (Mormons), the research may require only a trip to the local Family History Center. For reel numbers see below in the section for the Church of Jesus Christ of Latter-day Saints.

Extracted data from the reels of French-copied Algerian records for the cities of Constantine and Oran is available through *Etsi* which responds to requests about specific names and towns, if the request is accompanied by a self-addressed stamped envelope or an international postal response coupon.[2] The data extracted from these reels consists of:

Constantine:
  131 marriages, 1846–58 (reel 210)
  1,232 Jewish deaths, 1843–93 (reel 211)
  95 Jewish and European deaths, 1866–70, 1880 (reels 225 and 227, respectively)
Oran:
  687 births, 1856–59, 1861–62 (reels 282 and 283, respectively)
  45 deaths, 1891 (reel 475)

Ministere des Affaires Étrangeres, Service Central de l'Etat Civil
Address: 11 rue Maison Blanche, 44941 Nantes Cedex 9, France
Website: www.france.diplomatie.fr/francais/etatcivil/attrib.html

This archives holds copies of some Algerian records that are less than a hundred years old.[3] The copied record collection is not complete. If exact event dates and names are known, copies of civil records held by the agency may be obtained by direct descendants of the persons researched. A group of volunteers at the *Cercle de Généalogie Juive* in Paris have indexed some of these records from Algeria. To date the civil records indexed are for Constantine: 131 marriages, 1846–58; 1,232 Jewish deaths, 1843–93; 61 Jewish and European deaths, 1866–70; and for Oran: 156 births for 1856–59 and 1861–62, and 45 deaths, 1891.

Alliance Israelite Universelle Archives
Address: 45 Rue la Bruyere, 75009, Paris.
Archives: by appointment
Téléphone: 01 53 32 88 55

---

[2] *Etsi*, c/o L. et P. Abensur, 77 bd Richard-Lenoir, 75011 Paris, France. Website: www.geocities.com/enchanted Forst/1321.
[3] They also hold some records for French citizens of Morocco and Tunisia.

Fax : 01 48 74 51 33
Email : biblio@aiu.org
Website: www.aiu.org
Access: Monday, Tuesday, Thursday, 1–6 pm; Wednesday, 1–7:30 pm

In the 19th century the Alliance Israelite Universelle established schools in many locations in North Africa. The AIU archive contains information mostly about the schools, the teachers, and student statistics, and only a few students' personal details or name lists. Philip Abensur and Laurence Hazan-Abensur of Paris have spent the last two years methodically researching and documenting these archives. They describe them as containing 12 alphabetically named groups of documents of which the series E for *"ecoles"* contained the most genealogically useful information.

Church of Jesus Christ of Latter-Day Saints
Address: 35 North West Temple Street, Salt Lake City, Utah, 84150-3400
Telephone: 801-240-2331 or 800-453-3860 ext 22331
FAX: 801-240-1584
E-mail: fhl@ldschurch.org
Website: www.familysearch.org
See also www.jewishgen.org/databases/FHLC for Jewish items

The Mormons have microfilmed some Algerian civil registrations for the period 1832–92. Reel numbers of films of interest include 1811448–1811457 and 1811893–1811894. It is important to remember that many Algerian place names have changed since independence (see Place Names section below).

Tombstone inscriptions for some Jewish cemeteries in Algeria are on reel 2026232.

NATURALIZATION APPLICATIONS

Although Jews who lived in Algeria automatically gained French citizenship as a result of the 1870 Cremieux decree, some had applied for French citizenship before that date. The *Cercle de Généalogie Juive* in Paris has a 19-page list of these applications for French citizenship (see website, www.genealoj.org).

JEWISH CEMETERIES

Jewish cemeteries in Algeria are largely abandoned and most are in poor repair. Cemeteries include, with alternate names in parenthesis, Ain Defla (Duperre), Ain El Arba, Ain Temouchent, Alger (Saint-Eugene), Annaba (Bone), Azaba (Jemmapes), Bejaia (Bougie), Beni Saf, Blida, Bordj Bou Arreridj, Chelghoum El Aid (Chateaudun-du-Rhumel), Constantine, El Eulma (Saint-

Arnaud), El Kala (La Calle), El Malah (Rio Salado), Guelma, Hadjout (Marengo), Maghnia (Marnia), Mascara, Medea, Miliana, Mostaganem, Oran (Tamashouet), Oued Rhiou (Inkerman), Relizane, Sidi Bel Abbes, Skikda (Philippeville), Souk Ahras, Tenes, Tiaret, and Tlemcen.[4] Additional details about these cemeteries and photographs of them can be obtained directly from M. Roger Latapie, Le Beverly, 226 avenue de la Lanterne, 06200, Nice, France.

In 1888, Isaac Bloch published inscriptions of 48 Jewish tombstones from ancient Algerian cemeteries, some going back to the 1600s. In his abstract of names, Philip Abensur notes that a majority of the cemetery's population seems to have come originally from Majorca.[5]

PLACE NAMES

With independence, many places in Algeria changed their names. Some of the name changes from the LDS files are:

Ain-Benian (*see* Vesoul Benian, 1852)
Ain-Taya (*see* Rassauta. 1854–62)
Alma (*see* Fondouk, 1858–62)
Aomar (*see* Tizi Ouzou, 1883–92)
Azazga (*see* Tizi Ouzou, 1883–92)
Azeffoun (*see* Tizi Ouzou, 1883–92)
Baba-Hassen (*see* Douera, 1853–62)
Birmandreis (*see* Birkadem, 1853–62)
Bir-Rabalou (*see* Aumale, 1860–62)
Boghni (*see* Tizi Ouzou, 1883–92)
Bois Sacre (*see* Tizi Ouzou, 1883–92)
Bordi Menaiel (*see* Tizi Ouzou, 1883–92)
Bou Ismael (*see* Castiglione, 1848–52)
Bou Medfa (*see* Ain Benian, 1851–52)
Bouzareah (*see* Mustapha, 1853–62)
Camp-du-Marechal (*see* Tizi Ouzou, 1883–92)
Cap-Dinet (*see* Tizi Ouzou, 1883–92)
Chabet el Ameur (*see* Tizi Ouzou, 1883–92)
Crescia (*see* Douera, 1853–62)
Dellys (*see* Tizi Ouzou, 1883–92)
Djurdjura (*see* Tizi Ouzou, 1883–92)
Drariah (*see* Dely Ibrahim, 1853–62)
Dra-el-Mizan (*see* Tizi Ouzou, 1883–92)
El Achour (*see* Dely Ibrahim, 1858–62)

---

[4] Roger Latapie, "*Etat actuel des cimitieres juifs d'Algerie*," Etsi 1, no. 3 (1998): 3-4.
[5] Philip Abensur, "*Releve de tombes des anciens cimitieres juifs d'Alger*," Etsi 1, no. 3 (1998) 5.

El Biar (*see* Mustapha, 1852–62)
Fort-de-l'Eau (*see* Rassauta, 1858–62)
Fort Napoleon (*see* Fort National, after 1862
Fort National (*see* Tizi Ouzou, 1883–92)
Guyotville (*see* Cheragas, 1860–62)
Haussonvillers (*see* Tizi Ouzou, 1883–92) (includes Camp du Marechal, 1885–91)
Haut Sebaou (*see* Tizi Ouzou, 1883–92) (includes Azazga, 1883–92 and Yakouren, 1892)
Hussein Dey (*see* Kouba, 1853–62)
Issers (*see* Tizi Ouzou, 1883–92) (includes Camp de Marechal, 1883–85)
Isserville (*see* Tizi Ouzou, 1883–92) (includes Chabet el Ameur, 1883–92)
Joinville (*see* Blida, 1849)
Kouanin (*see* Tizi Ouzou, 1883–92)
La Ferme (*see* Orléansville, 1853–62)
Mahelma (*see* Douera, 1853–62)
Maison Blanche (*see* Rassauta, 1852–72)
Maison Carrée (*see* Rassauta,1852–69)
Massias (*see* Ain Benian, 1851–52)
Mekla (*see* Tizi Ouzou, 1883–92)
Michelet (*see* Tizi Ouzou, 1883–92)
Mirabeau (*see* Tizi Ouzou, 1883–92)
Montenotte (*see* Tenes, 1853–62)
Montpensier (*see* Blida, 1849)
Ouled Fayet (*see* Dely Ibrahim, 1853–62)
Pirette (*see* Tizi Ouzou, 1883–92)
Pointe Pecade (*see* Mustapha, 1853–62 or Saint-Eugène, 1868)
Ponteba (*see* Orleansville, 1853–62)
Rebeval (*see* Tizi Ouzou, 1883–92)
Reghaia (*see* Fondouk, 1858–62)
Rivet (*see* Arba, 1860–62)
Rouiba (*see* Rassauta, 1858–62)
Rovigo (*see* Arba, 1853–62)
Saint-Eugène (*see* Pointe Pescade, 1835–67)
Saint-Ferdinand (*see* Douera, 1853–62)
Sainte-Amelie (*see* Douera, 1853–62)
Sidi Ferruch (*see* Cheragas, 1853–62)
Sidi Moussa (*see* Arba, 1862)
Staoueli (*see* Cheragas, 1862)
Tefeschoun (*see* Castiglione, 1848–62)
Tigzirt (*see* Tizi Ouzou, 1883–92)
Tizi Reniff (*see* Tizi Ouzou, 1883–92)

Vesoul Benian (*see* Ain Benian, 1851–52)
Yakouren (*see* Tizi Ouzou, 1883–92)
Zeralda (*see* Cheragas, 1853–62)

Suggested Reading

With the absence of direct access to many records in Algeria, oral histories and the study of family surnames take on added importance. Several publications are particularly valuable. Prominent among these is Eisenbeth's book.

Abensur, Philip. *Releve de tombes des anciens cimitieres juifs d'Alger* (Recordings of tombs in the ancient cemeteries of Alger). *Etsi* 1, no. 3 (1998): 5.

Cercle de Genealogie Juive. *Comite Algerien d'Etudes Sociales: Le livre d'or du Judaisme Algerien (1914–1918). 1er fascicule, Septembre 1919* (Algerian committee for social studies: The golden book of Algerian Judaism [1914–1918]). First printed in 1919. Reprint Paris: Cercle de Genealogie Juive, 2000. This small manuscript lists Algerian Jews who had died fighting for France during World War I. The reprint includes an index of its two thousand names.

Chouraqui, André N. *Between East and West: A History of the Jews of North Africa.* Philadelphia: Jewish Publication Society, 1968.

Eisenbeth, Maurice. *Les Juifs de l'Afrique du Nord: Démographie et onomastique* (Jews of North Africa: Demographics and onomastics). Algiers: Imprimerie du Lycée, 1936. Recently reprinted by the Cercle de Genealogie Juive in Paris. Eisenbeth, former chief rabbi of Alger, based his 1936 work on a study of the 1831 official lists of Jewish inhabitants throughout Algeria. The book presents demographic population tables and the names of Algerian Jewish families and their origins.

Gilbert, Martin. *The Jews of Arab Lands: Their History in Maps.* London: Board of Deputies of British Jews, 1976.

Haddad, Heskel M. *Jews of Arab and Islamic Countries.* New York: Shengold publishers, 1984.

Lewis, Bernard. *The Jews of Islam.* Princeton, N.J.: Princeton University Press, 1984.

Stillman, Norman A. *The Jews of Arab Lands.* Philadelphia: Jewish Publication Society, 1979.

21.

TUNISIA

BRIEF HISTORY

According to the ancient historians Herodotus and Strabon, Jews were known to have been in Tunisia since the days of the ancient Phoenicians, whose ships carried Jews and Jewish settlements throughout the Mediterranean coast. Jewish settlements existed in Tunisia during Roman times, and Jewish artifacts have been discovered in Carthage and environs.[1] These early settlements were greatly augmented by a large influx of Jewish refugees following the destruction of the second Temple in 70 C.E. in Jerusalem. Famous Tunisian luminaries such as Rabbi Aba and Rabbi Hanina are mentioned in the Talmud, evidence of a significant intellectual life in Tunisia in the first millennium.

In the seventh century the Arab armies' rapid conquests included North Africa, and the city of Kairouan (the camp, in Arabic) was founded in 670 C.E. It became a noted Jewish center of learning with a 10th–11th century *yeshiva* that rivaled its Babylonian counterparts. The Babylonian masters spoke of the men of Kairouan in whom Torah and wisdom, Jewish and secular learning, were singularly combined.[2] Its teachers included R. Hanan'el ben Hushiel (11th century), Rabbi Nissim ben Jacob, and grammarian and philosopher Dunash ben Tamin. Learned men moved to Kairouan, as did the Egyptian physician Izhak Israeli and the Babylonian Mar Ouqba. In 1057 C.E. the Fatimids of Egypt conquered Kairouan (*the camp*) and declared it a holy Moslem city, forbidden to Jews and nonbelievers,[3] and the era of the Kairouan *geonim* ended. A dark period followed; Jews were repeatedly pillaged, enslaved, and impoverished by the conquering armies of Charlemagne, Spain, and Turkey.

During the 17th century, European Jews arrived mostly from Leghorn (Livorno) and Palermo. These Jews formed the Grana community in Tunis, which remained separate from the local Tuansa Jews until well into the 20th century.[4] The two communities maintained separate synagogues, butchers, cemeteries, and records.[5]

---

[1] A bronze Jewish candelabra and parts of a Jewish gravestone were found in the ruins of Carthage and a synagogue mosaic in Hamam-Lif.
[2] Max L. Margolis and Alexander Marx, *A History of the Jewish People* (New York: Athenaeum, 1927), 277.
[3] The prohibition continued until 1881.
[4] Grana is the plural of *Gorni* meaning from Leghorn (Ligorna, in Arabic). Tuansa is the plural of *Tounsi*, which means Tunisian in Arabic.
[5] Three volumes of the *ketubot* registers of the Spanish-Portuguese community of Tunis (Grana

The Grana Jews wore European (Italian) dress, with capes and hats totally unlike the garb of the local Tuansa Jews. The Grana Jews established themselves as a foreign "Jewish nation" independent of the control of the local Bey. They established a printing press, which published in 1768 the writings of Rabbi Itzhak Lumbroso. At various times during the 19th century, Great Britain and France protected the Jews when threatened by the local Moslem authorities in Tunisia In 1910, Jews could opt for French citizenship.

GRANA COMMUNITY OF TUNIS

When the Jews were expelled from Spain in 1492 and several years later from Portugal, they sought refuge wherever they could. Large numbers went to Morocco, The Netherlands and the welcoming Ottoman Empire. Others ventured further afield to the Caribbean and elsewhere in the New World and others settled in Eastern Europe.

In 1592, when Ferdinand I (di Medici), Grand Duke of Tuscany, invited Jews to settle and practice their religion freely in Pisa and Livorno, many expelled Sephardim eagerly accepted his offer. Thus was established the community of Sephardic Livornese Jews.

Trading from the Italian port of Livorno, the Jews spread throughout the Mediterranean. During the 18th century some settled in Tunis, first as agents for the repurchase of Christian slaves from North African pirates, and later as trading agents for their relatives in Livorno. These were the Grana Jews who called themselves the Portuguese Jewish community of Tunis. In the 19th century the Livornese Jews favored a protectorate under Italy, while the local Tuansa Jews favored France.

Because the Portuguese community kept detailed records, one can easily construct several complex genealogies. In their excellent source books *on these marriage records*, Robert Attal and Joseph Avivi reprint in their first volume two of ten marriage registers, with French translations of the text of the more than a thousand *ketubot* found in the registers.[6] The authors published a second volume of 233 *ketubot* in 2000.[7] The list of surnames mentioned in the *ketubot* is presented in appendix G.

Using just the first Attal book, the author found *ketubot* from the 18th and 19th centuries of an unrelated branch of the Malka family that enabled creation of a detailed genealogy tree including divorces, remarriages, and amount of money

---

community) have been published by Robert Attal, in Hebrew and French versions. See notes.
[6] Robert Attal and Joseph Avivi, *Registres Matrimoniaux de la Communaute Juive Portugaise de Tunis, XVIII-XIX siecles* (Marriage records of the Portuguese Jewish community of Tunis, 18th and 19th centuries) (Jerusalem: Ben Zvi Institute, 1989).
[7] Robert Attal and Joseph Avivi, *Registres Matrimoniaux de la Communaute Juive Portugaise de Tunis, 1843–1854* (Marriage records of the Portuguese Jewish community of Tunis, 1843-1854) (Jerusalem: Ben Zvi Institute, 2000).

of the *ketubah*, which (when compared with others) gave clues about their relative financial state.[8] One learns that Abraham Malka's son Moses married, "according to the traditions of Toledo," Luna, daughter of Solomon Israel, on October 12, 1791. They had two sons and a daughter. In 1803, their daughter Esther Malka married Isaac, son of Sam Pansir, while their sons David and Solomon Malka married Rebecca Medina and Anne Moreno in 1818 and 1853, respectively. Rebecca and David Malka also had two sons and a daughter. Esther Malka married Ruben Louizada, Isaac Malka married Esther Abdias, and Elie Malka married Judica Elhaik. A different Abraham Malka had a daughter Luna who married Solomon Bais (1855), only to divorce him and marry Benjamin Enriques in 1860. A year later her younger brother Moses Malka married her husband's sister Sara Enriques. Luna's sister married Moses Tapia while her other brother Jacob Malka married Reine Abocara.

This narrative demonstrates the level of detailed information available from the published *ketubot*. Many similar genealogies and family alliances can be developed easily for many other Sephardic families who happened to be part of the Portuguese community of Tunis.

ARCHIVES

ISRAEL
Central Archives for the History of the Jewish People (CAHJP)
Address: Hebrew University Campus, Sprinzak Bldg, Givat Ram, Jerusalem, Israel.
Mailing address: P.O. Box 1149, Jerusalem 91010
Telephone at (972)-2-5635716

This repository holds *pinkassim* (registers) and documents of the Portuguese community of Tunis covering the period 1710–1936. Uncatalogued and unindexed, these collections include information that is at present unavailable to the genealogist offsite.[9]

FOREIGN CONNECTIONS

Many Tunisian Jews sought foreign state protections, especially from Italy and France. Additional information may be found in Italian sources (see chapter 26, Italy) and French archives (see chapter 19, Morocco) or by searching the consulate records of countries such as Italy, France, and Great Britain.

---

[8] Attal and Avivi, *Registres Matrimoniaux*.
[9] The archives has a list of the documents it holds of the Portuguese community of Tunis. Lionel Levy in *La Nation Portugaise (Livourne, Amsterdam, Tunis, 1591-1951)* reports that Itshaq Abrahami wrote a thesis in 1997 at Bar Ilan University based on this list.

TUNISIA

A list of 19th- and 20th-century Portuguese Jews under Dutch protection is held at the *Archives Tunisiennes* (diplomatic sources), Souk El Attarine, Tunis (Levy, *La Nation Portugaise*).[10]

SUGGESTED READING

Attal, Robert, and Joseph Avivi. *Registres Matrimoniaux de la Communaute Juive Portugaise de Tunis, XVIII-XIX siecles* (Marriage records of the Portuguese Jewish community of Tunis, 18th and 19th centuries). Oriens Judaicus. Jerusalem: Ben Zvi Institute, 1989. Lists marriages in the Portuguese Jewish community of Tunis (from Leghorn/Livorno).

———. *Registres Matrimoniaux de la Communaute Juive Portugaise de Tunis, 1843–1854* (Marriage records of the Portuguese Jewish community of Tunis. 1843-1854). Oriens Judaicus. Jerusalem: Ben Zvi Institute, 2000. Additional marriages of the Portuguese Jewish community of Tunis.

Avrahami, Hannah. "The Jews of Livorno and their Relations with Tunis in the 17th and 18th centuries" (in Hebrew). Thesis, Ramat Gan University, 1979.

Chouraqui, André N. *Between East and West: A History of the Jews of North Africa.* Philadelphia: Jewish Publication Society, 1968.

Cohen, Benyamin Rafael. *Malkhei Tarshish* (Prominent Rabbis of Tarshish). Jerusalem, 1986. Extensive Hebrew-language biographical list of rabbis of Tunisia.

Filippini, Jean-Pierre. *Livorno e gli Ebrei dell' Africa del Nord nel settecento* (Livorno and the Jews of North Africa during the 1700s). Florence: Ed. Olschski, 1990.

Levy, Lionel. *La Nation Juive Portuguaise. Livourne, Amsterdam, Tunis 1591–1951* (The Portuguese Jewish Nation. Leghorn, Amsterdam, Tunis 1591–1951). Paris: L'Harmattan, 1999.

Tanugi, Y. *Toldot Hakhamei Tunis* (Generations of Tunis rabbis). Jerusalem: Bnei Brak, 1988.

Toledano, Joseph. *Une histoire des familles: Les noms de famille Juifs d'Afrique du Nord* (Family history: Family names of the Jews of North Africa). Jerusalem: Author, 1999.

---

[10] Lionel Levy, *La Nation Portugaise: Livourne, Amsterdam, Tunis, 1591-1951* (The Portuguese Nation: Leghorn, Amsterdam, Tunis, 1591-1951) Paris, France: L'Harmattan, 1999.

22.
EGYPT

HISTORY

Home to such Jewish notables as Jacob and Joseph, Moses, Philo of Alexandria, the prophet Jeremiah, Moses ben Maimon (Maimonides), the Gaon Saadiya and others, and boasting the oldest known synagogue (Ben Ezra) and the second-oldest Jewish cemetery (Bassatine), the historical link between Jews and Egypt is an ancient one. After the exodus from Egypt, Jews are known to have returned to Egypt in 586 B.C.E. and then maintained an uninterrupted presence in that land ever since.[1] Some say that Jews have always been in Egypt since the days of Joseph. Fargeon, editor of the 1942 *Annuaire des Juifs d'Egypte et du proche orient* (Yearbook of Jews in Egypt and the Near-East), for one, asserted that when Moses led the Israelites out of Egypt, some Jews remained in Egypt and settled in Asyut, where they formed a warrior tribe—thereby maintaining a Jewish presence in Egypt since early biblical days.[2]

In the early 20th century, the multilingual and cosmopolitan Jews of Egypt maintained 37 synagogues in Cairo alone, six B'nai B'rith lodges,[3] several all-Jewish orchestras, three Jewish theaters (one in Yiddish), nearly a dozen Jewish newspapers in a variety of languages, a Jewish hospital that treated 43,000 patients in 1936, old-age homes, and numerous charitable organizations.[4] In 1938, Cairo Jewish community schools[5] enrolled 8,462 children, approximately 51 percent of all Jewish children.[6] Many other children enrolled in several private Jewish schools, such as the Jabes or the Green schools and the Petit Lycée de

---

[1] Ralph Bennett, "History of the Jews of Egypt," *Avotaynu*, 10 (1994): 30.
[2] Maurice Fargeon, ed., *Annuaire des Juifs d'Egypte et du proche orient* (Annuary of the Jews of Egypt and the Near East) (Cairo: La Societe des Editions Historiques Juives d'Egypte, 1942).
[3] *B'nai B'rith* was founded in New York in 1843. A mere 44 years later saw the founding of the Maimonides Lodge in Cairo. Other lodges include the Eliaho Hannabi Lodge in Alexandria, Ohel Moche Lodge in Tanta, Magen David Lodge in Mansoura, Israel Lodge in Port Said, and the Benzion Costi Lodge in Khartoum.
[4] Maurice Fargeon, ed. *Juifs d'Egypte: Images et Textes* (Jews of Egypt: Images and texts) 2d ed. Paris: Les Editions du Scribe, 1984.
[5] Some Jewish schools were run by the Jewish community and others operated privately.
[6] Maurice Fargeon, ed. *Les Juifs en Egypte: Depuis le Origines jusqu'a ce jour* (Jews in Egypt: From the origins to this day) (Cairo: Imprimerie Paul Barbey, 1938).

Sakakini.[7] The Jewish aristocracy entertained and hobnobbed with both Egyptian and European royalty, and served at high levels of the government.[8]

Largely European in outlook, the 20th-century Egyptian Jewish population can be divided into four main groups. The most populous were the Sephardim, followed by the indigenous Egyptian Jews, Ashkenazim, and the ancient Karaites.[9] The Sephardim and Ashkenazim were mainly francophone in language and culture. Italian, Yiddish, and Judeo-Spanish were also common spoken languages. Members of the other two groups, who had inhabited Egypt for more than a millennium, were more likely to speak Egyptian Arabic and to wear Egyptian-style clothing. Even so, nearly all the Jews in Egypt felt themselves distinct from the surrounding Egyptian Arab culture.[10]

As a result of the several Israeli-Arab wars and the deteriorating economic and political situation under Egyptian President Gamal Nasser, in the 1950s most of the Jews of Egypt either left or were expelled, forced to leave behind all their property, jewelry, and cash. The present Jewish population is composed of fewer than 50 elderly Jews in Cairo and an even smaller number in Alexandria.

At its most recent population peak in 1948, 70,000 to 80,000 Jews lived in Egypt, about 55,000 in Cairo and most of the rest in Alexandria, with smaller communities in Port Said and smaller towns.[11] Of relevance to genealogists searching for documents, 5,000 to 10,000 Jews held Egyptian citizenship, 40,000 were stateless, and 30,000 were foreign nationals (Italian, French, British, and other), though most of those holding foreign nationality had been born in Egypt.[12]

The Sephardim began arriving in the 12th century (Maimonides came to Egypt in 1165). Their numbers were augmented by a large influx of Iberian exiles in 1492 and ensuing years.[13] Their ranks were further swelled in the 19th century by Sephardim from other areas of the Ottoman Empire, mainly Aleppo, Baghdad, Izmir, Livorno, Salonica, and Tunis.[14]

The indigenous Jews, possibly 20,000 in number, had lived in Egypt for centuries and were Egyptian in both language and culture. They worked mostly as goldsmiths and merchants, and often lived in Cairo's *harat al Yahud* (Jewish

---

[7] Fargeon, *Les Juifs en Egypte*.
[8] Fargeon, *Les Juifs en Egypte; Juifs d'Egypte: Images et Textes*.
[9] Karaites are an ancient Jewish sect that base their Judaism on the five books of Moses and reject subsequent rabbinical interpretations.
[10] Raphael Patai, *The Vanished Worlds of Jewry* (New York: Macmillan, 1981).
[11] Joel Beinin, *The Dispersion of Egyptian Jewry: Culture, Politics, and the Formation of a Modern Diaspora* (Los Angeles: University of California Press, 1998).
[12] Patai, *Vanished Worlds of Jewry*.
[13] Patai, *Vanished Worlds of Jewry*.
[14] Patai, *Vanished Worlds of Jewry*.

lane) neighboring *harat al barabra* (foreigners' lane), and in Alexandria's port district.

Almost all the Ashkenazim came to Egypt in the late 19th century, fleeing pogroms and anti-Semitism in Russia, Romania, and elsewhere. Their original presence in Egypt dates back, however, to the 16th century. As a sign of his favor, Sultan Suleiman the Magnificent granted Yosef ben Shlomo, a Jew of Budapest who in 1525 delivered the keys of Budapest to his triumphant Ottoman armies, the unique privilege that Yosef and his descendants would be perpetually exempt from taxation and have total religious freedom within his domains. Fargeon reports that descendants of the Aleman family, as they became known, were still present in Egypt as late as 1914, still taking advantage of their ancient tax exemption.[15]

Ashkenazim often were economically poorer than the local Sephardim, and many lived in an ancient area of Cairo known as *harat al barabra*. In time some Ashkenazim accumulated significant wealth and moved to Cairo suburbs. They spoke Yiddish and maintained in Cairo their own separate synagogues,[16] an Ashkenazic B'nai B'rith lodge (*Loge Maimonide No. 366*), a Yiddish theater and a Yiddish radio station that broadcast as late as 1950. The main Ashkenazic synagogue in Cairo, located at Haret El Noubi, Rue Farouk of the *harat el barabra*, was founded in 1865 and was known locally as the *Temple de la rue Farouk*.

Relatively less known are the Karaite Jews, who numbered about 5,000 in Egypt in 1947 and lived primarily in Cairo, where they maintained separate synagogues. The Karaites are a Jewish sect that broke away from rabbinic Judaism in the first millennium C.E. Rejecting rabbinic interpretations (such as the Talmud), they base their religion and practices on the written texts of the five books of Moses (*kara'a* means "to read'" in Hebrew) and maintained their own separate synagogues.[17]

In the 20th century, the largest remnants of Karaites lived in Egypt (5,000) and Russia (10,000), but unlike the Karaites of Lithuania, Poland, and the Crimea, who did not consider themselves Jews (a designation that, fortunately for them, both fellow rabbinic Jews and the Nazis accepted), in Egypt both Karaites and rabbinic Jews considered Karaites a Jewish sect, although both groups banned marriage with each other's members.[18] While many lived elsewhere, the traditional home of the Karaites was in Cairo's *harat al yahud al kar'in* (Karaite Jewish lane), which adjoins the *harat al yahud*. They buried their dead in their separate half of the Jewish Bassatine cemetery of Cairo, separated by a wall from the portion used by the rabbinic Jews. Arabic speakers, this community of

---

[15] Fargeon, *Les Juifs en Egypte*.
[16] In Alexandria, they formed a single community with the Sephardim.
[17] Leon Nemoy, *Karaite Anthology* (New Haven: Yale University Press, 1952, 1980).
[18] Beinin, *Dispersion of Egyptian Jewry*.

numerous goldsmiths and jewelers produced several notable poets and playwrights. Their last chief rabbi in Egypt was Tuvia Bakovitch (1934–56). Like the rest of Egyptian Jewry, they, too, have left Egypt. They can now be found mostly in the San Francisco area and elsewhere in the United States.

There were two chief rabbinates in Egypt, one in Cairo and the other in Alexandria. Jewish communities in other Egyptian towns reported to and were administered by one or the other of these chief rabbinates. In Cairo the Jews organized themselves in three autonomous communities (Sephardic, Ashkenazic, and Karaite), each administered separately. In Alexandria, where the Ashkenazim were just as numerous as in Cairo, they formed a single Jewish community with the Sephardim, a community that also included the fewer than 20 Karaite Jews of Alexandria.

Alexandria was once the home of several grand synagogues and Jewish schools both private and community based, a dozen Jewish benevolent societies,[19] B'nai B'rith Lodge,[20] a 140-bed Jewish hospital, several Alexandria-based Jewish periodicals,[21] and a very active Jewish presence; the Jewish presence is now non-existent.

Of great importance to genealogists is the knowledge that the grand rabbinate of Alexandria, at the turn of the last century when it was also the grand rabbinate of Egypt, ordered that all *ketubot* would be prepared in two copies. One copy was given to the bride; the other copy was kept at the rabbinate. This means that there are copies at the rabbinates of *ketubot* of all Jewish marriages contracted in Egypt at least during the 20th century. Access to these archives, however, is not an easy task.

Because of the dwindling Jewish population and lack of funds, only three synagogues remain functioning in Cairo, Shaar Hashamayim, Meyr Biton, and Ben Ezra. The Cairo Jewish community struggles to maintain and restore the others with the sporadic assistance of badly needed donations from its diaspora.

Ben Ezra synagogue in old Cairo (Fostat-Goshen) is the world's oldest known synagogue. Believed to have been founded by Ezra the Scribe half a millennium before the Common Era, it stands, according to both Jewish and Coptic tradition, at the site where Moses was retrieved from the Nile by Pharaoh's daughter. The waters of the Nile still flood its basement. The medieval Jewish traveler Benjamin of Tudela visited this synagogue in his travels in 1169.[22] In the forgotten *geniza*, (storehouse of discarded sacred documents) of the Ben Ezra synagogue were

---

[19] *Societe de Bienfaisance Israelite* (founded 1885), *Societe Bikour Holim* (medical care of the indigent), *Sedaka Bassiter* (discrete assistance to those embarassed to ask), *Mechibat Nafechu* (medical care for poor children), *Hessed Veemet* (elderly medical care), *Nohar Habetoulot* (for dowries to poor girls), *Goutte de Lait* (children's breakfasts), and a half dozen others.
[20] Loge Eliahu Hannabi.
[21] *Le Messager Sioniste, La Revue Israelite d'Egypte, La Voix Juive,* and *La Tribune Juive.*
[22] Elkan Nathan Adler, *Jewish Travellers in the Middle Ages* (New York: Dover, 1987).

found the treasure of ancient documents that have yielded so much information about medieval Jewish history, especially from around the 10th century. Preserved in London, they do not hold genealogically useful information.

Shaar Hashammayim is today the main Cairo synagogue and well worth a visit now that it has been restored.

Jewish Records

Cairo
Jewish Community Center of Cairo
Address: #13 Sabil El Khazinder Street, Abbassia, Cairo, Egypt.
Telephone: 20 2 482-4613
Fax: 20 2 482 4885
Access: hours irregular; call 20 2 482-4613 for appointment

Records in the Jewish archives are disorganized and written in either Sephardic Hebrew, French or Arabic script. At present, the only way to obtain information from these voluminous Jewish registers is to request such information from the Jewish community. Even academics have been denied permission to search the archives themselves.[23] Written requests must be accompanied by a donation of US $100–150 to the Jewish community center at the time of the request, with a similar amount sent when notified that the information is ready. Because of the archival disarray, information may take years to obtain—if it comes at all. No successful research has been reported, even after sending the requested down payment.

As noted in the history section above, since the turn of the century, the rabbinates in Egypt have maintained copies of all *ketubot* issued for marriages in Egypt. The elderly members of the Jewish Community Center would like to host volunteers from abroad who are knowledgeable in Hebrew to spend time helping to organize the records.

Jamie Lehman Collection held by New York's Yeshiva University
Address: Yeshiva University Archives, 500 West 185th Street, New York, NY 10033, USA
Telephone: 212 960-5451
Website: www.yu.edu/libraries/arch
Access: by appointment, call 212 960-5451

This collection is a small subset of the Cairo archives that were spirited out of Egypt and today are housed in the university archives.[24] Catalogued but

---

[23] Beinin, *Dispersion of Egyptian Jewry*.
[24] Jamie Lehman Collection. Yeshiva University Archives, 500 West 185th Street, New York, NY 10033.

unindexed, they consist of a mix of rabbinic records and letters, Cairo B'nai B'rith records, and accounts of the charity activities of the community. The collection is part of the Yeshiva University Archives. Advance permission is needed to use it. Figure 15 is an example of one of many passport applications held in this collection. Besides the applicant's name, occupation, and address, the passport application includes father's name, occupation, and address; father's land of origin; how long in Egypt; and name and address of two witnesses. The archives publishes a guide to the collection that can be purchased by writing directly to the archives.[25]

ALEXANDRIA
Jewish Community Center of Alexandria
Address: 69 Rue Nebi Daniel, Alexandria, Egypt

As in Cairo, the Jewish population of Alexandria has dwindled to a few elderly individuals, and the Jewish community center has a skeleton staff. Some visitors have been allowed access to the extensive but unindexed, disorganized records of the community. In the 1950s a warehouse fire destroyed a portion of these precious records.

According to egyptologist Morris Bierbrier of the British Museum in London, the Alexandria Jewish community has death records from 1860 (although not all burials were registered there), marriage records from about 1907, and birth records (not in consecutive order because families often delayed the registration of births).

Requests for record searches should be addressed to Jewish Community Center of Alexandria, 69 Rue Nebi Daniel, Alexandria, with a donation. Due to almost nonexistent personnel, responses are slow to come, although a few have been received. A visit in person is more likely to be successful.

JEWISH COMMUNITIES IN SMALL TOWNS OF EGYPT

Jews lived in several outlying towns in Egypt. These small towns are largely ignored in most accounts of Egyptian Jewry but could contain missing links in many genealogies. Some localities were quite large and others, like Tantah, were wealthy and the birthplace of many of Egypt's most prominent Sephardic families. Appendix K lists tombstone inscriptions from these outlying smaller towns with Jewish populations.

---

[25] Roger S. Kohn, *Inventory to the Jamie Lehmann Memorial Collection-Records of the Jewish Community of Cairo, 1886-1961*.

Library of Jewish Heritage in Egypt

The largest Jewish studies library in Cairo is located at the century-old Chaar Hashamayim synagogue on Adly Street. The library of Jewish history in the historic Ben Ezra synagogue is smaller but holds some useful material.

Cemeteries

Cairo Bassatine Cemetery

The main Jewish cemetery of Cairo, the Bassatine is the second-oldest Jewish cemetery in the world, second only to the cemetery on the Mount of Olives in Jerusalem. The cemetery is divided by a wall into halves for separate Karaite and rabbinic Jewish burials. The Karaite half has been sold, and today only the rabbinic section remains. In the 1960s, marble stones were ransacked en masse from the Bassatine by vandals to be used in the building boom in Cairo, and hoodlums set up homes and businesses in the deserted mausoleums. This sad state of affairs is in process of being reversed under the energetic leadership of the Cairo Jewish community center, the extraordinary 90-year-old Esther Weinstein and her 70-year-old daughter Carmen. Through their aggressive efforts, funds were found and a wall built around the cemetery; a proposed Cairo ring beltway that would have desecrated three hundred graves was diverted and instead uses an overpass.[26] To visit the Bassatine, it is necessary to contact the Jewish community center for permission. A substantial donation towards cemetery upkeep is requested for either a visit or information.

Private Jewish Cemeteries in Cairo

Cairo has a number of smaller private cemeteries belonging to some of its prominent Jewish families such as the Ades, Cattaui, Levy, Mosseri, and Sapriel families. Walled and with private watchmen, these cemeteries are better preserved and can be visited separately; make arrangements through the Jewish Community Center of Cairo.

Alexandria Jewish Cemeteries

Alexandria has three Jewish cemeteries, two in Chatby and one in Mazarita (sometimes called Chatby 1 cemetery). All three Alexandria cemeteries are walled and largely have escaped vandalism. They are overgrown with vegetation at some times of the year, but the gravestones show only the ravages of time and weather. The Alexandria Jewish community has a list of burials in its archives, although obtaining information or a response is difficult, as noted above.

---

[26] This is a remarkable achievement; the road goes through and desecrates two Moslem and one Christian cemetery. Thus, the Jewish cemetery received special treatment.

Egyptian Civil Records

Vital records are kept on microfilm at the *wezaret el maleyah* (ministry of finance), *masslahet el dara-eb el Tigariyah* (department of commercial taxes) in the El Mokatam[27] district of Cairo. Records for the first half of the 20th century are reportedly found here. Although the ministry holds civil registrations of births and deaths, marriage records apparently were held only by religious authorities.

To request birth or death certificates from Egyptian civil authorities, one must know the exact date and the specific health district in Cairo or Alexandria where the event occurred. Requests for certified copies (*Sourat Tibk el Asl*) can be made on special forms obtained from Egyptian consulates in countries throughout the world. Onsite requests in Cairo are more likely to succeed if one knows the exact date and health district, goes in person to the proper place (see above), and monetarily persuades the official in charge to look through the records. Even then, nothing may be found.

Montefiore Censuses

The Montefiore censuses of the Jewish population of Palestine conducted in 1839, 1849, 1855, 1866, and 1875, also include (on reel 3) a census of the Sephardim of Alexandria, Egypt, taken in 1840. The Montefiore censuses are kept at Jews College, Albert Road, London NW$ 2SJ England. A microfilm copy is at the Jewish National and University Library in Jerusalem from which copies of the census may be purchased for $120.

Egyptian Diaspora

With the dispersion of Egyptian Jewry, groups have formed around the world, especially in Israel; Adelaide and Sydney, Australia; London Brooklyn, New York; and Geneva, Switzerland. Members may be useful sources of information. These groups include:

- Association of Jews from Egypt in Israel, 56 Pinsker Street, Tel Aviv, telephone: 03-528-5534
- International Association of Jews from Egypt, a group headed by Victor Sanua, Ph.D., St. John's University, 2416 Quentin Road, Brooklyn, New York 11229, telephone: 718-339-0337. The association aims to preserve the memories and culture of expatriates before they are lost. Lectures are given and articles published in *Image Magazine*, www.imageusa.com, 1985 West 6th Street, Brooklyn, NY 11223, Telephone: (718) 627- 4624.
- Historical Society of Jews from Egypt, P.O. Box 230445, Brooklyn, NY 11223, e-mail: information@hsje.org. The society's literature states that its aims are "to preserve, maintain and coordinate the implementation, and to convey our

---

[27] *Mokatam* is the name of the small mountain on which part of Cairo is built.

rich heritage to our children and grandchildren, using all educational means at our disposal to bring into being the necessary foundations." The society wishes to create a museum of Egyptian Jewry in New York with *sepherim* (religious books) and other objects from Egypt that illustrate the life of Jewry in Egypt.

SOURCES OUTSIDE EGYPT

Birth, marriage, and death records from 1866 onward for Egyptian Jews who held foreign nationalities may be found at the Dutch, French, and Italian consulates in Alexandria and Cairo, as well as in British consular records in the Public Records Office, London.

INTERNET RESOURCES

Some Internet resources focus specifically on Egyptian Jewry. Among the most interesting are:
- Bassatine News, www.geocities.com/RainForest/Vines/5855, website of the Jewish Community Center of Cairo. The Jewish Community Center provides updates of its efforts to restore and preserve Egyptian Jewish cemeteries and landmarks as well as presents news of the remaining community. Requests for record searches may be made through this website, but responses are slow.
- Raafat. www.egy.com/judaica. Samir Raafat is an Egyptian writer of books and numerous articles in Egyptian newspapers about Cairo and its history in the 19th and 20th centuries. Although not Jewish himself, he has written excellent histories of some of the notable Egyptian Jewish families and events. This website presents many of his articles.
- Egyptian Jewish Identities. http://shr.stanford.edu/shreview/5-1/text/beinin.html presents an interesting perspective on Egyptian Jewry in the 19th and 20th centuries and their identity conflicts.
- Cattaui Family Tree, www.geocities.com/RainForest/Vines/5855/cattaui.htm
- Jabes Family Tree, www.geocities.com/RainForest/Vines/5855/jabes1.htm

SUGGESTED READING

Bennett, Ralph. "History of the Jews of Egypt." *Avotaynu* 10, no. 1 (1994): 30.

Beinin, Joel. *The Dispersion of Egyptian Jewry: Culture, Politics and the Formation of a Modern Diaspora.* Los Angeles: University of California Press, 1998.

Editions du Scribe. *Juifs d'Egypte: Images et textes* (Jews of Egypt: Images and texts), 2d ed. Paris: Author, 1984. Compendium of photographs and images from private collections.

Fargeon, Maurice, ed. *Annuaire des Juifs d'Egypte et du proche orient* (Yearbook of the Jews of Egypt and the Near East). Cairo: La Societe des Editions Historiques Juives d'Egypte, 1942, 1943.

———. *Les Juifs en Egypte: Depuis les origines jusqu'a ce jour* (Jews in Egypt: From the origins to this day). Cairo: Imprimerie Paul Barbey, 1938.

Kramer, Gudrun. *The Jews in Modern Egypt, 1914–1952.* Seattle: Univ of Washington Press, 1989. This is the most comprehensive study of that period.

Laskier, Michael M. *The Jews of Egypt, 1920–1970.* New York: New York University Press, 1992. History of the last decades of the Jewish community of Egypt.

Malka, Eli. *Jacob's Children in the Land of the Mahdi: Jews of the Sudan.* Syracuse, N.Y.: Syracuse University Press, 1997. Sole book in existence on this Sephardic community, composed largely of Jews from Egypt. Contains list of all Jewish marriages in the Sudan 1907–63.

Mostyn, Trevor. *Egypt's Belle Epoque: Cairo 1865–1952.* London and New York: Quartet Books, 1989.

FAMILY TREES AND RESEARCH

Aciman, Andre. *Out of Egypt.* New York: Farrar Straus Giroux, 1994. An Alexandrian Jewish family.

Alhadeff, Gini. *The Sun at Midday: Tales of a Mediterranean Family.* New York: Pantheon Books, 1997. Family story of the Alhadeff-Pinto families in Turkey, Rhodes, Egypt, and South America.

Alhadeff, Vittorio. *La cita en Buenos Aires Saga de una gran familia Sefaradi* (Appointment in Buenos Aires: Saga of a grand Sephardic Family). Buenos Aires: Grupo Editor Latinoamericano, 1996. Family story of the Alhadeff family of Rhodes.

Perera, Victor. *The Cross and the Pear Tree: A Sephardic Journey.* New York: Knopf, 1995. Author searches for his ancestors in Egypt and elsewhere.

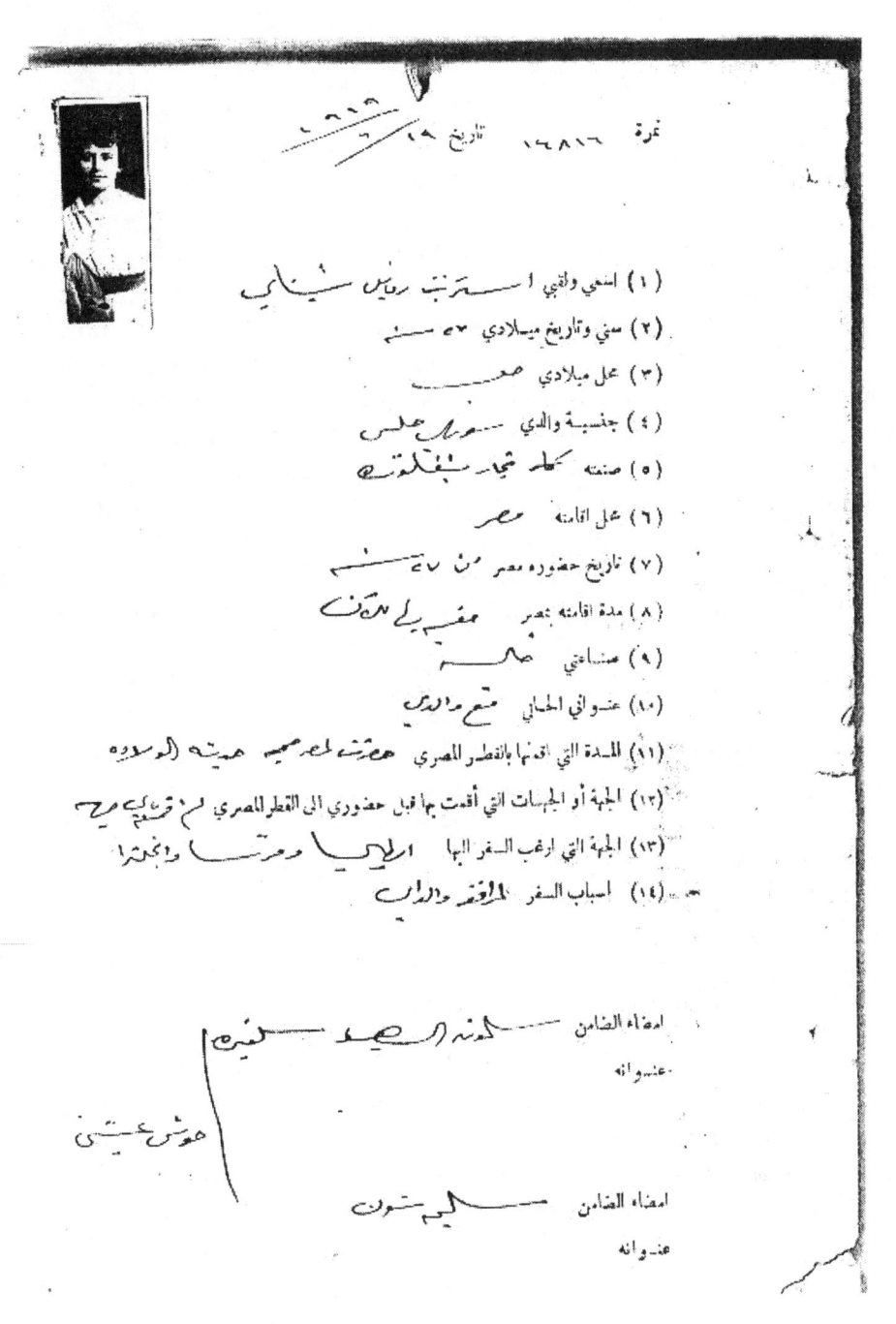

Source: Jaimie Lehmann Memorial Collection, Yeshiva University Archives, New York, N.Y.

Figure 15. Egyptian Passport Application from 1919

23.

SUDAN

The largest country in Africa, Sudan lies just south of Egypt and has a long, shared history with Egypt. Jewish history started in the Sudan in the late 19th century when a half dozen Jews from Egypt traveled south to start businesses in what was then a still-not-fully-charted African interior. These early settlers endured a turbulent time as prisoners of a fundamentalist Moslem leader known as the Mahdi.[1] The Mahdi routed both British and Egyptian armies and ruled the Sudan for 13 years until the British finally defeated him.

Building on these adventuresome beginnings, a flourishing Jewish community developed under the security blanket of British rule and the leadership of Shlomo Malka, a young rabbi recruited from Tiberias, Israel, in 1906. An elaborate synagogue was built and served a united congregation of Sephardim and Ashkenazim who lived mostly in Khartoum. A number of Jewish institutions evolved, including a large Jewish recreation club, Maccabi athletic teams, and the only B'nai B'rith lodge in the African interior.[2] Jewish businesses flourished, and Jews served in positions of leadership in many of the largest British and foreign trading companies.[3]

The Arab-Israeli conflict spelled doom for this small but vigorous Jewish community, causing a mass exodus to England, Israel, Switzerland, and the U.S. No Jews live in the Sudan today.

Members of the exiled Sudan community prospered abroad well out of proportion to their numbers. They donated millions of dollars to Jewish and Israeli causes, revived the World Sephardic Federation, provided huge subsidies and scholarships to universities in Israel, owned and ran deluxe hotels and international firms in Israel and throughout the world, and became major contributors to Jewish and Sephardic causes wherever the need arose. The ancient Adli synagogue in Cairo was refurbished with a $700,000 grant from Nessim Gaon, the most prosperous exile of the Sudan community. Funds from other Sudan Jews helped preserve the Bassatine cemetery in Cairo.[4]

---

[1] Lawrence Olivier starred as the Mahdi in the movie "Khartoum."
[2] Ben Sion Coshti Lodge.
[3] Eli Malka, *Jacob's Children in the land of the Mahdi: The Jews of the Sudan* (Syracuse, N.Y.: Syracuse University Press, 1998).
[4] Malka, *Jacob's Children in the land of the Mahdi*.

JEWISH ARCHIVES

JEWISH NATIONAL AND UNIVERSITY LIBRARY IN JERUSALEM

Address: Hebrew University Givat Ram, Jerusalem, Israel
Mailing Address: P.O.Box 503, Jerusalem 91004, Israel
Website: http://jnul.huji.ac.il
Access: varies according to department; mostly Sunday-Thursday, 9am-1or 5 pm; most departments closed Friday afternoon and Saturday

The only remaining archival material concerning the Jewish community of the Sudan are the rabbinic records maintained by Rabbi Malka. These records are difficult to use because they are written in the Sephardic cursive script.[5] They include copies of *ketubot* from all Jewish marriages that occurred in the Sudan.

Around the turn of the century the grand rabbinate of Alexandria, at that time the grand rabbinate also of Egypt, ordered that copies of all *ketubot* be kept by the rabbinates. The Sudan Jewish community maintained this custom and, as a result, the rabbi kept copies of all the *ketubot* in the Sudan. An index of these marriages appears in Malka's *Jacob's Children in the Land of the Mahdi*.[6]

BEN ZVI INSTITUTE[7]

Address: 12 Abravanel St., P.O.Box 7660, Jerusalem 91076 Israel
Telephone: 972-2-5398844
Fax. 972-2-5612329
Library: 13 Ibn Ezra, Jerusalem
Telephone (Library): 02-5398811
Website: www.ybz.org.il/menu/eng-index.html
E-mail: mahonzvi@h2.hum.huji.ac.il

Several hundred articles written by Rabbi Shlomo Malka in the Cairo Jewish periodical *Al Shams* (the Sun)[8] were found by Nahem Ilan, deputy director of the Ben Zvi Institute in Jerusalem. Ilan studied these records intensively and has written and lectured about them and about Rabbi Malka. The articles cover a broad range of religious, political, and social topics, and present a good picture of the thinking of the time, particularly of what Dr. Ilan believes are Rabbi

---

[5] See chapter 9, Sephardic Languages.
[6] Malka, *Jacob's Children in the Land of the Mahdi*, 215-22.
[7] The Yad Ben Zvi library holds 50,000 volumes, 3,000 manuscripts (chiefly the religious heritage of Sephardi and Oriental Jewry), 300 antique ketubot (marriage contracts) from Sephardic communities, an extensive collection of periodicals and other publications in Judeo-Spanish, Keter Aram Tzova , the 10th century Aleppo Codex, and 10,000 offprints.
[8] There were two Jewish weeklies in Egypt in the 1940s, both founded in 1936, *La Tribune Juive* at 7 Rue Tewfik, Alexandria and *Al Shams* at 6 Rue Mouski, Immeuble Rateb Pacha, Cairo.

Malka's progressive views of modern Judaism especially concerning women's issues and their role in Jewish society. The articles do not, however, supply direct genealogical information.

SUDAN JEWISH CEMETERY

The Jewish cemetery in Khartoum was vandalized and desecrated after the Jews left in the late 1950s. Many of the gravestones were overturned or broken. As a result many relatives arranged to transfer the remains of their rabbi and families for reburial in Israel within the Sudan section of Jerusalem's Givaat Shaul cemetery.

24.
TURKEY AND THE OTTOMAN EMPIRE

The word Ottoman is derived from the Turkish name *Uthman* (Osman). Khan Osman I (Uthman, in Turkish), who ruled from 1299 to 1326, founded the Osmanli dynasty that ruled Turkey and the Ottoman Empire for the next six hundred years. Known to his Turkish tribesmen by the traditional title *khan*, Osman I also came to be known by the more familiar and grand title of sultan. The powerful sultans of Turkey ruled over an empire that spanned three continents and held many other official titles among which were *padishah* (Persian for high king or emperor) and the Moslem religious title of *Imam*.

Legislation within the Ottoman Empire would come forth in the form of a *firman* (decree) issued by and in the name of the reigning sultan. The day to day governance of the empire was however directed by the Sultan's grand vizier who would meet with the imperial council in a special building.[1] The entranceway to this special building was known as *Babiali* (Sublime Porte) from which arose the term Porte that came to be commonly used in literature and everywhere else as a synonym for the Imperial Ottoman government itself.

MODERN TURKEY

Mustafa Kemal (1881-1938), born in Salonica (today Thessalonica, Greece), established in 1923 the modern Turkish republic. Kemal became known as Ataturk, "father of the Turks." Ataturk's objective was to modernize and Europeanize the country, and thus transform it from the "sick man of Europe," as it had become known for more than a century, to a nation that could compete favorably with the modern Western European countries that were then the models of successful world powers. His successor, Ismet Inonu (Ismet Pasha), continued Ataturk's reforms and, in the late 1940s, presided over the first democratic Turkish elections.

OTTOMAN GOVERNMENT

The Ottoman system of government was a surprisingly minimalist one. Society was divided into two groups: a small ruling class that paid no taxes and a large subject class. The role of the ruler and state was to ensure justice and security for the subjects, who in turn could create wealth and pay taxes to support the state. The ruling class's functions were primarily to ensure order and border security,

---

[1] The provinces or *viyelat* (or *eilat*) were ruled by governors who at times had enormous military and local powers.

and to collect the taxes used to maintain the state (*devlet*) and the military. The military's role was to maintain the ruler in power and to provide for the state's expansion and security, which in turn permitted subjects to prosper and create more wealth to generate taxes.

The subject class governed itself in all matters relating to its members. Under this system, religious entities within the Ottoman realm were organized into autonomous, self-governing bodies known as *millets* (nations). There were four *millets*, or religious communities, originally arranged in order of rank: Moslem, Greek, Armenian, and Jewish.[2] The individuals within a *millet* dealt with the ruling class through their own leaders.[3] Jews, a recognized religious entity, were organized into a self-governing millet under the chief rabbi (*hakham bashi*) of Istanbul.[4] The millet organized all aspects of life for its members, including education, religion, local justice, hospitals, old-age homes, etc. For Jews this system offered a much greater level of autonomy and freedom than they enjoyed anywhere else, especially in Christendom, and one that attracted many beleaguered Jews from Europe and elsewhere to the Ottoman Empire—even before the expulsion from Spain.

The Ottoman Empire was organized into provinces (*vileyet*). There are 67 *vileyets* in today's Turkey, each governed by a pasha with vast administrative and military powers. The *vileyets* themselves contained the original basic Turkish unit called a *sancak*, or sub-province, governed by a bey.[5] Each sub-province was subdivided into districts (*caza*), towns, and villages (*koy*). *Merkez kazasi* is the capital city of a *sancak*.

SEPHARDIM IN TURKEY

Benbassa and Rodrigue discuss the difficulties in relating a history of post-expulsion Jews of the eastern Mediterranean because of the long neglect by academic historians and the subsequent overlay of myths that has enveloped what is known of that history.[6] They mention the myths of tolerance, symbiosis, and

---

[2] See Bernard Lewis, *What Went Wrong:* **Western Impact and Middle Eastern Response.** (Oxford: Oxford University, 2002) and Cevdet, *Tezakir* (Reminiscences) (Ankara: Türk Tarih Kurumu Basimevi, 1953-1967), 67.

[3] Individuals could move from the subject class into the ruling class if they fit certain exacting criteria that included being a Moslem, loyalty to the Sultan and the Ottoman system of government and thirdly, education particularly in its exacting customs and patterns of behavior. Similarly, members and children of the ruling class who did not maintain these requirements could move out of the ruling class into the subject class.

[4] *Hakham* (sometimes written *haham*) is the term used for rabbi among Sephardim. *Basha, başi*, or *bashi* (pasha) is a Turkish honorific signifying chief rabbi.

[5] *Sancak (Sanjak)*, or sub-province, literally means banner. The original Ottoman state was a single *sancak*.

[6] Benbassa, Esther, and Aron Rodrigue, *Sephardi Jewry: A History of the Judeo-Spanish Community, 14–20th Centuries* (Berkeley: University of California, 2000).

golden age in a romanticized and idealized Spain. These myths ignore the periods of intolerance and hardship that culminated in the 1492 expulsion from their adopted land. The myth of 400,000 exiles recent historians dispel, indicating that the numbers probably did not exceed 50,000.[7] The myths of a Jewish right to Iberia based on the early settlement of Jews on that peninsula or that of the extraordinary welcome by the Turkish sultan that ignores other aspects of Turkish rule.[8] Partial truth resides in all these myths, but they glamorize a reality with many shades of gray.

To Sultan Beyazid II (1481–1512) is attributed the statement, "They say the king of Spain is a wise man, and yet he impoverishes himself by expelling such an industrious people. His loss will be my gain." Whether or not he uttered those words, he welcomed the exiled Spanish Jews to his domains—and is said even to have sent ships to sail them to Turkey.

Clearly the Ottoman sultan had motivations other than altruism in encouraging the Sephardic Jews to move to his realm. The population of Constantinople had declined from 400,000 inhabitants to 50,000 by the time it fell in 1453 into Ottoman hands, and he had great need for populations to inhabit it and other parts of his realm. By order of the sultan, entire populations of Romaniot Jews from throughout Anatolia and the Balkans had been transferred in 1456 to Constantinople to help repopulate the area.[9] When the Sephardic exiles came to the eastern Ottoman Empire, they found Romaniot Jews who had inhabited the Byzantine world since Roman times (synagogue ruins in Turkey date back to 200 B.C.E.) and Ashkenazic Jews who had found refuge there from the most recent pogroms of Christendom.

Contrary to common belief, the exiled Sephardim did not come to Istanbul en masse in 1492, but migrated in several waves after a number of intermediate stops along the way. The early arrivals were Spanish Jews who had chosen exile rather than conversion to Christianity, mainly artisans and small shopkeepers. Later came the more secular and assimilated *conversos* with their greater wealth, education, and expertise in large-scale trading. In the eastern Mediterranean the Sephardim prospered and rapidly became the numerically and culturally dominant Jewish group in Turkey and the surrounding Ottoman Empire. They established large communities in Izmir (Smyrna), Istanbul, Salonica, and Rhodes, among others.[10]

---

[7] See also the discussion of the depletion of Spanish Jewry before 1492 in chapter 3, Spanish Diaspora.

[8] For instance, there were times when Jewish women were forbidden to wear gold and diamond jewelry on the streets and Jewish men had to wear modest hats instead of the fancier headware of the period. See Shlomo Avraham Rozanes, *Korot Hayehudim Beturkia Vebeartzot Hakedem: Divrei Yemai Yisrael Betogarma Al-Pi Mekorot Rishonoim* (History of the Jews of Turkey and of the Middle East). 6 vols. (Vol. I, Tel Aviv: 1930; Vol II-V, Sofia, Bulgaria: 1934-8; Vol. VI, Jerusalem: 1948).

[9] Romaniot, or Greek, Jews were the Jews who had lived and suffered for centuries under Greek Byzantine rule. The entire population of Salonica was moved to satisfy the repopulation needs of the Ottoman government.

[10] Salonica became an essentially Jewish city. Ladino was spoken everywhere and the town's businesses closed on the Jewish Sabbath.

Many of the local Ashkenazic and Romaniot Jews adopted the dominant Sephardic culture and language; this phenomenon explains the presence of such surnames as Russo (Russian), Hamizrachi (eastern Jew), Romi (Roman), Soriano (from Soria, Italy) and Ashkenazi (German) among the Ottoman Sephardim.

Istanbul

The 18th century was a turning point for both the Ottoman Empire and its Jews. By then the Jews of Istanbul, the new home of refugees from Spain and other parts of Europe, represented one of the largest Jewish communities in the world. The majority of Sephardim belonged to the poorer classes or worked as small tradesmen, but a highly successful and wealthy elite yielded great power and controlled large commercial and other enterprises and provided physicians and served as councilors to the rulers. Though still subject to the *dhimmi* laws (see chapter 5, Jews under Islam),[11] some Jews rose to play major roles as *sarraf* (court bankers) and administrators. From these positions, they were powerful spokesmen for the concerns and interests of the Jewish community. They reached their greatest heights of power with the mid-16th century arrival of the *converso* house of Nasi, in the persons of Dona Gracia (born Beatriz de Luna Mendes) and her son, the powerful duke of Naxos.[12]

After the failed Turkish siege of Vienna in 1683, the Ottoman Empire started its slow decline, and Turkey's Jews shared in that decline. The Armenians, who had been the long-time jewelers of the Sultan,[13] took over the influential post of *sarraf* from the Jews and in 1758 took control of the Constantinople mint. In time, both the Christian Greek and the Armenian communities wrested power from the hands of the Jews; because of their historic enmity and opposing interests, that change was to the great detriment of the Jewish community.

Janissaries (from the Turkish *yeni ceri*) were special Turkish troops whose privileges sometimes went to their heads. They were formed from Christian children who had been taken as a special levy from the subject class, the young children were converted into Islam and put through a prolonged special training for their military role as imperial bodyguards. By becoming military men, they de facto became part of the ruling class with all its many privileges. Jews and Armenians were not subject to this special child levy, but the advantages were such that some Moslems even pretended their children where Christian as a means of gaining them entry into the ruling class. The year 1826, saw Sultan Mahmut II crack down on a janisaries rebellion. He bombarded the janissary

---

[11] A colorful sidenote: To distinguish among their various non-Moslem *dhimmi* subjects, the Ottomans obliged their *dhimmi* to wear turbans of different colors. Armenians wore purple turbans, Jews blue, and Greeks black.

[12] Cecil Roth, *The House of Nasi: 1. Dona Gracia* (Philadelphia: Jewish Publication Society of America, 1977).

[13] The Armenian Duyzan family were the court jewelers.

barracks and pursued all that had any connection with them. A Jewish financier, Behor Carmona, was caught in that web. Carmona was strangled and his possessions confiscated simply because of his officially appointed role of provisioner to the janissaries. Jews fled the country including among others the wealthy Cammondo family. The Cammondos were a fabulously wealthy Sephardic family, known as the Rothschilds of the East, who after their flight from Turkey ultimately moved to France where they lived in great style, endowing France with palaces, theaters, and art. The entire Cammondo family was caught in the World War II turmoil and died in German death camps in 1943-44. The 19th century saw the Jews of Constantinople become financially and culturally impoverished.

Turkish Imperial Archives

Addresses: Ankara: Ivedik Cad. 59, Yenimahalle/Ankara, Turkey
Istanbul: Ticarethane Sok. 12 Sultanahmet/Istanbul, Turkey
Email: ysarinay@devletarsivleri.gov.tr
Website: www.turkses.com/culture/newspot/access_to_documents_and_conditio.htm; see also http://ottoman.home.mindspring.com

Sultan Mehmet II (reigned 1451-1481) is credited with being the first to order the creation of the registers known as *defter e Hakani*. These registers listed all the inhabitants of his vast realm, their taxes due, general revenues, and sums allotted to various expenditures. In these *defters*, individuals are listed by first name and father's name, and a brief description is given of the individual.

The Turkish Imperial Archives contain 100-150 million documents. The contents of the archives are found today in two main collections: one in the Topkapi palace, the other in the Prime Minister's Archive.

Research Requirements

To search the archives, a research permit and a resident visa are required. In addition, in some cases, the researcher must demonstrate ability to read the Ottoman script. Both the research permit and the resident permit can be obtained from a Turkish embassy abroad before leaving for Turkey; it typically takes about a month to receive the documents. If one is already in Turkey on a tourist visa, the research permit may be obtained directly from the Prime Minister's Archives in either Istanbul or Ankara, a matter of a few days according to Shaw. The resident permit can be obtained from the local police station. Several passport photos are needed to complete the process.[14]

---

[14] Stanford J. Shaw, *Jews of the Ottoman Empire and Turkish Republic* (New York: New York University Press, 1991).

Ostensibly to ensure the continuing need for their professional services, Ottoman scribes labored to make their script *difficult* to decipher. For the average Jewish genealogist, this situation translates into the need for professional archivists and scholars to help research the records, written in the Turkish language in Arabic script.

Stored in mice-infested storerooms, the Ottoman Archives hold vast amounts of data of great genealogical interest, covering more than 20 different countries that belonged at one time to the Ottoman Empire—often the only archives for these countries. Yet it remains a barely touched resource. A recent report revealed that from 1921 to 2000, only 3,000 foreign researchers have accessed the Ottoman archives and one can be certain that a very tiny percentage, if any, of these were Jewish genealogists.[15] Turkish officials announced in 1998 an effort to digitize the archives and make them available on the Internet, as well as to provide tools to assist researchers with the language difficulties described above; no progress reports have been received.

Genealogical research in the Turkish archives is difficult not only because of the need to read the indecipherable Turkish script, but a researcher must also understand the language, convert Turkish dates, and be familiar with Turkish administrative units used in the archives. The following will provide a brief introduction and point to sources of additional information (see bibliography). Also see appendix C for examples of Arabic script and appendix H on the Turkish calendar.

TURKISH SCRIPT

The Latin alphabet was adopted in Turkey in 1928. Earlier the Turkish language was written in Arabic script and known as Osmanlica. To access official documents, newspapers, and books written prior to 1928, it is necessary to read the Arabic script as well as to understand Turkish. For examples of Arabic script and its transliteration equivalent, see appendix C and the section on Arabic in chapter 9, Sephardic Languages.

TURKISH CALENDAR

For centuries Turkey used the traditional Islamic calendar. In 1789 a civil calendar, known as the *sene i maliye* (*maliye* for short) or *sene i rumiye*, based on the Julian calendar, was adopted for official use.[16] Like the Julian calendar, there were 12 months in the *sene e maliye*: maret, nisan, mayiis, haziran, temuz, agustos, eilul, tishrin-ievvel (tishrin-ewel), tishrin-thani, kannun-ievvel, kannun-thani, shubatt.

---

[15] In 1929, a 1513 copy of Columbus's map, forgotten for centuries, was found in the Ottoman archives. See Lewis, *What Went Wrong*.

[16] *Sene* means year. *Maliye* is financial and *rumi* refers to the Europeans (or Romans).

Official documents such as birth certificates usually would use the *maliye* calendar, although some might use the older Islamic calendar. Dates written in Osmanlica can be difficult to decipher, partially because scribes' rapid and sometimes slurred handwriting varied in legibility as much as handwriting would today, but it is also because of the tendency to write the names of the months not only in Arabic script (right to left) but also splitting word portions over two or three lines, each part written below the other. For instance the portion "*thani*," meaning second, would often be written below the first part of the month's name instead of following it. This created a more aesthetic writing style, but one that creates difficulty for the person unaccustomed to Arabic script styles.

Finally as part of the westernization efforts of the modern Turkish republic, the Gregorian calendar was adopted in 1926.

Several tables can help convert Turkish dates to their modern equivalents. One tool is the "computus" conversion program developed by Gerhard Behrens. It can be downloaded free from the Internet from www.lib.umich.edu/area/Near.East/computus.html. Despite its small size (only 29K), this tool accurately converts dates between the Jewish, Christian (Gregorian/Julian), Ottoman *maliye*, Hijra (lunar), Hijra (solar/Iran), Jalali (*Malikshah*), Persian (*Yezdegerd*), Coptic, Great Armenian, French Revolution, and Julian (Old Style) calendars.

GENEALOGICAL RESOURCES

Sephardic genealogic research in Turkey very much in its infancy, needs volunteers to develop it further. Among the documents of value to the Jewish genealogist are *ketubot* (Jewish marriage certificates), synagogue records, official censuses, and Turkish birth certificates (only exist since 1922).

JEWISH RECORDS

Jewish records consist of synagogue records of births, circumcisions, marriages, and deaths. Most of these types of documents of interest to the Sephardic genealogist in Turkey are written in Judeo-Spanish using Rashi Sephardic Hebrew or Solitreo script (see chapter 9, Sephardic Languages). Unfortunately they do not exist before the twentieth century.

The **Ashkenazic** community office (Banker sokak No.10, Karakoy, Istanbul) has birth, marriage, and death records starting in 1847 written with Latin characters. The early documents are in German; by the 1930s, the language is Turkish in Latin characters.

Besides *ketubot* held in private hands, collections of Sephardic *ketubot* are held in Israeli museums and archives such as the Ben Zvi Institute, National Library of Hebrew University, and the Central Archives for the History of the Jewish People.

CENTRAL ARCHIVES FOR THE HISTORY OF THE JEWISH PEOPLE

Address: Hebrew University Campus, Sprinzak Bldg, Givat Ram, Jerusalem, Israel.
Mailing address: P.O. Box 1149, Jerusalem 91010
Telephone: (972)-2-5635716

This repository has some *pinkassim* (registers) of the Istanbul rabbinical court (1839–41) and the Izmir community archives (1760–70). CAHJP holds a copy of a 10-book census of Izmir families from around 1906. Written in Solitreo,[17] families are listed in alphabetical order with birth dates (from the 19th century), birthplaces, occupations, and parents' names.

The CAHJP's Ashkenazic family collection includes Izmir marriage registers for the period 1819–1933.

TURKISH RABBINATE OFFICE IN ISTANBUL

Address: *Turkiye Hahambasiligi*, Yemenici Sokak 23, Beyoglu 80050 Tunel, Istanbul, Turkey

This repository holds a number of records, researchers must appear in person; due to personnel shortage staff does not respond to mail requests. The records are written mostly in Solitreo.

IZMIR RABBINATE, *Harahan*, Alsancak quarter in Izmir. This rabbinate has two registers of interest, the *cazamientos*, or marriage register, and the *nacimientos*, or birth records. Both contain records in Judeo-Spanish from 1909 to the present. The rabbinate holds a 10-book census of Izmir families that dates from around 1906, with birth dates that extend back to the 19th century. A copy is also held at Central Archives of the Jewish people.

Dov Cohen, a professional genealogist in Israel, has prepared a transcribed list of 7,300 Jewish brides and grooms who married in Izmir during the years 1883–1901 and 1918-1933.[18] Of the surnames listed, 20 percent were carried by 70 percent of the population with Cohen and Levi being the most common and alone accounting for 7 percent of the population studied.[19]

---

[17] Judeo-Spanish was written in cursive Hebrew Sephardic script and later Latin characters. The word solitreo is said to come from the Portuguese word *soletrar*, to spell, presumably because one had to "spell" or transcribe Judeo-Spanish into Hebrew or Latin letters.

[18] Dov Cohen, *Izmir: List of 7300 Names of Jewish Brides and Grooms who married in Izmir between the years 1993-1901 and 1918-1933, List no 1*, 1997. A copy of the unpublished list is available at the Jewish Genealogy Society of Greater Washington.

[19] Roland Taranto, "Les noms de famille juifs à Smyrne" (Jewish Surnames in Smyrna) *Etsi*, Vol. 5 No 16, March 2002.

CEMETERIES

Sephardic cemeteries in the Istanbul area include:
- Kuzguncuk Cemetery, dating back to the 1500s
- Haskoy Cemetery, dating back to 1582
- Ortakoy Cemetery, dating back to the 1800s
- Arnavutkoy Cemetery, dating from 1920
- Hemdat Israel Cemetery at Kadikoy
- Italian Cemetery[20]

Jewish tombstones in Turkey have been extensively studied and photographed by Minna Rozen of Tel Aviv University; study results are not yet published or available. Included in Rozen's study is the Haskoy Cemetery of Istanbul, for which partial data has been published.[21] The middle of the cemetery was destroyed when a road was built through the cemetery. During construction, remains were moved to other parts of the cemetery.

An index to the 3,000 burials in the Ashkenazic Yukeskkaldirim Cemetery from the work of Erdal Frayman was posted online by Daniel Kazez at http://userpages.wittenberg.edu/dkazez/fam/turk-bur/.

Burial lists from the Kadikoy, Yukeskkaldirim, and Kuzguncuk cemeteries are to be posted in the JewishGen Online Worldwide Burial Registry (JOWBR) at www.jewishgen.org/databases/Cemetery, courtesy of Daniel Kazez.

The Ashkenazic cemetery Arnavutkoy-Ulus was inaugurated in 1916; its records go back to that year. Before 1916, Ashkenazic Jews were buried in Sephardic cemeteries such as Haskoy.

CIVIL RECORDS

Turkish civil registration of births began in 1922. Birth certificates apparently can be obtained by writing to local Turkish consulates giving the person's exact name, year of birth, and town of birth. But computer glitches may produce the wrong certificate. Ottoman birth certificates list date of birth, religion, birth name, father's and mother's names, and a brief physical description.

In Istanbul birth, marriage and divorce records can be found at the Turkish Nufus Mudurlugu district offices for that city. It is essential to know which of the 32 Istanbul districts to look in. Additional information about these Istanbul districts can be found on the web at http://rehber.ibb.gov.tr. No special permission is necessary to access these records.

---

[20] Daniel Kazez, personal communication.
[21] Mina Rozen, "Jewish Cemeteries in Turkey." In Esther Juhasz, ed., *Sephardi Jews of the Ottoman Empire: Aspects of Material Culture* (Jerusalem: Israel Museum and Jerusalem Publishing House, 1990).

SALNAME

A series of *salname* books is available for purchase from www.lib.uchicago.edu/e/su/mideast/Vilayet_Salname.html. These are Ottoman yearbooks that contain names and varying levels of information. Written in Osmanlica, (Turkish language in Arabic script), they are difficult to use.

SUGGESTED READING

Attal, Robert. *Les Juifs de Grece de l'expulsion d'Espagne a nos jours: bibliographie* (Jews of Greece from the expulsion from Spain to our days: Bibliography). Jerusalem: Institute Ben Zvi and Hebrew University, 1984. Includes 2,297 references in Greek, Hebrew, Ladino, French, and English. Index to subjects, authors, and places.

―――. *Les Juifs de Grece de l'expulsion d'Espagne a nos jours: Bibliographie. Additifs a la premiere edition.* (Jews of Greece from the Spanish expulsion to our days: Bibliography: Additions to the first edition). Jerusalem: Ben Zvi Institute and Hebrew University, 1984. Includes 940 references in Greek, Hebrew, Ladino, French, and English. Index to subjects, authors, and places.

Benbassa, Esther, and Aron Rodrigue. *Sephardi Jewry: A History of the Judeo-Spanish community, 14-20th centuries.* Berkeley: University of California Press, 2000. Account of post-expulsion Balkan Sephardim.

Bunis, David M. "The History of Judezmo Orthography." Working papers in Yiddish and East European Jewish Studies. Max Weinreich Center for Advanced Studies, *YIVO* 2 (1974): 1-55.

Carasso, Elie, ed. *Les Juifs de Salonique, 1492-1943* (Jews of Salonica, 1492-1943). Tarascon, France: Cousins de Salonique, 1993. Synagogues, name lists, Michel Molho, AIU schools, Carasso family.

Farhi, Gentille. "La situation linguistique du sephardite a Istanbul" (The linguistic situation of Sephardite in Istanbul). *Hispanic Review* 5 (1937), 151-58,.

Franco, Moise. *Essai sur l'histoire des Israelites de l'Empire Ottoman depuis les origines jusqu'a nos jours* (Essay on the history of the Jews of the Ottoman Empire from its origins to our days). Paris: Dularcher, 1897. The 1897 edition has no index, but many names are mentioned.

Frayman, Erdal. *Yuksekkaldirim'da Yuz Yillik bir Sinagog/Askenazlar* (A hundred year-old synagogue in Yuksekkaldirim/Ashkenazic Jews). Istanbul: 2000. Complete list of 3,000 Ashkenazic burials in Istanbul.

Galante, Avram. *Histoire des Juifs d'Istanbul* (History of the Jews of Istanbul). 2 vols. Istanbul: Husnutabiat, 1941, 1942.

―――. *Histoire des Juifs de Turquie* (History of the Jews of Turkey). e vols. Istanbul: Editions ISIS, 1985.

Harris, Tracy. "The Prognosis for Judeo-Spanish: Its Description, Present Status, Survival and Decline, with Implications for the Study of Language Death in General." Ph.D. diss., Georgetown University, 1979.

Emmanuel, Isaac S. *Matsevot Saloniki* (Salonican Tombstones). 2 vols. Jerusalem: Ben Zvi Institute, 1963–68).

Jerusalmi, Isaac. *From Ottoman Turkish to Ladino*. Cincinnati, Oh.: Ladino Books, 1990. Guide to transliteration from Osmanlica into Latin characters.

Levy, Avigdor. *Jews of the Ottoman Empire*. Washington, D.C.: Darwin Press, 1994.

Lewis, Bernard. *What Went Wrong: Western Impact and Middle Eastern Response*. Oxford: Oxford University, 2002.

Mitchell, T.F. *Writing Arabic: A Practical Introduction to the Ruq'ah Script*. Oxford: Oxford University Press, 1990. A good guide to the Arabic script.

Molho, Michael. *Literatura sefardita de Oriente* (Sephardic literature of the Orient). Madrid: Instituto Arias Montano, 1960.

Moissis, Asher. *Les noms des juifs de Grece* (Names of Jews from Greece). Gordo, France: Carasso, 1991.

Nehama, Joseph. "*Le dialecte Judeo-espagnol et le Ladino*" (Judeo-Spanish dialect and Ladino). *Tresoro de los judios sefardies* 6 (1964): 57–64.

Roth, Cecil. *A History of the Marranos*, 4th ed. New York: Hermon Press, 1974.

———. *The House of Nasi: 1. Dona Gracia*. Philadelphia: Jewish Publication Society of America, 1948.

———. *The House of Nasi: 2. The Duke of Naxos*. Philadelphia: Jewish Publication Society, 1948.

Rozanes, Shlomo Avraham. *Korot Hayehudim Beturkia Vebeartzot Hakedem: Divrei Yemai Yisrael Betogarma Al-Pi Mekorot Rishonoim* (History of the Jews of Turkey and of the Middle East). 6 vols. Vol. I, Tel Aviv: 1930; Vol II-V, Sofia, Bulgaria: 1934-8; Vol. VI, Jerusalem: 1948.

Sola-Cardoza, Anne de. "Spanish-Jewish Nobility of Aleppo, Syria" *Avotaynu* Vol. VII: 1991, 17–8.

Shaw, Stanford J. *History of the Ottoman Empire and Modern Turkey*. 2 vols. Cambridge and New York: Cambridge University Press, 1976.

———. *Jews of the Ottoman Empire and Turkish Republic*. New York: New York University Press, 1991.

25.

THE BALKANS

To discuss the Jews of the Balkans is to describe a community that largely has been destroyed. The final death blow was administered by the Nazi Holocaust that decimated the Jewish populations of the Balkans, Greece, and Salonica, but these communities had already been in decline for some time, and deteriorating economic conditions had provoked emigration to other regions of the world during the 19th century.

The Eastern Sephardim of the Balkans have the distinction of being the group of Spanish exiles that most successfully maintained their Judeo-Spanish language and culture. The Spanish exiles who went south to North Africa, except for some towns in Northern Morocco and Tunisia, merged with the more numerous local Jews to form a Sephardized cultural blend. The exiles who settled in Europe and the Americas were already quite assimilated into the Spanish or Portuguese Catholic cultures from which they had come and they, too, absorbed the cultures and languages of their adoptive countries. In the eastern Mediterranean and Balkans, however, Spanish exiles numerically overwhelmed the local Jews. Though here, too, they absorbed local Ottoman cultural traits, as a majority Jewish culture, they succeeded in preserving more of their northern Spanish language and culture. By contrast, many of the local pre-existing Romaniot and Ashkenazic populations were culturally absorbed by the Iberian newcomers.

The Balkan Peninsula is subdivided into several countries whose borders and names have changed periodically. Today the Balkans are considered to include Albania, Bulgaria, Greece, Turkey in Europe, Slovenia, Croatia, Bosnia and Herzegovina, Yugoslavia, Macedonia and Romania.

Many of these countries achieved independence only in the late 19th century. Earlier they had been part of the Ottoman Empire, and the Jews of the Balkans shared great cultural affinity and cohesiveness with the Eastern Sephardim of Turkey and Salonica. Bulgaria, Yugoslavia and Salonica are discussed in this chapter.

BULGARIA

Jews have inhabited Bulgaria since the first century C.E., having arrived as part of the Roman presence in the area. Referred to in the Talmud and other Jewish texts as *romanim* (or in its Greek form, *Romaioi*), Bulgarian Jews named their synagogues *kahal kadosh romaniah* (Romaniah holy congregations). When Jewish exiles from Spain arrived in Bulgaria in 1494, they found older Romaniot (Greek) and Ashkenazic Jewish communities dating back long before the 1396 Ottoman conquest of Bulgaria. Bulgarian Jewry in the 20th century was a mixture of Romaniot, Ashkenazic, and Sephardic Jews. All three groups had adopted Judeo-Spanish as the common language of Bulgarian Jews.[1]

Prior to the 14th century little evidence of anti-Semitism in Bulgaria existed, even after it became Christian in 864. In 1335, however, King Ivan Aleksandur divorced his queen Teodora to marry his Jewish love, Sara. Even though Sara converted to Christianity and was crowned as Queen Teodora, the marriage provoked a backlash. A synod was convened that condemned Jews and several Christian heresies that then flourished in Bulgaria.[2]

After five centuries of prosperity and tolerance for Jews under the Ottomans (1366–1878), Bulgaria's war of independence saw Jewish homes and businesses destroyed and many Jews expelled, while others fled the country to avoid similar treatment. Most expelled and fleeing Bulgarian Jews fled to Istanbul and Adrianopolis.[3]

Russia emerged victorious from the Russo-Turkish war (1877–78) with a much-enlarged Bulgaria as its protectorate. Concerned that Russia might now extend its influence to Istanbul and the Suez Canal, England and Austria imposed the Treaty of Berlin (1878) on a Russia weakened by its recent war. The treaty divided Bulgaria into three parts: Romania, Montenegro, and Serbia were recognized as independent; Austria occupied Bosnia and Herzegovina; and a diminished Bulgaria. The Treaty of Berlin also officially restored the civil rights of Bulgarian Jews but reality was otherwise and popular anti-Semitism and government discrimination persisted.

During World War II anti-Jewish laws declared Jews enemies of the state and excluded them from professions, voting, property and car ownership, corporate boards, and marriage with non-Jews. Jewish organizations were banned, and Jews were to receive one quarter the war ration for non-Jews. Bulgarian Jews with Jewish-sounding names were forced to change their names (creating an additional hurdle for genealogists later researching government documents).[4] In 1941 Bulgaria joined a Nazi alliance and the subsequent Nazi occupation resulted in 11,000 Bulgarian Jews dying in Nazi camps. Vigorous protests by Peshev, an influential Bulgarian parliamentary leader, however, succeeded in saving another 40,000 Bulgarian Jews from the gas chambers.

In 1944, the Soviet army occupied Bulgaria. By 1950, the combination of a poor economy and popular anti-Semitism prompted close to 50,000 Bulgarian Jews to leave the country. Almost all went to Israel, where there already existed an 1895 settlement of early Bulgarian Zionists. Bulgarian Jews were active early in the

---

[1] Vicky Tamir, *Bulgaria and Her Jews: The History of a Dubious Symbiosis* (New York: Sepher-Hermon Press, for Yeshiva University Press, 1979).
[2] Tamir, *Bulgaria and Her Jews*.
[3] Heskel M. Haddad, *Jews of Arab and Islamic Countries* (New York: Shengold, 1984).
[4] Tamir, *Bulgaria and Her Jews*, 166-73; Mathilde Tagger, "Bulgarian Jewish Names in the Second World War Period," *Sharsheret Hadorot* 10, no. 1 (April 1996).

Zionist movement, and the Central Zionist Archives at 8 Ha Maalot Street, Jerusalem, Israel may therefore hold records of value to researchers of Bulgarian Jewish families.

GENEALOGICAL RESOURCES

Diaspora Museum (Beth Hatefutsoth)
Address: Tel Aviv University Campus, Klausner Street, Ramat Aviv,
Mailing address: P.O.B. 39359, Tel Aviv 61392
Telephone: 972 3 646 2020; Fax: 972 3 646 2134
Website: http://www.bh.org.il/
E-mail: bhwebmas@post.tau.ac.il
Access: Sunday-Tuesday, 10:00 am - 4:00 pm; Wednesday, 10:00 am - 5:00 pm

The museum holds copies of Jewish documents from the State Archives in Sofia, which includes all Bulgarian Jewish communities from the 16th century to 1960, with the exception of the small towns of Vidin and Ruse. Also held here is information on the history of Bulgarian Jewry and its institutions (1895–1968) prepared by the Union of Bulgarian Jews in Israel.

American Sephardic Federation
Address: 15 West 16th Street, NewYork, N.Y. 10011, USA
Telephone: (212)294-8350
Fax: (212) 294-8348
Website: http://www.asfonline.org/portal/
Email: mustaev@cjh.org

The federation holds annual books on Sephardic Jews in Bulgaria prepared by the Bulgarian-Jewish Association.

Alliance Israelite Universelle Archives
Address: 45 Rue la Bruyere, 75009, Paris.
Archives: by appointment
Télephone: 01 53 32 88 55
Fax : 01 48 74 51 33
Website: www.aiu.org
Email : biblio@aiu.org
Access: Monday, Tuesday, Thursday, 1–6 pm; Wednesday, 1–7:30 pm

The Alliance Israelite Universelle opened its first school in Bulgaria in 1870, followed by others in cities such as Shumen, Ruse, and Samokov. The archives, records are organized into 12 groups of documents, of which the series E for *ecoles* (schools) offer the most genealogically useful information.

Church of Jesus Christ of Latter-day Saints
Address: 35 North West Temple Street, Salt Lake City, Utah, 84150-3400
Telephone: 801-240-2331 or 800-453-3860 ext 22331
FAX: 801-240-1584
E-mail: fhl@ldschurch.org
Website: www.familysearch.org
See also www.jewishgen.org/databases/FHLC for database of Jewish items.

The Mormons hold copies of civil registrations in Bulgaria which, although they do not identify Jews as such, include Jews. The reels are listed by locality in Bulgaria.

Mathilde Tagger, a noted Sephardic genealogist in Israel, has researched family trees for the Eliahou, Hako, Levy, and Mechoulam families of Bulgaria and Israel (1790–1983), and the Tagger family from Bulgaria and Israel (1825–1970).

Yugoslavia

Though Sephardic communities first settled in Yugoslavia following their 1492 expulsion from Spain, Jews are known to have inhabited that land since at least the second century B.C.E. Sephardic Jews first settled mainly in Macedonia and Bosnia-Herzegovina and later in Belgrade and northern Yugoslavia. In the 19th century a large number of Ashkenazic Jews from the Austro-Hungarian Empire migrated to Yugoslavia, settling mainly in the more urban, westernized regions of the north. While under Ottoman rule, conditions of relative tolerance prevailed for the Jews of Yugoslavia, as they did elsewhere in the Ottoman Empire.

By 1939, on the eve of World War II, the Jewish population of Yugoslavia was 72,000, of whom 39,000 were Sephardim concentrated mainly in Serbia, Bosnia, Macedonia, and Dalmatia. The Nazis occupied Yugoslavia in 1941 and subsequently exterminated all but 14,000 of the country's Jews, starting first with the Jews of Serbia. During World War II, Macedonia was under Bulgarian control; all its Jews were deported to perish in Nazi death camps. Thousands of Yugoslavia's Jews were rounded up and shot. Others died in concentration camps (Samjiste near Belgrade, Auschwitz, Treblinka, and others).

Some Jews escaped to Italy, Switzerland, or the United States, while an estimated 2,000 to 3,000 fought with Tito's partisans. After the war, 12,495 Jews were left in Yugoslavia, about 8,000 of whom sought refuge and settlement in Israel between 1948 and 1952.[5]

---

[5] Harriet Pass Freidenreich, *The Jews of Yugoslavia: A Quest for Community* (Philadelphia: Jewish Publication Society, 1979).

GENEALOGICAL RESOURCES

Jewish Historical Museum of Belgrade

Address: Kralja Petra 71A, Belgrade, Serbia, Yugoslavia
Mailing address: *Jevrejski Istorijski Musej*, Kralja Petra 71A, 11000 Beograd, Serbia, Yugoslavia
Telephone: 622-624,
Fax: 626-674
Email: muzej@eunet.yu
Website: www.beograd.org.yu/srpski/upoznaj/religija/jevreji
and www.jim-bg.org

Belgrade's Jewish Historical Museum holds records of the Federation of Jewish Communities in Yugoslavia from 1919 to the present. Its collection of documents and records from the prewar period includes holdings of older Jewish communities, papers of prominent people, and records of Jewish organizations.

Professor Mina Rozen has microfilmed these records, currently held at the Museum of the Diaspora in Tel Aviv (see below).

Ottoman Archives

The archives in Istanbul, Turkey hold records for the period during which much of Yugoslavia was under Ottoman rule. These *Mufassal defters* for Yugoslavia are written in Osmanlica and, therefore, difficult to use (see chapter 9, Sephardic Languages).

Yad Vashem Holocaust Museum

Address: Yad Vashem, The Martyrs' and Heroes' Remembrance Authority, P.O.B. 3477, Jerusalem 91034 Israel
Telephone: +972 2 6443400
Fax: +972 2 6443443
Website: http://www.yad-vashem.org.il
Email: general.information@yadvashem.org.il
Access: Sunday-Thursday 9 am-5 pm; Fridays and Holidays Evenings, 9 am-2 pm
Archives: Sunday-Thursday 8:30 am-5:00 pm Books and files must be ordered by 3:00 pm
Library: Sunday-Thursday 8:30 am – 5:00 pm

Isaac Nehama describes Nazi registers containing 1,031 persons and 270 photos of Jews from Monastir (Bitola) in Yad Vashem.[6] The Museum has published a series of books on various Jewish communities including *Pinkas hakehilot Yugoslavia* about Yugoslavian Jewish communities. The book can be

---

[6] Personal communication, September 2002.

purchased at the museum or through its distributor Rubin Mass, Ltd., P.O. Box 990, Jerusalem 91009, Israel.

Museum of the Diaspora (Beth Hatefutsoth)
Address: Tel Aviv University Campus, Klausner Street, Ramat Aviv, P.O.B. 39359, Tel Aviv 61392
Telephone: 972 3 646 2020
Fax: 972 3 646 2134
Website: www.bh.org.il
E-mail: bhwebmas@post.tau.ac.il
Access: Sunday–Tuesday, 10:00 am–4:00 pm; Wednesday, 10:00 am–5:00 pm

The museum has copies of the archives of the Jewish community of Belgrade and Slovenia.

United States Holocaust Memorial Museum in Washington D.C.
Address: 100 Raoul Wallenberg Place, SW, Washington, D.C., 20024, U.S.A.
Website: http://www.ushmm.org
Access: 10 am–5:30 pm every day including weekends
Library: 10 am–5 pm
Archives: 10 am–5 pm, Monday–Friday

The Osobyi Archives (Center for Preservation of Historical Documentary Collections) in Moscow holds extensive archives of Jewish and Holocaust records confiscated by the Red Army from Nazi Germany at the end of World War II. These records had been unavailable to researchers until recently.

Copies of most of this collection are now held at the United States Holocaust Memorial Museum in record group RG 11.001 (especially 11.001.20). The collection also includes B'nai B'rith records for Yugoslavia and Greece. Isaac Nehama also describes Nazi registers containing 1,360 photos of Jews from Monastir (Bitola).[7]

The United States Holocaust Memorial Museum also holds the following useful publications:
- *Jugoslevni u Koncentracion Legoru Ausvic 1941–45*, by Tomislav Zugic, which lists 17,000 Yugoslavs deported to Auschwitz
- *Deca Na Lomaci Rata u Neza Visnoj Drza vi Hrvatskoj 1941–45 Jasenovac* which lists 19,500 children killed in the Jasenovac concentration camp
- a list of 6,000 Croatian-Jewish victims and a list of Belgrade Jews whose property was expropriated.

---

[7] Personal communication, September 2002.

- *Jews in Macedonia during the Second World War 1941–45* which lists 7,148 Macedonian Jews who were deported to Treblinka.

American Jewish Archives, Cincinnati, Ohio
Address: 3101 Clifton Ave., Cincinnati, OH 45220
Telephone: 513-221-1875
Fax: 513-221-7812
Email: AJA@huc.edu

The archives holds in its World Jewish Congress Holocaust archival collection (groups 274/10 and 274/47) lists of Jews living in Yugoslavia.

SALONICA

Known as the Jerusalem of the Balkans, Salonica, was the pride of the eastern Mediterranean Sephardic community because of its cultural prestige and community size. As early as 1530, half Salonica's population of 40,000 was Jewish—the second largest Jewish community in the world at the time. Half Salonica's Jews spoke Ladino and were of Sephardic culture.[8]

When chronicler Benjamin of Tudela visited Salonica in the 12th century, he found a mere five hundred oppressed Jews living in the city. The population grew when the city came under Ottoman rule in 1430, and relative tolerance of the regime towards minorities caused Jews from Europe and elsewhere to settle there.

But it was the massive influx of Spanish exiles in the 16th century that, because of its size and vigor, definitively imprinted its culture and language on the city. Sephardic Jews soon controlled all the commerce and trades in the city, which became essentially a Jewish city. Its residents had commercial ties with Jews throughout the Mediterranean, especially with Venice, an important trading partner at the time.

When the Sephardic exiles settled in Salonica, they established separate communities and synagogues reflecting the localities from which they had come, as they did wherever they settled. Members of each community spoke their separate languages, lived within their circumscribed areas, and typically did not infringe upon the others. The earliest Sephardic communities believed to have existed in Salonica were those of Aragon, Gerush-Sepharad, Yishma'El (Calabra), Mayor (Majorca), Sicilia, Catalonia, and Castilla.[9] By the end of the 16th century,

---

[8] H.M. Sachar, *Farewell Espana: The World of the Sephardim Remembered* (New York: Vintage Books, 1995).
[9] Elie Carasso, ed. *Les Juifs de Salonique, 1492-1943* (Jews of Salonica, 1492–1943) (Tarascon, France: Cousins de Salonique, 1993).

30 such *kehillot* (Jewish communties) existed—Sephardic, Romaniot, and Ashkenazic—each with its own separate leaders and synagogues. Multiple fires destroyed these early wooden synagogues; none remain today. As the Sephardic communities increased in numbers, both Ashkenazic and Romaniot Jews assimilated into the dominant Sephardic culture.

In 1912, Greece gained its independence and recaptured Salonica. Jews then began to leave the city, reducing its population to 56,000 by 1939. Thousands of Salonican Jews were deported by the Nazis to Auschwitz and Bergen-Belsen, where 95 percent of them died.

SYNAGOGUES

A 1917 fire destroyed much of Salonica and, along with it, most Jewish records prior to that date.

Michael Molho provides descriptions of 16th-century Salonican Sephardic synagogues and, of interest to genealogists, the surnames associated with each in 1525.[10] See Table 2 below and Table 8 in appendix L, Surnames and Synagogue Affiliations in 16th-Century Salonica. The association of these surnames with specific areas of the Sephardic world is of great value to Sephardic families attempting to identify their possible origins. Indeed, on the 8th of July 1525, the leaders of the various communities met in the *Ashkenaz* synagogue and promulgated a series of rules, including one that forbade, under pain of excommunication, any individual from leaving his community to join another Jewish community![11]

The *Ashkenaz* synagogue, established in Salonica in 1470, is not mentioned in Molho's list[12] but is included in Table 5, appendix L. Also, communities from Andalusia and southern Spain are conspicuous by their absence as are also Hispanic-sounding names which are typical of *converso* families.

The following table lists the Sephardic communities (*Kehillah Kedoshah*) and Synagogues in 16th-century Salonica.[13] With the *Ashkenaz* synagogue that Molho does not mention, there were a total of 30 synagogues.

---

[10] Michael Molho, "*Les Synagogues de Salonique*" (Synagogues of Salonica), in Carasso, *Les Juifs de Salonique, 1492–1943*.

[11] Carasso, *Les Juifs de Salonique, 1492–1943*.

[12] The *Ashkenaz* synagogue was also known as *El Kal de la Moshka* (congregation of the "fly", a play on the word for Moskow). A *Haggadah* published in Thessalonica in 1970 lists its members as Pessah, Ouri, Menahem, Tsadik, Sion, Tazartes, Shimshi, Eskinazi, Simha, Saadi (Levi), Shaoul, Faisevi, Halevy, Hanoh, Touvi and Lapas. From Elie Carasso, ed. *Les Juifs de Salonique*.

[13] The *Har Gavoah* and *Beth Aharon* synagogues only appear elsewhere in the literature as of the 17th century.

Table 2. Synagogues in 16th-Century Salonica

Community (*Kehillah Kedoshah*)	Synagogues
Ets ha Haim and *Ets Ha Daat*, also known as *de los Gregos* (of the Greeks)	*Ets ha Haim*
Provincia for the Jews of Provence, France	*Provincia, Har Gavoah*
Pulia for the Jews of Apulia in the kingdom of Naples	*Pulia, Neve Shalom, Neve Tsedek*
Portugal or *Portugezim*	*Portugal*
Calabria Calabria also known as *Yishma'El, Calabrezis, Calabrizim,* or *Gerush-Calabrezis*	*Yishma'El*
Castilla	*Castilla, Geroush Sepharad*
Shalom for ex-*conversos* from western Europe	*Shalom*
Kyana or *Cana* for Jews from Lucania in Italy	*Kyana*
Catalan also known as *Catalunia, Catalanish, Catalnits, Gerush-Catalan*	*Catalan Yashan, Catalan Hadash*
Otranto also known as *Ontrento* for Jews from Naples	*Otranto*
Evora for Jews from Evora in Portugal	*Evora*
Italia also known as *Italiani* or *Italiano*	*Italia Yashan, Italia Hadash, Italia Shalom*
Estrok a splinter group from the *Otranto* synagogue	*Estruk*
Aragon	*Aragon*
Beth Aharon a splinter group from *Sicilia* synagogue	*Beth Aharon*
Yehya (from ben Yehya family) also known as *Kehillah Kedoshah Orehim* (host synagoghue) for Jews not part of any other synagogue	*Yehia* (or *Orehim*)
Lisboa also known as *Lisbonne*, and *Lisbonna*	*Lisbonne Yashan, Lisbonne Hadash*
Mayor for Jews from Majorca	*Mayor*
Sicilia	*Sicilia Yashan, Sicilia Hadash*
Mograbis for Jews from North Africa	*Mograbis*

Source: Michael Molho "Les Synagogues de Salonique" (Synagogues of Salonica) in Carasso, *Les Juifs de Salonique, 1492–1943*. Reproduced with permission of publisher, Elie Carasso.

GENEALOGICAL RESOURCES
Turkish Imperial Archives
Because of the centuries Salonica was part of the Ottoman Empire, the Prime Minister's Archives (*Bashbakanlik Arshivi*) in Istanbul is an extremely important resource, but under-utilized because of language difficulties previously discussed. See chapter 14, Turkey and the Ottoman Empire, for more details.

Macedonian State Archives, Athens.
The Macedonian State Archives holds a 1912 census of Salonica, in Turkish, taken just before ceding the city to Greece.

Jewish National and University Library
Address: Hebrew University Givat Ram, Jerusalem, Israel
Mailing Address: P.O.Box 503, Jerusalem 91004, Israel
Website: http://jnul.huji.ac.il
Access: varies according to department; mostly Sunday-Thursday, 9am-1or 5 pm; most departments closed Friday afternoon and Saturday

The library holds copies of *pinkasssim* (registers) of Salonika (and Janina) in its Institute of Microfilmed Hebrew Records.

Central Archives for the History of the Jewish People
Address: Hebrew University Campus, Sprinzak Bldg, Givat Ram, Jerusalem, Israel.
Mailing address: P.O. Box 1149, Jerusalem 91010, Israel.
Telephone: (972)-2-5635716

The Central Archives for the History of the Jewish People has records from Salonika, mostly of historical rather than genealogical value.

United States Holocaust Memorial Museum in Washington D.C.
Address: 100 Raoul Wallenberg Place, SW, Washington, D.C., 20024, U.S.A.
Access: 10 am–5:30 pm every day including weekends
Library: 10 am–5 p.m
Archives: 10 am–5 pm, Monday–Friday

The Osobyi Archives (Center for preservation of Historical Documentary Collections) in Moscow holds extensive archives of Jewish and Holocaust records confiscated by the Red Army from Nazi Germany at the end of World War II. These records had been unavailable to researchers until very recently. Copies of most of this collection are now held in Washington D.C. in record group RG

11.001 (especially 11.001.20) and include 450 files for Greece, the majority of which are for Salonika and the rest for Athens. They are written mostly in Solitreo and include rabbinical records of circumcisions, marriages, and deaths, and records from the Eretz Israel office in Salonika detailing migration from Salonika and other parts of Greece to Palestine.[14] They also include B'nai B'rith records for Yugoslavia and Greece.

YIVO Institute for Jewish Research, New York.
Address: YIVO Institute for Jewish Research, The Center for Jewish History,
    15 West 16th Street, New York, NY 10011-6301, USA
Telephone: (212) 246-6080
Fax: (212) 292-1892
Email: yivomail@yivo.cjh.org
Website: www.yivoinstitute.org
Access: reading room is open to researchers, Monday-Thursday, 9:30 am-5:30 pm

YIVO holds a collection of Jewish vital records of Salonika from the 1920s.

SUGGESTED READING

Angel, Marc D. *The Jews of Rhodes: The History of a Sephardic Community*. New York: Sepher-Hermon Press, 1978.

———. *La America: The Sephardic Experience in the United States*. Philadelphia: Jewish Publication Society of America, 1982.

Arditti, Benjamin. *Yehudei Bulgaria bishnot hamishtar hanatsi, 1940–1944* (Jews of Bulgaria during the years of the Nazi regime, 1940–1944). Tel Aviv, Author, 1962.

Benbassa, Esther, and Aron Rodriguez, eds. *A Sephardi Life in Southeastern Europe: The Autobiography and Journal of Gabriel Arie, 1863–1939*. Seattle: University of Washington Press, 1998.

Carasso, Elie ed. *Les Juifs de Salonique, 1492–1943* (Jews of Salonica, 1492–1943). Tarascon, France: Cousins de Salonique, 1993.

Chary, Frederick B. *The Bulgarian Jews and the Final Solution 1940–1944*. Pittsburgh: University of Pittsburgh Press, 1972.

Elazar, Daniel. *The Balkan Jewish Communities: Yugoslavia, Bulgaria, Greece, and Turkey*. Lanham, Md.: University Press of America, 1984.

Emmanuel, Isaac Samuel. *Gedole Salonica le doratam* (Great Jews of Salonica). Tel Aviv: Defus A. Strod, 1936.

———. *Histoire des Israelites de Salonique* (History of the Jews of Salonica). Paris: Thonon, 1936.

---

[14] Yitzhak Kerem, "Sources on Greek Jewry in the Special Archives in Moscow," *Sharsheret Hadorot* 7, no. 2 (April 1993).

———. *Matsevoth Saloniki* (Salonican tombstones). Jerusalem: Ben Zvi Institute, 1963.

Entsiklopedyah shel galuyot (Encyclopedia of the Jewish diaspora), c.f. Bulgaria.

Freidenreich, Harriet Pass. *The Jews of Yugoslavia: A Quest for Community.* Philadelphia: Jewish Publication Society, 1979.

Gaon, Solomon and Mitchell M. Serels, eds. *Del fuego: Sephardim and the Holocaust.* New York: Sepher-Hermon Press, 1995.

Kerem, Yitzhak. "Sources on Greek Jewry in the Special Archives in Moscow." *Sharsheret Hadorot* 7, no. 2 (April 1993).

Matkovski, Alexander. *A History of the Jews in Macedonia.* Skopje, Yugoslavia: Macedonian Review Editions, 1982.

Mezan, Saul. *Les Juifs Espagnols en Bulgarie* (Spanish Jews in Bulgaria). Sofia, Bulgaria: Amichpat, 1925.

Modiano, Mario. *Hamehune Modilliano: The Genealogical Story of the Modiano Family from ~1570 to Our Days.* Athens: Author, 2000.

Molho, Michael. "Les Synagogues de Salonique" (Synagogues of Salonica). In Carasso, Elie, ed. *Les Juifs de Salonique, 1492–1943* (Tarascon, France: Cousins de Salonique, 1993).

Nehama, Joseph. *Histoire des Israélites de Salonique* (History of the Jews of Salonica). 7 vols. London : World Sephardi Federation, 1935–78. History of the early Jewish community of Salonica.

Recanati, David, ed. *Zichron Saloniki, Gedulata Vehurvata Shel Yerushalayim Debalkan.* Tel Aviv: Havaad Lehotsaat Sefer Kehilat Saloniki, 1972.

Rozanes, Shlomo Avraham. *Korot hayehudim beturkia vebeartzot hakedem: Divrei yemai yisrael betogarma al-pi mekorot rishonoim* (History of the Jews of Turkey and of the Middle East). 6 vols. Vol. 1, Tel Aviv, 1930; Vols 2–5, Sofia, Bulgaria, 1934–8; Vol. 6, Jerusalem, 1948.

Tamir, Vicky. *Bulgaria and Her Jews: The History of a Dubious Symbiosis.* New York: Sepher-Hermon Press for Yeshiva University Press, 1979.

Source: Reprinted with permission of the publisher. Esther Benbassa and Aron Rodrigue, *Sephardi Jewry: A History of the Judeo-Spanish Community, 14th-20th Centuries. Berkeley, California*: University of California Press, 2000.

Figure 16. Map of the Ottoman Empire in Europe, 1574

Source: Reprinted with permission of the publisher. Esther Benbassa and Aron Rodrigue, *Sephardi Jewry: A History of the Judeo-Spanish Community, 14th-20th Centuries*. Berkeley, California: University of California Press, 2000.

Figure 17. Map of the Ottoman Empire in Europe, 1813

Source: Reprinted with permission of the publisher. Esther Benbassa and Aron Rodrigue, *Sephardi Jewry: A History of the Judeo-Spanish Community, 14th-20th Centuries*. Berkeley, California: University of California Press, 2000.

Figure 18. Map of the Balkans after World War I

202 • *Sephardic Genealogy: Discovering Your Sephardic Ancestors and Their World*

26.
ITALY

Jewish presence in Italy is ancient indeed; Jews composed 10 percent of the population of the Roman Empire in the Mediterranean region (see Table 1.). Jewish communities existed in Imperial Rome and in several other locations in Roman Italy. Yet the numbers of Jews on the Italian Peninsula remained relatively small compared to the significant proportion of the general population of Jews represented on the Iberian Peninsula.

Facing discrimination, forced to live in ghettos,[1] and prohibited by law from owning land, Jews were unable to join the vast majority of the surrounding population that earned its livelihood from agriculture; they were forced, therefore, into becoming money lenders and merchants. Ironically, these livelihoods made them relatively prosperous as a group.

From antiquity on, Jews continued to live in Italy until modern times. The largest concentrations have been in Rome and the Kingdom of the Two Sicilies. In 1492, the Jewish presence in Italy was augmented by Jews expelled from Spain, and, a century or more later, by *conversos* escaping from Portugal.

HISTORY

Although the history of Italy is complex, it is essential to have a basic understanding before researching Italian ancestry. The reader is referred to the Suggested Reading section at the end of this chapter for additional references on the history of Italy and other topics of genealogical interest.

During the Middle Ages, Italy was composed of as many as 15 separate states. By the 15th century, the number of states had shrunk to 10, but it was not until 1861 that a unified Italy came into existence. First a monarchy in 1861 with Turin as its capital,[2] in 1946 Italy became a republic.

Before unification, the northern Italian states had been under Austrian influence and the southern mainland part of the Kingdom of the Two Sicilies, ruled by the Bourbons from Naples. Between these two areas lay the Papal States ruled by the Pope in Rome. These states all differed in history and attitudes, dialect and culture. They also differed in how they treated their Jewish

---

[1] The generic term ghetto is said to have arisen from the name of the Venice Ghetto (foundry) in Italy.

[2] Victor Emmanuel II was the first king of an Italy newly unified through the efforts primarily of his prime minister Cavour and Garibaldi's "red-shirts" followers. At that time Rome still belonged to the Vatican and the Papal state. Rome did not become incorporated into the Kingdom of Italy until 1870.

inhabitants. Historians point out that until the mid-19th century, Latin, not Italian, was the lingua franca on the peninsula and that as late as 1860, only one of eight Italians could speak Italian. Because the history and conditions of Jews varied so markedly, one cannot make broad generalizations about Jewish life in Italy before the 20th century.

Although it is commonly believed that northern Italy's Jews are primarily Ashkenazic and Jews in the south are Sephardic, careful scrutiny reveals many exceptions. Livorno in northern Italy was a Tuscan port developed by Sephardim and populated by Spanish and some North African Jews. Many Sephardic families in North Africa and Turkey came originally from Venice or other towns throughout Italy.

At the southern tip of Italy, the Kingdom of the Two Sicilies was a dependency of the Crown of Aragon. Therefore, in 1493, the Crown forced its Sicilian Jews, too, to choose between conversion or expulsion. Many of the expelled southern Italian Jews moved north to the Papal States, while some sought refuge outside Italy. Congregations of Sicilian Jews established themselves in Salonica,[3] Istanbul, Greece (in the towns of Patras, Lepanto, Arta, Yanina, and others), Syria (Damascus[4] and Syrian Tripoli), Cairo, and many other places. Where they settled, these Sicilian congregations endeavored to retain their language and their familiar Sicilian rite. Schwarzfuchs relates that Sicilian *hazzanot* (cantorial prayers) were still being said in Salonica as late as 1935 and were published in Venice in 1580 and 1585 under the title "*hazorim* according to the usage of the Maghrebines (north Africans) who lived in Sicily."[5] In most cases, however, Italian Sephardim gradually merged into the surrounding, frequently Spanish-speaking congregations, losing their Italian dialect and adopting Spanish dialects and the Spanish rite. They thus became part of the complex blend of Jews now referred to as Sephardim.

When Spain expelled its Jews, many sought refuge in Naples, among them such notables as Isaac Abrabanel. Unfortunately, most of these Jews were later expelled from the Naples area, partially in 1510 and then finally in 1541, and forced to seek refuge elsewhere. A surprisingly large number of Sephardic families have Italian ancestry, sometimes unknown to them. Prominent Sephardic families such as the Abrabanels of Spain, the Camondos of Turkey, the Montefiores of England, and the Mosseris of Egypt are among the many Sephardic families that trace their origins to Venice or other towns in Italy.

---

[3] Salonica had three communities of Sicilian Jews: Old Sicily (Kal de Madero), New Sicily (Kal de los pescadores), and the Beth Aaron congregation.

[4] In 1521 Damascus had three Sephardic synagogues: one for each of its Spanish, Moriscos, and Sicilian congregations.

[5] Simon Schwarzfuchs, "The Sicilian Jewish Communities in the Ottoman Empire" *Italia judaica: Gli ebrei in Sicilia sino all'espulsione del 1492: atti del convegno internazionale, Palermo, 15–19 guigno 1992.* Rome: Ministero per I beni culturali e ambientali, Ufficio centrale per I beni archivisti, 1995.

Italy is an important resource in the genealogy of Sephardim who believe their roots began elsewhere—because many Jews throughout North Africa and the Balkans claimed Italian ancestry or Italian protection for political or business reasons. A person's right to Italian nationality is based on providing proof of the family being of Italian ancestry that had never officially been renounced. The exact requirements for this proof varied in different countries. Many Sephardim living in North Africa and Balkan countries found it advantageous to claim Italian ancestry based on such claims of Italian ancestry. Some of these claims were legitimate, but sometimes Italian consulates in North Africa or Turkey granted Italian nationality with little scrutiny of the evidence for these claims. Sometimes Italian nationality or protection was granted for political reasons.

Once Italian nationality was bestowed and a person was recorded as an Italian living abroad, the Italian consulates attempted to keep records of their families and forwarded the birth, death, and marriage information they collected to the Italian ancestral municipalities of record—where the researcher would find them today.

RESEARCH STRATEGIES

In the Italian townships after 1870, birth, death, and marriage information has been collected on standard forms, usually at the mayor's office. These records are kept in the municipal archives (*archivi communale*).

Registrations from smaller villages (*frazioni di communi*) with no mayors or archives are kept in the municipal archives in their parent administrative area. An annual index of vital records (*stato civile*) is maintained by the same authorities, a valuable research aid to the researcher.

Provincial state archives (*archivi di stato*) typically hold registrations and records before 1870 and also receive from municipal authorities copies of vital records older than 75 years.

With rare exceptions, only archives employees are authorized to search municipal records. Because the employees do not do extensive searches, the researcher must give information as accurately as possible on a person's name and dates. In the regional *archivio di stato*, genealogists can do their own searches. At the archives, it is important to ask for an extract (*estratto del'atto*) of the vital records and not just a certificate. The former contains much more information than the latter.[6] The Church of Jesus Christ of Latter-day Saints (Mormons) has microfilmed many records of the *archivi di stato*. These microfilms can be accessed easily through the Family History Centers the church maintains all over the world (see below).

---

[6] John Philip Colletta, *Finding Italian roots: the complete guide for Americans* (Baltimore, Md.: Genealogical Pub. Co., 1996).

How does one find the ancestral town of origin in Italy? The first steps are to interview the elders in the family and to scrutinize family documents or published genealogies. The name of the ancestral town may become evident by consulting Schaert's *I Cognomi degli Ebrei d'Italia* (Surnames of the Jews of Italy) which lists the ancestral towns of many Italian families.[7] Then consult Sacerdoti's *Guida all'Italia Ebraica* (Guide to Jewish Italy), which has information on the many current or former Jewish communities in Italy.[8]

Vital Records

Besides the ancestor's original Italian name (which may be a variant of the current family name) and the time period in Italy for the ancestor to be searched, the most important bit of information is the name of the ancestral town of origin. Vital records (*stato civile*) of birth, death, and marriage in Italy repose, not in a centralized national or even regional repository, but in municipal archives (*archivi communale*) of the townships and cities of Italy. Similarly, Jewish records that still exist will be found in the synagogues in these ancestral towns, although some older records may have been transferred to the state archives (*archivio di stato*).

An understanding of Italy's history—especially since Napoleon Bonaparte's invasion—and the structure of the modern state is essential for a meaningful and productive search of vital records in Italy.

In 1796, Napoleon Bonaparte invaded and conquered Italy. He named himself king of a unified Italy (1796–1815) that extended throughout Italy, except for the islands of Sicily and Sardinia. This conquest was a landmark event for genealogists. Napoleon organized Italy into a centralized administration with essentially the same system of regions, provinces, and municipalities (*communi*) that exists today. Napoleon also instituted civil registration of births, deaths, and marriages throughout Italy using standardized forms to record information uniformly throughout the kingdom. (For the period prior to universal registration, records available to researchers are mostly those of persons of importance or those who were wealthy enough to be taxed.) After Napoleon's defeat in 1815, the Congress of Vienna once again divided Italy into smaller individual states and restored all the old rulers and boundaries. The civil registrations Napoleon had instituted were discontinued in most of Italy, with some exceptions.[9]

---

[7] Samuele Schaert, *I Cognome degli Ebrai d'Italia* (Surnames of the Jews of Italy) (Florence: Casa Editrice Israel, 1925).

[8] Annie Sacerdoti, *Guida alla'Italia Ebraica* (Guide to Jewish Italy) (Casale Monferrato, Italy: Casa Editrice Marietti, 1986). There is a somewhat abridged English version: Annie Sacerdoti *Guide to Jewish Italy*. (Brooklyn, N.Y.: Israelowitz, 1989). Though not as extensive as the Italian original, it is useful for those who have trouble reading Italian.

[9] Colletta notes that the records of the province of Toscana are continuous since 1808, and the

Registration of births, deaths, and marriages resumed on a national scale during the period 1866–70, after Italy was again unified within today's borders, a gradual unification begun in 1850 and completed in 1870. These vital records consist of birth records (*atto di nascita*), death certificates (*atto di morte*), and marriage certificates (*atto della solenne prommessa di celebrare il matrimonio*). As noted above, they are kept in municipal archives (*archivi comunale*) throughout the country. The Mormons have microfilmed many of the archived records.

Today's Italy is composed of 20 regions (*regioni*) subdivided into 94 provinces (*provincie*) that bear the name of their principal cities (see Figure 19 and Table 3). Each province has a provincial state archive (*archivio di stato*), with an additional central archive in Rome (*Archivio Centrale dello Stato*). The 94 Italian provinces are composed of townships and villages. The Central State Archive (*Archivio Centrale dello Stato*) in Rome is the national Italian archive, the repository for governmental records of relatively little genealogical value.

Church of Jesus Christ of Latter-day Saints (Mormons)
Address: 35 North West Temple Street, Salt Lake City, Utah, 84150-3400
Telephone: 801-240-2331 or 800-453-3860 ext 22331
FAX: 801-240-1584
E-mail: fhl@ldschurch.org
Website: www.familysearch.org
See also www.jewishgen.org/databases/FHLC for database of Jewish items.

The Mormon Library holds copies of:
- *Registri dello stato civile* (Births, marriages, deaths, census), Parma, 1817–1845 (film 755727)
- *Registri dello stato civile* from the district of the Università Israelitica of Urbino, Pesaro e Urbino, 1861–1865 (film 1962979)
- Holocaust war crimes cases, 1945–1959 (numerous films)
- *Registri dello stato civile*, Mantova, 1770–1899, (films 1618972 , 1618698-1646524).
- *Registri dello stato civile*, Modena, 1681–1852 (films 1114773-75, and 1102179)
- *Registri dello stato civile*, Reggio Emilia, 1689–1894, (films 1424445, 1424447, 1442485, and 1443230)

Censuses
National Italian censuses (*censimenti*) exist for the years 1861, 1871, 1881, 1891, and 1901, and at varying intervals for the years beyond 1921. Censuses taken

---

registrations in the kingdom of Sicily, which remained under French control, are continuous since 1820. Some records on the mainland extend continuously to 1809.

before 1921 are open to the public and may be consulted in the state archives (*archivi di stato*).

JEWISH RECORDS

Because Jews have lived in Italy for so long, some Jewish records exist that are much older than government records. Records of Jewish congregations in Italy usually still can be found in the local synagogues or in the municipal archives (*archivi comunali*) or state archives (*archivi di stato*). Livorno has marriage records from the 17th century and birth records from the 18th century.[10] Censuses of Livorno Jews from 1809 and 1841 are available in published form.[11] Copies of many Italian Jewish community records can also be found in Israel.

Many ancient Jewish cemeteries remain throughout Italy. Consult Sacerdoti's *Guida alla'Italia Ebraica* or *Guide to Jewish Italy*.[12] *Etsi* has published a detailed list of archival resources for the Jews of Leghorn (Livorno) and Pisa.[13] Because of the unique history of Livorno as a sanctuary for exiles from Spain,[14] Livorno is often a useful focus of Sephardic research. The *Etsi* article also includes a long list of names extracted from an 1809 document declaring Jewish names from Livorno, Pisa, and Portoferraio.

NOTARIAL RECORDS

Some Italian notarial records go back to the 14th century, and much information about Jews can be gleaned from them. Notarial records documented sales of land, loans of money, and other transactions. Italian notarial records can be as informative as those of Spain (see chapter 2, Early Spanish Records), but they have not been as extensively mined as they could be.

In 1986 Shlomo Simonsohn collected, translated into English, and printed in a four-volume set all the notarial records he found concerning Jews who lived in the Milan area in the period from the Middle Ages to the 16th century. The collection provides insight into the wealth of genealogical information contained in Italian notarial records.[15]

---

[10] Morris L. Bierbrier "Tracing your ancestry in Italy and the Ottoman Empire" Madelyn Travis ed. *Syllabus: 21st International Conference on Jewish Genealogy* (London: JGS 2001, 2001).
[11] For the 1841 Livorno census, see Luzzatto, *Ebrei di Livorno tra due censimenti (1841–1938): Memoria familiare et identita* (Jews of Livorno through two censuses (1841-1938): Family memories and identity). (Livorno: Commune di Livorno Belforte, 1990). This book, and several others, also provide extensive genealogy charts for several Jewish families. The 1809 Livorno census is published in J. F. Filippini, *Rivista Italiana di Studi Napoleonici* 19 (1982), 77–113.
[12] Sacerdoti, *Guida alla'Italia Ebraica*.
[13] Nardo Bonomi "The Jews of Leghorn : Archival sources" Etsi 4, no 13 (June 2001).
[14] See also chapter on Tunisia and its *grana* community.
[15] Shlomo Simonsohn, *Bibliografia per la storia degli Ebrei in Italia, 1986–1995* (Bibliography of the history of the Jews of Italy, 1986-1995). *Biblioteca Italo-ebraica*. Rome and Tel Aviv: Menorah University, 1997. (Publication of the Diaspora Research Institute).

OTHER RECORDS

Certificate of family status (*Certificato di stato di famiglia*) is a uniquely Italian document. Most townships have tried to maintain them since 1911; for some towns they exist from 1870. This certificate lists the known members of an Italian family, including such genealogically useful information as their ages; birth, death, and marriage dates; and much more. When available, this certificate can be obtained from the office of vital records (*ufficcio di stato civile*) of the township in which the family resided.

Certificates of residency (*certificato di residenza*) obtainable from municipal authorities (mayor's office) record ancestors' addresses of record in Italy. This certificate is the basis for the issuance of the Identification cards (*carta d'identita*) Italians carry with them. For ancestors still living in Italy after Italy's unification in 1870, these documents can provide valuable information, including unsuspected relatives and dates when they may have moved into or out of Italy.

Draft registration lists (*registri degli uffici di leva*), available since 1870, are kept in the National Archives (*Archivio Central dello Stato*) in Rome. After unification, all Italian males were required to register for military conscription. As a result, these records can provide useful information for Italians during the years following unification.

Property and tax records (*catasti or rivelli*), some of which go back to the 14th century, may be useful. They are usually found in the state archives (*archivi de stato*), except for those of the Papal States, which are kept in Vatican Secret Archives (*Archivio Secreto del Vaticano*).

ITALIAN SCRIPT

Ancient documents written in Italian script can present difficulties for researchers unaccustomed to the style. Many of the individual letters are easily confused with other letters. A guide to decipher this ancient writing style is found in Nelson's *A Genealogist's Guide to Discovering your Italian Ancestors*.[16]

WEBSITES

The reader is referred to Part IV, Internet for a list of websites that could be helpful for Italian genealogy.

SUGGESTED READING

Abensur Hazan, Laurence. *Les Pontremoli: Deux dynasties rabbiniques en Turquie et en Italie: Sources et documents* (The Pontremoli: two rabbinic dynasties in Turkey and Italy: Sources and documents). Paris: Author, 1997.

---

[16] Lynn Nelson, *A Genealogist's Guide to Discovering your Italian Ancestors* (Cincinnati, Ohio: Betterway Books, 1997).

Avrahami, Hannah. *The Jews of Livorno and Their relations with Tunis in the 17th and 18th Centuries* (in Hebrew). Thesis, Ramat Gan University, 1979.

Bruckmayer, Daniel. *Dizionario degli ebrei* (Dictionary of the Jews). Rome: Ed. Carucci, 1985.

Caselli, Paola. *Italia judaica: Gli ebrei in Sicilia sino all'espulsione del 1492* (Jews in Sicily after the 1492 expulsion) *[in Atti del V convegno internazionale, Palermo 15-19 giugno 1992]*. Rome: Ministero per i beni culturali e ambientali, Ufficio centrale per i beni archivistici, 1995.

Cole, Trafford R. *Italian Genealogical Records: How to Use Italian Civil, Ecclesiastical, and Other Records in Family History Research.* Salt Lake City: Ancestry, 1995.

Colletta, John Philip. *Finding Italian Roots: The Complete Guide for Americans.* Baltimore: Genealogical Publishing Co., 1996.

Filippini, Jean-Pierre. "*Le Port de Livourne et la Toscane, 1676-1814*" (Port of Leghorn and Tuscany, 1676-1814). Doct. thesis, University of Paris, 1990.

———. *Livorno e gli Ebrei dell' Africa del Nord nel settecento* (Leghorn and the Jews of North Africa during the 1700s). Florence: Ed. Olschski, 1990.

Frattarelli Fisher, Lucia. "*Portoghesi, ebrei ponentini ed ebrei levantini nella Toscana dei Medici (1549-1737)*" (Portuguese, Pontine and Levantine Jews in Medici's Tuscany (1549-1737). *Le migrazioni internazionali dal medioevo all'età contemporanea: Il caso italiano, Roma 11-12 gennaio 1990.* Rome, 1990.

Luzzatto, Aldo. *Biblioteca Italo-Evraica* (Italian-Jewish library). Milan: Franco Angeli Libri, 1989. Bibliography in multiple languages.

———. *Ebrei di Livorno tra due censimenti (1841-1938): Memoria familiare et identita* (Jews of Livorno through two censuses (1841-1938): Family memoires and identity). Livorno: Commune di Livorno Belforte, 1990. Family trees and list of Jews in the 1841 census, with details of their ages, addresses, citizenship status, professions, and family members, and additional remarks.

———. *La communita ebraica di Venezia e il suo antico cimitero* (Jewish community of Venice and its ancient cemetery). 2 vols. Milan: Il Polifilo, 2000. Biographical references and index.

Mack Smith, Dennis. *Italy: A Modern History.* Ann Arbor: University of Michigan, 1969.

Nelson, Lynn. *A Genealogist's Guide to Discovering your Italian Ancestors.* Cincinnati, Oh.: Betterway Books, 1997.

Pavoncello, Nello. *Antiche famiglie ebraiche italiane* (Ancient Jewish Italian families). Rome: Carucci editore, 1982. Several old Jewish families and their names.

Sacerdoti, Annie. *Guida alla'Italia Ebraica* (Guide to Jewish Italy). Casale Monferrato, Italy: Casa Editrice Marietti, 1986.

———. *Guide to Jewish Italy.* Brooklyn, N.Y.: Israelowitz, 1989. Abridged version of the Italian-language book by the same author.

Schaert, Samuele. *I Cognome degli Ebrai d'Italia* (Surnames of the Jews of Italy). Florence: Casa Editrice Israel, 1925. Many Italian Jewish family names.

Schwarzfuchs, Simon. "The Sicilian Jewish Communities in the Ottoman Empire". *Italia judaica: Gli ebrei in Sicilia sino all'espulsione del 1492: atti del convegno internazionale, Palermo, 15–19 guigno 1992*. Rome: Ministero per I beni culturali e ambientali, Ufficio centrale per I beni archivisti, 1995.

Simonsohn, Shlomo. *Bibliografia per la storia degli Ebrei in Italia, 1986–1995* (Bibliography of the history of the Jews of Italy, 1986–1995) (in Italian and Hebrew). *Biblioteca Italo-ebraica*. Rome and Tel Aviv: Menorah University, 1997. (Publication of the Diaspora Research Institute.

Toaff, Renzo. *La Nazione ebrea a Livorno e a Pisa, 1591–1700* (Hebrew Nation in Livorno and Pisa). Florence: Ed. Olschski, 1990.

Yerushalmi, Yosef Hayim. *From Spanish Court to Italian Ghetto: Isaac Cardoso, a Study in Seventeenth-Century Marranism and Jewish Apologetics*. New York: Columbia University Press, 1971; Seattle: University of Washington Press, 1981.

Source: Lynn Nelson, "A Genealogist's Guide to Discovering Your Italian Ancestors" copyright © 1997 by Lynn Nelson. Used with permission of Betterway Books, an imprint of F&W Publications, Inc. All rights reserved.

Figure 19. Modern Italy: Regions and Provincial Capital Cities

Table 3. Italian Provinces and Archival Addresses

Region	Province Today	Province Name before 1870	State Archive Address
Abruzzo	Chieti	Abruzzo Citra	Archivio di Stato di Chieti Via F. Ferri, 27 66100 Chietti, Italia
	L'Aquila	Abruzzo Ultra	Archivio di Stato di L'Aquila Piazza della Republica, 9 67100 L'Aquila, Italia
	Pescara	Abruzzo Ultra 1	Archivio di Stato di Pescara Piazza della marina, 2/4 65126 Pescara, Italia
	Teramo	Abruzzo Ultra 1	Archivio di Stato di Teramo Via Delfico, 16 64100 Teramo, Italia
Basilicata	Matera	Basilicata	Archivio di Stato di Matera Via Stigliani, 25 75100 Matera, Italia
	Potenza	Basilicata	Archivio di Stato di Potenza Via Due Torri, 33 85100 Potenza, Italia
Calabria	Catanzaro	Calabria I'Ltra 2	Archivio di Stato di Catanzaro Piazza Rosario, 6 88100 Catanzaro, Italia
	Cosenza	Calabria Citra	Archivio di Stato di Cosenza Via Miceli, 67/71 87100 Cosenza, Italia
	Reggio Calabria	Calabria I'Ltra 1	Archivio di Stato di Reggio Calabria Argine Destro Annunziata, 59/61 89100 Reggio Calabria, Italia
Campania	Avellino	Principato I'Ltra	Archivio di Stato di Avellino Via S. Soldi, 9 83100 Avellino, Italia
	Benevento	Principato I'Ltra	Archivio di Stato di Benevento Via dei Mulini, 148 82100 Benevento, Italia
	Caserta	Molise, Principato I'Ltra, Terra Di Lavoro	Archivio di Stato di Caserta Via Appia, 1 81100 Caserta, Italia
	Napoli	Lavoro	Archivio di Stato di Napoli Piazzetta Grande Archivio, 5 80138 Napoli, Italia

Chapter 26: Italy

Region	Province Today	Province Name before 1870	State Archive Address
	Salerno	Napoli, Terra Di Lavoro, Principato Ctira	Archivio di Stato di Salerno Piazza Abate Conforti, 7 84100 Salerno, Italia
Emilia-Romagna	Bologna	Bologna	Archivio di Stato di Bologna Piazza Celestini, 4 40123 Bologna, Italia
	Ferrara	Ferrara	Archivio di Stato di Ferrara Corso Giovecca, 146 44100 Ferrara, Italia
	Forli	Forli	Archivio di Stato di Forli Via dei Gerolimini, 6 47100 Forli, Italia
	Modena	Modena, Bologna	Archivio di Stato di Modena Corso Cavour, 21 41100 Modena, Italia
	Parma	Parma, Modena	Archivio di Stato di Parma Via d'Azeglio 43100 Parma, Italia
	Piacenza	Parma	Archivio di Stato di Piacenza Piazza Cittadella, 29, 29100 Piacenza, Italia
	Ravenna	Ravenna	Archivio di Stato di Ravenna Via Guaccimanni, 51 48100 Ravenna, Italia
	Regio Emilia	Modena	Archivio di Stato di Reggio Emilia Via B. Cairoli, 6 42100 Reggio Emilia, Italia
Fruili-Venezia Guilia	Gorizia	Part of Austria	Archivio di Stato di Gorizia Via dell'Ospitale, 2 34170 Gorizia, Italia
	Pordenone	Belluno, Udine	Archivio di Stato di Pordenone Via Monreale, 7 33170 Pordenone, Italia
	Trieste	Part of Austria	Archivio di Stato di Trieste Via La Marmora, 17 31139 Trieste, Italia
	Udine	Udine	Archivio di Stato di Udine Via Urbanis, 1 33100 Udine, Italia
Lazio	Frosinone	Frosinone	Archivio di Stato di Frosinone Piazza de Mattheis, 41 03100 Frosinone, Italia

Region	Province Today	Province Name before 1870	State Archive Address
	Latina	Velletri, Frosinone	Archivio di Stato di Latina Via dei Piceni, 24 04100 Latina, Italia
	Rieti	Rieti	Archivio di Stato di Rieti Viale Ludovico Canali, 7 02100 Rieti, Italia
	Roma	Roma	Archivio di Stato di Roma Corso Rinascimento, 40 00186 Roma, Italia
	Viterbo	Civita Vecchia, Viterbo	Archivio di Stato di Viterbo Via Romiti 01100 Viterbo, Italia
Liguria	Genova	Genova	Archivio di Stato di Genova Via Tommaso Reggio, 14 16123 Genova, Italia
	Imperia	Savona	Archivio di Stato di Imperia Via Matteotti, 105 18100 Imperia, Italia
	La Spezia	Genova	Archivio di Stato di La Spezia Via Galvani, 21 19100 La Spezia, Italia
	Savona	Savona	Archivio di Stato di Savona Via Quarda Superiore, 7 17100 Savona, Italia
Lombardia	Bergamo	Bergamo	Archivio di Stato di Bergamo Via Tasso, 84 24100 Bergamo, Italia
	Brescia	Brescia	Archivio di Stato di Brescia Via Galilei, 44 25124 Brescia, Italia
	Como	Como	Archivio di Stato di Como Via Briantea, 8 22100 Como, Italia
	Cremona	Cremona	Archivio di Stato di Cremona Via Antica Porta Tintoria, 2 26100 Cremona, Italia
	Mantova	Mantua	Archivio di Stato di Mantova Via Ardigo, 11 46100 Mantova, Italia
	Milano	Milano, Lodi, Pavia	Archivio di Stato di Milano Via Senato, 10 20121 Milano, Italia

Chapter 26: Italy • 215

Region	Province Today	Province Name before 1870	State Archive Address
	Pavia	Allessandria, Novara, Vercelli	Archivio di Stato di Pavia Via Cardano, 45 27100 Pavia, Italia
	Sondrio	Sondrio	Archivio di Stato di Sondrio Largo Mallero Cadorna, 28 23100 Sondrio, Italia
	Varese	Como, Milano	Archivio di Stato di Varese Via Col. di Lana, 5 21100 Varese, Italia
Marche	Ancona	Ancona, Urbino	Archivio di Stato di Ancona Via Maggini, 80 60127 Ancona, Italia
	Ascoli Piceno	Macerata	Archivio di Stato di Ascoli Piceno Via S. Serafino da Montegranaro 8/c 63100 Ascoli Piceno, Italia
	Macerata	Ancona, Macerata	Archivio di Stato di Macerata Corso F Cairoli, 175 62100 Macerata, Italia
	Pesaro-Urbino	Urbino	Archivio di Stato di Pesaro Via Neviera, 44 61100 Pesaro, Italia
Molise	Campobasso	Capitanata, Molise	Archivio di Stato di Campobasso Via Orefici, 43 86100 Campobasso, Italia
	Isernia	Molise	Archivio di Stato di Isernia Via Testa, 27 86170 Isernia, Italia
Piemonte	Alessandria	Alessandria	Archivio di Stato di Alessandria Via Solero, 42, 15100 Alessandria, Italia
	Asti	Coni	Archivio di Stato di Asti Piazzetta Dell'Archivio, 1 14100 Asti, Italia
	Cuneo	Coni	Archivio di Stato di Cuneo Via Monte Lovetto, 28 12100 Cuneo, Italia
	Novara	Novara	Archivio di Stato di Novara Via Archivio, 2 28100 Novara, Italia
	Torino	Torino	Archivio di Stato di Torino Via S. Chiara, 40 10100 Torino, Italia

Region	Province Today	Province Name before 1870	State Archive Address
	Vercelli	Vercelli	Archivio di Stato di Vercelli Via Manzoni, 11 13100 Vercelli, Italia
Puglia	Bari	Terra di Bari	Archivio di Stato di Bari Via L. Bissolati, 3 70125 Bari, Italia
	Brindisi	Terra d'Otranto	Archivio di Stato di Brindisi Piazza Santa Teresa, 4 72100 Brindisi, Italia
	Foggia	Capitanata	Archivio di Stato di Foggia Piazza XX Settembre 71100 Foggia, Italia
	Lecce	Terra d'Otranto	Archivio di Stato di Lecce Via Carafa, 15 73100 Lecce, Italia
	Taranto	Terra d'Otanto	Archivio di Stato di Taranto Via di Polonia (Palma) 74100 Taranto, Italia
Sardegna	Cagliari	Cagliari	Archivio di Stato di Cagliari Via Gallura, 2 09125 Cagliari, Italia
	Nuoro	Nuoro	Archivio di Stato di Nuoro Via Oggiano, 22 08100 Nuoro, Italia
	Oristano	Nuoro	Archivio di Stato di Oristano Via Ciuso, 2 09170 Oristano, Italia
	Sassari	Sassari	Archivio di Stato di Sassari Corse Angioy, 1 07100 Sassari, Italia
Sicilia	Agrigento	Caltanisetta, Girgenti	Archivio di Stato di Agrigento Via Mazzini, 187 92100 Agrigento, Italia
	Caltanissetta	Caltanisetta	Archivio di Stato di Caltanissetta Via Borsellino, 2-2a 93100 Caltanissetta, Italia
	Catania	Catania	Archivio di Stato di Catania Via Vittorio Emanuele, 156 65131 Catania, Italia
	Enna	Catania	Archivio di Stato di Enna Via Scifitello, 20 94100 Enna, Italia

Region	Province Today	Province Name before 1870	State Archive Address
	Messina	Messina	Archivio di Stato di Messina Via 24 maggio, 291 98100 Messina, Italia
	Palermo	Palermo	Archivio di Stato di Palermo Corso Vittorio Emanuele, 31 90133 Palermo, Italia
	Ragusa	Siragosa	Archivio di Stato di Ragusa Viale del Fante, 7 97100 Ragusa, Italia
	Siracusa	Siragosa	Archivio di Stato di Siracusa Via F. Crispi, 66 96100 Siracusa, Italia
	Trapani	Trapani	Archivio di Stato di Trapani Via Liberta, 31 91100 Trapani, Italia
Toscana	Arezzo	Arezzo	Archivio di Stato di Arezzo Via Albergotti, 1 52100 Arezzo, Italia
	Firenze	Firenze	Archivio di Stato di Firenze Viale Giovane Italie, 6 50122 Firenze, Italia
	Grosseto	Grosseto	Archivio di Stato di Grosseto Piazza Socci, 3 58100 Grosseto, Italia
	Livorno	Pisa, Grossetto	Archivio di Stato di Livorno Via Fiume, 40 (Palazzo del Governo) 57100 Livorno, Italia
	Lucca	Lucca	Archivio di Stato di Lucca Piazza Guidiccioni, 8 55100 Lucca, Italia
	Massa Carrara	Modena	Archivio di Stato di Massa Carrara Via Sforza, 3 54100 Massa, Italia
	Pisa	Pisa	Archivio di Stato di Pisa Largo Arno Mediceo, 17 56100 Pisa, Italia
	Pistoia	Firenze	Archivio di Stato di Pistoia Piazza Scuole Normali, 2 51100 Pistoia, Italia
	Siena	Siena	Archivio di Stato di Siena Via Binachi di Sotto, 52 53100 Siena, Italia

Region	Province Today	Province Name before 1870	State Archive Address
Trentino-Alto Adige	Bolzano	Part of Austria	Archivio di Stato di Bolzano Via Armando Diza, 8 39100 Bolzano, Italia
	Trento	Part of Austria	Archivio di Stato di Trento Via Maccani, 161 38100 Trento, Italia
Umbria	Perugia	Perugia	Archivio di Stato di Perugia Piazza G. Bruno, 10 06100 Perugia, Italia
	Terni	Perugia, Orvieto	Archivio di Stato di Terni Via Pozzo, 2 05100 Terni, Italia
Valle D'Aosta	Aosta	Aosta	Archivio di Stato di Aosta Via de Sales, 3 11100 Aosta, Italia
Veneto	Belluno	Belluno, Treviso	Archivio di Stato di Belluno Via S. Maria dei Battuti, 3 32100 Belluno, Italia
	Padova	Padova	Archivio di Stato di Padova Via dei Colli, 24 35143 Padova, Italia
	Rovigo	Polesina	Archivio di Stato di Rovigo Via Sichirollo 45100 Rovigo, Italia
	Treviso	Treviso	Archivio di Stato di Treviso Via A. Marchesan, 11/a 31100 Treviso, Italia
	Venezia	Venezia	Archivio di Stato di Venezia Contrado S. Polo, 3005 30100 Venezia, Italia
	Verona	Verona, Vicenza	Archivio di Stato di Verona Via Franceshine, 2/4 37122 Verona, Italia
	Vicenza	Vicenza	Archivio di Stato di Vicenza Via Borgo Casale, 91 36100 Vicenza, Italia

27.
THE NETHERLANDS

Descendants researching families that were part of the Sephardic community of The Netherlands are both very lucky and very unlucky: lucky because the records available are superb; unlucky because, sadly, the Nazis massacred most of Holland's Sephardic families. Only 25 Dutch Sephardic families have members who have survived to this day. The genealogical records available in The Netherlands are truly superb. Not only do detailed circumcision, marriage, and death records of the Sephardic community go back centuries, but records exist of civil government registrations that started in The Netherlands in 1795. In addition a wealth of other documentation and photographs is available to search through.

RECORDS AND ARCHIVES

Genealogists researching Sephardim in The Netherlands have access to civil records and Jewish community records. Civil records include the civil registrations instituted under French rule in 1796 and 1811. Local population records were kept starting in 1850; they now are found in the Central Bureau of Genealogy (*Centraal Bureau voor Genealogie*). After 1920 population records were written on family record cards (*gezinskaarten*) and between 1938 and 1994 on personal record cards (*persoonskaarten*). The archive also holds extensive newspaper, photo, and historical archives; corporation minutes;[1] and other documents that permit one to flesh out and bring to life the ancestral history, all easily accessible to the researcher.

The civil registration system consists of local registration offices (*burgerlijke*), where births, deaths, and marriages are initially recorded. These records are then transferred to city archives (*gemeentearchief*) and then progressively on to state, provincial, and national archives. Each municipality maintains its own registers. Registers created before 1925 are deposited in the municipal archives and are open to the public. Registers created after 1925 are kept at the registrar's office in each municipality, but they are closed to the public because of privacy considerations. Civil registration records are written in duplicate. The duplicates of the pre-1925 records are kept at the state's archives in the provinces. At the Central Bureau of Genealogy, microfilms of civil registration records of Amsterdam and other municipalities can be viewed on microfilm.

---

[1] Because the Dutch Sephardim played a major part in the Dutch East Indies Company and the Dutch West Indies Company, the history and minutes of these companies may also yield valuable information.

The most useful repositories of documents of interest to the Jewish genealogist in The Netherlands are the Municipal Archives of Amsterdam, the Central Bureau for Genealogy in The Hague, Netherlands Institute of War Documentation, Bibliotheca Rosenthaliana, and the Sephardic cemetery at Ouderkerk.

RESOURCES IN THE NETHERLANDS

Municipal Archives of Amsterdam (*Gemeentearchief Amsterdam*)
Street address: Amsteldijk 67, 1074 HZ Amsterdam
Telephone: +31 (0)20 572 0202
Mailing address: Post Box 51140, 1007 EC Amsterdam, The Netherlands
Website: www.gemeentearchief.amsterdam.nl
E-mail: secretariaat@gaaweb.nl
Access: Monday–Friday, 8:45 am to 4:45 pm

The Municipal Archives of Amsterdam is one of the largest city archives in the world, with its 35 kilometers of documents; one million illustrations; 700,000 photos; 150,000 books; 20,000 maps; a newspaper collection that dates from 1672; and records of corporations, family histories, and professional organizations. The following discussion highlights records of particular interest to researchers of Sephardic genealogy held by the archives.

A list of Sephardic surnames from the civil records of Amsterdam can be viewed at *www.sephardim.com/index.html*.

CIVIL RECORDS

- Birth records from 1811 to 1892. Marriage records from 1811 to 1912. Death records from 1811 to 1940
- Census records from 1851 to 1893
- Registers of residents up to 1920
- Index of family names from 1893 to 1939

JEWISH RECORDS

- Sephardic congregation, 1,200 registers (archival code PA 334), including among others:[2]
  - Family index (fathers) of births, 1736–1937 (archival code PA 334-338; microfilm 6047)
  - Burials (alphabetical list) at Ouderkerk to 1937 (archival code PA 334-340, PA 334-929; microfilm 4164)

---

[2] Vibeke Sealtiel-Olsen, "Sephardic Genealogical Investigations in Amsterdam," *Etsi* 2, no. 6 (October 1999): 10-13.

- Members (alphabetical list) of the Sephardic congregation of Amsterdam (archival code PA 334–502)
- Archives of Jewish institutions, persons, companies, seminaries, and charitable institutions. Also non-Jewish records about Jews and Jewish topics. Included are records of the Portuguese Jewish congregation from 1614 to 1975, printed inventory of the Amsterdam Portuguese Congregation records from 1870 to 1964, and list of archival documents for the period 1871–1943.
- Archives of the rabbinical school Etz Haim and the Ashkenazic Jewish community of Amsterdam from 1640 to 1943
- Documents from Jewish communities outside The Netherlands such as the Sur Israel in Brazil from 1645 to 1654
- Documentary film collection (viewable onsite), including films about Jews in Amsterdam through the World War II era

The book *Trouwen in Mokum* contains a list of 15,000 Jewish marriages.[3] Researcher Vibeke Sealtiel-Olsen has published an alphabetical list of about 700 Sephardic family names from Amsterdam from the period 1598 to 2000.[4] Sealtiel-Olsen collected these names primarily from the records of the Sephardic Congregation (PA 334 in the *Gemeentarchief*).

Central Bureau for Genealogy (*Centraal Bureau voor Genealogie*)
Reading rooms: Prins Willem-Alexanderhof 22, The Hague, The Netherlands
Mailing address: *Centraal Bureau voor Genealogie*, Postbus 11755, 2502 AT Den Haag, The Netherlands
Telephone: +31 -70 3150500
Genealogical and heraldic inquiries: +31 -70 3150570 www.cbg.nl/contact/cnt_enquiry.htm
Website: www.cbg.nl/english/englishpag.htm
Access: Monday–Friday, 9:30 am to 5 pm; Saturday, 9:00 am–1:00 pm; Tuesday, 6:00 pm–9:30 pm
Entrance fee: NLG 7.50

The Central Bureau of Genealogy (CBG) was founded in 1945 in order to centralize the country's genealogical collections. Its holdings include:
- 100,000 volumes of genealogical interest, mostly about genealogy, heraldry, history, and the countries of Dutch emigration and immigration
- 60,000 files (dossiers) of genealogical manuscripts and biographical data

---

[3] D. Verdooner, *Trouwen in Mokum* (Jewish marriage in Amsterdam) (Gravenhage: Warray, 1992).
[4] Vibeke Sealtiel-Olsen, "Sephardic Family Names in Amsterdam, 1598-2000" *Etsi* 3, no. 10 (October 2000): 8-14.

- Millions of newspaper cuttings (*familieadvertenties*) and family announcements (*familiedrukwerk*) of births, marriages, and deaths (from about 1795 to the present)
- Primary genealogical data in the form of microfilm copies of thousands of registers of births, baptisms, marriages, and burials in The Netherlands, in the former Dutch East India and Dutch West India, and the border areas of The Netherlands.
- The CBG also holds copies of population registrations up to about 1910, and the personal record cards used in the population registration from 1939 to 1994. For privacy reasons, population cards are not open to the public. If the full name and location is known, researchers can obtain copies of the cards for a fee by written request to the *Centraal Bureau voor Genealogie*. Only cards of the deceased are stored at the CBG. Registration after 1994 was electronic, and the information reaches the CBG in that form.
- Collection of the Royal Dutch Society for Genealogy and Heraldry

A searchable catalog (*CBG Catalogus*) may be accessed at www.cbg.nl/english/englishpag.htm. It covers the archive's collections of books, family records, family notices until 1970, files, newspaper clippings and family announcements, and obituary cards (surnames A-H only). Additional details of the collections can be found at the website www.cbg.nl/english/englishpag.htm.

The CBG also has an excellent online English-language guide for genealogy in The Netherlands at www.cbg.nl/english/eng_researchguide.htm. Staff conduct research but only if requested in writing or online using the research questionnaire on its website, www.cbg.nl/contact/cnt_enquiry.htm.

Netherlands Institute of War Documentation (*Nederlands Instituut voor Oorlogs–documentatie*)
Address: Herengracht 380, 1016 CJ Amsterdam, The Netherlands
Telephone: +31 20 5233800
E-mail: info@oorlogsdoc.knaw.nl
Website: www.riod.nl/engels/english.html
Access: Monday-Friday, 9:00 am–5:00pm

The Netherlands Institute of War Documentation, founded in 1945, holds documents from the Dutch resistance during World War II and collections of illegal newspapers and pamphlets, posters, photographs, books, and articles from that era. The collection includes documents from Dutch possessions such as the Dutch East Indies.

Bibliotheca Rosenthaliana
Street address: Singel 425, 1012 WP Amsterdam, The Netherlands

Mailing address: Postbus 19185, 1000 GD Amsterdam, The Netherlands
Telephone: 020 525 2366
E-mail: ros@uba.uva.nl
Website: www.uba.uva.nl/nl/bibliotheken/bibros.html

Bibliotheca Rosenthaliana, the Rosenthal Collection of Hebraica and Judaica of the Amsterdam University Library is one of the largest and most important collections of Hebraica and Judaica in the world. It holds 500,000 volumes, of which 100,000 are printed works from the 15th century to the present, 1,500 periodicals from the 17th century, 1,000 manuscripts, and 25 meters of archival material. Among its contents are the complete works of Menasseh ben Israel, the noted scholar and diplomat who founded the first Hebrew printing press in The Netherlands in 1626.

Beth Haim Cemetery at Ouderkerk aan de Amstel, in use since 1614, contains 27,000 graves. Because of the *converso* backgrounds of the persons interred, many tombstones have carvings and decorations not normally permitted in a Jewish synagogue. Before the opening of *Ouderkerk*, burials of Sephardim from Amsterdam took place at Groet near Alkmaar.

WEBSITES

♦ Many websites are available for research on Dutch Jews on the Internet. See Part IV, Internet.

ISRAEL RESOURCES

Of special interest are the following resources:
Diaspora Museum (Beth Hatefutsoth) in Tel Aviv
Address: Tel Aviv University Campus, Klausner Street, Ramat Aviv
Mailing address: P.O.B. 39359, Tel Aviv 61392, Israel
Telephone: 972 3 646 2020
Fax: 972 3 646 2134
Website: http://www.bh.org.il
E-mail: bhwebmas@post.tau.ac.il
Access: Sunday-Tuesday: 10:00 am–4:00 pm; Wednesday: 10:00 am–5:00 pm

Center for Research on Dutch Jewry
Address: Hebrew University of Jerusalem, Mount Scopus, 91905 Jerusalem, Israel
Fax: 972-2-5880242
Website: http://dutchjewry.huji.ac.il/upload/about/odot.html
E-mail: dutchjew@cc.huji.ac.il

Access: Monday-Wednesday, 8:30 am–2:00 pm (call in advance for an appointment)

Central Archives for the History of the Jewish People
Address: Hebrew University Campus, Sprinzak Bldg, Givat Ram, Jerusalem, Israel.
Mailing address: P.O. Box 1149, Jerusalem 91010, Israel
Telephone: (972)-2-5635716

The Central Archives holds microfilmed copies of the Portuguese community archives covering the 17th to the 20th centuries.

SUGGESTED READING

Sealtiel, Robert. "Genealogical Research in Holland." Paper presented at the 19th Annual Conference on Jewish Genealogy, 1999.

Sealtiel-Olsen, Vibeke. "Sephardic Genealogical Investigations in Amsterdam." *Etsi* 2, no. 6, (October 1999): 10–13.

———. "Sephardic Family Names in Amsterdam, 1598–2000." *Etsi* 2, no. 10, (October 2000): 8–14.

———. "Aliases in Amsterdam." *Etsi* 4, no. 12, (March 2001): 3–7.

Yogev, Gedalia. *Diamonds and Coral: Anglo-Dutch Jews and 18th Century Trade.* New York: Leicester University Press, 1978.

28.
IRAQ

Unfortunately, almost nothing is known about where to find genealogical records of the Jews of Iraq and Syria, other than perhaps in Israeli archives. A great deal has been written about the history of the Jews in Iraq, but very little knowledge is in the public realm about vital records and the like.

HISTORY

Birthplace of Abraham (the biblical Ur, 1500 B.C.E.), Iraq was known in ancient times as Mesopotamia and later as Assyria and Babylonia. The year 720 B.C.E. saw the deportation of Jewish captives to Assyria following the defeat of the Northern Kingdom of Israel by the Assyrian ruler Sargon. In 586 B.C.E. Nebuchadnezzar conquered the kingdom of Judea, destroyed the first Jerusalem Temple, and exiled Jewish captives to Babylonia. See also chapter 8, Geonim.

For the following two and a half millennia, Jews have lived in Iraq. Under the 14 centuries of Moslem rule, Iraq's Jews fared well at first, though they suffered under rulers such as Harun al Rashid (786–809), frequently mentioned in the Arabian Nights, and Al Muqtadi (1075–1094), who forced Jews to wear distinctive colored patches for identification as Jews.[1] Under the Mongol ruler who conquered the region in 1258, Jews were appointed to high-ranking positions within the government, but conditions deteriorated markedly. By the 14th century many Jews were forced to convert to Islam, resulting in a massive flight of Jews from Baghdad. Haddad states that 50,000 Jews settled in the Crimea and southern Russia.

In 1534, Ottoman rule improved the lot of Iraq's Jews. By the 19th century Jews controlled most of Iraq's commerce, several held high government posts and were avid Zionists. Haddad states that in the years 1920–25 Iraqi Jews contributed two to three times more per capita than Polish Jews to the Zionist Shekel, the Golden Shekel, and to Keren Hayessod and gave 90 times more per capita to the Jewish National Fund—possible sources of useful genealogical information. When Iraq became independent in 1932, subsequent riots and Jewish massacres (900 dead in a 1941 riot alone) made life precarious for Iraq's Jews. Despite travel restrictions, most Jews fled the country. Of 150,000 Jews in

---

[1] Most of the historical information on Iraq is derived from Heskel M. Haddad, *Jews of Arab and Islamic Countries* (New York: Shengold, 1984).

226 • *Sephardic Genealogy: Discovering Your Sephardic Ancestors and Their World*

1947, there were only 6,000 Jews remained in 1951.[2] To leave the country Iraqi Jews had to abandon all their property and other assets.

Far-East Interlude

In the 17th, 18th and 19th centuries, attracted by the lack of religious persecution and commercial possibilities, Jews from Baghdad, Basra and Aleppo (Syria) settled in northern India, mostly in Surat, Bombay and Calcutta. From India they also spread to other parts of the British Empire such as Burma, Hongkong, Shanghai and Singapore.

The Middle-Eastern Jews of India included such notables as the wealthy Sassoon bankers, Ezra and Elias real estate and cotton merchants (builders of the Magen David synagogue and the Ezra hospital), and numerous merchants, teachers, bakers and shopkeepers.

India gained independence from Britain in 1947 at which time it was partitioned into India and Pakistan. Fearing a backlash against minorities—which in the mind of the Indian population were associated with British rule—as well as potential political insecurity many Jews left for Israel, the United States, England and Australia. From a peak population of over 6,000 Middle-Eastern Jews, less than a thousand still remain in India.[3] Mavis Hyman, a descendant of the Baghdadi Jews of Calcutta describes the history of this Jewish population in her book *The Jews of the Raj*.[4]

Genealogical Resources

Very little is known about available resources, although a great deal is likely to exist in community records in Iraq. Other possibilities include:

- Museum of the Heritage of Babylonian Jewry, 83 Ha'Hagana Street, Or Yehuds, Israel
- Thesite2000.virtualave.net/iraqijews/index2.html, an Internet website whose a genealogy section presents a number of Iraqi family trees
- Alliance Israelite Universelle.[5] The first AIU school was inaugurated in Baghdad in 1864; AIU archives in Paris might yield useful information about children and teachers in their schools in Iraq.[6]
- Ottoman Archives contain useful documents for the periods they ruled the area. See chapter 24, Turkey.

---

[2] Haddad, *Jews of Arab and Islamic Countries*.
[3] Haddad, *Jews of Arab and Islamic Countries*.
[4] Mavis Hyman, *Jews of the Raj* (London: Hyman Publishers, 1995).
[5] For access information see chapter 19, Morocco.
[6] Philip Abensur, "Les élèves de l'école de l'Alliance de Baghdad entre 1865 et 1879" (Students of the Baghdad Alliance School between 1865 and 1879) *Etsi* 5, no. 16 (March 2002), 10-17.

- In 1909 Jews became eligible for the draft in Iraq. Iraqi draft records, when available, as well as records of the special *bedel-il-askar* tax Iraqi Jews paid prior to 1909 in lieu of military service.
- The periodical *The Scribe: Journal of Babylonian Jewry*.[7]

SUGGESTED READING

Cohen, Mark R. *Under Crescent and Cross: The Jews in the Middle Ages.* Princeton, N.J.: Princeton University Press, 1994.

Gaon, Moshe David. *Yehudei haMizrah beEretz Yisrael* (Oriental Jews in Eretz Yisrael). Jerusalem: 1928. Index and some biographical data pertaining to 2,882 Sephardic rabbis and notables were abstracted by Mathilde Tagger, www.sephardicstudies.org/gaon.html.

Gilbert, Martin. *The Jews of Arab Lands: Their History in Maps.* London: Board of Deputies of British Jews, 1976.

Haddad, Heskel M. *Jews of Arab and Islamic Countries.* New York: Shengold, 1984.

Hyman, Mavis. *Jews of the Raj.* London: Hyman, 1995.

Lewis, Bernard. *The Jews of Islam.* Princeton, N.J.: Princeton University Press, 1984.

Raphael, Chaim. *The Road from Babylon: The Story of Sephardi and Oriental Jews.* New York: Harper & Row, 1985.

Rejwan, Nissim. *The Jews of Iraq: 3000 Years of History and Culture.* Boulder, Colo.: Westview Press, 1985.

Stillman, Norman A. *The Jews of Arab Lands.* Philadelphia: Jewish Publication Society, 1979.

Sutton, Joseph A.D. *Magic Carpet: Aleppo-in-Flatbush: The Story of a Unique Ethnic Jewish Community.* New York: Thayer-Jacoby, 1979.

---

[7] Published by The Exilarch's Foundation, 20 Queen's Gate Terrace, London SW7 5PF

29.
IRAN (PERSIA)

Jews have lived in Iran (formerly Persia)[1] at least since the days of Cyrus and possibly even earlier as part of the diaspora from the Assyrian conquest of the 10 tribes that formed the Northern Kingdom of Israel.[2] Nebuchadnezzar, king of Babylonia, conquered the kingdom of Judea in 586 B.C.E. He destroyed the first Temple in Jerusalem and took back to Babylon as captives the Jewish royal family, Jewish nobility, and the priest leadership. In 539 B.C.E., Cyrus II, the first Persian king of a united Persia and Media, conquered the Babylonian empire. A year later, in 538 B.C.E., Cyrus allowed the exiled Jews of Babylon (and other captive nations) to return to Judea. He even ordered the Jerusalem Temple booty be restored to Judea and reparations paid to rebuild the Jewish Temple.

Not all the captive Jewish nobility and clergy whom Nebuchadnezzar had brought to Babylonia elected to return to Judea. Many stayed in Babylonia. Their descendants in later centuries spread to cities in Babylonia, Persia and further east. The Jews apparently were treated well and multiplied greatly under Persian rule, under the Parthian dynasty that followed (249 B.C.E.–226 C.E.), and finally under the Sassanids (226–642 C.E.). In 642 C.E. Persia, which had been independent for centuries, was conquered by the Arab Moslem armies of the first century of Islam and came under the rule of the Umayyad caliphs of Damascus and, later, the Abbassid caliphs of Baghdad. With Moslem rule, Persian scribes who until then had written in Babylonian cuneiform script began using the Arabic alphabet and script. Under Islamic rule, Jews found themselves downgraded to *dhimmis* and, therefore, social and legal inferiors.

Under Persian Sassanid rule, Babylonian Jewish academies produced the Babylonian Talmud and ushered in the era of the *geonim*. Jews continued to be represented at the Persian court by the Jewish exilarch (Jewish king in exile; see chapter 8, Geonim).

The social turbulence caused by the shift to Islamic rule saw the development of breakaway Jewish movements. The Jew Abu Isa, who saw himself as the

---

[1] Persia is derived from *Pars*, a southern province of today's Iran. There being no "p" in the Arabic alphabet, it was known by the Moslems as *Fars*, from which is derived the name of the language, *Farsi*.

[2] According to Habib Levi, descendants of these 10 tribes are said to include (among others) the Jews of Kurdistan (and the Nestorians of Kurdistan said to be descended from the tribes of Dan and Naftali); inhabitants of the old Khorasan area of Afghanistan, which includes the Afghan tribes of Durrani, Yusafzai, and Afridi, which Afghan tradition says are descended from King Saul; and inhabitants in the Caucasus, Bokhara, and Samarkand. See Habib Levi (Lavi), *Comprehensive History of the Jews of Iran: The Outset of the Diaspora*. Trans. by George W. Maschke. Costa Mesa, Calif.: Mazda Publishers, in association with the Cultural Foundation of Habib Levi, 1999.

messiah, developed a following that later became known as the Isfahanians.[3] The Karaite sect developed under the leadership of Anan.

Yet the early centuries of Islamic rule also allowed Jewish merchants and bankers to develop considerable wealth—as remarked on by numerous Jewish and Moslem authors of the period. Despite being second-class citizens (*dhimmis*) in a Moslem country, Persian Jews managed reasonably well until the 14th century. At the end of the 13th century, Jews even achieved considerable political power under the Mongol ruler Hulaga who abolished their *dhimmi* designation. Sa'ad a'Daula, a Jew, became Hulaga's chief *vizier*, and Jewish governors served in Baghdad, Shiraz and Mosul.[4]

The situation deteriorated for the Jews of Persia through the 14th and 15th centuries, and especially when Shi'ite Islam was adopted as the state religion in the 16th century by the Safawid dynasty.[5] The fundamentalist Shi'ites enforced the Pact of Omar to the maximum (see chapter 5, Jews under Islamic Rule), and Persian Jews suffered great persecution and continual public humiliations (*jud baazi*).[6] Forced to wear an identifying badge on their clothes and multicolored hats identifying them as Jews, Jews in the 19th century also were labeled ritual polluters by Moslem clerics and forbidden to touch food destined for or purchased from Moslems. These and other restrictions effectively forced the Jews out of agriculture and further reduced their options for earning a living. Even walking in the rain was forbidden because it would pollute rainwater cascading off them. Excluded from the guilds and suffering under multiple restrictions and degradations, Jews were forced into service occupations forbidden to Moslems, such as money lending (where Moslem borrowers could not legally be forced to repay) or gold and silver smithing (where Islamic law ruled they could charge only for the value of the gold, not their labor). Other Jews became itinerant peddlers, entertainers, or midwives to survive. With Jewish possessions subject to confiscation by any Moslem who desired to do so, Jews learned to hide their wealth in the walls and floors of their homes and to pretend abject poverty while avoiding antagonizing the neighboring Moslems in any way. These conditions remained in effect until mollified over parts of the country by the shah of Iran in 1926.

Despite these atrocious conditions in Shi'ite Persia, Jewish life persisted. Loeb, who studied the Jews of Shiraz, reports that religious leaders known as councils of the pious and *dayanim* (judges) successfully maintained Jewish education and services through the centuries. Loeb describes secular representation of the

---

[3] The city of Isfahan in Persia was founded by Jews; formerly it was known as Yahudiya (Jewish).
[4] L.B. Loeb, "Dhimmi Status and Jewish Rules in Iranian Society" in *Jews among Muslims*, Deshen and Zenner, eds. (New York: New York University Press, 1996).
[5] Bernard Lewis sees the origin of Shia in Persia as a rebellion of Persian rural serfs against their Arab landlords.
[6] *jud baazi* means Jewish baiting.

Jewish community through a government approved *rais* (leader) aided by *eine ha'eda* (eyes of the community), positions that apparently exposed their holders to considerable danger.

Loeb also describes the 17th-century law of apostasy. This law made any *dhimmi* who converted to Islam legally entitled to inherit the entire estates of all his relatives as far as seven generations away.[7] As a consequence Jews developed a variety of ways to survive and pass some inheritance to their children, including hiding their wealth or conveying it to their children in the form of early marriages and dowries. Another consequence of this law was that few Jews in Shiraz would acknowledge their ability to name relatives beyond their grandparents, a significant obstacle to genealogists trying to retrace these family histories. It is possible, of course, that Loeb simply encountered reluctance to discuss personal family details with a European stranger. It should also be noted that Loeb conducted his research mainly in the more traditional Shiraz in the 1960s, at a time when the majority of Persian Jews lived in Teheran.

In the 19th century, European Jewry had pressured Persian rulers to improve the lot of their Jews, though with little success at first. In 1898 the first *Alliance Israelite Universelle* school opened in Teheran. It was only in the 20th century, however, that the situation improved for Jews. The 1906 Persian constitution granted Jews civil rights, but life became significantly better for the Jews only when Shah Reza Pahlavi took over the government (1925-41) and excluded the *mullahs* from the political arena. However, the World War II period saw the shah befriend Hitler and change the name of Persia to Iran (to highlight its Aryan nature), and anti-Semitism became a factor in Iran.

In 1941 the Allies forced the shah to abdicate. Iranian Jews finally saw a period of tranquility and prosperity under his son Mohammed Reza Shah (1941-79). Mohammed Reza secularized the tone in the country and allied himself with leading Iranian Jews, who helped modernize and develop the country. On the other hand, when the shah was overturned in 1979, the backlash against his modernization and secularization efforts included renewed oppression of the Jews of Iran, as Ayatollah Khomeni reinstated an Islamic theocracy.

Daniel Elazar reports that 95,000 Jews lived in Iran in 1948 and that 60,000 Jews emigrated to Israel between 1948 and 1970, with another 10,000 in the following decade.[8] Still others left Iran for Europe or the United States, especially California. But knowledgeable Iranian Jews find these numbers unlikely. Counting the Jews in smaller towns, as many as 150,000 Jews may have lived in Iran and only 30-50,000 went to Israel, sometimes with the financial support of their more affluent relatives in Iran who continued to assist them in Israel.

---

[7] L.B. Loeb, "Dhimmi Status and Jewish Rules in Iranian Society" in *Jews among Muslims* ed. Deshen and Zenner (New York: New York University Press, 1996).
[8] Daniel J. Elazar, *The Other Jews: The Sephardim Today* (New York: Basic Books, 1989).

Iranian Jews who could afford to, preferred to go to Europe or the United States, settling mostly in New York (Kings Point) and California (Beverly Hills. Those who went to Israel were motivated to some extent by a combination of poverty and idealistic feelings. In Israel they faced discrimination and hardship. Many moved on to the United States or elsewhere as soon as they could.[9]

Genealogical Resources

Little is known about archives or records useful to genealogists. Records of genealogical value may be found in the *Alliance Israelite Universelle* archives, or the Jewish Distribution Committee records; these two organizations provided significant aid to Iranian Jews during much of the 20th century. Iranian historian Schelly Dardashti believes that there are Jewish archives connected with the chief rabbi's office in Teheran, but is unaware if copies or microfilms of them exist elsewhere. The Center for Iranian Jewish Oral History in Los Angeles is also building a collection of oral histories and photographs.[10]

Jewish cemeteries exist in many locations in Iran, including the historic Sara bat Asher cemetery outside Isfahan.[11] None have been catalogued to date.

Suggested Reading

Levi (Lavi), Habib. *Comprehensive History of the Jews of Iran: The Outset of the Diaspora*, trans. George W. Maschke. Costa Mesa, California: Mazda Publishers Cultural Foundation of Habib Levi, 1999.

Lewis, Bernard. *The Jews of Islam*. Princeton, N.J.: Princeton University Press, 1984.

Littman, David. *Jews under Muslim Rule: The Case of Persia*. Wiener Library Bulletin 34, nos. 49–50, (1979).

Loeb, L.B. "Dhimmi Status and Jewish Rules in Iranian Society" in *Jews among Muslims*, Deshen and Zenner, eds. New York: New York University Press, 1996.

Netzer, Amnon, ed. *Padyavand* (in English and Farsi). 3 vols. Costa Mesa, California: Mazda Publishers, 1997, 1998.

Patai, Raphael. *Jadid al Islam: The Jewish "New Muslims" of Meshed*. Detroit: Wayne State University Press, 1997.

Raphael, Chaim. *The Road from Babylon: The Story of Sephardi and Oriental Jews*. New York: Harper & Row, 1985.

Sarchar, Houman, ed. *Esther's Children*. Philadelphia: Jewish Publication Society, 2002.

---

[9] Schelly Dardashti. Personal communication, 2001.
[10] Center for Iranian Jewish Oral History website: www.cijoh.org
[11] *Sara bat Asher* is a very large cemetery located in Pir Bakran, also known as Linjan.

30.
SYRIA

HISTORY

Jews have inhabited Syria since at least the era of King David (1009–969 B.C.E.). King David's conquests extended Israel's rule to include most of today's Syria and were followed by the settlement of many Jews in the region. The Jews of Syria were oppressed, however, for most of their three millennia. Rome's war to quell the rebellion in Judea that culminated in the 70 C.E. destruction of the second Temple in Jerusalem also saw the massacres of thousands of Jews in Syria, massacres that continued both for the next four centuries and later under the Christianized Byzantine Empire.[1]

The Moslem conquest of Syria in 631 C.E., welcomed by Syria's Jews, provided a brief respite that ended with the arrival of the Abbassid dynasty in 750. The new rulers brought forced conversions and oppression. For the next eight centuries foreign armies continually invaded the country, making life miserable for the Jews in their paths.

Conditions improved with the advent of Ottoman rule (1516) and with the arrival of Spanish exiles, mostly to the town of Aleppo. The Farhi family rose to prominence in government during the 18th century. In the 19th century, the deteriorating local economy led Jews to migrate to more promising regions, such as Lebanon, Egypt (with its Suez Canal employment opportunities), and Palestine, then a part of the Ottoman Empire.[2] Ottoman laws made Jews eligible for the draft in 1909, precipitating flight of more Syrian Jews to other countries, including the United States.

Syria gained its independence in 1945, whereupon it became illegal for Jews to leave the country. Oppression and riots in Aleppo, which in 1947 destroyed many synagogues and Jewish shops, incited a hasty flight of Jews, mostly to Lebanon.[3]

GENEALOGY RESOURCES

Little is written about sources of genealogical data. Sources certainty remain to be identified. Several are discussed below.

Haddad identifies three different groups of Syrian Jews:

---

[1] Most of the historical information on Syria is derived from Heskel M. Haddad, *Jews of Arab and Islamic Countries* (New York: Shengold, 1984).
[2] Haddad, *Jews of Arab and Islamic countries.*
[3] Ibid.

- Jews from the town of Aleppo. Many descend from Spanish exiles and some have retained surnames such as Silvera, Picotta, Davan, Harari, and Laniado.
- Jews of Damascus. Of more ancient families, many claim descent from the era of the destruction of the Second Temple in Jerusalem.
- About 500 Jews whose parents came to Kamishli, Syria, in 1925-26 from Nusaybin, Turkey.[4]

An interesting tradition held by some Jews of Syrian descent relates to the Spanish exiles who found refuge in Aleppo. Initially the exiles had difficulty gaining acceptance from local Jews, but they were finally accepted before the Jewish festival of Hanukah. Aleppo Spanish exiles developed a tradition of lighting an extra candle (actually a second *shamash*) every day during Hanukah to commemorate the new miracle of finding refuge in Syria and being accepted by the local Jews. Descendants of some families (Attie, Betesh, Tawil, Sutton, and Haber, among others) still light an extra Hanukah candle today.

Genealogical resources include:
- Ottoman Archives in Istanbul
- Archives Diplomatiques de Nantes (17 rue du Casterneau, 44000, Nantes, France), notarial documents from the French protectorate of Syria
- *The Scribe: Journal of Babylonian Jewry*, www.bsz.org/lsyrianjewsbrooklyn.htm, an international periodical[5]
- Website www.bsz.org/lsyrianjewsbrooklyn.htm for Syrian Jews in Brooklyn
- Syrian synagogue Shaare Zion, 2030 Ocean Parkway, Brooklyn, NY

SUGGESTED READING

Cohen, Mark R. *Under Crescent and Cross: The Jews in the Middle Ages.* Princeton, N.J.: Princeton University Press, 1994.

Gaon, Moshe David. *Yehudei haMizrah beEretz Yisrael* (Oriental Jews in Eretz Yisrael). Jerusalem: 1928. Index and some biographical data pertaining to 2,882 Sephardic rabbis and notables were abstracted by Mathilde Tagger, www.sephardicstudies.org/gaon.html.

"Genealogies of 30 Families from Aleppo Documented." *Avotaynu* 10, no. 4, 61.

Gilbert, Martin. *The Jews of Arab Lands: Their History in Maps.* London: Board of Deputies of British Jews, 1976.

Haddad, Heskel M. *Jews of Arab and Islamic Countries.* New York: Shengold, 1984.

Lewis, Bernard. *The Jews of Islam.* Princeton, N.J.: Princeton University Press, 1984.

---

[4] Ibid.
[5] *The Scribe* is published by The Exilarch's Foundation, 20 Queen's Gate Terrace, London SW7 5PF.

Raphael, Chaim. *The Road from Babylon: The Story of Sephardi and Oriental Jews.* New York: Harper & Row, 1985.

Stillman, Norman A. *The Jews of Arab Lands.* Philadelphia: Jewish Publication Society, 1979.

Sutton, Joseph A.D. *Magic Carpet: Aleppo-in-Flatbush: The Story of a Unique Ethnic Jewish Community.* New York: Thayer-Jacoby, 1979.

31.
CARIBBEAN

Jews resided in most of the Caribbean Islands prior to the 19th century. This chapter touches on selected communities for which there is documentation of genealogical value. These include Curaçao, St Eustatia, St Maarten, Jamaica, St Croix, St Thomas, and Nevis. For other communities, see Malcolm Stern's excellent summary of the history of Jewish communities in the Caribbean and see the forthcoming Avotaynu Guide to Jewish Genealogy.[1] Stern also points out the presence of genealogical records in the collections of:

- Zvi Loker, former Israeli ambassador to Haiti (32 Palmach Street, Jerusalem, Israel)
- Mordechai Arbell, former Israeli ambassador to Colombia and Central America (50 Pinkas St., Tel Aviv, Israel)
- Florence Abrahams (library of the Historical Society of Pennsylvania, 1300 Locust Street, Philadelphia, PA 19107), notebooks that contain data from the periodical *Caribbeana* (London, 1910–19).

CURAÇAO, ST. EUSTATIA AND ST. MAARTEN

Curaçao

In 1634 the Dutch captured the island of Curaçao from Spain. Among the members of the conquering Dutch fleet was a Portuguese New Christian, the interpreter Samuel Cohen. After an unsuccessful search for gold, Cohen returned to Amsterdam, leaving behind another New Christian, Juan Araujo.

Following the Dutch takeover, several Jews settled on the island but they did not stay permanently. In 1659, 70 Jews, residents of Brazil who had been forced by the Portuguese conquest to flee to Amsterdam, sailed to Curaçao where they formed the first permanent Jewish settlement on the island. They founded the Mikve Israel Congregation, which established a Jewish cemetery and in 1732 built Curaçao's historic Mikve Israel synagogue. This synagogue, with its sand floor designed to muffle footsteps in the *marrano* tradition, is today the oldest surviving synagogue in the Western Hemisphere. In 1746 a breakaway group from the congregation established another synagogue, Neve Shalom, which continued in use until 1817, after which its congregants moved elsewhere.

---

[1] Malcolm Stern, "Portuguese Sephardim in the Americas," Martin A. Cohen and A.J. Peck, eds. *Sephardim in the Americas: Studies in Culture and History* (Tuscaloosa and London: University of Alabama Press, 1993); Sallyann Amdur Sack and Gary Mokotoff, eds. *Avotaynu Guide to Jewish Genealogy* (Bergenfield, New Jersey: Avotaynu, in press).

By the year 1745 the island's Jewish population reached 1,500, a number at that time greater than the total Jewish population in the rest of North America. Besides their three and a half centuries of Jewish life on the island, Curaçao's Jews were instrumental in the development of Jewish communities in the United States. Its wealthy Jewish population donated significant funds, and many served as founders of a number of the early Jewish congregations on the North American mainland.

Curaçao's ancient Mikve Israel cemetery has been damaged by industrial fumes. Fortunately, however, Rabbi Emmanuel carefully studied the cemetery's tombstones and recorded the data in his book *Precious Stones of the Jews of Curaçao, 1656–1956*.[2]

The American Sephardic Federation,[3] holds the Curaçao Jewish community's congregational records, including births, 1723–1891; deaths, 1883–1912; and lists of community members.[4]

St. Eustatia

Jews from Curaçao first settled in St. Eustatia in 1660. A 1722 census reveals the presence of 21 Jews.[5] Congregation Honen Dalim was founded in 1737, but in retaliation for Jewish support of the American Revolution, the British expelled Jewish males from the island in 1781.[6] The Jewish population subsequently dwindled. Most of the expelled Jews settled in St. Thomas and St. Croix.

St. Maarten

Some St. Eustatian Jews expelled by the British went to the Dutch half of the island of St. Maarten and built a synagogue, but they soon moved elsewhere.[7]

JAMAICA

David Silvera has a special interest in researching the genealogy of Jews in Jamaica. His website for Jamaican Jewish genealogy[8] lists resources including:

Synagogue Records from Jamaica
- Kingston. Kaal Kadosh Shahar Ashamain. Register of births, deaths, and marriages, 1809–1907. American Jewish Archives record group SC-13463 and microfilm no. 3003.

---

[2] Isaac S. Emmanuel, *Precious Stones of the Jews of Curaçao, 1656–1956* (New York: Block Publishing, 1957).
[3] 15 West 16th Street, New York, N.Y.
[4] AJHS Record Group I-112.
[5] Stern, "Portuguese Sephardim".
[6] Johannes Hartog, *The Jews and St. Eustatius: The Eighteenth Century Jewish Congregation Honen Dalim, and Description of the Old Cemetery* (St. Maarten, Netherlands Antilles: T.M. Pandt, 1976).
[7] Hartog, *Jews and St. Eustatius*; Isaac S. Emmanuel and Suzanne A. Emmanuel, *History of the Jews of the Netherlands Antilles*. (Cincinnati and Curaçao: American Jewish Archives, 1970).
[8] Located at www.sephardim.org/jamgen/index.html

- Kingston. Kaal Kadosh Shahar Shaangare Yosher. Register of births and marriages, 1788–1918. American Jewish Archives record groups SC-13464 and microfilm no. 3003.
- See also Mormon holdings under St. Croix, St. Thomas, and Nevis section.

Silvera also lists many of the Sephardic family names from Jamaica from 1664 on, as well as several other useful resources and pointers for research in Jamaica. See also Barnett and Wright, *The Jews of Jamaica: Tombstone Inscriptions 1663–1880*.[9] For Mormon and British resources on Jamaican genealogy, see www.sephardim.org/jamgen/jgLDSresources.html.

ST. CROIX, ST. THOMAS, AND NEVIS
St. Croix and St. Thomas

Most of the Jews exiled from St. Eustatia settled in St. Thomas, which had been colonized by Denmark in 1672. St. Thomas is the site of the oldest Jewish congregation in continuous existence in the United States. Congregation Bracha u Shalom was founded in 1796 and reinforced by Sephardic Jews from Curaçao during the British occupation of the island (1807–16), Jamaica and the United States.[10] At its peak population in 1837 400 Jews constituted nearly half the island's white population. Fire destroyed the early synagogues; the most recent was built in 1833 as Bracha u Shalom u Gemulut Hassidim. Hurricanes, a deteriorating economy, and a 1895 cholera epidemic diminished the Jewish population. Many Jews also left to settle in Panama. In 1917 the United States purchased the island of St. Thomas.

An early Jewish cemetery had gravestones marked from 1792 and 1802; a newer cemetery was purchased and has been used from 1837 on. In 1965, Margolinsky studied and published 299 epitaphs from the newer Jewish cemetery of St. Thomas.[11]

The American Jewish Historical Society, has three rolls of microfilm containing vital records of 18th to 20th century Jews of St. Thomas. The historical society also holds a family tree for a family of Joshua Piza and his descendants.

St. Croix had a synagogue in 1760, but the Jewish community ceased to exist by the end of the 19th century. Stern reports that the Jewish cemetery has 11 decipherable epitaphs.[12]

Church of Jesus Christ of Latter-day Saints
Address: 35 North West Temple Street, Salt Lake City, Utah, 84150-3400
Telephone: 801-240-2331 or 800-453-3860 ext 22331

---

[9] R.D. Barnett and P.Wright. *The Jews of Jamaica: Tombstone Inscriptions. 1663–1880*. (Jerusalem: Ben Zvi Institute, 1997).
[10] Stern, "Portuguese Sephardim".
[11] J. Margolinsky *299 Epitaphs on the Jewish Cemetery in St. Thomas, W.I. 1837-1916: Compiled from Records in the Archives of the Jewish Community in Copenhagen* (Copenhagen, 1965).
[12] Stern, "Portuguese Sephardim".

FAX: 801-240-1584
E-mail: fhl@ldschurch.org
Website: www.familysearch.org
See also www.jewishgen.org/databases/FHLC for database of Jewish items.

The Mormons holds copies of:
- St Thomas Synagogue birth records, 1786–1954 (film 882930)
- Transcript of 298 epitaphs from the Jewish Cemetery in St. Thomas, W. I., 1837–1916, with index (film 1013426 Item 18); Jewish marriage records, Jamaica Kingston, 1788–1920; St. Thomas & Jamaica circumcision records, 1800s; St. Thomas & Jamaica birth records, 1800s-1950; St. Thomas & Jamaica death records, 1796–1824 (film 1012748)
- Birth records, 1786–1954, Cards arranged by year containing brief information about Jews in the Virgin Islands (film 1001639)
- St. Thomas & Jamaica circumcision records, 1800s; St. Thomas & Jamaica birth records, 1800s-1950; St. Thomas & Jamaica death records, 1796–1824 (film 1012748)

Suggested Reading

Arbell, Mordechai. " 'La Nacion': Los Judios Hispano-Portugueses del Caribe" ("The Nation": Spanish-Portuguese Jews of the Caribbean). *Sephardica* 1, no. 1 (March 1984): 85–94. Jewish communities established in the Caribbean by Marranos after their expulsion from Brazil.

———. *Portuguese Jews of Jamaica*. Kingston, Jamaica: Canoe Press, University of West Indies, 2000.

Barnett, R.D., and P. Wright. *The Jews of Jamaica: Tombstone Inscriptions 1663–1880.* Jerusalem: Ben Zvi Institute, 1997.

Bennett, Ralph. "The Jewish of Exotic Surinam and Their History," *Avotaynu* 8, no. 2 (1992): 2, 16.

———. "History of the Jews of the Caribbean." *Los Muestros* (1993): 11.

Bejarano, Margalit. *La Comunidad Hebrea de Cuba: La memoria y la historia* (Hebrew community of Cuba: Memory and history). Jerusalem: Hebrew University, 1996.

Bentes, Abraham Ramiro. *Primeiros immigrantes hebreus na Amazonia: Instillacao da primeira communidade israelite brasiliera* (First Jewish immigrants in the Amazon: Installation of the first Brazilian Jewish community). Rio de Janeiro: Gráficos Borsoi, 1987.

———. *Das Ruinas de Jerusalem a Verdajante Amazonia* (Ruins of Jerusalem in the Green Amazon). Rio de Janeiro: Edicoes Bloch, 1987.

Bohm, Gunter. "The First Sephardic Synagogues in South America and in the Caribbean Area." *Studio Rosenthaliana* 22, no. 1 (Spring 1988): 1–14.

Boyd-Bowman, Peter. *Indice geobiografico de 56 mil pobladores de America* (Geobiographical index of 56,000 American villagers). 2 vols. Mexico City: Fondo de Cultura Economica, 1985.

Cahen, *"Les Juifs de Martinique"* (Jews of Martinique). *Revue des etudes juives* 31: 102–114. Contains census lists of Jews in Martinique for 1680 and 1683.

Cohen, M.A., and Peck, A.J., eds. *Sephardim in the Americas: Studies in Culture and History.* Tuscaloosa and London: University of Alabama Press, 1993.

Emmanuel, Isaac S., *Precious Stones of the Jews of Curaçao, 1656–1956.* New York: Block Publishing, 1957. Describes the Jewish cemetery in Curaçao.

Emmanuel, Isaac S. and Suzanne A. Emmanuel. *History of the Jews of the Netherlands Antilles.* 2 vols. Cincinnati and Curaçao: American Jewish Archives, 1970.

Fidanque. *Kol Shearith Israel: Cien años de vida judía en Panamá, 1876–1976* (Kol Shearith Israel: A hundred years of Jewish life in Panama, 1876–1976). Panama: Igmar, 1977.

Goldemberg, Isaac, ed. *El gran libro de la America judia* (Grewat book of Jewish America). San Juan: Editorial de la Universidad de Puerto Rico, 1998.

Hartog, Johannes. *The Jews and St. Eustatius: The Eighteenth Century Jewish Congregation Honen Dalim, and Description of the Old Cemetery.* St. Maarten, Netherlands Antilles: T.M. Pandt, 1976.

Hilfman, P.A. "Notes on the History of the Jews of Surinam." *Publications of the American Jewish Historical Society* 18: 179 ff. Describes birth, marriage, and death records of the Portuguese Congregation (microfilm, in American Jewish Archives).

Levine, Robert. *Tropical Diaspora: The Jewish Experience in Cuba.* Gainesville: University Press of Florida, 1993.

Liebman, Seymour B. *The Inquisitors and the Jews in the New World.* Miami: University of Miami Press, 1975. Following a brief introduction, lists Inquisition records in the New World. Good source for *converso* names in the New World.

Margolinsky, J. *299 Epitaphs on the Jewish Cemetery in St. Thomas, W.I. 1837–1916. Compiled from Records in the Archives of the Jewish Community in Copenhagen.* Copenhagen, 1965.

Obejas, Achy. *Days of Awe.* New York: Ballantine, 2001. Not genealogy, but a semi-autobiographical novel about Cuban crypto-Jews.

Porter, Stephen. *Jamaican Records.* stephen.porter@virgin.net.

Postal, Bernard, and Malcolm H. Stern. *Tourist's Guide to Jewish History in the Caribbean.* New York: American Airlines, 1975.

Ricard, R. *"Notes sur l'immigration des Israelites marocains en Amerique espagnole et au Bresil"* (Notes about the immigration of Moroccan Jews in Spanish America and in Brazil). *Revue Africaine* (1944).

Rosenzweig. *"Judios en la Amazonia Peruana, 1870-1949"* (Jews in the Peruvian Amazon, 1870-1949). *Majshavot: Pensiamentos* 4 , nos. 1-2. (1967): 19-30.

Segal, Ariel. *Jews of the Amazon: Self Exile in Earthly Paradise*. Philadelphia: Jewish Publication Society, 1999. Study of the Jewish *mestizos* of Iquitos at the western edge of the Amazon. Lists names of people buried at Iquitos Jewish Cemetery and names of Jews who settled in the Peruvian Amazon.

Stern, Malcolm. "Portuguese Sephardim in the Americas." Martin A. Cohen and A.J. Peck, eds. *Sephardim in the Americas: Studies in Culture and History* (Tuscaloosa and London: University of Alabama Press, 1993).

Wiznitzer, Arnold. *The Records of the Earliest Jewish Community in the New World*. New York: American Jewish Historical Society, 1954.

———. *Jews in Colonial Brazil*. New York: Columbia University Press, 1960.

Wolff, Egon, and Frieda Wolff. *Sepulturas de Israelitas* (Jewish tombstones). 4 vols. Sao Paolo: Centro de Estudos Judaicos, 1976-1989. Names from Jewish cemeteries in Brazil.

———. "Sephardic Jews in Northern Brazil in the 19th Century." *Avotaynu* 9, no. 4, (1993).

32.
SOUTH AMERICA

ARGENTINA

Though not specifically targeted at Sephardic resources, Diana Nimcowicz has authored an excellent infofile about resources available for genealogical research in Argentina. It can be found on the Internet at www.jewishgen.org/infofiles/Argentina.html.

Asociación de Genealogía Judía de Argentina
Address: Juana Azurduy 2223 8°,C.P. 1429, Buenos Aires, Argentina
Website: www.agja.org.ar

The association's Internet site contains a listing of names for whom the Argentinian genealogical association has found information in Argentina. The name list is derived from cemetery lists, marriages performed in the Chalom community of Buenos Aires, passenger ships and other sources.

Cemeteries
There are 4 specifically Sephardic cemeteries in Argentina:
- Avellaneda (Moroccan, 2200 registries),
- Ciudadela (Syrian Jews from Aleppo, 4400 registries),
- Lomas De Zamora (Jews from Damascus, 6000 registries)
- Bancalari (Ladino speakers, 3700 registries.)

The Jewish Genealogy Association of Argentina holds the registers from the above cemeteries.

Argentine Israelite Mutual Association
Associacion Mutual Israelita Argentina or AMIA
Address: Pasteur 633, C.P 1028, Buenos Aires, Argentina
Website: www.amia.org.ar

The Associacion Mutual Israelita Argentina is the central Kehilla organization for Argentinian Jewry and has information about the various temples, many of which have their own membership and marriage information.

Latin American Center for Studies of Migrations
Centro de Estudios Migratorios de America Latina: CEMLA

242 • Sephardic Genealogy: Discovering Your Sephardic Ancestors and Their World

Address: Independencia 20, C.P. 1099, Buenos Aires, Argentina
Website: cemla@ciudad.com.ar

The center holds list of passengers who arrived at the port of Buenos Aires from 1882 to April 1926. The lists include surnames, first names, nationalities, marital status, age, profession, religion, port of embarkation, name of ship and date of arrival. A search can be requested for $25.

Registry Office (*Registro Civil*)
Address: Uruguay 753, C.P. 1018, Buenos Aires, Argentina
Website: www.registrocivil.gov.ar

Civil registration began in Argentina in August 1886.[1] The Registry Office will search and provide birth, death, and marriage certificates if provided with a full name and year ($20). These certificates can provide such information as birth, sex and name of the child, name, address and I.D. numbers of the parents and of the attending doctor for the birth certificates; bride and groom names, ages, nationalities, I.D. numbers and parents' names in the marriage certificates; and date of birth, name, I.D. number and sex of the deceased, and parents' names.[2]

Immigration Registration

For immigrants prior to 1882 records are held at the National Archives (*Archivo General de la Nacion*) at Leandro N. Alem 246, C.P. 1003, Buenos Aires, Argentina. For arrivals after 1882, the records are held at the *Direccion Nacional de Migraciones*, Antartida Argentina 1355, (1104) Buenos Aires. The Department of Written Documents (*Soportes Escritos*), located within the National Archives has the arrival lists of passengers from 1821 to May 15, 1869.

Central Archives for the History of the Jewish People (CAHJP)

Hebrew University Campus, Sprinzak Bldg, Givat Ram, Jerusalem, Israel. The archives can be contacted at P.O. Box 1149, Jerusalem 91010 or by telephone at (972)-2-5635716. CAHJP holds records from Argentina, documenting the Baron de Hirsch agricultural colonies.

BRAZIL

By 1645, there were as many as 1,450 Jews living in New Holland, and the Dutch controlled Pernambuco province of Brazil where it bulged out into the Atlantic. Together these Jews formed the Ben Zur congregation in the capital on the island of Recife and the Magen Abraham congregation in Mauricia on the

---

[1] Oscar Pardo "Argentina" *Avotaynu* 2, October 1986.
[2] Oscar Pardo "Argentina" *Avotaynu* 3, Summer 1987, 18-23.

mainland. In 1641 they were led by Rabbi Isaac Aboab da Fonseca of Amsterdam and Rabbi Moses Rafael de Aguilar. The Dutch held on to their New World possession for about three decades but in 1654, they finally surrendered to the Portuguese forces besieging the city. With the intolerant Portuguese back in control, the Dutch and all the Jewish inhabitants left Brazil, mostly on ships returning to Holland, bringing to a close that chapter of Sephardim in Brazil. It was one of these returning ships that, through misadventure, ended up in New Amsterdam (New York) as described in the chapter on the United States.[3]

Earlier in this book, in the chapter on the Amazon, the reader was briefly introduced to another group of Brazilian Sephardim. These were Moroccan Sephardim who came to the Amazon during the second half of the nineteenth century. Egon Wolff[4] who researched these immigrants found it difficult to find the names of the earliest ones. There were no burial registries found, and most of the information retrieved was from naturalization documents of the Jews who sought Brazilian nationality and from newspapers of the time. Despite the absence of burial registers, Wolff was able to retrieve the inscriptions on about 700 tombstones in Brazilian Jewish cemeteries.[5] The commonest Sephardic surnames they found were Benchimol (a family related to Aguiar, Dahan, Franco and Gabbay), Siscu, Azulay, Serruya and of course Cohen and Levy, the latter found in combinations with Benchimol, Benoliel, Benzaquen, Bencheton, Israel, Obadia and Serrulha. These Sephardim appeared to intermarry amongst themselves because 361 of the surnames were related to each other.[6] Though most of them were businessmen, several members of the Bentes family became prominent in the Brazilian military reaching the grades of General.[7]

Vital Records

Civil registration of births and marriages begin in Brazil November 15, 1889 after it became a republic. Prior to that births, marriages and deaths were registered only in the parish church and therefore do not include Jews for that period.

Records of marriages among foreigners were sometimes recorded in the appropriate consulates. Notations in family Bibles and announcements in newspapers are a possible source of information. Prior to 1970 there was no legal divorce in Brazil.

---

[3] Arnold Wiznitzer *Jews in Colonial Brazil* (New York, 1960).
[4] Wolff "Sephardic Jews in Northern Brazil in the 19th Century" *Avotaynu*, Vol. IX, Number 4, 1993.
[5] Egon Wolff and Frieda Wolff *Sepulturas de Israelitas*. 2 vols. (Sao Paulo, 1976 & 1983).
[6] Wolff "Brazil" *Avotaynu*, Vol. VI, Number 1, 1990.
[7] Abraham Ramiro Bentes *Das Ruinas de Jerusalem a Verdajante Amazonia* (Rio de Janeiro: Edicoes Bloch, 1987) and *Primeiros imigrantes hebreus na Amazonia* (Rio de Janeiro: Author, 1987).

Cemeteries

Non-denominational cemeteries (municipal) date back to the 1840s and contain Jewish graves. Wolff has identified a number of these and published his findings.[8] The earliest Jewish cemetery was the one used in Recife during the Dutch occupation of that city (1630 to 1654). It no longer exists and the next oldest Jewish cemetery dates back to 1921. Researchers should note that death certificates in Brazil do not mention religion.

Naturalization

Naturalization documents are preserved at Brazil's National Archives. Data often includes applicant's parents, spouse, children, and witnesses (often also Jewish).

Wills, commercial contracts of firms with Jewish partners, death announcements mentioning children and other relatives, newspaper clippings, memoirs of parents, grandparents and other relations provide additional information.[9]

Alain Bigio at the Jewish genealogy Society of Brazil (Sociedade Genealógica Judaica do Brasil) is a good source for information about Jewish genealogy in Brazil. He can be reached through the society's website at www.netjudaica.com.br/sgjb..

Marc Raizman has written a concise history of Jews in Brazil which is on the Internet at www.jewishgen.org/infofiles/BrazilianJewry.htm. Though not focused on Sephardim, it does provide useful information about the Jews of Brazil.

SUGGESTED READING

Bentes, Abraham Ramiro. *Primeiros immigrantes hebreus na Amazonia: Instillacao da primeira communidade israelite brasiliera* (First Jewish immigrants in the Amazon: Installation of the first Brazilian Jewish community). Rio de Janeiro: Gráficos Borsoi, 1987.

———. *Das Ruinas de Jerusalem a Verdajante Amazonia* (Ruins of Jerusalem in the Green Amazon). Rio de Janeiro: Edicoes Bloch, 1987.

Novinsky, Anita. *Cristãos novos na Bahia: história* (New Christians of Bahia: history). Sãn Paulo: Editôra Perspectiva, 1972.

Pardo, Oscar. "Argentina." *Avotaynu* 2, October 1986.

---

[8] Egon Wolff and Wolff, Frieda. *Sepulturas de Israelitas* (Jewish tombstones) (San Paolo: Centro de Estudos Judaicos, 1976–1989).

[9] Egon Wolff "Brazil" *Avotaynu*, Vol. VI, Number 3, 1990.

Ricard, R. "Notes sur l'immigration des Israelites marocains en Amerique espagnole et au Bresil" (Notes on the immigration of Moroccan Jews in Spanish America and in Brazil). *Revue Africaine*, 1944.

Wolff, Egon, and Frieda Wolff. *Sepulturas de Israelitas* (Jewish tombstones). 4 vols. San Paolo: Centro de Estudos Judaicos, 1976–1989.

———. *Dicionário biográfico* (Biographical Dictionary). Rio de Janeiro: Author, 1986.

———. *Guia histórico da comunidade judaica de São Paulo* (Historical Guide for the Jewish Community of Sao Paulo). São Paulo: Editora B'nei B'rith, 1988.

———. "Sephardic Jews in Northern Brazil in the 19th Century." *Avotaynu* 9, no. 4, (1993).

33.

UNITED STATES

Sephardic Jews have come to the United States in three major waves and at other times, too. The very first Jews who came to the United States were Sephardim. A community of Sephardic merchants had lived in an area of Brazil conquered by the Dutch in the 1630s. When the Portuguese regained possession from the Dutch in 1654, the Jews set sail from Recife to seek safety elsewhere and avoid prosecution by the imported Portuguese Inquisition. Some Jews went to French-controlled Martinique and Barbados, but the majority sailed back to Holland. One ship in a flotilla of 16 ships intent on returning to Holland was separated from the others and captured by a Spanish ship, which then planned to turn the Jews over to the Inquisition. Before they could do so, a French ship rescued the prisoners, who were able to find refuge in French-controlled Florida.[1]

In the same year another ship with Dutch Jews departing from Recife was captured on the high seas by a Spanish ship, but the intercession of the Dutch government saved its Jews from the Inquisition and on September 7, 1654, the 23 Jews (four men, six women, and 13 youngsters) landed in Dutch New Amsterdam (the future New York City). New Amsterdam's Governor Peter Stuyvesant opposed Jews settling in his colony. He became particularly incensed when later that year, they were joined by another five wealthy Sephardic families sailing directly from Holland. His objections were overruled when the Sephardim resorted to the powerful connections they wielded among fellow Dutch Sephardim—who were major investors in the Dutch West India Company that employed Stuyvesant.

The first Sephardic congregation, Shearith Israel (remnant of Israel), was established in New York City. It was soon followed by the establishment in Newport, Rhode Island, of Touro Synagogue, in 1658, and in turn by synagogues in Savannah, Georgia, and Charleston, North Carolina.

A second, larger wave of Sephardim were among the millions of immigrants from all nations who arrived at U.S. ports at the end of the 19th and beginning of the 20th centuries. Thirty thousand Sephardic Jews from the eastern Mediterranean were part of this massive migration. They, along with Eastern European immigrants, settled on the Lower East Side of New York, where they congregated in cafes known as *cavanes*. Fewer than 3,000 came to the U.S. from 1890 to 1907, but the flow of immigrants from Turkey and elsewhere in the Ottoman Empire increased dramatically in 1908 as military-age Jews fled the

---

[1] H.M. Sachar, *Farewell Espana: The World of the Sephardim Remembered* (New York: Vintage Books, 1995): 362.

country following the Young Turk Revolt, a conflict that suddenly rendered them draftable. Ten thousand Balkan Jews came to the U.S. during the period 1908–14 to escape dire poverty; a series of natural disasters; and conscription into the Turko-Italian War of 1911–12, the Balkan wars of 1912–13, and World War I.[2] There was a lull in immigration during the First World War, and then another 10,000 Balkan Jews came between 1920 and 1924.

For an account of life at the turn of the last century for the Balkan contingent of Sephardic immigrants, Marc Angel's *La America* is excellent reading.[3] In his book, named for the New York Ladino-language newspaper, Angel recreates the lost world of the Balkan and Turkish Sephardic immigrants during the first decades of the 20th century.

The third wave of Sephardim arrived in the 1950s, consisting mostly of Jews expelled from Arab lands. These arrivals are recent enough that some older family members may still be around to tell their stories.

Genealogical Resources

If you are researching a family that was already in the U.S. by 1840—when an estimated 10,000 Jews lived in the U.S.—you may be in luck. Malcolm Stern published two books of family trees of Jewish families in the United States before 1840. The later, more complete book is *First American Families*, in which he includes six hundred family trees of Jewish families in the U.S. during the period 1654 through 1988.[4] Although not specifically about Sephardic families, a large number of the families during this early era were Sephardim.

For the massive wave of immigrants at the beginning of the 20th century, prime resources for American genealogists are records of arrival and naturalization. Arrival records include passenger ship records maintained at the various U.S. ports of entry, as well as records kept at European ports from which the emigrants embarked. Many U.S. immigrants were subsequently naturalized, and their naturalization records also provide useful information.

Upon arrival in the United States, the new immigrants began creating records of great value to their descendants. Their records include vital records, census records, World War I and II draft registration records, military service records, corporate records (if they ran businesses), city directory listings, newspaper announcements or articles, and synagogue or brotherhood association records, among countless others. If the immigrants and their descendants died in the U.S.,

---

[2] Marc D. Angel, *La America: The Sephardic experience in the United States* (Philadelphia: Jewish Publication Society of America, 1982).
[3] Ibid.
[4] Malcolm H. Stern, *First American Jewish Families: 600 Genealogies 1654–1988*, 3d ed. (Baltimore: Ottenheimer Publishers, 1991).

obituaries, Social Security death index records, testamentary wills, and cemeteries may provide additional information about them.

Jewish and general genealogical research methodologies are well developed in the United States. Information about resources and where to find and use them is widely available, both in books and on the Internet. The best Jewish genealogy resource on the Internet is JewishGen at www.jewishgen.org. See the extensive infofiles on Sephardim and a variety of Jewish genealogy topics and the SIG (Special Interest Group) for Sephardic genealogy at www.jewishgen.org/sefardsig.

Brief details of several types of records are presented below to give the reader a flavor for the richness of the resources and how to use them. This is not a comprehensive list of records for United States genealogical research.

NATURALIZATION RECORDS

The process by which immigrants became U.S. citizens has varied over the years. Until 1906, persons wishing to become citizens could go before any local, state, or federal court, or justice of the peace, and simply swear allegiance to the state and country. No federal papers were filed. Starting in September 1906, naturalization records were filed with the federal government. Earlier records vary greatly both in location and content.

Until 1922 women derived citizenship from their fathers or husbands, as did males under age 16. The citizenship process after 1906 consisted of three steps reflected by three documents: Declaration of Intent or "first papers," Petition for Naturalization, and Certificate of Citizenship. The necessary time of residency in the United States between the first and final papers was frequently five years of residency, but that varied, especially in the earlier periods, as did other requirements for citizenship.

Of the three sets of documents, the first two provide the most information, especially after 1906. Information after 1906 includes the original name of the person before arrival in the United States and aliases used; the U.S. port, date and ship they arrived on; names of family members; street address; ages; and sometimes a photograph. The final Certificate of Citizenship is the least informative, but the certificate number can help track down earlier papers.

Naturalization records (at least for 1906 and later) are kept by the Immigration and Naturalization Service (INS), and researchers can request records under the Freedom of Information Act (FOIA). It is important to mention the FOIA in the request for the INS to release the information; be sure to request "all documents" in the file, not just naturalization documents. Naturalization records and some indexes are also kept at the U.S. National Archives, whose main offices are in Washington, D.C., but which maintains regional offices across the country. These offices can be visited in person or one can write to them. Visiting in person is more likely to be successful, since an interested person is more likely to be persistent and creative in the search for records.

Copies of naturalization records are available from Mormon Family History Centers. The Church of Jesus Christ of Latter-day Saints (LDS) maintains Family History Centers for genealogy researchers in numerous cities throughout the country. Microfilms or materials not held by a local Family History Center can be requested from the Family History Library in Salt Lake City for a nominal fee.[5]

Passenger Ship Records

The majority of Jews who came to the U.S. in ships did so through the port of New York. In the latter part of the 20th century, Jews may have come by plane or overland via the northern or southern borders. During the massive immigrant influx at the turn of the last century, the United States government kept lists of the incoming ship passengers. These can provide considerable genealogical information. Not only are the name, age, nationality and language of the person listed, but often how much money they had, who met them at the port, and their destination address.

Until 2001, finding these records meant going to the National Archives, locating the proper microfilm reel, and then patiently searching page by microfilm page. In 2001, volunteers from the LDS entered the information for passengers arriving through New York into a database available on the Internet at www.ellisislandrecords.org permitting direct name searches. This database does not include passengers who came to the United States other than through New York or outside the period covered. Once the individual name is identified, the passenger list for that ship can be viewed on screen and downloaded or printed.

Because searching through the database on the internet requires a number of steps, Stephen Morse developed a one step search form that shortens the process considerably and adds additional searching capability. Morse's form can be used from his website at http://www.jewishgen.org/databases/EIDB/ellis.html. A variant designed to search for Jewish passengers is found at http://www.jewishgen.org/databases/EIDB/ellisjw.html.

Census Records

A federal census is taken in the United States every 10 years; these records are open to the public after a 72-year period. The most recent census available to the public for research is the 1930 enumeration. These federally mandated census records are found at national and regional archives. Some censuses are indexed for some localities. It is necessary to know at least the city or county the person lived in, if not the actual city.

---

[5] See chapter 18, Spain, for access information.

JEWISH RECORDS

HEBREW IMMIGRANT AID SOCIETY

HIAS records provide information about turn-of-the-20th-century Sephardic immigrants. Although HIAS records concern mostly Eastern European Jewish immigrants, HIAS also tried to help Sephardic immigrants. They developed a poorly funded "Oriental Bureau," often manned by one or two Sephardic part-time volunteers to assist Turkish and Balkan Sephardim through the immigration process.[6]

INDUSTRIAL REMOVAL OFFICE

The records of the Industrial Removal Office (IRO) may also be helpful in researching early 20th-century immigrants. Financed by the Baron de Hirsch Fund, IRO was a Jewish organization that sent many immigrants from New York to places such as Seattle, Gary, Cincinnati, Toledo, Columbus and Cleveland, where it was felt they might have a better chance to succeed than in congested and overcrowded New York.

SEPHARDIC BROTHERHOOD ORGANIZATIONS

Early 20th-century Sephardic immigrants from the same locality of origin founded self-help fellowship organizations in New York.[7] The societies include:

- Union and Peace Society, founded in 1899. The society's relatively wealthy English-speaking members hailed from Turkey, Morocco and elsewhere. Many worshiped at Shearith Israel.
- Oriental and Progressive Society, founded in 1904, was short-lived. Its members were primarily Ashkenazic Jews from Turkey who spoke Yiddish and English.
- *Hebra Ahava ve-Ahvah Janina* (Love and Brotherhood Society of Janina), founded in 1907. Membership consisted primarily of Greek Jews from Janina.
- *Hesed ve Emet* (Mercy and Truth) society. Founded by Jews from Kastoria, Greece, the membership was reinforced by Ladino-speaking Jews from Kastoria who were part of the Janina group.
- *Tikvah Tovah* society, founded in 1907. Greek-speaking members included Jews from Janina, Kastoria, Salonica, and Izmir. It tended to work in tandem with members of *Ahava ve-Ahvah Janina*.
- *Ahavath Shalom* society (Love of Peace), founded in 1910. Members were Jews from Monastir (Bitola in Yugoslavia).

---

[6] Angel, *La America*.
[7] Ibid.

- *Ez Hahayim* society, founded in 1912. Ladino-speaking Jews from Salonica founded the society.
- Salonican Brotherhood (renamed the Sephardic Brotherhood in 1921), *Haskalah* (Enlightenment), Angora Union, *Ahim Mevorakim* (blessed Brothers) were other Sephardic societies, each catering to its constituency of Jews originating in various areas of the Levant and Palestine. A list of members of the Sephardic Brotherhood on March 10, 1916, appears at www.jewishgen.org/sefardsig/seph_ brotherhood. htm.

The early immigrants from the Balkans remained largely fragmented, forming many small societies for members of various towns of origin. They remained suspicious and jealous of each other and of the helping hand of Shearith Israel, whose mode of operation was different from that to which they were accustomed.[8]

Associations of Sephardim who fled their homes in the mid-20th century, mostly from Middle-Eastern Arab countries, include the Historical Society of Jews from Egypt (HSJE), a particularly active group with a website at www.hsje.org and a newslist where exiles from Egypt or their descendants share memories and help each other.[9] The library and records at the historic Shearith Israel, the Spanish Portuguese synagogue in New York City, and the more recent Sephardic congregations in Brooklyn provide additional valuable resources well worth a visit.

SUGGESTED READING

Angel, Marc D. *La America: The Sephardic Experience in the United States.* Philadelphia: Jewish Publication Society of America, 1982.

Hordes, Stanley. *The Crypto-Jewish Community of New Spain, 1620–1649: A Collective Biography.* PhD. Diss. Tulane University, 1980.

Nidel, David S. "Modern Descendants of Conversos in New Mexico". Western States Jewish Historical Quarterly 16, no. 3: 194–292.

Stern, Malcolm H. *First American Jewish Families: 600 Genealogies 1654–1988*, 3rd ed. Baltimore: Ottenheimer Publishers, 1991

Sutton, Joseph A.D. *Magic Carpet: Aleppo-in-Flatbush. The Story of A Unique Ethnic Jewish Community.* New York: Thayer-Jacoby, 1979.

---

[8] Angel, *La America*.
[9] To subscribe, send e-mail to hsje-subscribe@yahoogroups.com.

Part IV
Internet

Jewish Genealogy Websites

- **JewishGen.** www.jewishgen.org
- **JewishGen's Infofiles.** www.jewishgen.org/infofiles
- **International Association of Jewish Genealogical Societies.** www.jewishgen.org/ajgs
- **Jewish Encyclopedia Online.** www.jewishencyclopedia.com/index.jsp
- **Reading Hebrew Tombstones.** www.jewishgen.org/infofiles/tombstones.html
- **Church of Jesus Christ of Latter-day Saints (LDS).** www.familysearch.org Not Jewish, but contains the largest collection of genealogical records. See also www.jewishgen.org/databases/FHLC for database of Jewish items.

Sephardic Websites

Several websites focus on Sephardic genealogy in general. Other websites highlight specific countries.

Genealogy-Related Websites

- **Sephardic Genealogy Resources.** www.orthohelp.com/geneal/sefardim.htm. An award-winning website created and personally maintained by the author, this extensive resource provides articles and information on many aspects of Sephardic genealogy.
- **JewishGen's SefardSIG.** www.jewishgen.org/sefardsig. JewishGen is the largest and most extensive website for Jewish genealogy. See the Sephardic **section and infofiles.**
- **JewishGen's KahalLinks.** www.jewishgen.org/sefardsig/kahallinks.htm. A section of JewishGen's SefardSIG, KahalLinks provides information about countries with significant Sephardic communities.
- **Foundation for the Advancement of Sephardic Studies and Culture.** www.sephardicstudies.org. This New York City publishing firm includes good genealogy content on its website, primarily on Turkish and Greek Sephardic genealogy, but it posts good material about other areas as well.
- **Sephardim.** www.sephardim.org. Extensive list of family names and heraldry.
- *Etsi*. www.geocities.com/EnchantedForest/1321. *Etsi*, "my tree" in Hebrew, is the home of the periodical *Etsi* with articles in English and French (with summaries of each article in the other language); it is the only periodical devoted solely to Sephardic genealogy and history.
- **Central Archives for the History of the Jewish People.** http://sites.huji.ac.il/archives. Lists summary of the archives contents.

Part IV: Internet • 255

- **Saudades.** www.saudades.org. Beautiful site on Portuguese Sephardic history. Provides information about surnames.
- **The Sephardi Connection.** sephardiconnect.com/Welcome.html. A discussion and educational site, with a large Sephardic forum.
- **Jewish National and University Library, Jerusalem.** http://jnul.huji.ac.il/dl/ketubbot. 1,200 *Ketubot* from its manuscript collection (and other collections, including the US Library of Congress, the Lehmann collection and several others) are digitized online.
- **International Association of Jewish Genealogical Societies.** www.jewishgen.org/iajgs/ajgs-jgss.html. Lists societies and special interest groups.
- **Cindy's List - Jewish.** www.cyndislist.com/jewish.htm

BACKGROUND INFORMATION OF SEPHARDIC INTEREST

The following sites have little genealogy content, but they may be of interest to the Sephardic genealogist. These sites provide history and background information that give body and meaning to an otherwise dry family tree.

- **American Sephardi Federation.** www.amsephfed.org
- **Dinur Center for Research in Jewish History,** Hebrew University of Jerusalem. www.hum.huji.ac.il/Dinur/internetresources/gen.htm
- **History of Sephardim in New Jersey.** http://home.earthlink.net/~etzahaim/ceajhist.html
- **Bnai Sepharad.** www.geocities.com/SouthBeach/8341/SEPHARD1.HTM#sites
- **Pedagogic Center, Diaspora, Spain.** www.jajz-ed.org.il/diaspora/europe/spain.html
- **Middle East and Jewish Studies, Columbia University.** www.columbia.edu/cu/lweb/indiv/mideast/cuvlj/sephardic.html
- **Museo Sefardi of Madrid.** www.servicom.es/museosefardi. Website focusses on Toledo's Sinagoga del Transito.
- **Sephardi European Institute.** www.sefarad.org
- **History of Rabbi Yosef Caro.** www.kinneret.co.il/betdavid/betkaro/welcome.html
- **Biographies of Selected Sephardic Rabbis.** www.jewishgen.org/sefardsig/leaders.htm
- **Bernard Gui Inquisitorial Technique (c.1307–23).** www.fordham.edu/halsall/source/heresy2.html
- **Barcelona Haggadah.** www.facsimile-editions.com/bh_page.htm
- *Juderias* **in Spanish Towns.** www.redjuderias.org/eng/index.html
- **Malaga (Malaca) History Tour.** www.us-israel.org/jsource/vjw/Malaga.html

- **Ladino and other Jewish Languages (Columbia University Department of Middle East and Jewish Studies).** www.columbia.edu/cu/libraries/indiv/area/Jewish/langs.html
- **Ladino: A Lost Language.** www.jewishworldreview.com/0798/Ladino1.asp
- **Judeo-Spanish as a Language of Liturgy and Religious Identification.** www.sephardicstudies.org/americanization2.html
- **Sephardic Medical Roots.** www.apfmed.org/chevra/sephardic.htm
- **Portuguese Jews.** www.apol.net/dightonrock/odyssey_of_port_jews.htm
- **Reading Hebrew Tombstones.** www.jewishgen.org/infofiles/tombstones.html

Anusim or Crypto-Jews

Genealogy-Related Websites

- **Bloom SouthWest Jewish Archives on Crypto-Jews.** http://dizzy.library.arizona.edu:80/images/swja/crypto.htm
- **Crypto-Jews.** http://home.earthlink.net/~benven. Benveniste homepage.
- **Portuguese Sephardim and Crypto-Jews.** www.saudades.org
- **Names of Portuguese Inquisition victims (from Archives Torre do Tombo).** http://home.earthlink.net/~bnahman/NamesFromPortugueseInquisitionArchives.html

Background

- **Institute for Marrano-Anusim Studies.** www.casa-shalom.com
- **Halapid: Society for Crypto-Judaic Studies.** sephardiconnect.com/halapid/halapid.htm
- **Revista Raices: Titulos publicados Spanish Jewish Cultural Review.** www.eunet.es/InterStand/raices/index-rev.html
- **Crypto-Jews in Portugal.** www.lusaweb.com/comunidades/dias2.html
- **Crypto-Jews in the Canary Islands.** http://members.aol.com/artbenven/artbenven.html
- **Crypto-Jews and the Mexican Inquisition.** www.geocities.com/Athens/Acropolis/7016/Jews2.htm
- **Crypto-Rituals.** www.lusaweb.com/comunidades/rituals.html
- **Crypto-Jews of Brazil.** http://home.earthlink.net/~benven/cryptoJewsofBrazil.htm

Balkans, Turkey, Greece

Genealogy-Related Websites

- **Central Archives for the History of the Jewish People.** http://sites.huji.ac.il/archives/page3.htm
- **Rhodes Jewish Museum.** www.rhodesjewishmuseum.org

- **Rhodes Headstones.** www.rhodesjewishmuseum.org/plots.htm. 800 tombstones from Rhodes Jewish cemetery.
- **La Pagina Rodas.** www.rodas.com.ar
- **Monastiri Research List.** http://feefhs.org/mon/monrl.html
- **List of Jews Deported from Monastir in 1943.** www.jewishgen.org/yizkor/bitola/bitola.html
- **Family Names of the Jews of Monastir (Bitola).** www.sephardicstudies.com/monastir.html
- **List of Names, Salonika (Greece) Jewish Community, 1943.** www.sephardicstudies.com/recanati.html
- **Names from Haskoy cemetery (from Minna Rozen's *Haskoy Cemetery: Typology of Stones*).** www.sephardicstudies.org/haskoy.pdf
- **List of Jews Deported from Florina (Greece) by the Nazis.** www.jewishgen.org/Yizkor/florina/florina.html
- **Index of Names from Joseph Nehama's "Histoire des Juifs de Salonique."** www.sephardicstudies.org/nehama.html
- **Translation of *Zikron Salonike: Gedulata ve-hurbana shel Yerushalim de-Balkan: grandeza I destruyicion de Yerushalim del Balken*.** www.jewishgen.org/Yizkor/Thessalonika/Thessalonika.html
- **Jewish Thessaloniki (Salonica).** www.hri.org/culture97/eng/eidika_programmata/koinothtes/jewish_community
- **A Genealogist's Research Trip to Istanbul.** www.jewishgen.org/sefardsig/istanbul_algaze.htm
- **Resources in Ottoman and Turkish Studies at Harvard.** www.fas.harvard.edu/~turkish/resources.html
- **Bulgarian Jewish Names.** www.sephardicstudies.org/b-names.html

Background
- **Turkish Alphabet.** http://umbc7.umbc.edu/~dkusic1/arabtrsl.html
- **History of Turkish Jews.** www.mersina.com/lib/turkish_jews
- **Jews of Turkey.** www.bsz.org/aturkishjews.htm
- **Sefaradi of Monastir (Bitola).** www.jump.net/%7Eelie/Cassorla_Monastir/Monastir.html#Mona_J_Hist
- **Jewish History of Florina.** www.jewishgen.org/yizkor/florina/florina1.html
- **Rhodes Jewish Museum.** www.rhodesjewishmuseum.org/index.htm

Caribbean
Genealogy-Related Websites
- **Jamaican Jewish Families.** www6.pair.com/silvera/jamgen/index.html
- **Cemetery on Curaçao.** www.saudades.org/cur.htm

- **Naming Patterns of Curaçao Sephardim.** www.tc.umn.edu/~terre011/Surnames.html
- **Jewish Cemetery on Nevis.** www.tc.umn.edu/~terre011/Cemetery.html

BACKGROUND
- **Jews of Cuba.** www.jewishcuba.org
- **Sephardim and Fidel Castro.** www.ruthbehar.com
- **Jewish Community of Nevis Archaeology Project.** www.tc.umn.edu/~terre011/Nevis.html
- **350 Years Mikve Israel-Emanuel Curaçao.** www.snoa.com/350/introduction/index.html

EGYPT
See also North Africa.
GENEALOGY-RELATED WEBSITE
- **Resources in Egypt.** www.orthohelp.com/geneal/egypt.htm

BACKGROUND
- *Bassatine News*: **Cairo Jewish Community Website.** www.geocities.com/RainForest/Vines/5855
- **Friends of the Jewish Community in Cairo.** www.geocities.com/jewsofcairo
- **Historical Society of Jews from Egypt.** www.hsje.org
- **Samir Raafat's Articles about Cairo's Jews.** www.egy.com/judaica
- **Taylor-Schechter Genizah Research Unit at Cambridge University Library.** www.lib.cam.ac.uk/Taylor-Schechter
- **Association of Egyptian Jews in France.** www.ajoe.org
- **Albert Mizrahi.** http://mapage.noos.fr/amizrahi

FRANCE
GENEALOGY-RELATED WEBSITES
- **Cercle de Généalogie Juive.** www.genealoj.org
- **Genami.** http://asso.genami.free.fr/english/anglais.htm
- **French Naturalizations, including Algerian and Tunisian Jews 1830–1920.** http://perso.wanadoo.fr/geneagm/ABCD.htm

BACKGROUND
- **Alliance Israelite Universelle.** www.aiu.org
- **Carpentras in the Comtat.** www.col.fr/communautes/carpentras
- **Jewish Community of Tahiti, French Polynesia.** www.col.fr/communautes/polynesie

- French Jewish Communities. www.col.fr/communautes/index.html

The Netherlands
Genealogy-Related Websites
- *Gemeentearchief Amsterdam* (Amsterdam Municipal Archives). www.gemeentearchief.amsterdam.nl
- *Centraal Bureau voor Genealogie* (Central Bureau for Genealogy). www.cbg.nl/english/englishpag.htm
- *Nederlands Instituut voor Oorlogsdocumentatie* (Netherlands Institute of War Documentation). www.riod.nl/engels/english.html
- Netherlands Society for Jewish Genealogy. www.nljewgen.org
- Dutch Jewish Genealogy Homepage. http://web.inter.NL.net/users/DJGH
- Hebrew University, Jerusalem: Dutch Jewish Genealogy. http://dutchjewry.huji.ac.il
- Dutch Jewish Genealogical Database. http://dutchjewry.huji.ac.il/upload/genealogy/main.html
- Bibliotheca Rosenthaliana. www.uba.uva.nl/nl/collecties/rosenthaliana/index.html
- Sephardic Emigrations from Amsterdam, 1757–1813. http://maxpages.com/donadeli/migration
- Amsterdam Sephardic Family Names. http://maxpages.com/donadeli/FamilyTrees

Background
- *Marranos Celebrate Yom Kippur in Amsterdam.* www.chabadonline.com/scripts/tgij/paper/Article-tishrei-text.asp?ArticleID=576
- Esnoga (Amsterdam Synagogue). www.esnoga.com
- Menasseh Ben Israel. http://menasseh.uba.uva.nl/en/collections/rosenthaliana/menasseh
- Jewish Historical Museum. www.jhm.nl/e_home.htm
- Cemetery at Ouderkerk aan de Amstel. www.euronet.nl/users/mnykerk/ouderkrk.htm

Iraq and Syria
Genealogy-Related Websites
- Iraqi Jews, Genealogy. http://thesite2000.virtualave.net/iraqijews/index1.html

Background
- Babylonian Jewry Heritage Center. www.BabylonJewry.org.il

- **Jews of Iraq.** www.us-israel.org/jsource/anti-semitism/iraqijews.html
- **Loolwa Khazzoom website.** www.loolwa.com/workshops.html
- **Syrian Jews of Brooklyn.** www.bsz.org/lsyrianjewsbrooklyn.htm
- **Iraqi Jews Who Left Baghdad during the 1960s and 1970s.** http://thesite2000.virtualave.net/iraqijews/index1.html
- **Jews of Bombay.** www.kashrus.org/asian/bombay.html
- **Baghdadi Jews.** http://theory.tifr.res.in/bombay/history/ethnic/baghdadi-jews.html
- **Scribe Journal.** www.dangoor.com/scribe.html. Photos, family trees.
- **Iraqi Jews of Shanghai.** www.dangoor.com/71page16.html

ISRAEL
GENEALOGY-RELATED WEBSITES
- **Israel Genealogy Society.** www.isragen.org.il
- **Galilee Genealogical Society.** www.geocities.com/Heartland/Hills/9698
- **Beth Hatefutsoth.** www.bh.org.il
- **Central Archives for the History of the Jewish People.** http://sites.huji.ac.il/archives
- **Yad Ben Zvi, Jerusalem.** www.ybz.org.il/menu/eng-index.html
- **Jewish National and University Library.** http://jnul.huji.ac.il

ITALY
GENEALOGY-RELATED WEBSITES
- **Italian Genealogy Page.** www.italiangenealogy.com
- **Marco Soria's Homepage.** www.geocities.com/CapeCanaveral/8037
- **Italian Genealogy, Culture, Heritage, and Databases.** www.cimorelli.com/pie/piemenu.htm
- **Italian Ancestors.** www.geneaita.org/emi. Search for *"Juifs"* (Jews)

BACKGROUND
- **Medici Archive Project Jewish Initiative: The Jews and the Medici.** http://jhuniverse.jhu.edu/~medici/jewish/jewishb.htm
- **Medici Archive Project Jewish Initiative: Documents Relating to Jewish History.** http://jhuniverse.jhu.edu/~medici/jewish/docstoc.htm
- **Jews of Italy.** http://haruth.com/JewOfItaly.html
- **Jewish Community of Livorno (Leghorn).** www.comunitaebraica.org
- **Jewish Ghetto of Venice.** www.doge.it/ghetto/indexi.htm
- **Antico Ghetto di Venezia il Museo Ebraico.** www.doge.it/ghetto/oggetti.htm
- **I-TAL-YA: L'Isola della Rugiada Divina.** www.italya.net

Part IV: Internet • 261

Mexico

Genealogy-Related Websites
- Crypto-Jews and the Mexican Inquisition. www.geocities.com/Athens/Acropolis/7016/Jews2.htm
- *Conversos* Tried by the Mexican Inquisition, 1528–1815. www.geocities.com/Athens/Acropolis/7016/Jews2.htm

Background
- Kulano: Mexican Hanukah. www.ubalt.edu/kulanu/mexican.html

Morocco

Genealogy-Related Websites
- Central Archives for the History of the Jewish People. http://sites.huji.ac.il/archives/page3.htm
- Moroccan Jews in the Amazon. www.orthohelp.com/geneal/amazon.htm
- Index of Maghrebian Surnames. www.al-andaluz.com/gen.html
- Moroccan Jews deported from France (W.W.II). www.sephardicstudies.org/maroc_depor_fr.pdf

Background
- Jewish Morocco. http://rickgold.home.mindspring.com
- Judeo Maghrebi Literature. www.geocities.com/Paris/Jardin/2471/judeo_maghrebi_lit/index.html
- Images of Daily Life in Morocco. http://geogweb.berkeley.edu/GeoImages/Miller/millerone.html
- Les Affinitees Recouvrees: 3 Minutes Down A Street in Morocco. http://artnetweb.com/artnetweb/gallery/code/rubin/rubin.html
- Sephardic-Moroccan Page. www.geocities.com/CapitolHill/1717

North Africa

See also Egypt and Morocco.

Genealogy-Related Websites
- Resources in Egypt. www.jewishgen.org/sefardsig/egypt.htm
- Resources in Morocco. www.jewishgen.org/sefardsig/morocco.htm
- Central Archives for the History of the Jewish People. http://sites.huji.ac.il/archives/page3.htm
- French Naturalizations, including those of Algerian and Tunisian Jews 1830–1920. http://perso.wanadoo.fr/geneagm/ABCD.htm
- Tunisian Jews deported from France during W.W.II www.sephardicstudies.org/tunis_dep_fran.pdf

- ♦ **Church of Jesus Christ of Latter-day Saints (Mormon), Resources for Algeria.** www.pieds-noirs.org/echanges/registre.htm

BACKGROUND
- ♦ **Jews of Libya.** http://sunsite.berkeley.edu/LibyanJews
- ♦ **Jews of Tunisia.** www.harissa.com/accueileng.htm
- ♦ **Jews of Malta.** www.angelfire.com/al/AttardBezzinaLawrenc
- ♦ **Bassatine News: Cairo Jewish Community.** www.geocities.com/RainForest/Vines/5855
- ♦ **Friends of the Jewish Community in Cairo.** www.geocities.com/jewsofcairo
- ♦ **Historical Society of Jews from Egypt.** www.hsje.org
- ♦ **Samir Raafat's Articles about Cairo's Jews.** www.egy.com/judaica
- ♦ **Judeo Maghrebi Literature.** www.geocities.com/Paris/Jardin/2471/judeo_maghrebi_lit/index.html
- ♦ **Jews of Cape Verde and the Azores.** www.saudades.org/jewscapev.html

SOUTH AMERICA
GENEALOGY-RELATED WEBSITES
- ♦ **Argentina: Sociedad Argentina de Genealogia Judia.** www.agja.com.ar
- ♦ **Pablo Chami's Page from Argentina.** www.pachami.com/English/chamiE.htm
- ♦ **Brazilian Genealogy** (not Jewish) http://Genealogias.Org

BACKGROUND
- ♦ **Jews in Chile.** http://members.tripod.com/~sefard/index.html
- ♦ **Herencia Del Norte.** www.herencia.com
- ♦ **Bibliography: Latin American Jewish Studies** by Judith Laikin Elkin. http://h-net2.msu.edu/~latam/bibs/bibjewish.html
- ♦ **Brazilian Jewish bibliography** in Portuguese. http://utopia.com.br/ahjb
- ♦ **Brazilian Jewry: A Concise History.** www.jewishgen.org/infofiles/BrazilianJewry.htm
- ♦ **CISICSEF: Centro de Investigacion y Difusion de la Cultura Sefardi** in Argentina. www.cidicsef.org.ar

UNITED STATES
GENEALOGY-RELATED WEBSITES
- ♦ **JewishGen.** www.jewishgen.org
- ♦ **Ellis Island DataBase** (ship passenger lists of immigrants to New York). www.ellisislandrecords.org

- **Stephen Morse One-Step Search Engine.** http://www.jewishgen.org/databases/EIDB/ellis.html. Simplifies Ellis Island Data Base searches.
- **Hamburg Passenger Lists.** www.hamburg.de/LinkToYourRoots/english/welcome.htm
- **Steamship Historical Society of America** (photos of trans-Atlantic immigrant ships). http://archives.ubalt.edu/steamship/photo.htm
- **JewishGen's infofiles.** www.jewishgen.org/infofiles
- **Social Security Death Index.** www.ancestry.com
- **U.S. Bureau of the Census.** www.census.gov
- **U.S. National Archives.** http://lcweb.loc.gov/rr/genealogy

SEPHARDIC FAMILY PAGES

Personal websites on the genealogies of specific Sephardic families include:

Aboaf. http://members.aol.com/aboafaa
Alhadef and Kazes. http://userpages.wittenberg.edu/dkazez/dk/elh-kaz-fre.html
Amzalak. www.geocities.com/Heartland/Plains/5286
Arditi. www.netvision.net.il/php/arditi76
Attie. *See* Matalon.
Barrocas. www.barrocas.com
Bensaude. www.bensaude.org
Benveniste. http://home.earthlink.net/~benven
Berdugo, Botbol, Sebbag, Cohen-Scali. http://dept-info.labri.u-bordeaux.fr/~loeb/tree/index.html
Bigio. *See* Matalon.
Botbol. *See* Berdugo.
Cardozo. www.cardozo.org/genealogy
Cassorla. www.jump.net/%7Eelie/Cassorla_Monastir/Cassorla.html
Cassuto. www.bobcassuto.fr.st
Cattaui (in Egypt). www.geocities.com/RainForest/Vines/5855/cattaui.htm
Cazes. *See* Kazez
Cohen-Hadria. www.ifrance.com/cohenhadria
Cohen-Scali. *See* Berdugo
Elazar. www.geocities.com/Athens/Acropolis/6527/elazar.html
Farhi. www.farhi.org
Forrester. *See Hays.*
Gabbai. www.netspace.net.au/~rwagner/welcome.html
Garcia. www.jerrygarcia.co.uk
Gomez. www.gomez.org/gomez.html
Hakim. www.webstazy.com/hakim
Hays/Myers/Touro/Forrester. http://eyesofglory.com

Jabes (in Egypt). www.geocities.com/RainForest/Vines/5855/jabes1.htm
Hodara. www.hodara.com
Kazez, Cazes. http://userpages.wittenberg.edu/dkazez/fam/Kazez-Cazes.html
Levy-Bencheton. www.alex.alexandre.com/genealogy
Maduro. *See* Delvalle.
Maimon (Maimonides). www.ttec.com/maimon/hist.htm
Malka-Gelfand. www.orthohelp.com/geneal
Matalon, Bigio, Attie. www.angelfire.com/sk/bigiofamilytree
Maya. http://familytreemaker.genealogy.com/users/c/o/h/Michael-L-Cohen/index.html
Maymi. http://users.erols.com/gascue-maymi
Melca. www.melca.info/genealogy.html
Mendes da Costa. www.mendesdacosta.com
Myers. *See* Hays
Nahman (of Gerona). http://home.earthlink.net/~bnahman
Ottolenghi. www.ottolenghi.org
Pinheiros (of Nevis and Barbados). www.tc.umn.edu/~terre011/tree.html
Salomon. www.salamon.net
Sebbag. *See* Berdugo
Seruya (in Rio). www2.netpoint.com.br/elloco
Shaltiel. www.shealtiel.org
Suissa. www.alex.alexandre.com/genealogy
Tobias. http://genforum.genealogy.com/tobias
Toledano. http://members.tripod.com/~Yacov_Tal
Touro. *See* Hays
Zakine-Cerf. http://geocities.com/Paris/Musee/9390

GAZETTEERS

Gazetteer. Locations of towns and villages, including old names. www.calle.com/world
Mapquest. www.mapquest.com

PEOPLE SEARCH PAGES

Anywho. www.anywho.com
Four 11. www.411.com
Google. www.google.com
InfoSpace. www.infospace.com
Lycos's Whowhere. www.whowhere.lycos.com
Switchboard. www.switchboard.com
Worldpages. www.worldpages.com
Yahoo. http://people.yahoo.com

Reverse directories. Use when:
— a person's address or telephone number is known, but not the names:
    www.teldir.com (international directories)
    http://reversedirectory.langenberg.com
    www.thinkdirectmarketing.com/freesearch
— an e-mail address is known, but not the name:
    http://my.email.address.is/efreverse.htm

Family Finders:
    www.orthohelp.com/geneal/family_sites.htm (Sephardic families)
    www.jewishgen.org/jgff (Jewishgen Family Finders)
    www.jewishgen.org/gedcom
    www.ancestry.com

Search for births, deaths, and marriage records:
    http://vitalrec.com
    www.knowx.com
    http://familysearch.org (LDS Library catalog)
    www.jewishgen.org/cemetery

U.S. Social Security Death Index. www.ancestry.com/search/rectype/vital/ssdi/main.htm?rc=locale%7E&us=0

APPENDIXES

APPENDIX A.
ETYMOLOGY OF SELECTED SEPHARDIC NAMES

The sample of common Sephardic surnames in Table 4 illustrates their variants, origins, and meanings.[1] Most *converso* surnames of Hispanic origin, such as Rodriguez, Gomez, Mendez, and Henriquez, are not included; except for names originating from places, they are usually adopted Christian surnames and have no underlying Jewish meaning or origin. The notations "ben.." and "avin.." mean the variant includes the ben or avin prefixes.

Table 4. Selected Sephardic Surnames: Variants, Languages, Meanings

Name	Variants	Original Language	Meaning	Notes
Abenrey	Malka, Ben Rey, ibn Rey, Avenreyna, Ben Melekh, Reyno, Soberano	Hispanic-Arabic	Son of king	
Abensour	Abensur	Hebrew	Son of rock (*tsour*)	
Abitbol	Toboul, Abitboul (*see also* Botbol)	Arabic	Drummer (*taboula*)	
Abouaf	Aboab, Abuhab	Arabic	Dispensor of goods	
Abrabanel	Abravanel	Unknown	Unknown	Ancient family, said to descend from King David
Abulafia	Boulafia, Alafia	Arabic	Possessor of health or well being (*afia*)	Name also borne by Moslem families
Aknin	Aqnine, ben Aknine	Berber	Jacob	
Albaz	Elbaz, Elvas, ben..	Arabic	Falconer, also locality in Spain	

---

[1] Sources: Abraham Laredo, *Les Noms des Juifs du Maroc* (Names of the Jews of Morocco) (Madrid: Institut Montano, 1978); Jose Maria Abecassis, *Genealogia Hebraica: Portugal e Gibraltar, Secs. XVII a XX* (Jewish genealogy: Portugal and Gibraltar, 17th to the 20th centuries); Joseph Toledano, *La Saga des Familles: Les Juifs du Maroc et leurs noms*. (Family sagas: The Jews of Morocco and their names) (Tel Aviv: Stavit, 1983). Joseph Toledano, *Une histoire des familles: les noms de famille Juifs d'Afrique du Nord* (Family history: The family names of the Jews of North Africa). (Jerusalem: Author, 1999); Maurice Eisenbeth, *Les Juifs de l'Afrique du Nord: Démographie et Onomastique* (Jews of North Africa: Demographics and onomastics) (Algiers: Imprimerie du lycée, 1936).

Name	Variants	Original Language	Meaning	Notes
Alfasi	Elfassi, Fasi, Defaz	Arabic	From Fez, Morocco	
Alhadeff	Alkhadif, Alhadyb	Arabic	*Kedif*, or chief	
Anonios		Greek	Eternal	Found in Janina
Aragon	De Aragon	Spanish	From Aragon	Name borne by both Moslems and Jews
Arapis		Greek	Arab	Found in Janina.
Arditi		Italian	Ardent	
Ashkenazi	Eshkanazi, Eskinazi	Hebrew	German	
Assouline	Asulin, ben.., Benasuly	Berber	Rocks	
Attal		Arabic	Porter	
Azulay	ben..	Berber	Good	
		Spanish	Blue eyes	
Barcilon	Barchilon, Barcilon, Bargeloni	Hebrew Bar-shelona (our coast)	Old name of Barcelona	
Barmalil		Hebrew	Son of the word	Mostly in Morocco
Benatar	ibn Attar, Abenatar, Alatar	Arabic	Druggist, perfumer	
Ben Sushan	ben Sussan	Persian	Ancient Persian capital (Suze)	
Benveniste	Benvenist, Abenvenisti, Bensiti	Spanish	Welcome (translation of *shalom*)	A noted Benvenisti family came from Narbonne.
Bitton	Betoun, Beton	Spanish	Life	
Botbol	Tebol, Boutbol (*see also* Abitbol)	Arabic	Drum maker or seller	
Cabalero	Caballero, Cabaliero	Spanish	Knight, horseman	
Cardoza	Cardozo, Cartoso	Spanish/ Portuguese	From towns in Guadala-jara (Spain) or Viseu (Portugal) A vegetable (*cardo*)	
Carmi	Karmi	Hebrew	Vineyard keeper	

Name	Variants	Original Language	Meaning	Notes
Caro	Habib	Spanish	Dear, beloved	
Carvalho	Cabalo	Portuguese	Town in Portugal	
Castelnuevo		Italian	New castle	
Castorianos		Greek	From Castoria	
Castro	Decastro	Spanish	Jewish fortress in Leon	
Charbit	Sharbit	Hebrew	Scepter	
Cohen	Exists as part of multiple combined names	Hebrew	Priest	
Cohen-Scali		Hebrew-Spanish	From "Scali Sevillan"[2]	Morocco and Egypt
Corcos		Spanish	Town in Castile	
Crespin	Crispin; aven.., ben...	Spanish	Curly (hair)	
Dalyan	Dalven	Turkish	Fishnets/fishpond	Found in Ioannina
Danon	Dondon, aben.., Abendanno	Spanish/Hebrew	Judge	
Dayan		Hebrew	Judge	
De Aragon	Ragon (see also Aragon)	Spanish	Kingdom in Spain	
De Fez	Alfasi	Arabic	From Fez, Morocco	
De Silva	Da Silva	Spanish	From the forest (*silva*)	
De Soto	Soto, Del Soto	Spanish	Marsh land	
Farhi	Hafarhi	Hebrew	From Florenza (*perahi* = flowered)	
		Arabic	From *farha* (joy)	
Ferreres	Ferares, ben..	Spanish	Blacksmith. From towns in Majorca or Zamora	
Foinquinos	Follinquinos, Foyinquinos	Greco-Latin	Phoenician	
Franco	Franca (also given as	Spanish	Freed (from	

---

[2] Scali denotes a gold-thread industry conducted in Seville during the Middle Ages; the numerical equivalent of Saddock, denoting descent from that direct Cohen line.

Appendix A: Etymology of Selected Sephardic Names • 271

Name	Variants	Original Language	Meaning	Notes
	first name)		taxes or bondage)	
Gabbay	Gabai, Avin.., Cabay	Hebrew	In talmudic era. alms collectors; in Spain, tax collectors	
Gaguin	Gagin	Spanish	Town in Pontevedra, Spain	
Galanos		Greek	Blue-eyed	
Guedalia	Guadella, Guedalha	Hebrew	Elevated by God	
Hakim	Elhakim, Alhakim, Hkim	Arabic	Physician, sage	
Halfon	Khalfon, Jalfon, Alfon, Halpen	Arabic	given to child "replacing" a dead person (like first name, Makhlouf)	
Hamu	Hammou, Hamuy	Arabic	Father-in-law; heat (from *hams* Hebr); Berber tribe	
Hasdai	Hasday, Chasdai, ben.., Acday, Azday	Aramaic	Goodness	
Hazan	Azan, Chasan, Ha-Hazan	Hebrew	Official, cantor	
Kampanaris		Greek	Bells	Found in Janina.
Kokkinos		Greek	Means red (redhead?)	
Laredo		Spanish	Town in Santander, Castile	
Levy	Halevy, Levita	Hebrew	Levy tribe	
Lombroso		Spanish	Translation of Hebrew *nehora* or *eir*, meaning luminous	
Lugasi	Lugashi	Arabic	From town of Lugas in Oviedo	

Name	Variants	Original Language	Meaning	Notes
Maimon	ben.., Mainonides, Mimon, Maymo	Hebrew	Fortunate, lucky	
Malka	ben Melekh, Soberano, ibn Rey, Reino, Malki, Abimelekh	Aramean	King	
		Hebrew	From Malaga (Malaca)	
Malqui	Malka, Almalqui, Almalki, Maleque, Malaki	Spanish	From Malaga (Aramean: *Malaca*)	
Mandil		Arab	Apron	
Marciano	Martziano	Spanish	From Murcia	Mostly in Morocco
Marcus	Marcos	Spanish	Plural of *Marco* (measuring weight)	
Medina	De Medina	Hebrew	State	
		Arabic	Several towns in Spain	
Mizrahi	*See also* Ben Ashurqui, De Levante, Shuraqui	Hebrew	Eastern	
Montefiore		Italian	From placename: Montefiore	Originates in Papal States
Moreno	ben..	Spanish	Brown	
Nahon		Hebrew/Spanish	From town of Naon in Oviedo, Spain	
Nahman	ben Nahman	Hebrew	Lord will heal (or console)	Biblical name.
Navaro	Nabaro	Spanish	Kingdom of Navarre	
Obadya	Obadiah, Ovadia, Abdias	Hebrew	Servant of God	
Ohanna	O'Hana, Bohana, Abuhana, Abuhenna	Berber	Son of Hanna	Prefix *O* means son in Berber name
Ohayon		Berber Hebrew (*hayon*)	Son of Life (*Hayon*)	Prefix *O* means son in Berber name

Appendix A: Etymology of Selected Sephardic Names

Name	Variants	Original Language	Meaning	Notes
Oiknine	Waknin, Ouaknin, ben..	Berber	Son of Jacob	
Patish	Betache	Hebrew	Hammer	In Greece and North Africa
Perez		Hebrew	Grandson of Jacob	Biblical
Perreira		Portuguese	Pear tree	Many Jews forced to convert to Chritianity took on the names of trees
Pinto	De Pinto, Pynto	Spanish	Town near Madrid	
Pisa		Italian	Town in Italy	
Rabi	Ribbi, ben..	Hebrew	My rabbi	
Rofe	Ha Rofe, Roffe, Rophe, (see also Del Medico)	Hebrew	Physician	
Rosales	Rozales	Spanish	Rose bush; also from some towns in Spain	
Sabah	Caba	Arabic	Morning	
Sacerdoti		Italian	Priest (Cohen)	
Saltiel	Shaltiel, Chaltiel	Hebrew	Asked of God	
Santob	Shemtob, Sentob, Sento	Hebrew	Good name	
Sasson	Sassoon, ben..	Hebrew	Happiness, joy	
Sebag	Sabag, Assabagh, Essebagh	Arabic	Dyer of cloth	
Senor	Senior, Bonsenyor, Ben Senor, Bonsignour	Spanish	Elder, sir	
Serero		Spanish	Candle-maker	
Serfati	Sarfati, Zarfati, Ha-Zarfatti, Hasserfaty	Hebrew	Frenchman	
Sevillano		Spanish	From Seville, Spain	
Shalom	ben..	Hebrew	Peace	
Shuraqui	ben, Souraqi, Shouraqui (see also Mizrahi)	Arabic	Easterner	
Soberano	see also Malka	Spanish	Sovereign	
Sofer	HaSoffer, Soffer, Sopher	Hebrew	Scribe,	

Name	Variants	Original Language	Meaning	Notes
			notary	
Soriano		Spanish	From Soria in Castile	
Soto	De Soto, Del Soto	Spanish	Marsh land	
Sultan	Bensultan, Ibenrey, Malka	Arabic	Sultan, king	
Taranto	Toranto	Italian	Town in Italy	
Tangier	Tanjir, Tanzir, Tandjir	Berber	Clay cooking pot	
Toledano		Spanish	From Toledo	
Turqui	El Turqui, Eturki, Atturki	Arabic	Turk	
Uaknin	Waknin (*see* Oiknine)	Berber		
Uziel	Oziel, Uzziel, Ouziel	Hebrew	God is my strength	Biblical
Valensi	Balenci	Arabic, Spanish	From Valencia	
Veniste	Beniste, Benveniste	Spanish	You came	
Verdugo	Berdugo	Spanish	Branch (of a tree)	
Vidal	Vital, Vitalis, Bitales, Viton, Hayyim	Latin	Life	
Yahia	ibn Yahia	Arabic	Life, from *Chiya* (Aramaic) and *Haim* (Hebrew)	ibn Yahia family descended from Yahia al Daoudi (Yahia of Davidic descent)
Zadoq	Sadoc, Zadoc, Acencadoque, Aben Cadoc, Sadox	Hebrew	Just	Biblical
Zafrani	Ezafrani, Alzafrani	Arabic and Persian	From Zafaran, in Persia	

Appendix B.
Sephardic Cursive Alphabet

Source: Adapted from a table by Mark Lidzbarsky in the Jewish Encyclopedia, 1901–06.

Table 5. Recent Sephardic Hebrew Scripts

Name	Block letters (meruba)	Rashi print	Sephardic cursive	Ashkenazi cursive
aleph	א	אּ	ſ	IC
aleph-lamed	ﬥ	ﬥ	ﬥ	
vet, bet	ב בּ	ב בּ	ב בּ	ב בּ
gimel	ג	ג	∿	ʓ
dalet	ד	ד	ʏ	ʓ
heh	ה	ה	∾	ה
vav	ו	ו	ן	ן
zayin	ז	ז	ſ	ʒ
khet	ח	ח	ת	ח
tet	ט	ט	ט	ﻉ
yod	י	י	׳	׳
khaf/sofit/kaf	כ ך כּ	כ ך כּ	כ ך כּ	כ ך כּ
lamed	ל	ל	ﻝ ℓ	ʃ
mim/sofit	מ ם	מ ס	מ ס	מ N
noon/sofit	נ ן	נ ן	נ ן	ן J
samekh	ס	ס	ø	O
ayin	ע	ע	y	⅄
fe/sofit/pe	פ ף פּ	פ ף פּ	פ ף פּ	פ ף פּ
tsad/sofit	צ ץ	צ ץ	ʒ ʃ	ʒ ʋ
kaf	ק	ק	ʃ	ק
resh	ר	ר	ʃ	ר
sin/shin	ש שׁ	שׁ שׁ	ש ש	e e
tav	ת תּ	ת	∾	ת ת

Appendix B: Sephardic Cursive Alphabet • 277

APPENDIX C.
ARABIC ALPHABET

Arabic Alphabet

Name	Alone	Sound	Initial (before ن)	Middle (between ص ر)	Terminal (after ص)
alif	ا	*a*ward	ان	صار	صا
ba	ب	*b*all	بن	صبر	صب
ta	ت	*t*ime	تن	صتر	صت
tha	ث	*th*ink	ثن	صثر	صث
jeem	ج	*j*oke	جن	صجر	صج
ha	ح	*h*acham	حأ	صحن	صح
kha	خ	ha*ch*am	خأ	صخن	صخ
dal	د	*d*ollar	دن	صدر	صد
zal	ذ	*th*at	ذن	صذر	صذ
ra	ر	*r*ush	رن	صرر	صر
za	ز	*z*ion	زن	صزر	صز
sin	س	*s*am	سن	صسر	صس
shin	ش	*sh*am	شن	صشر	صش
sud	ص	strong S	صن	صصر	صص
dud	ض	strong D	ضن	صضر	صض
Ta	ط	strong T	طن	صطر	صط
za	ظ	strong TH	ظن	صظر	صظ
ayn	ع	Hebrew *ayn*	عن	صعر	صع
rhayn	غ	Hebrew *rhayn*	غن	صغر	صغ

fa	ف	found	فن	صفر	صف
qaf	ق	strong K	قن	صقر	صق
kaf	ك	king	كن	صكر	صك
lam	ل	lamp	لن	صلر	صل
mim	م	mother	من	صمر	صم
nun	ن	none	نن	صنر	صن
ha	ه	hat	هن	صهر	صه
waw	و	wound	ون	صور	صو
ya	ي	yellow	ين	صير	صي

Appendix D.
Sephardic Documents at the Central Archives for the History of the Jewish People

Name	Place	Period	Reference, *File No.*
Ashkenazi	Tiberias, Safed	1803–1965	Inv6671, *10*
Assouline	Fedala, Morocco	18th century–1990	Inv6777, *187*
Bonaventura, Enfo	Italy		P191, *38*
Bonfiglioli, Giuliu	Italy		F186, *39*
Corcos		1842–1929	HM2/928, *791*
Curiel	Italy	16th–20th centuries	Inv1882, *531*
De Picciotto	Lebanon, Syria		IT1189; Inv8598, *148*
De Sola	Lisbon	1670–1910	Inv3116, *705*
De Vries	Holland	17th–20th centuries	Inv5782, *766*
Del Vecchio	Italy		IT1208; IT1274; Inv5935, *387*
Del Vecchio	Italy		IT1211, *589*
Delblanco			AHW753, *315*
Elias		1715–1947	Inv1863; Inv5761, *353*
Henrique	Amsterdam	1802–04	Inv280/5, *645*
Henriques		1682–1737	HM2/1015, *813*
Moscati	Italy		IT1211, *588*
Picciotto			*See* De Picciotto
Pinto	Groningen		Inv353, *634*
Sealtiel	Hamburg	1712–1970	P178, *159*
Vas Dias	Holland	1724–1973	Inv6595, *765*
Vitale	Italy		IT1211, *590*
Zarfati			Inv3244, *741*

Source: Sallyann A. Sack, *A Guide to Jewish Genealogical Research in Israel*, rev. ed. (Teaneck, N.J.: Avotaynu, 1995), 133.

Appendix E.
Sephardic Register and Record Books at the Jewish National and University Library

Place	Description	Period	Access #
Jerusalem	Sephardi kollel	1772–1806	4 1037
Jerusalem	Sephardi kollel	1851–80	4 95
Jerusalem	Sephardi kollel	1854	8 259
North Africa	Births and *milahs*	1902–7	8 5246
Reggio, Italy		1742–78	8 985
Reggio, Italy	*Pinkhas*	1840	M.V 319
Salonica	Births	1917–24	4 851
Salonica	Help to needy	1919–40	4 853
Salonica	Deaths	1934–40	4 701
Salonica	*Bet Din*	1935–37	4 861
Salonica	Official papers	1938–40	8 852
Sefrou, Morocco	Accounts	1887–96	8 4117
Sudan	*Ketubot*	1907–63	Heb 4 7306/1–2

Source: Sallyann A. Sack, *A Guide to Jewish Genealogical Research in Israel*, rev. ed. (Teaneck, N.J.: Avotaynu, 1995), 177

APPENDIX F.
GENEALOGY FORMS

Genealogy Research Log

Researched Name/Item

Goals *(parents of ..., etc)* | Locality

Date of Search	Location Call #	Description of source (Author, title, year, page)	Comments (purpose of search, results, years and names searched)	Doc. number

Correspondence Record Sheet

Surname: _____ Researcher: _____

Entry	Date Sent	Follow-up Response	Charge Refund	Addressee & Address	Subject or Citation	Results	Doc. No.
1							
2							
3							
4							
5							
6							
7							
8							

Check if continued on other side ☐

Appendix F: Genealogy Forms • 283

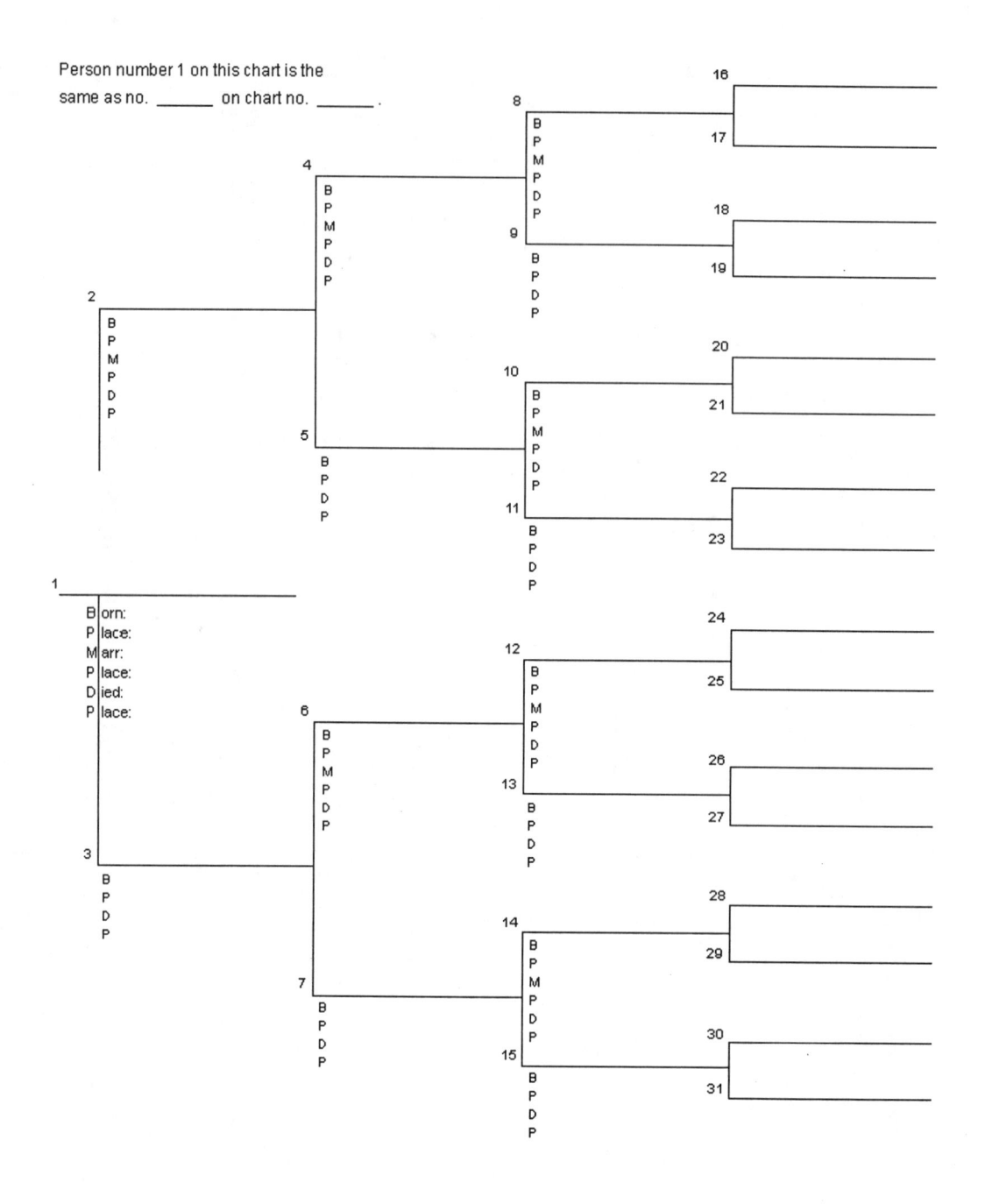

Person number 1 on this chart is the same as no. _____ on chart no. _____ .

Pedigree Chart

284 • *Sephardic Genealogy: Discovering Your Sephardic Ancestors and Their World*

Family Record Sheet

                                                                                                  Source

Husband: _____ _____

    Born on: _____ Place: _____ _____
    Married: _____ Place: _____ Div? _____
    Prior Spouse: _____ Place: _____ Div? _____
    Died on: _____ Place: _____ _____
    Military Service: _____ _____
    Father: _____ _____
    Mother: _____ _____

Wife: _____ _____

    Born on: _____ Place: _____ _____
    Died on: _____ Place: _____ _____
    Father: _____ _____
    Mother: _____ _____

Child # 1: _____ _____

    Born on: _____ Place: _____ _____
    Died on: _____ Place: _____ _____
    Prior Spouse: _____ Place: _____ Div? _____
    Father: _____ _____
    Mother: _____ _____

Child # 2: _____ _____

    Born on: _____ Place: _____ _____
    Died on: _____ Place: _____ _____
    Married: _____ Place: _____ Div? _____
    Father: _____ _____
    Mother: _____ _____

Child # : _____ _____

    Born on: _____ Place: _____ _____
    Died on: _____ Place: _____ _____
    Married: _____ Place: _____ Div? _____
    Father: _____ _____
    Mother: _____ _____

Additional Notes:

Prepared by and Date:

Chart of Family Relationships

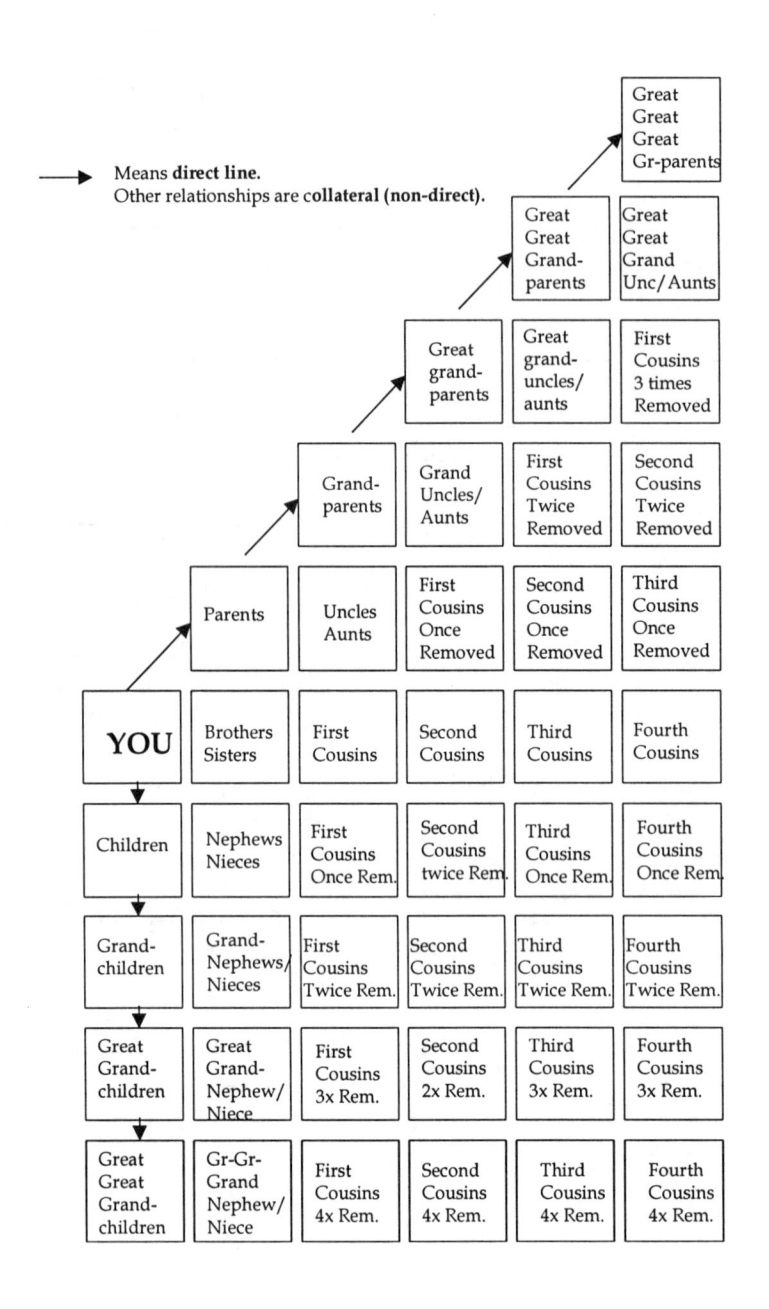

→ Means **direct line**.
Other relationships are **collateral (non-direct)**.

						Great Great Great Gr-parents
				Great Great Grand-parents	Great Great Grand Unc/Aunts	
			Great grand-parents	Great grand-uncles/ aunts	First Cousins 3 times Removed	
		Grand-parents	Grand Uncles/ Aunts	First Cousins Twice Removed	Second Cousins Twice Removed	
	Parents	Uncles Aunts	First Cousins Once Removed	Second Cousins Once Removed	Third Cousins Once Removed	
YOU	Brothers Sisters	First Cousins	Second Cousins	Third Cousins	Fourth Cousins	
Children	Nephews Nieces	First Cousins Once Rem.	Second Cousins twice Rem.	Third Cousins Once Rem.	Fourth Cousins Once Rem.	
Grand-children	Grand-Nephews/ Nieces	First Cousins Twice Rem.	Second Cousins Twice Rem.	Third Cousins Twice Rem.	Fourth Cousins Twice Rem.	
Great Grand-children	Great Grand-Nephew/ Niece	First Cousins 3x Rem.	Second Cousins 2x Rem.	Third Cousins 3x Rem.	Fourth Cousins 3x Rem.	
Great Great Grand-children	Gr-Gr-Grand Nephew/ Niece	First Cousins 4x Rem.	Second Cousins 4x Rem.	Third Cousins 4x Rem.	Fourth Cousins 4x Rem.	

Sephardic Genealogy: Discovering Your Sephardic Ancestors and Their World

APPENDIX G.
JEWISH NAMES IN PRINTED SOURCES

Use the following lists to identify sources where the names are mentioned. Refer to the sources where these names are found for additional information.

Abecassis, Jose Maria. *Genealogia Hebraica: Portugal e Gibraltar* (Jewish Genealogy: Portugal and Gibraltar). (Lisbon: Author, 1990).

Four volumes present carefully documented Jewish family trees from Portugal and Gibraltar, listed alphabetically.

Volume 1:
   Abeasis, Abecassis, Abensur, Abitbol, Aboab, Abohbot, Absidid, Abudarham, Acris, Adrehi, Aflalo, Albo, Alkaim, Amar, Amram, Amselem, Amzalak, Anahory, Asayol, Askenazi, Assayag, Athias, Atrutel, Auday, Azancot, Azavey, Azerad, Azuelos, Azulay, Balensi, Banon, Baquis, Barchilom, Baruel, Berlilo, Benabu, Benady, Benaim, Benamor, Benarus, Benatar, Benbunan, Benchaya, Benchetrit, Benchimol, Bendahan, Bendelack, Bendran, Benelisha, Beneluz, Benhayon

Volume 2:
   Beniso, Benitah, Benjamim, Benjo, Benmergui, Benmiyara, Benmuyal, Benoalid, Benoliel, Benrimoj, Benros, Bensabat, Bensadon, Bensaloha, Bensaude, Benselum, Bensheton, Bensimon, Bensliman, Bensusan, Bentata, Bentubo, Benudis, Benyuli, Benyunes, Benzacar, Benzaquen, Benzecry, Benzimra, Berdugo, Bergel, Bibas, Blum, Bohudana, Brigham, Brudo, Buzaglo, Bytton, Cagi, Cansino, Cardoso, Carseni, Castel, Cazes, Cohen, Conquy, Coriat, Cubi, Danan, Davis, Delmar, Elmaleh, Esaguy, Esnaty, Farache, Ferares, Finsi, Foinquinos, Fresco

Volume 3:
   Gabay, Gabizon, Garson, Hadida, Hassan, Hatchuel, Israel, Kadoshi, Katzan, Labos, Laluff, Laredo, Lasry, Lengui, Levi, Malca, Maman, Marques, Marrache, Martins, Massias, Matana, Megueres, Melul, Moreira, Mor-Jose, Mucznik, Muginstein, Muller, Nahon, Namias, Nathan, Obadia, Ohana, Oliveira, Pacifico, Pallache, Pariente, Pimienta, Pinto, Querub, Roffe, Ruah, Rygor, Sabath, Salama, Sananes, Saragga, Schocron, Sebag, Segal, Sequerra, Serfaty

Volume 4:
   Serequi, Serrafe, Seruya, Sicsu, Tangi, Tapiero, Taregano, Taurel, Tedesqui, Tobelem, Toledano, Tuati, Uziel, Varicas, Wahnon, Waknin, Wolfinsohn, Zafrany, Zagury

Laredo, Abraham. *Les noms des Juifs du Maroc.* Madrid: Institut Arias Montano, 1978.

This extensive work presents family names of Sephardic Jews of Morocco, including their origins and variants. Lists historical occurrences of the names with a summary of available data with documented sources. Because of its extensive detail, this out of print book is an indispensable source for Sephardic research, even if the family did not originate in Morocco.

Philip Abensur, editor of *Etsi*, indexed the names from Laredo's book; the index may be accessed at www.geocities.com/EnchantedForest/1321/ laredo_1.htm.

Toledano, Joseph. *La saga des familles: Les juifs du maroc et leurs noms.* Tel Aviv: Stavit, 1983.

This book is less extensive than Laredo's work, but includes photographs of individuals when available.

Abecassis, Abehsera, Abensour, Abergel, Abdallah, Abetan, Abikhzer, Abisror, Abitbol, Abizmil, Aboab, Abou, Aboudraham, Aboulafia, Abourmad, Abourbia, Abrabanel, Adi, Adrotiel, Aflalo, Afriat, Akoka, Akrich, Albaranes, Albo, Alcheikh, Alfonta, Almaalem, Alloul, Altaraz, Altit, Amar, Amiel, Amor, Amozeg, Amghar, Amselem, Amzallag, Amsili, Anconina, Ankri, Anfaoui, Anidjar, Annaquab, Arajel, Arrouas, Arama, Asbili, Assabti, Assaraf, Assor, Assouline, Attar, Auday, Altia, Azencot, Azerad, Azar, Azeroual, Aziza, Azogui, Azoulay, Azuelos, Azran, Bahloul, Bahtit, Banon, Barchilon, Barsheshet, Belahdeb, Baruk, Belahsen, Belicha, Benadiba, Benaksas, Benaim, Benamram, Benamara, Benaroch, Benaudis, Benazeraf, Ben Baroukh, Benchlmol, Bendavid, Ouyoussef, Bendrao, Bendelak, Benelzra, Benezra, Beniciki, Bengio, Benibgui, Benghouzi, Benhaim, Benisty, Benkemoun, Benmaimon, Benlolo, Bensaude, Benshabat, Bensimon, Bentolila, Benwalid, Ben Waish, Benyair, Benzaquen, Benzenou, Berdugo, Beriro, Betito, Bettach, Bibas, Bitton, Bodoch, Bohbot, Botbol, Bouaziz, Boucfti, Bouhadana, Bouganim, Boussidan, Bouzaglo, Bouskila, Cabessa, Candero, Cardozo, Caro, Castiel, Cazes, Charbit, Chetrit, Choukroun, Chkeiran, Chlouch, Chriqui, Cohen, Cohen, Maquin, Cohen-Scali, Corcos, Conqui, Coriat, Dabela, Dades, Dadoun, Dahan, Dadia, Danan, Danon, Danino, Dayan, Delmar, Deloya, Dery, Diwan, Drihem, Elalouf, Elbaz, Elgrabli, Elfassi, Elhadad, Elharar, Elhyani, Elkabas, Elkayim, Elkeslassy, Elmekies, Elkouby, Elkrief, Elmaleh, Elmoznino, Encaoua, Eskouri, Etedgui, Ezerzer, Fedida, Fouinquinos, Fhima, Gabay, Gagurn, Garzon, Gavison, Ghozlan, Guedalia, Guigui, (Ben) Haco, Hadida, Haliwa, Hamou, Hamron, Harboun, Hassan, Hassine, Hatchwel, Hazan, Houta, Hazot, Haziza, Himi, Ifergan, Iflah, Ifrah, Illouz, Israel, Iscini, Itah, Katan, Khalfon, Kadoch, Kakon, Karsenti, Khalifa, Kessous, Knafo, Lahmy, Laredo, Lasry, Lazimi, Levy, Levy-Ben-Yuli, Librati, Loeb, Loubaton, Lougassy, Louk, Lousky, Mahfoda, Maimran, Malka, Mamane, Mansano, Marache, Marciano, Mareli, Medioni, Meloul, Meran, Mergui, Messas, Monsonego, Moreno, Moryoussef, Moyal, Mreien, Myara, Nahmany, Nahmias, Nahon, Nahori, Nezri, Nidam, Obadia, Ohana, Ohnouna, Ohayon, Oliel,

Ouaknine, Ouakrat, Ouanounou, Ouazana, Outmezguin, Ouziel, Pariente, Pallache, Perez, Pimienta, Pinto, Rebibo, Revah, Riboh, Rouah, Rimokh, Rouach, Rosilio, Ruti, Ruimy, Saba, Sabah, Sadoun, Sananes, Saporta, Sarfati, Saraga, Sasson, Sayag, Sebag, Seban, Selouk, Serero, Shoushana, Siboni, Siksu, Sisso, Soudry, Soussan, Suissa, Sultan, Sunbal, Tapiero, Tangui, Tawil, Temstet, Toblem, Tobali, Tobi, Toledano, Torjman, Vidal, Wahnish, Wizgan, Wizman, Ymar, Zabaro, Zafrani, Zagury, Zamero, Zaoui, Zazon, Zekri, Zini, Znati, Zrihen, Zimra

Malka, Eli S. *Jacob's Children in the Land of the Mahdi: Jews of the Sudan.* Syracuse, N.Y.: Syracuse University Press, 1997. Includes index.

Surnames mentioned in the text include:

Abboudi, Ades, Aeleon, Aghion, Aharoni, Ani, Baroukh, Bassiouni, Battan, Belilos, Bellenstein, Benbassa, Ben-David, Ben-Ezra, Benin, Ben-Lassin, Ben-Malka, Benou, Ben-Rubi, Ben-Sion, Bergmann, Bernstein, Blau, Bloch, Braunschweig, Braunstein, Btesh, Carmona, Castro, Cattaoui, Cohen, Dahan, Dannon, Daoud, Douek, Dwek, El-Eini, Ezra, Farhi, Forti, Gabbai, Gabra, Gabriel, Gaon, Goldenberg, Goldring, Gwertzman, Haim, Hakim, Harari, Hayon, Hazan, Heiman, Hemou, Hornstein, Inglizi, Ishaq, Israel, Kaminski, Kanarek, Kane, Kantzer, Klein, Kudsi, Levy, Lieberman, Mafinfeker, Malka, Mani, Marcos, Marcovitch, Marnignone, Mashiah, Massoud, Mazuki, Menasce, Menasse, Mendel, Merzan, Metzger, Mousky, Mosseri, Nadler, Nahmias, Nahum, Novecks, Ohanna, Ortasse, Pinto, Polon, Pontremoli, Prato, Qattawi, Reich, Risenfeld, Rodriguez, Romy, Rubin, Safadi, Safra, Saleh, Salem, Salvator, Sasson, Schechter, Schlesinger, Seroussi, Shaoul, Shapiro, Shoua, Siboani, Silvera, Simoni, Sinauer, Smouha, Sokolov, Suleiman, Soriano, Steinhart, Tammam, Tamman, Toledano, Tueta, Turetsky, Tuval, Weinberg, Wolf, Yacoub, Yettah

Appendix I in Eli Malka's book lists all Jewish marriages in the Sudan. Names in the records include:

Abboudi, Abdalla, Ades, Aeleon, Ani, Baroukh, Behar, Belilos, Ben Rubi, Benaim, Bennou, Berchmann, Berkowitz, Berlenstein, Bigo, Bossidan, Braunstein, Carmona, Cavaliero, Cohen, Coshti, Dannon, Daoud, David, Dayan, Drigg, Dwek, Eini, Feinstein, Franco, Gabra, Gabriel, Gaon, Gershon, Goldenberg, Goldring, Greenberg, Hakim, Harari, Heber, Heimani, Hemmo, Herman, Hindi, Ishag, Ishkinazi, Israel, Kanzer, Khaski, Konein, Kramer, Kudsi, Leilibh, Levitin, Levy, Loupo, Malka, Mannifker, Marcos, Masasini, Mashi, Alon, Menovitch, Mizrahi, Moshe, Mourad, Moussa, Ohanna, Ortasse, Palombo, Pinto, Saada, Safadia, Sagrani, Saltoun, Sasson, Seroussi, Shakra, Shama, Shaoul, Shapiro, Shenouda, Shoua, Sidis, Sinai, Soriano, Stulmacher, Tammam, Vago, Wahba, Wais, Weinberg, Yetah, Yona

Appendix G: Jewish Names in Printed Sources • 289

Arie, Gabriel. Généalogie de la famille Arie de 1766 a 1929. 1929. (Pamphlet).

Gabriel Arie (1863–1939) of Samakov, Bulgaria, was a well-known teacher and director of *Alliance Israelite Universelle* schools in various countries. Family surnames in his pamphlet include:

Abdala, Acher, Adroxi, Aguilar, Aharon, Alcalay, Almalech, Amada, Arav, Arditti, Arie, Aslan, Assa, Baruch, Baruh, Bassan, Behar, Behmoaras, Benaroya, Benyaech, Beraha, Calderon, Calef, Camhi, Canetti, Carasso, Cario, Cohen, Cohen-Hemsi, Conforte, Conorte, Crespin, Decaro, Donna, Elias, Eliezer, Faraggi, Farhi, Fortunee, Gerson, Gueron, Haim, Hananel, Henri, Houyomdji, Jacob, Jacobson, Joseph, Kaplan, Koffler, Kokachoeli, Kouyumdjulu, Levy, Maggar, Manoach, Mazaltov, Melamed, Mevorah, Mitrani, Molho, Moscona, Moshe, Ninio, Panigel, Papo, Policar, Presente, Rachel, Rahamim, Raphael, Rivca, Rudiac, Schnur, Semach, Shabetay, Sidi, Soref, Tagger, Uziel, Varsano, Venezia, Weill, Weinstein, Zonana

Ujlaki (comp). Sophia (Bulgaria) Jewish Cemetery. Budapest: Ujlaki, 1997.

Abilash, Adroki, Aftalion, Alabalah, Aladjem, Albalah, Albas, Albasa, Albuhayre, Alfandari, Alhalel, Alkabes, Alkalai, Alkolukbre, Almaleh, Almoznino, Anavi, Anzhel, Apsheh, Arditti, Arama, Arye, Aroyo, Arucheti, Asael, Assa, Asseo, Astrik, Astrug, Astuk, Atias, Avigdor, Avishay, Azriel, Bakish, Barnathan, Baruh, Basan, Betzalel, Behar, Behmoaram, Benaroy, Benatov, Benbasat, Benyozef, Benmayor, Benoasat, Beniesh, Bentura, Benvenisti, Beraha, Bidzherano, Biyla, Burla, Cemah, Tchitchek, Daca, Dafret, Danon, David, Davitchon, Dekalo, Delareya, Djain, Djaldeti, Dzherasi, Djiba, Eshkenazi, Elazar, Eli, Ezdra, Faraggi, Farhi, Faruy, Fintzi, Florentin, Fransiz, Garti, Gershon, Djivany, Haimov, Hazan, Hazday, Hezkiya, Ilel, Isak, Izrael, Katzuni, Kalderon, Kalev, Kamhi, Kapo, Kapon, Karakash, Katalan, Katarivas, Kemalov, Konfino, Konforti, Konorti, Kordova, Koren, Kovo, Koyen, Krusrin, Levi, Lidzhi, Lossia, Lupo, Luna, Madzhar, Magrilo, Mamad, Mamon, Mandil, Manoah, Mashiah, Mashiyah, Melamed, Menashe, Merkado, Mesulam, Mevorah, Mezan, Mihael, Mizrahi, Molhov, Moshe Moscona, Nahnias, Nardeya, Natan, Navon, Niego, Ninyo, Oliver, Ovadya, Pandjuro, Panizhel, Paparo, Papo, Pardo, Pardov, Penhas, Perera, Peretz, Pidzhi, Piyade, Pilosof, Pinctzu, Pinkas, Polikar, Prezente, Primo, Rahaminov, Rahamim, Refetov, Rodrig, Ronko, Rosanes, Shamli Shaulov, Salmi, Shabat, Sabitau, Sabitay, Samuel, Sarfati, Sason, Seliktar, Seviliya, Sidi, Spinadel, Tadzhes, Talvi Tagger, Tagjer Taranto, Uziel, Varsano, Zahariya, Yarhi, Yeroham Yerushalmi, Yeshua, Yomtov, Yona, Yuazari, Yulzari

Leon Tello, Pilar. *Judios de Toledo.* Madrid: Institut Arias Montano, 1979.

A list of names in this book, prepared by Ben Nahman, may be accessed at http://home.earthlink.net/~bnahman/toledohtm.htm.

Elnecave, Nissim. *Los Hijos de Ibero-Franconia.* Buenos Aires: Ediciones La Luz, 1981.

Names in this book were extracted by Ben Nahman and listed here with his permission. "/" means variant of same name.

Aalamani, Aaron, Aba, Abadi, Abas, Abazardiel, Abdalah, Abendana, Abengeld, Abenhateus, Abensur, Abira, Aboab, Aboab Mualim, Aboav, Aboav Da Fonseca, Abod, Abotbol, Aboulker, Abrabanel, Abraham, Abraham/Fonseca, Abraham-debalmes, Abramico, Abravalla, Abravanel, Abravanel/Dormido, Abudaraahan, Abudarraham, Abulafia, Abulker, Abulner, Adadi, Adas, Adato, Adatto, Adjiman, Adret, Adron, Adut, Aelion, Aflalos, Aghmati, Aguado, Aguilar, Aharon, Ahim, Akin, Aknin, Al-Jirizi, Al Tusari, Alalouf, Alamanni, Alami, Alashkar, Alashkaz, Alaskar, Alatino, Albala, Albala De Levy, Albalia, Albo, Alburzhi, Alcabets, Alcaforada, Alcalay, Alchekh, Alcoforado, Al-Corsi, Al-Dahari, Al-Damari, Alegre, Alemano, Alfacar, Al-Fakharmeir, Alfandari, Al-Faradzh, Alfasi, Al-Fayumi, Alfonso, Algazi, Alhaik, Al-Hak, Al-Harizi, Al-Harizi, Aljadef, Aljanati, Al-Jarizi, Al-Kabisi, Ali, Alkabets, Alkalay, Allemano, Almaleh, Almosnino, Almoznino, Akawa, Alroi, Alsheij, Alsheikh, Alshij, Al-Taban, Altaras, Altauso, Aluch, Alvarenga, Alvares De Barros, Al-Yamani, Amadia, Amar, Amon Yaari, Amor, Amram, Amzalag, Anashiksan, Anatoli, Andalusi/Fasi/Sikili, Anenturiel, Anfaoni, Angel, Antebi, Anzancot, Archivolti, Ardutiel, Arenus, Arneti, Aroio, Arragel, Artemion, Artom, Artom, Arueste, Aruguet, Aruj, Ascarelli, Aseo, Asher, Ashkenazi, Askari, Assa, Asser, Assusi, Astruc, Ata, Atar, Atataros, Athias, Atias, Atrani, Attal, Attar, Attias, Attiias, Atunes/Rois, Aviad, Avigador, Aviz, Avraham, Awad, Ayash, Azar, Azareff, Azaria, Aziz, Azubid, Azulay

Bachi, Bagrat, Bakrat Y Khalas, Bakri, Balam, Baldomir, Bale, Banco, Banin, Barajel, Barazani, Barchillon, Barel, Bar-Natan, Baron, Baros Basto, Baruj, Barun, Barzilai, Basan, Basilea, Basola, Bassan, Bassani, Basto, Basula, Battat, Bauri, Bautista Peres, Bazilay/Bargueloni, Bedersi, Behar, Beirav, Bejar, Belasco, Belforte, Ben, Ben Adriat, Ben Israel, Ben Veniste, Ben Yosef, Ben Zeev, Benamu, Ben-Atar, Ben-Ayon, Benas, Benazeref, Benbassat, Benchimol, Bendelac, Bengio, Benhamu, Benjamin, Benjeresh, Ben-Kikis, Benmozegh, Benoliel, Bensabat, Bensantchi, Bensid, Benvalia, Benveniste, Benzaquen, Berab, Beraha, Beraja, Berajia, Berdugo, Berechia, Berejia, Beretvas, Berez, Bernardete, Bernays, Bertinore, Bertinoro, Berujim, Bessis, Betsalel, Bezalel, Bibas, Bitton, Bivas, Blanca, Boghachadji, Bonacosa, Bonafos, Bonan, Bonanasco, Bonastruc, Bonchara, Bondabi, Bondavin, Bonet Sarfati, Bonfil, Bonfils, Bonjorn, Bonjuhes, Bordzhel, Botton, Bragadini, Bravo, Brito, Bueno, Bueno/De Mesquita, Bul-Faradzh, Busach, Busal, Busnach, Buzaglio

Cabra, Cabral/Da Gama, Caceres, Cadeau, Cadoche, Cadoche, Calson, Calvo, Candiote, Candioti, Canias, Cansino, Cantarini, Capon, Capsali, Caraco, Carcassona, Cardoso, Cardozo, Carmona, Caro, Carsinet, Carvajal, Carvalho, Carvallo, Cases, Cassin, Cassuto, Castel Nuevo, Castiglioni, Castro, Castyright, Catalano, Catalini, Cataui, Cattaui, Cavalleria, Cazes, Chaprut, Chaufan, Chehebar, Chiriki, Chumaceiro, Cicurel, Cillalongo, Cohen, Cohenbenoliel, Colon, Colorini, Colorni, Combriso,

Appendix G: Jewish Names in Printed Sources • 291

Comtino, Cona, Conambriel, Constantino, Corcos, Cordovero, Coriat, Corsino, Costantini, Cremieux, Cremieux/Moie, Crescas, Crespin, Crudcoriat, Culi, Curiel

D'pomi, D'rossi, D'vecchi, da Costa, da Fonseca, da Mercado, da Peschera, da Pisa, da Rosa, da Silva, Dabah, Dabbah, Dabella, Dahan, Dall'arpa, Dana, Danan, Danan, Dangoor, Daniel, Danon, Dapiera, Dari, Darman, Darnim, Dasilva, Dato, Daud, David, Daviddepomis, Dayan, de Acevedo, de Barrios, de Castro, de Couto, de La Rosa, de Lara, de Lavega, de Lemon, de Leon, de Lis/de Castro, de Oya/Delonga, de Loyola y Haro, de Mierbeave, de Oliveira, de Oria, de Pomi, de Roma, de Sale, de Samuel, de Armiento, de Silva, de Sola, de Sola Pool, de Sousa, de Tarso/de Pablo, de Toledo, de Torres/Abecassis, de Victorio/Victoria, de Voltera, de Volterra, de Avila, de Betinoro, de Camondo, de Estrella, de Fonseca, de Fulda, de Herat, de Jorena, de Jorjena, Del Medigo, de Lattes, de Leon, Delgado, Della Torre, Delmar, Delmedigo, de Luna, Demaestre, de Mercado, de Modena, de Montalto, de Pina, de Pina/Sarfatti, de Pisa, de Rossi, de Sequeyra, de Symons, de Tolosa, de Tudela, Devir, de Volterra, di Capua, di Nigarelli, di Segni, Dias, Dias/Santiago, Diena, Dina, Disegni, Ditrani, Divekar, Donnolo, Dosa, do Vale, Drago, Drago de Lemos, Dunio, Duran, Durant, Duwayk, Dzhalil, Dzhama, Dzhamil, Dzhian, Dzian

Ebreo, Ecija, Edni, Efendi, Effendi, Efrati, Ejica, El-Ankawa, Elbaz, Eleazar, Elia, Eliah, Eliakim, Elias, Eliezer, Elmaleh, Elnecave, Elyashar, Emasllen, Emsani, Encaona, Ephraim, Erera, Ereza, Ereza, Ergas, Escapa, Escobar, Eshkenazi, Eshkol, Espinoza, Evans, Ezdras, Ezekiel, Ezequias, Ezobi, Ezra

Faba, Falaquera, Falcon, Fano, Faquimi, Farhi, Farisol, Farissol, Farji, Farrar, Farrisol, Favela, Fayumi, Fermi, Fernandes, Fernandes/Brandao, Fernandez, Fernandez/Carvajal, Figo, Finzi, Fiorentino, Florentin, Fonseca, Fonseca/Nassi, Formiggini, Foz, Frances, Franco, Franses, Fresco, Furtado

Gabail, Gabari, Gabay, Gabirol, Gabizon, Gabriol, Gadol, Gaguin, Galante, Galicchi, Galico, Galimidi, Galipapa, Gallico, Gamaliel, Gambach, Gaon, Garcia, Garji, Garzon, Gatanio, Gavison, Gedelicia, Gegate, Gerondi, Gershan, Gershom, Gilbert, Girondi, Gitakila, Godefroi, Gomez, Gozaglo, Gozlan, Gracia, Gracian/Pambuk, Gradis, Granata, Graziani, Guedalia, Guenun, Guershom, Gurdzhi

ha Cohen, ha Nasi, Haam, ha-Babli, ha-Bargueloni, ha-Bavli, Habib, ha-Cohen, ha-Cohen/ha-Sefardi, ha-Dani, Hadani, ha-Darshan, Hadida, Hagege, Hagiz, Haguiz, ha-Haver, ha-Hazan, Haim, Hakashlari, Hakhmon, Hakim, ha-Kohen, Halac, Ha-Levi, Halevi, Halevtrani, Halevy, Halevy/Caslari, Haley/Elie, Halfon, Ha-Maravi, Hamon, Hamon, Ha-Naguid, Ha-Nakdan, Hanania, Ha-Nasi, Hana, Hananel, Hanasi, Haness, Ha-Paytan, Harari, Harizi, Haroma, Harun, Hasday, Ha-Siboni, Hasson, Hatchuel, Hatwil/Hatshmil, Havivai, Hayat, Ha-Yishari, Hayon, Hazan, Hekmat, Hemsi, Henriquez, Henriquez/Gomez, Henriquez/Senior, Herrera, Hibat/Alah, Hilel, Hin, Hina, Hiya, Hoshama, Hoyada, Huino, Hushiel

Ibn Ezra, Ichay, Imach, Imola, Isaac, Iskandari, Israel, Israeli, Issaev, Isserles

Jacob, Jagel, Jagiz, Jaim, Jaion, Jais, Jakun, Jalfon, Jalshush, Jamtsi, Jamuy, Janan, Janoj, Jaquete, Jardon, Jasday, Jasid, Javilla, Jay, Jayudzh, Jazan, Jezkia, Jida, Jinin, Josefo, Joseph, Josfe, Juda, Judah, Juejati, Jushiel, Jushiel/Ben Efraim/Yosef, Juzin

Kadoorie, Kafa, Kafih, Kafusi, Kagig/Cazes, Kahani, Kalonimus, Kamaniel, Kamniel, Kanian, Kashifi, Kastoria, Katsin, Kayra, Kazaz, Kehimkar, Khalas, Khalfon, Kiki, Kimhi, Kimji, Knafo, Kuraish

Labadon, Labatt, Labrat, Laguna, Lanaido, Laredo, Laski, Latimi, Lattes, Lavi, Lazarus, Jacobs, Lealtad, Leao, Leeser, Leon, Lernopranti, Lev, Levi, Levi-Bacrat, Levita, Levi-Valensi, Levy, Levy/Yuly/Moses, Ligier, Loez Fonseca, Lombroso, Lopes, Lopes/Simoes, Lopes/Dubec, Lopez, Lopez/Laguna, Louzada, Lumbroso, Luria, Lusitanus, Luzada, Luzzato

Madmun, Madriaga, Maduro, Madzhani, Magangaki, Magriso, Maimi, Maimon, Majzir, Maldonado De Silva, Maleha, Mali, Mallah, Maltzan, Maman, Manases, Manass/Israel, Mandes/Seixas, Mandolino, Manoel, Mantin, Mantino, Malka, Maracha, Mari, Marini, Marour, Marzuk, Masajaway, Mascaran, Massarani, Massarini, Masud, Matalon, Mataraso, Matita, Maymeran, Mayques, Mazliaj, Medola, Meiggs, Meir, Meiri, Mejzir, Meknes, Meldola, Melili, Melkitsedek, Melli, Memmi, Menajem, Menasche, Menashe, Mendes, Mendes/France, Mendez, Mendoza, Merman, Mesa, Meshal, Meshulam, Mevorakh, Mezan, Migash, Miledi, Milhau, Mishan, Mizrahi, Mizraim, Mizraji, Moatti, Moatti, Modena, Modigliani, Modigliano, Modon, Moha, Moise, Moises, Molho, Moljo, Monsano, Monsanto, Monsino, Montagnana, Montagu, Montalto, Montefiore, Montefioree, Montefiori, Morais, Morban, Mordejay, Moresco, Moron, Morpurgo, Mortara, Morteira, Moscato, Mosconi, Moses, Moses de Palermo, Moshe, Moskoni, Moyal, Mozesh, Mrezhen, Muatti, Muiz, Munk, Munoz, Munoz Maldonado, Murad, Musa, Musafia

Nadjara, Nadzbran, Nadzhar, Nadzhara, Nafusi, Nahama, Nahman, Nahon, Nahoum/Effendi, Nahum, Najmuli, Nakawa/Elnacave, Narro, Nasi, Nata, Natan, Navarra, Navarro, Navon, Nayas, Nedebo, Nedivot, Nehemias, Neria, Netanel, Netira, Nicanor, Nicholas, Nieto, Nifoci, Nimir, Nissim, Nissim Gambach, Noah, Nono, Noraim, Nunes De Mattos, Nunes Wais, Nunez, Nunez De Silva, Nunez/Carvalho, Nunez-Cardoso

Olmo, Omar, Orabuena, Orsani, Orvieto, Ossuna, Ottolenghi, Ovadia, Ovadia De Bertinoro, Oz, Ozmo

Pacheco, Pacifico, Padilla, Pakuda, Palache, Palaggi, Panigel, Paparrabalos, Pardo, Paredes, Pariente, Pejiel, Penso, Penso Mendes, Perahia, Pereira, Perez, Perfet, Pergola, Piade, Piatelli, Pichon, Pincherele, Pinehas, Pinto, Piza, Planes, Pontremoli, Portaleone, Porto, Prato, Primo, Proops, Pyrrhus

Querido

Raban, Rachel, Rahabi, Rajpurkar, Raka, Ramirez, Ratsbashi, Ratshabi, Ravena, Ravenna, Recanati, Reggio, Remos, Reuven, Reuveni, Ribeiro, Ricardo, Ricchi, Rieti, Robles, Rodrigues, Rodrigues/Mendes, Rodrigues/Pereire, Rodriguez, Rodriguez/Sanches, Rogelio, Romanelli, Romano, Rosanes, Rossi, Rovigo, Rubin, Rubio

Saadi, Saadia, Sabor, Sacchetto, Sacerdoti, Sada, Sadaga, Sad-Aldawla, Safir, Saguiz, Saieg, Saimen, Sakri, Sala, Salamon, Salamon De Trani, Salamons, Salas, Salem, Salih, Salom, Salomon, Salvador, Samama, Samaya, Samlaich, Samokovlio, Samson, Samuel, Santiago, Sanu, Sapir, Saportas, Saragosti, Saraval, Sardas, Sarfati, Sarmad, Sarok, Saruk, Sas Portas, Sason, Sasoon, Sasporta, Sasportas, Sasportas/Saportas, Sasson, Sasson (Effendi), Sassoon, Saul, Sciaky, Sedacca, Sedequias, Sefaradi, Sefas/Alfasi, Sefata, Seloaf, Semaj, Senior, Senoriu, Senyor, Sequerra, Sereni, Sereno, Serfati, Seror, Serrerosarfaty, Sevi, Sevy, Sforno, Shabazi, Shabetay, Shabrabak, Shagi, Shahun, Shakri, Shalom, Shalom/Kujayl, Shaltiel, Shama, Sharabi, Shaul, Shelemo, Shelush, Shemaria, Shemuel De Acco, Sherira, Sheshet, Shimjon, Shimoni, Shindook, Shofet, Shoshan, Shushan, Siboni, Sid, Sidi, Sidun, Sieff, Siesu, Sigmar, Siliera, Simeon, Simon, Simone/Simha, Slelatt, Sodicky, Sofat, Soiano, Soliman, Solomon/David, Somej, Somekh, Soncino, Soriano, Sosportos, Soulam, Spinoza, Stora, Sullam, Sunbal, Sunbal, Sussan, Svevo

Tabiana, Tabit, Tabul, Tadjer, Tagliocozzo, Taitashak, Tam, Tamim, Tartas, Taurel, Tawa, Tayb, Tayeb, Tayeb, Teboul, Teixeira, Teixeira/Pinto, Templo, Terracini, Terrasina, Testa, Teubal, Tibbon, Tiboli, Tivoli, Toledano, Toledo, Tomas, Tores, Torres, Touro, Trani, Treves, Tsahalon, Tsalaj, Tsarefati, Tsemaj, Tsevi, Tsova

Ukba, Ulhoa, Uriah, Usque, Uzan, Uziel

Vadzhar, Vaez, Ventura, Verga, Vetura, Vidash, Viegas, Vital, Volterra

Wakar, Wakasa

Yaakov, Yacob, Yafe, Yahia, Yahuda, Yahudi, Yaish, Yajya, Yakar, Yakub, Yana, Yanez, Yatah, Yayez, Yedidia, Yehiel, Yehoshua, Yehuda, Yejiel, Yekutiel, Yekutiel/Kohen, Yerushalmi, Yesha, Yeuda, Yijah, Yishag, Yisjak, Yitsaki, Yitsjak, Yitzak, Yojay, Yom Tov, Yona, Yosef, Yoseph, Yuda, Yuda/Roussillon, Yusef

Zacut, Zacuto, Zacutus Lusitanos, Zahit, Zahula, Zakar, Zakay, Zaken, Zaky, Zarefati, Zeevi, Zelvi, Zemat, Zequi, Zerbib, Zhuli, Zimra, Zuta

Attal, Robert, and Joseph Avivi. *Registres Matrimoniaux de la Communaute Juive Portugaise de Tunis: XVIII-XIX siecles.* Jerusalem: Ben Zvi Institute, 1989.

Names in 1,031 *ketubot* from the Sephardic Portuguese community (Grana or Leghorn [Livorno] Jews) of Tunis, including the following:
Abdias, Aboccara, Aboucaya, Achour, Adahan, Adi, Albaili, Alban, Alloro, Almaizi, Amar, Amorborgo, Anakas, Arbib, Arikas, Arous, Artona, Ascoli, Ashkenazi, Assafar, Assfar, Assuied, Astrologo, Atazouri, Attal, Attia, Attias, Azoulay, Bais, Bargansa, Bargas, Barnes, Baron, Baruch, Basivi, Bassan, Battan, Belhassen, Bellaiche, Bembaron, Ben Adi, Ben Baron, Ben Simeon, Ben Yaiche, Bendana, Berda, Bessis, Betito, Bijaoui, Bises, Bismuth, Biziz, Boccara, Boiro, Bonan, Bondi, Bonfia, Borcatsa, Borgel, Boublil, Boucarra, Boujenah, Boukhobza, Brami, Bueno, Calo, Calvo, Camio, Campus, Capoua, Caravallio, Cardozo, Cariglio, Carmi, Caro, Cartozo, Cassuto, Castelnuevo, Castro, Cattan, Cavallio, Cesana, Chemla, Cittanova, Cohen, Cohen de Lara, Cohen Solal, Cohen Tanougi, Constantine, Corcos, Coronel, Coscas, Costa, Crimas, Crimisi, Curiel, Dadoune, Dahan, Daian, Dardour, Darmon, Darmouni, David, De Pas, Delouya, Dias Palma, Dicunia, Diouani, Douali, Elahmi, Elajim, Elfassi, Elhaik, Elkana, Elmalih, Elportogues, Elpronti, Eminenti, Enajar, Enriques, Errera, Espinoza, Etazer, Etouil, Ezberro, Fellous, Finaro, Finia, Finiro, Finsi, Finzi, Fiorentino, Fitoussi, Flah, Forti, Fougi, Franchetti, Franco, Freoa, Funaro, Gabai, Gabay, Gabison, Gandus, Garci, Garsin, Garson, Ghalula, Ghanem, Ghozlan, Gidilia, Gimsi, Gonzales, Grego, Guedalia, Guetta, Guez, Guiguiati, Guttieres, Hababou, Habib, Hacohen, Haddad, Hadida, Hagege, Hakouk, Hakoun, Halevy, Halevy de Albaili, Halevy de Leon, Halevy Sonsine, Halimi, Hanouna, Hasda, Hassid, Hattab, Hayoun, Hazaken, Heskouni, Hiskouni, Houri, Iflah, Isaac, Isaaki, Israel, Israel Enriques, Jami, Jano, Jarmon, Jazo, Jerafa, Josue, Journo, Kali, Khalaf, Khalfon, Khayat, Khoshkhash, Khrief, Koresh, Ksabi, Ktorza, Lahmi, Lampronti, Lara, Lebe, Leon, Leotagi, Levi, Levy, Levy de Albaili, Levy de Leon, Lodriguez, Lodriguez Dicunia, Lodriguez Enriques, Lodriguez Silvera, Lopes Perrera, Louizada, Louniel, Lumbroso, Lunel, Lussato, Maarek, Malabar, Malka, Margalit, Marini, Marouani, Martassi, Marzouk, Medina, Meimoun, Melloul, Mendes, Mendes Ossona, Mendoza, Messica, Messina, Mizrahi, Moati, Modiliano, Modon, Molco, Molho, Molina, Montefiore, Montillia, Moreno, Moron, Morpourgo, Morpugo, Naccache, Nahon, Nahum, Najar, Namias, Narboni, Nataf, Nounil, Nunes, Nunes Vais, Obadia, Obana, Ossona, Ouaiche, Palatgi, Paligi, Palma, Paltero, Paltigi, Pansir, Pansiri, Pariente, Parienti, Pas, Pasanno, Pavoncello, Peres, Perets, Pignero, Pinheiro, Pinto, Piperno, Pirosa, Platero, Polako, Pougi, Rignano, Roa, Rodriguez, Rodriques, Saada, Saadoun, Sabban, Sacouto, Sagdoun, Sala, Salom, Saltillana, Samama, Santaliana, Sarbia, Sarfati, Sberro, Sedbon, Semah, Semaha, Senouf, Servadio, Servi, Setbon, Setroug, Settouna, Sfez, Shalajar, Shalazar, Shalom, Sharabi, Sharabia, Sharabig, Shebokh, Shemama, Sicso, Signia, Silvera, Simeon, Sion, Sira, Sitri, Slama, Smaja, Solal, Solas, Solima, Sonino, Sonsine, Soria, Souzine, Spinoza, Spizzichino, Strologo, Suares, Suied, Tabib, Taieb, Taigan, Tanougi, Tapia, Tedeschi, Timsit, Tisignia, Tito, Tivoli, Tolicciano, Toubiana, Uzan, Vais, Valensi, Ventura, Vilariali, Voltera, Yaiche, Yakhia, Yehia, Younes, Zacout, Zacouto, Zafrana, Zaibi, Zaken, Zarka, Zazo, Zazoun, Zegbib, Zeitoun, Zerah, Ziki

Appendix G: Jewish Names in Printed Sources • 295

APPENDIX H.
MOSLEM CALENDAR

THE LAY YEAR

	Turkey	Egypt	Syria
January	kanun thani كأنون ثاني	yanayir يناير	kanun al thani كانون الثاني
February	shubatt شباط	fabrayir فبراير	shubatt شباط
March	maret مأرت	maris مارس	azar أذار
April	nisan نيسان	abreel أبريل	nissan نيسان
May	mayiis مايس	mayou مايو	ayar أيار
June	haziran حزيران	youniou يونيو	haziran حزيران
July	temouz تموز	youliou يوليو	tamouz تموز
August	agoustos أغسطس	aghoutous أغسطس	ab أب
September	eylul أيلول	subtambar سبتمبر	ayloul أيلول
October	tishrin evvel تشرين أول	oktobar أكتوبر	tishrin al awal تشرين الأول
November	tishrin thani تشرين ثاني	nofambar نوفمبر	tishrin al thani تشرين الثاني
December	kannun evvel كانون أول	disambar ديسمبر	kannun al awal كانون الأول

The Hijri (religious) year

mahram محرم	safr صفر	rabyah al awal ربيع الأول
rabyah al thani ربيع الثاني	jamadi al awal جمادي الأول	jamadi al thani جمادي الثاني
rajab رجب	shaaban شعبان	ramadan رمضان
shouwal شوال	zo al kaada ذو القعدة	zo al hajah ذو الحجه

APPENDIX I.
OTTOMAN RECORDS IN ISRAEL

The Israel State Archives holds a collection of the original Ottoman census and population registers (*nufus* registers) for Palestine. In 1979 the National Archives of Israel microfilmed these Ottoman registers for the period 1883 to 1917. These microfilms contain preliminary registers; basic registers; early population registers; registers of births, marriages, divorces, and changes of address; registers of men of military age; registers of foreigners; and *mukhtars'* registers for that period.

The Ottomans kept the registers for 10 geographical districts. Each district includes cities (divided into neighborhoods) and villages in present-day Israel and parts of Jordan and Egypt. Registration in each locality was conducted and listed according to religious affiliation. The collection also includes a catalog in English that gives general background information about the registers, a locality index, and detailed descriptions of the contents of each register.

The Table lists registers most likely to include Jewish content. Copies of the 84 microfilm reels are available at the Church of Jesus Christ of Latter-day Saints (LDS) Family History Centers. Reel numbers given in the table are those of the LDS collection. Item number refers to the order of appearance of the record group on the reel.

Table 6. Ottoman Census and Population Records

Place	Years	Population	Register Description	LDS Reel	Item
Jerusalem (city)	1905–12	Coptic Christian, Jewish	Preliminary, no. 35	1212763	Item 2
Jerusalem (city)	1883–1904	Jewish	Early population, no. 36	1212763	Item 3
Jerusalem (city)	1905–16	Jewish	Basic, no. 37	1212763	Item 4
Jerusalem (city)	1915–17	Jewish	Basic, no. 38	1212763	Item 5
Jerusalem (city)	1905–17	Jewish	Basic, no. 39	1212763	Item 6
Jerusalem (city)	1905–11	Jewish	Preliminary, no. 40	1212763	Item 7

Place	Years	Population	Register Description	LDS Reel	Item
Jerusalem (city)	1883–1901	Jewish	Early population, no. 41	1212763	Item 8
Jerusalem (city)	1883–1901	Jewish	Early population, no. 41 (cont.)	1212764	Item 1
Jerusalem (city)	1905–17	Jewish	Basic, no. 42	1212764	Item 2
Jerusalem (city)	1905–17	Jewish	Basic, no. 43	1212764	Item 3
Jerusalem (city)	1905	Jewish	Preliminary, no. 44	1212764	Item 4
Jerusalem (city)	1905–17	Jewish	Basic, no. 45	1212764	Item 5
Jerusalem (city)	1905–17	Jewish	Basic, no. 45 (cont.)	1212765	Item 1
Jerusalem (city)	1915–17	Jewish	Basic, no. 46	1212765	Item 2
Jerusalem (city)	1905–17	Jewish	Basic, no. 47	1212765	Item 3
Jerusalem (city)	1905–11	Jewish	Preliminary, no. 48	1212765	Item 4
Jerusalem (city)	1905–17	Jewish	Basic, no. 49	1212765	Item 5
Jerusalem (city)	1905–17	Jewish	Basic, no. 50	1212765	Item 6
Jerusalem (city)	1883–1904	Jewish	Early population, no. 51	1212766	Item 1
Jerusalem (city)	1905–17	Jewish	Basic, no. 52	1212766	Item 2
Jerusalem (city)	1905–12	Jewish	Preliminary, no. 53	1212766	Item 3
Jerusalem (city)	1915–17	Jewish	Basic, no. 54	1212766	Item 4
Jerusalem (city)	1905–10	Jewish	Preliminary, no. 55	1212767	Item 1
Jerusalem (city)	1905–17	Jewish	Basic, no. 56	1212767	Item 2
Jerusalem (city)	1905–17	Jewish	Basic, no. 57	1212767	Item 3
Jerusalem (city)	1905–11	Jewish	Preliminary, no. 58	1212767	Item 4
Jerusalem (city)	1915–17	Jewish	Basic, no. 59	1212767	Item 5
Jerusalem (city)	1915–17	Jewish	Basic, no. 60	1212767	Item 6

Place	Years	Population	Register Description	LDS Reel	Item
Jerusalem (city)	1905–17	Jewish	Basic, no. 61	1212768	Item 1
Jerusalem (city)	1894–1903	Jewish	Early population, no. 62	1212768	Item 2
Jerusalem (city)	1883?–1901	Jewish	Mukhtar's, no. 62/A	1212768	Item 3
Jerusalem (city)	1905–17	Jewish	Basic, no. 63	1212768	Item 4
Jerusalem (city)	1905–17	Jewish	Basic, no. 64	1212768	Item 5
Jerusalem (city)	1905	Jewish	Mukhtar's, no. 65	1212768	Item 6
Jerusalem (city)	1905	Jewish	Mukhtar's, no. 65 (cont.)	1212769	Item 1
Jerusalem (city)	1905	Jewish	Mukhtar's, no. 65/A	1212769	Item 2
Jerusalem (district)	1905–13	Moslem, Jewish	Preliminary, no. 72	1212770	Item 4
Jerusalem (district)	1905–12	Moslem, Jewish, Foreign Moslem	Preliminary, no. 73	1212770	Item 5
Jerusalem (district)	1905–12	Moslem, Jewish, Foreign Moslem	Preliminary, no. 73 (cont.)	1212771	Item 1
Jerusalem (district)	1905–17	Jewish	Basic, no. 74	1212771	Item 2
Jerusalem (district)	1905	Moslem, Jewish	Preliminary, no. 75	1212771	Item 3
Jerusalem (city and district)	1905–13	All religious communities	Birth, no. 161	1212789	Item 5
Jerusalem (city and district)	1916–17	All religious communities	Birth, no. 162	1212789	Item 6
Jerusalem (city and district)	1905–15	All religious communities	New registration, no. 163	1212789	Item 7
Jerusalem (city and district)	1905–14	All religious communities	Corrections of birth, no. 164	1212789	Item 8
Jerusalem (city and district)	1905–13	All religious communities	Death, no. 165	1212789	Item 9
Jerusalem (city and district)	1905–13	All religious communities	Death, no. 165 (cont.)	1212790	Item 1

Appendix I: Ottoman Records in Israel • 299

Place	Years	Population	Register Description	LDS Reel	Item
Jerusalem (city and district)	1914–17	All religious communities	Death, no. 166	1212790	Item 2
Jerusalem (city and district)	1905–10	All religious communities	Marriage, no. 167	1212790	Item 3
Hebron (city)	1915–17	Moslem, Jewish	Birth, no. 190	1212794	Item 5
Hebron (city and district)	1905–14	Moslem, Jewish	Marriage, no. 191	1212794	Item 6
Hebron (city and district)	1905–14	Moslem, Jewish	Marriage, no. 191 (cont.)	1212795	Item 1
Hebron (city and district)	1915–17	All religious communities	Changes of address, no. 193	1212795	Item 3
Hebron (city and district)	1905–14	All religious communities	Changes of address, no. 194	1212795	Item 4
Hebron (city and district)	1917	All religious communities	New registration, no. 195	1212795	Item 5
Hebron (district)	1914	All religious communities	Men of military age, no. 195/a	1212795	Item 6
Hebron (city and district)	1905–14	All religious communities	Divorce, no. 196	1212795	Item 7
Hebron (city and district)	1915–17	All religious communities	Divorce, no. 197	1212795	Item 8
Hebron (city and district)	1905–14	All religious communities	Death, no. 198	1212795	Item 9
Hebron (city and district)	1915–17	All religious communities	Death, no. 199	1212795	Item 10
Hebron (city and district)	1906–16	All religious communities	Changes of address, no. 200	1212795	Item 11
Hebron (city)	1918	Moslem, Jewish	Additions to families, no. 201	1212795	Item 12
Hebron (district)	1915–17	All religious communities	Men of military age, no. 236	1212802	Item 3
Hebron (district)	1915–17	All religious communities	Men of military age, no. 237	1212802	Item 4

Place	Years	Population	Register Description	LDS Reel	Item
Gaza (district)	1906-17	All religious communities	New registration, no. 241	1212803	Item 2
Gaza (district)	1913-17	All religious communities	Birth, no. 243	1212803	Item 4
Gaza (district)	1906-7	All religious communities	Men of military age, no. 245	1212803	Item 6
Gaza (district)	1906-17	All religious communities	Death, no. 255	1212806	Item 1
Gaza (district)	1906-13	All religious communities	Birth, no. 256	1212806	Item 2
Gaza (district)	1906-17	All religious communities	Correction of register, no. 257	1212806	Item 3
Gaza (district)	1905-16	All religious communities	Divorce, no. 275	1212809	Item 7
Gaza (district)	1906-17	All religious communities	Change of address, no. 276	1212809	Item 8
Gaza (district)	1908-13	All religious communities	Marriage, no. 279	1212810	Item 1
Nazareth (district)	1905-12	All religious communities	Birth, no. 298	1212813	Item 5
Nazareth (district)	1913-17	All religious communities	Corrections of registration no. 300	1212813	Item 7
Nazareth (city and district)	1885-1903	religious communities	Births, deaths, marriages, changes of address, no. 301	1212813	All item 8
Nazareth (city and district)	1885-1903	All religious communities	Births, deaths, marriages, changes of address, no. 301 (cont.)	1212814	Item 1
Nazareth (city and district)	1910-12	All religious communities	Death, no. 302	1212814	Item 2
Nazareth (district)	1891-1904	All religious communities	Births, deaths, changes of address, no. 330	1212818	Item 5
Nazareth (city and district)	1893-1910	All religious communities	Births, deaths, divorces, changes of address, no. 331	1212818	Item 6
Nazareth (city and district)	1902-09	All religious communities	Births, deaths, divorces, changes of address, no. 332	1212818	Item 7
Nazareth (city and district)	1913-17	All religious communities	Changes of address, no. 333	1212818	Item 8

Appendix I: Ottoman Records in Israel

Place	Years	Population	Register Description	LDS Reel	Item
Nazareth (city and district)	1910–11	All religious communities	New registration, no. 334	1212818	Item 9
Tiberias (city)	Undated	Moslem, Jewish	Early population, no. 361	1212822	Item 7
Tiberias (city and district)	1914	Moslem, Roman Catholic, Greek Catholic, Greek Orthodox, Jewish	Men of military age, no. 362	1212822	Item 8
Tiberias (city and district)	1879–82	Moslem, Jewish	Births, deaths, change of address, new registration, no. 363	1212822	Item 9
Haifa (city)	1911–18	All religious communities, foreigners	Preliminary, no. 371	1212824	Item 3
Haifa (district)	1912–18	All religious communities	Corrections of register, no. 372	1212824	Item 4
Haifa (district)	1912–18	All religious communities	New registration, no. 373	1212824	Item 5
Haifa (district)	1912–17	All religious communities	Men of military age, no. 374	1212824	Item 6
Haifa (district)	1912–18	All religious communities	Birth, no. 375	1212824	Item 7
Haifa (district)	1912–18	All religious communities	Death, no. 376	1212824	Item 8
Haifa (district)	1912–18	All religious communities	Marriage, no. 377	1212824	Item 9
Haifa (district)	1912–18	All religious communities	Divorce, no. 378	1212824	Item 10
Haifa (city and district)	1901–17	All religious communities	Foreigners, no. 379	1212824	Item 11
Haifa (district)	1911–16	Moslem, Jewish	Basic, no. 391	1212826	Item 6
Haifa (district)	1911–16	Moslem, Jewish	Basic, no. 391 (cont.)	1212827	Item 1
Haifa (district)	1900	Jewish	Early population, no. 396	1212827	Item 6
Haifa (district)	1915	All religious communities	Men of military age, no. 397	1212827	Item 7
Haifa (district)	1915	All religious communities	Men of military age, no. 397 (cont.)	1212828	Item 1
Nazareth (district)	1905	Moslem, Jewish	Preliminary, no. 398	1212828	Item 3

Place	Years	Population	Register Description	LDS Reel	Item
Haifa (district)	1912	All religious communities	Register of foreigners, no. 399	1212828	Item 4
Haifa (city)	1911–18	Roman Catholic, Maronite, Protestant, Jewish, Greek Orthodox	Basic register, no. 400	1212828	Item 5
Safed (city)	1911–18	Greek Catholic, Jewish	Basic, no. 401	1212828	Item 6
Safed (city)	1911–18	Jewish	Basic, no. 402	1212828	Item 7
Safed (city)	1911–18	Jewish	Basic, no. 402 (cont.)	1212829	Item 1
Safed (city)	1911–18	Jewish	Basic, no. 403	1212829	Item 2
Safed (city)	1911	Jewish	Preliminary, no. 404	1212829	Item 3
Safed (city)	1902–3	Jewish	Mukhtar's, no. 405	1212829	Item 4
Acre (city)	1905	Jewish, Greek orthodox, Greek Catholic, Roman Catholic, Protestant, Masons	Preliminary, no. 406	1212829	Item 5
Acre (district)	1913–18	All religious communities	New registration, no. 413	1212831	Item 2
Acre (district)	1912–18	All religious communities	Changes of address, no. 435	1212833	Item 8
Acre (city and district)	1915–16	All religious communities	Men of military age no. 436	1212833	Item 9
Acre (city and district)	1915–16	All religious communities	Men of military age, no. 436 (cont.)	1212834	Item 1
Acre (district)	1913–18	All religious communities	Corrections of register, no. 437	1212834	Item 2

Appendix I: Ottoman Records in Israel

Appendix J.
Inquisition Tribunals in Spain

The Spanish Inquisition began at different dates in different places throughout Spain. Table 5 is a list of the tribunals in Spain and the dates they were first installed. These dates help in locating the correct tribunal file.

Table 7. Locations and Dates of Spanish Inquisition Tribunals

Tribunal Locality	Date Installed	Tribunal Locality	Date Installed
Alcaraz	1488	Llerena	1512
Aracena	1481	Logroño	?
Avila	1490	Madrid	1648
Balaguer	1489	Medina Campo	1484
Barcelona	1483	Monzon	1486
Belalcazar	1486	Murcia	1488
Burgos	1489	Osma	1489
Calahorra	1491	Palencia	1493
Calatayud	1488	Palma	1488
Ciudad Real	1483	Pamplona	1512
Cordoba	1482	Plasencia	1487
Cuenca	1489	Salamanca	1488
Durango	1499	Santiago	1561
Estella	1513	Segovia	1486
Gerona	1489	Sevilla	1480
Granada	1526	Siguenza	1491
Guadalupe	1485	Tarragona	1489
Jaen	1484	Teruel	1484
Jerez	1491	Toledo	1485
Las Palmas	1507	Tudela	1513
Leon	1499	Valencia	1481
Lerida	1486	Valladolid	1485
		Zaragoza	1483

Source: Miguel Juan Blazquez, *La Inquisición* (Madrid: Ediciones Penthalon, 1988).

Appendix K.
Tombstone Inscriptions from Small Egyptian Towns

Although most Egyptian Jews lived in the major cities in that country, many Jews lived in several outlying towns in Egypt. Information is presented here about the cemeteries and tombstone inscriptions in some of these towns, Port Said, Ismailia, Suez, Damanhour, Kafr El Zayat, and Tantah. The names on the tombstones were culled from Fargeon's 1938 book *Les Juifs en Egypte: Depuis le Origines jusqu'a ce jour* (Jews in Egypt: From the origins to this day).[1] The book is difficult to find, but it offers additional information about these and other Jewish settlements in Egypt.[2]

Port Said

Graves in Port Said's Jewish cemetery date back to the founding of the city during the Suez Canal construction. The following are tombstone inscriptions in Port Said's Jewish cemetery:

Elie Abrebaya, died February 12, 1900
Sara Marie Albert, died June 6, 1890, at 26 years of age
Shemouel Arama, died 1903
Simon Arzt, died June 25, 1910, at 96 years of age
Mayer Arzt, died March 29, 1897
Fanny Helen Arzt, nee Schmidt, died June 9, 1918, 70 years old
Gamila Arzt, died in 1907
Rachel Hermine Barani, died December 14, 1890
Rebecca Benderly, died June 8, 1908
Shemuel Benveniste, died 1908
Bellina Braunstein, died December 20, 1906, 2 years old
Rosa Cassuto, wife of Youssef Cassuto, died in 1870, 76 years old
Mayer Coen, died 1891
Moche Ebbo, died 1884
Albert Joseph Falanca, died July 27, 1912

---

[1] Maurice Fargeon, *Les Juifs en Egypte: Depuis les origines jusqu'a ce jour.* (Jews in Egypt. From the origins to this day) (Cairo: Imprimerie Paul Barbey, 1938).
[2] Kafr el Zayat, Tantah, Mehalla el Kobra, Mansoura, Mit Ghamr, Zifta, Zagazig, Benha, Kouesna, Khelwet el Ghalban, and Sinbou.

Abraham Fredman, born 1813, died 1889
Jafa, wife of Nessim Halevi, died 1894
Yehouda Halevi, died 1888
Yomtob Halevi, died 1907
Chemouel Hakohen, died November 16, 1892
Yehouda Kakona [?], died 1885
Baroukh ben Kalmoun, died 1895
Marcello Abramo Krieger, died September 27, 1908
Yaacob Mansour, died 1913
Ezra Moche Mazliah, died 1888
Salomon Most, died 1890
Moise Liberman, died 1901 at 57 years of age
Nico Mustchi, died January 20, 1908
Frime Rosenfeld, died July 19, 1926, 75 years old
Sara de Salmona, died 1887
Esterina Yacum, born 1852, died July 7, 1900

Ismailia

Although Ismailia did not have a separate Jewish cemetery in 1938, a Jewish section of the European cemetery had 15 Jewish graves. Fargeon lists the following tombstone inscriptions:

Aron Altaras, died October 12, 1866
Joseph Betitou, died January 29, 1926, 50 years old
Bekhor M. Cohen, died October 29, 1933, 60 years old
Jacob I. Cohen, died March 13, 1927, 40 years old
Salomon Goldenberg, died September 15, 1937, 80 years old
Bernard Guttman, died December 18, 1914, 34 years old
Behor R. Hasson, died May 13, 1917, 27 years old
David Hassoun, died September 30, 1927, 19 months old
Meriam Hassoun, died February 2, 1930
Vivida Hassoun, died October 1921, 55 years old
Ibrahim Jacob Joury, died 26 December 1923, 50 years old
Berthe Soriano, nee Goldfarb, died January 9, 1937
Edouard Soriano, died June 3, 1936

Suez

The Jewish cemetery in Suez is in an area of cemeteries known as *al yahoudia* located at some distance from the town. *Al yahoudia* means "Jewish area" in Arabic. Fargeon theorizes that Jews inhabited this area during the Ptolemic era. Humidity has destroyed the inscriptions on some of the older tombstones, but Fargeon lists the following stones legible in 1938:

Vitali Agialmo, died February 17, 1936, 75 years old
Bramo Arughetti, died April 25, 1906, 56 years old
Eliakim M. Arughetti, died April 10, 1904, 39 years old
Lea Arughetti, died May 1891, 45 years old
Abraham G. Benatar, died October 2, 1928, 72 years old
Elisa Bensihum, died 1894
Simon Benvenisti, died March 8, 1918
Lucy Blumenthal, nee Goldstein, died December 16, 1921
Adela Brambir, died September 4, 1913
Albert Cazes, died February 5, 1917, 45 years old
Ezra Tou Cheba, died 1912
Joseph M. Cohen, died June 12, 1912
Tifaha Dangor, died April 21, 1918
Elie Shalom Dangour, died October 24, 1916
Moise A. Dangour, died October 14, 1917, 68 years old
Simha Dangour, died September 3, 1928
David R. Delbourgo, died December 24, 1920, 30 years old
Carlo Grunberg, died December 25, 1925
Rachel Grunberg, nee Abecassis, died May 22, 1907
Seva Yehouda Hacco, died February 6, 1920, 65 years old
Abram, *figlio de* [son of] Joseppe Israel, died October 19, 1902
Marguerite Leznover, died March 10, 1920
Rose Lichtenthal, died June 4, 1932, 50 years old
Salomon, son of Lipa, died March 15, 1871
Zimboul Maggiar, nee Eskenazi, died 1919, 62 years old
Nessim Nassi, died 5673 [1913]
Salomon Pezaro, died August 3, 1936, 49 years old
Isaac Rosenfeld, died January 30, 1917, 20 years old
Jacques Urbini, died July 14, 1922

DAMANHOUR

The cemetery of the town of Damanhour houses the tomb of the Moroccan rabbi Abu Hassira, which has become a site of pilgrimages and about 100 Jewish graves. Surrounding Abu Hassira's tomb are three marble tombstones with the names Moshe Michaali, Yehouda Pinto, and Yaacob Toledano.

Fargeon lists the following other tombstone inscriptions legible in 1938:

Isaak Baroukh, died 1912, 26 years old
Samaan Baroukh, died 1924
Daoud Farfara, died 1037
Heneina Fisson [?]

Aziza abu Haroun
Joseph Hassan, died 1930, 66 years old
Marietta Hassan, died 1919, 35 years old
Ishak Hayon, died 1913
Shlomo Hemmo
Rosine Levy, died 1904, 24 years old
Abraham Naphtali
Sultan Omara, died 1917
Yaacoub Saban
Esther Sabban

Kafr El Zayat

The town of Kafr El Zayat has an abandoned Jewish cemetery from which many marble tombstones had been stolen by 1938. Fargeon reports that some graves were pointed out to him as being those of Yaacoub Gabbai, Marco Maarabi, Moussa Gabbai, and Daniel Mars.

Tantah

The cemetery of the town of Tantah is some distance from the town. Tombstone inscriptions listed in 1938 by Fargeon are:

Moshe Azirad, died 1871
Louna Barcilon, died 1881
Haim Benzakein, died February 26, 1928
Masseoud Benzakein, died February 26, 1928
Victoria Benzakein, died 1896
Stella Berouchel
Bokhor Botton, died March 23, 1907, 62 years old
Louna Botton, died May 21, 1934
Moussa Botton, died 1920, 58 years old
Rahel Chababo, died 1916
Hezkiel Chimeon Cohen, died 1917
Moussa Cohen, died August 11, 1927
Saeda Bint [daughter of] Haim Cohen, died 5648
Mordekhai Dolmodou, died 1876
Flora Halfon
Maimoun Libhar
Moise Meshoullam, died 1915
Daoud Moshe, died 1895
Shalom Zammam [Tammam?], died 5657
Sultana Trounga, died 1886
Youssef Youda Zaga, died 1895
Nessim Levy Zeghel, died 1921

Appendix L.
Surnames & Synagogue Affiliations in 16th-Century Salonica

Salonican synagogues maintained lists of their members. Table 6 lists surnames found in 16th-century Salonica and the synagogues in which their names appear as members. Early Spanish and Portuguese exiles settled in communities based on their towns of origin where their neighbors spoke the same language and had similar customs. The membership lists of these early synagogues, therefore, provide clues as to where the families originated.

Striking is the predominance of surnames of Hebraic or Arabic origin. Except for surnames based on place names (Toledano, Taragano, Otranto, and Saragoussi, for example), Hispanic names such as Rodriguez, Henriquez, Nunes, da Costa, Gomez that are typical of *converso* families do not appear among these early Spanish Jewish exiles who preceded the *converso* diaspora. Similarly, Jewish families such as Allatini and Modiano that came from Leghorn (Livorno) in the 18th century are absent from the list. Of interest is the presence of Ashkenazim as shown by the handful of surnames listed as being part of the Ashkenazic synagogue membership.

Table 8. Surnames and Synagogue Affiliations in Salonica in the 16th Century

Surname	Synagogue	Surname	Synagogue
Abastado	Ets Haim	Alcheh	Catalan Hadash
Aboav	Evora	Algava	Neve Tsedek
Aboav	Shalom	Alhades	Sicilia Hadash
Aboulafia	Neve Shalom	Alhadef	Sicilia Hadash
Abravanel	Lisbon Hadash	Alhanati	Shalom
Acouni	Neve Shalom	Aleman	Catalan Yashan
Aelion	Mayor	Allalouf	Castilla
Aelion	Ets ha Haim	Allalouf	Ets Haim
Aelion	Portugal	Almosnino	Catalan Hadash
Afias	Lisbonne Yasham	Alfandari	Yehia
Agostari	Sicilia Hadash	Alfandari	Lisbonne Hadash
Aharon	Italian Yashan	Alfandari	Ets Haim
Aharon	Italian Shalom	Altaras	Evora
Aji	Ets Haim	Alvo	Lisbonne Hadash
Akiva	Har Gavoah	Alvo	Ets Haim
Alcalay	Yehia	Alvo	Shalom
Alcheh	Kyana	Amar	Sicilia Hadash

Surname	Synagogue	Surname	Synagogue
Amaradji	Castilla	Azriel	Mograbis
Almarilyo	Evora	Arnaldes	Yishma'El
Almarilyo	Yehia	Baena	Mayor
Amiel	Shalom	Bar Avraham	Har Gavoah
Amir	Sicilia Hadash	Bar David	Har Gavoah
Amir	Evora	Bar Elazar	Har Gavoah
Amiras	Sicilia Hadash	Bar Sion	Portugal
Amon	Castilla	Baraja	Mayor
Amram	Shalom	Baroukh	Italia Yashan
Angel	Otranto	Baroukh	Italia Hadash
Angel	Italia Shalom	Baroukh	Italia Shalom
Angel	Poulia	Baroukh	Lisbonne Hadash
Angel	Kyana	Baroukh	Neve Shalom
Arama	Neve Shalom	Baroukh	Portugal
Arama	Ets Hahaim	Baroukh	Provincia
Arari	Portugal	Baroukh	Catalan Hadash
Arditti	Catalan Yashan	Barouhiel	Geroush Sefarad
Arnaldes	Ishmael	Barzilay	Italia Shalom
Arokas	Catalan Yashan	Barzilay	Catalan Hadash
Aron	Yehia	Basso	Mayor
Arotchas	Mayor	Beja	Mayor
Arouh	Geroush Sefarad	Benadon	Pulia
Arouh	Neve Tsedek	Ben Atar	Ets ha Haim
Asher	Geroush Sefarad	Ben David	Lisbonne Yashan
Asher	Poulia	Ben Djoya	Geroush Sefarad
Asher	Shalom	Ben Djoya	Yehia
Ashkenazi	Provincia	Ben Ezra	Castilia
Assael	Neve Shalom	Ben Mayor	Mayor
Asseo	Shalom	Ben Natan	Sicilia Yashan
Attias	Evora	Ben Natan	Erts ha Haim
Attias	Aragon	Ben Nahmias	Lisbonne Hadash
Attias	Geroush Sefarad	Ben Santchi	Mayor
Attias	Portugal	Ben Santchi	Pulia
Avayou	Beth Aharon	Ben Santchi	Castilla
Avlas	Castilla	Ben Sarah	Castilla
Avraham	Italia Yashan	Ben Shoham	Geroush Sefarad
Avraham, Moshe	Neve Shalom	Ben Shoham	Catalan hadash
		Ben Shoham	Castilla
Avraham, Yaacov	Aragon	Ben Soussan	Castilla
		Ben Yaesh	Mayor
Ayash	Sicilia Hadash	Ben Zion	Catalan Hadash
Azaria	Italia Shalom	Ben Zion	Geroush Sefarad
Azaria	Yehia	Benadon	Pulia
Azouz	Aragon	Benardout	Aragon
Azouz	Shalom	Benforado	Geroush Sefarad

Surname	Synagogue
Benforado	Ishmael
Benforado	Lisbonne Yashan
Benforado	Neve Tsedek
Benouziglio	Otranto
Benouziyo	Lisbonne
Benouziyo	Aragon
Benron	Catalan Hadash
Benroubi	Aragon
Benroubi	Mograbis
Benveniste	Shalom
Benzion	Italia Yashan
Berakha	Sicilia Yashan
Berakha	Sicilia Hadash
Beressi	Catalan Hadash
Bessantchi	see Ben Santchi
Bezes	Italia Yashan
Bienvenido	Har Gavoah
Biniamin	Provincia
Biniamin	Kyana
Bitran	Sicilia Hadash
Bivas	Evora
Bivas	Ets ha Haim
Bonano	Yehia
Bonano	Castilla
Bonano	Pulia
Bourla	Kyana
Bourla	Yehia
Broudo	Ets ha Haim
Broudo	Shalom
Bueno	Portugal
Cabelli	Mograbis
Calorras	Aragon
Campano	Portugal
Campeyas	Catalan Yashan
Capouano	Estrug
Capouano	Pulia
Capon	Lisbonne Yashan
Capon	Sicilia Yashan
Carasso (Levi)	Shalom
Carasso (Levi)	Estrug
Cassuto	Beth Aharon
Castro	Beth Aharon
Castro	Geroush Sefarad
Castro	Lisbonne Hadash

Surname	Synagogue
Catan	Ets ha Haim
Catan	Provincia
Cazes	Portugal
Chelibon	Shalom
Chenio	Aragon
Chico	Ets ha haim
Chelebi	Italia Yashan
Chimino	Neve Shalom
Cimhi	See Kimhi
Cohen	Evora
Cohen	Italia Yashan
Cohen	Italia Hadash
Cohen	Geroush Sefarad
Cohen	Har Gavoah
Cohen	Yehia
Cohen	Lisbonne Hadash
Cohen	Lisbonne Yashan
Cohen	Mayor
Cohen	Neve Tsedek
Cohen	Neve Shalom
Cohen	Sicilia Yashan
Cohen	Sicilia Hadash
Cohen	Ets ha Haim
Cohen	Pulia
Cohen	Portugal
Cohen	Catalan Hadash
Cohen	Castilla
Cohen	Shalom
Cohen, Benardout	Aragon
Comprado	Ishmael
Conforte	Yehia
Cordovero	Yehia
Coune	Lisbonne Hadash
Counio	Italia Shalom
Coutiel	Yehia
Coutilo	Provincia
Covo	Shalom
Crespin	Yehia
Crespin	Shalom
Cuenca	Mayor
Dafan	Sicilia Yashan
Daniel	Italia Yashan
Dassa	Shalom

Surname	Synagogue	Surname	Synagogue
David	Italia Hadash	Galea	Italia Hadash
David	Italia Shalom	Galidi	Neve Shalom
David	Lisbonne Hadash	Gallego	Ets ha Haim
Djahon	Castilla Hadash	Gallego	Lisbonne Yashan
Djilletes	Sicilia Yashan	Gattegno	Aragon
Djirassi	Sicilia Yashan	Gavios	Lisbonne Yashan
Elazar	Otranto	Gavriel	Italia Hadash
Eliahou	Yehia	Gedalia	Italia Hadash
Eliahou	Italia Shalom	Gedalia	Yehia
Eliakim	Neve Tsedek	Gershon	Italia Hadash
Eliezer	Italia Hadash	Gordji	Yehia
Eliezer	Italia Shalom	Gormezano	Sicilia Hadash
Eliezer	Ets ha Haim	Grotas	Italia Yashan
Elimelekh	Evora	Habib	Shalom
Elisha	Lisbonne Yashan	Hacohen ha Guer	Yehia
Erera	Geroush Sefarad	Hadayo	Otranto
Erera	Provincia	Hagouel	Sicilia Hadash
Ergas	Evora	Haim	Italia Yashan
Ergas	Ets ha Haim	Haim	Provincia
Escaloni	Lisbonne Yashan	Halega	Castilla
Escapa	Castilla	Halevy	Ashkenaz
Esformes	Catalan Yashan	Halfon	Neve Tsedek
Escayo	Mograbis	Hamon	Castilla
Eskenazi	Ashkenaz	Hananel	Ets ha Haim
Estrougano	Pulia	Hanania	Aragon
Estrougano	Geroush Sefarad	Handali	Catalan Hadash
Estrougo	Estrug	Hanen	Neve Tsedek
Estrougo	Aragon	Hanen	Mograbis
Estroumsa	Castilla	Hanoh	Yehia
Ezrati	Sicilia Hadash	Hanoh	Ashkenaz
Faisevi	Ashkenaz	Hanoka	Aragon
Falcon	Yehia	Hanoka	Shalom
Faradji	Sicilia Yashan	Hasday	Lisbonne Yashan
Faradji	Etz ha Haim	Hassid	Aragon
Faradji	Aragon	Hassid	Italia Yashan
Faradji	Portugal	Hasson	Beth Aharon
Ferrera	Mayor	Hasson	Yehia
Fisso	Evora	Haver	Sicilia Hadash
Florentin	Italia Yashan	Hayatt	Aragon
Frances	Mayor	Hazan	Provincia
Frances	Etz ha Haim	Hazan	Neve Tsedek
Franco	Italia Yashan	Hazan	Sicilia Yashan
Franco	Beth Aharon	Hazan	Sicilia Hadash
Franco	Aragon	Hirida	Mayor
Gaguin	Lisbonne Hadash		

Surname	Synagogue	Surname	Synagogue
Hizkiya	Mograbis	Machorro	Portugal
Houdras	Aragon	Madiordo	Ets ha Haim
Houli	Sicilia Hadash	Madiordo	Aragon
Houli	Aragon	Maggioro	Evora
Immanuel	Pulia	Magriso	Beth Aharon
Immanuel	Italia Shalom	Mahalalel	Italia Yashan
Israel	Italia Hadash	Mair	Italia Yashan
Israel	Beth Aharon	Mallah	Provincia
Israel	Portugal	Mandel	Catalan Yashan
Israel	Provincia	Mano	Pulia
Israel	Castilla	Mansano	Castilla
Israel	Kyana	Maradji	Sicilia Hadash
Israel	Italia Hadash	Marcos	Lisbonne Hadash
Israel	Beth Aharon	Markezano	Estrug
Kalay	see Kalli	Massarano	Portugal
Kalli	Geroush Sefarad	Masseri	Yehia
Kalli	Ets ha Haim	Matalon	Neve Shalom
Kimhi	Sicilia Yashan	Matarasso	Aragon
Kimhi	Sicilia Hadash	Matarasso	Evora
Lapas	Ashkenaz	Matarasso	Ets ha Haim
Lea	Castilla	Matarasso	Otranto
Lea	Geroush Sefarad	Matsliah	Yehia
Lea	Neve Shalom	Matsliah	Portugal
Lea	Yehia	Mayissa	Geroush Sefarad
Leal	Beth Aharon	Mayissa	Catalan Hadash
Leja	Geroush Sefarad	Mazliah	Italia Hadash
Leon	Neve Shalom	Mazlou	Neve Tsedek
Leon	Portugal	Medina	Portugal
Levy	Italia Shalom	Meir	Italia Shalom
Levy	Aragon	Menahem	Ashkenaz
Levy	Beth Aharon	Menahem	Provincia
Levy	Geroush Sefarad	Menahem	Italia Shalom
Levy	Mayor	Menahem	Neve Shalom
Levy	Mograbis	Menashe	Geroush Sefarad
Levy	Neve Tsedek	Menashe	Yehia
Levy	Neve Shalom	Menashe	Sicilia Hadash
Levy	Sicilia Yashan	Merida	Yehia
Levy	Sicilia Hadash	Meshoulam	Estrug
Levy	Ets ha Haim	Meshoulam	Portugal
Levy	Provincia	Mevorah	Geroush Sefarad
Levy	Catalan Hadash	Michael	Otranto
Litchi	Neve Shalom	Mijan	Sicilia Yashan
Litchi	Shalom	Milo	Portugal
Louvil	Italia Yashan	Miranda	Portugal

Appendix L: Surnames and Synagogue Affiliations in 16th-Century Salonica

Surname	Synagogue	Surname	Synagogue
Misrahi	Estrug	Ouri	Ashkenaz
Mizrahi	Yehia	Ouriel	Neve Tsedek
Mitchi	Sicilia Yashan	Ouriel	Italia Yashan
Mitchi	Shalom	Ouziel	Italia Shalom
Modiano	Italia Yashan	Ouziel	Geroush Sefarad
Mokata	Beth Aharon	Ouziel	Mograbis
Molho	Shalom	Ouziel	Sicilia Hadash
Monina	Castilla	Ovadia	Evora
Montekio	Italia Shalom	Pachariel	Ets ha Haim
Mordechai	Italia Hadash	Paladino	Yishma'El
Mordoh	Pulia	Paladino	Provincia
Morea	Yehia	Papouchado	Yehia
Moshe	Otranto	Pardo	Sicilia Hadash
Moshe	Italia Yashan	Pardo	Shalom
Moshe	Italia Hadash	Parente	Pulia
Moshe	Ishmael	Passi	Uehia
Moshe	Catalan Hadash	Passi	Ets ha Haim
Moshon	Portugal	Pelossof	Neve Shalom
Moussa	Ets ha Haim	Perahia	Italia Yashan
Moussa	Catalan Hadash	Pereira	Portugal
Nar/Naar	Lisbonne Hadash	Perez	Italia Hadash
Madjari	Evora	Perez	Neve Tsadok
Nahman	Italia Yashan	Perez	Shalom
Nahman	Italia Hadash	Pessah	Evora
Nahmias	Evora	Pessah	Ashkenaz
Nahmias	Lisbonne Yashan	Pessah	Geroush Sefarad
Nahmias	Lisbonne Hadash	Pessah	Yehia
Nahmias	Yehia	Pesso	Evora
Nahmias	Mayor	Petelon	Otranto
Nahoum	Aragon	Pichi	Otranto
Nahoum	Sicilia Hadash	Pilo	Castilla
Naki	Provincia	Pilo	Shalom
Navarro	Ets ha Haim	Pinhas	Italia Hadash
Nefoussi	Kyana	Pinhas	Italia Shalom
Negrin	Yehia	Pinhas	Har Gavoah
Nehama	Italia Hadash	Pinhas	Mograbis
Nehama	Mograbis	Pinto	Aragon
Nissim	Otranto	Pipano	Castilla
Nissim	Geroush Sefarad	Pitchon	Har Gavoah
Nissim	Italia Hadash	Pitchon	Neve Shalom
Nissim	Lisbon Hadash	Policar	Geroush Sefarad
Nissim	Mograbis	Porfeta	Yishma'El
Nissim	Ets ha Haim	Rahamim	Shalom
Olivares	Mayor	Raphael	Italia Yashon
Oreja	Geroush Sefarad	Raphael	Italia Shalom

Surname	Synagogue	Surname	Synagogue
Raphael	Neve Shalom	Sasson	Ets ha Haim
Raphael	Portugal	Sasson	Geroush Sefarad
Razon	Sicilia Hadash	Sasson	Pulia
Recanati	Neve Tsedek	Sciaki	see Shaki
Reouven	Sicilia Hadash	Segoura	Sicilia Hadash
Reouven	Neve Tsedek	Segoura	Ets ha Haim
Revah	Sicilia Hadash	Senor	Lisbonne Yashan
Roha	Geroush Sefarad	Sephiha	Sicilia Hadash
Romano	Yishma'El	Serer	Mograbis
Romano	Shalom	Serero	Yehia
Rosales	Castilla	Sevilia	Shalom
Roubissa	Provincia	Shaban	Neve Tsedek
Rousso	Shalom Ishmael	Shaban	Sicilia Hadash
Rousso	Ishmael	Shami	Otranto
Rouvio	Evora	Shabato	Italia Shalom
Saadi	Ashkenaz	Shabetay	Italia Yashan
Saadi	Italia Yashan	Shabetay	Italia Shalom
Saadi	Yehia	Shabetay	Ets ha Haim
Saayas	Otranto	Shabetay	Provincia
Saayas	Pulia	Shaki	Yehia
Sadicario	Portugal	Shaki	Otranto
Sadok	Aragon	Shalom	Shalom
Safan	Neve Tsedek	Shalom	Pulia
Safan	Yehia	Shalom	Catalan Yashan
Salem	Catalan Hadash	Shalom	Catalan Hadash
Salamias	Italia Hadash	Shalom	Kyana
Salmon	Italia Hadash	Shami	Otranto
Salmona	Beth Aharon	Shami	Sicilia Hadash
Salmona	Yehia	Shaoul	Ashkenaz
Saloum	Shalom	Shaoul	Sicilia Hadash
Saltiel	Shalom	Shelomo	Italia Yashan
Saltiel	Ets ha Haim	Shelomo	Otranto
Samoura	Aragon	Shelomo	Italia Hadash
Saoul	Catalan Hadash	Shelomo	Italia Shalom
Saporta	Catalan Yashan	Shemouel	Italia Hadash
Saporta	Lisbonne Hadash	Shevah	Geroush Sefarad
Saragoussi	Beth Aharon	Shibi	Evora
Sarfati	Aragon	Shibi	Ets ha Haim
Sarfati	Geroush Sefarad	Shibi	Shalom
Sarfati	Sicilia Hadash	Shimon	Italia Hadash
Sarfati	Ets ha Haim	Shimon	Italia Shalom
Sarfati	Kyana	Shimshi	Ashkenaz
Sarfati	Shalom	Shitouvi	Lisbonne Yashan
Sarrano	Castilla	Shivilio	Shalom

Appendix L: Surnames and Synagogue Affiliations in 16th-Century Salonica

Surname	Synagogue	Surname	Synagogue
Shoel	Aragon	Varsano	Pulia
Shoulam	Yehia	Venezia	Sicilia Yashan
Shounina	Sicilia Yashan	Ventoura	Italia Yashan
Sides	Castilla	Ventoura	Italia Hadash
Sides	Shalom	Ventoura	Ets ha Haim
Sides	Yehia	Veyissid	Otranto
Simaha	Ashkenaz	Vital	Neve Shalom
Sion	Ashkenaz	Vosnali	Yehia
Sion	Aragon	Yacar	Portugal
Sirioti	Geroush Ashkenaz	Yacoel	Neve Tsedek
Sitbon	Neve Tsedek	Yahiani	Sicilia Yashan
Soto	Mayor	Yeheskel	Otranto
Soto	Otranto	Yehiel	Aragon
Soulam	Ets ha Haim	Yehiel	Pulia
Soulema	Italia Yashan	Yehiel	Yehia
Soulema	Italia Shalom	Yehoshoua	Har Gavoah
Soulema	Mayor	Yehouda	Catalan Hadash
Soulema	Sicilia Yashan	Yehouda	Provincia
Soustiel	Pulia	Yehouda	Shalom
Souyeni	Sicilia Hadash	Yehouda, Shelomo	Kyana
Taboh	Aragon	Yeni	Sicilia Yashan
Taboh	Catalan Yashan	Yermia	Lisbon Hadash
Talbi	Sicilia Hadash	Yerouham	Evora
Talbi	Yehia	Yehouroun	Yehia
Taragano	Neve Shalom	Yitshak	Italia Yashan
Tarfon	Catalan Hadash	Yitshak	Italia Shalom
Tazartes	Ashkenaz	Yitshak	Shalom
Tazartes	Shalom	Yitshak	Neve Shalom
Termin	Sicilia Hadash	Yoel	Lisbonne Yashan
Tevah	Mayor	Yomtov	Geroush Sefarad
Teveth	Sicilia Yashan	Yona	Aragon
Tiano	Italia Yashan	Yoseph	Italia Hadash
Toledano	Beth Aharon	Yoseph	Italia Shalom
Toledano	Yehia	Yoseph	Ismael
Toledano	Mograbis	Yoseph	Mograbis
Torres	Pulia	Yoseph	Castilla
Torres	Mayor	Zafaran	Har Gavoah
Touvi	Ashkenaz	Zakar	Neve Shalom
Touvi	Otranto	Zakay	Italia Yashan
Touvi	Beth Aharon	Zaraya	Otranto
Touvi	Portugal	Zaraya	Neve Shalom
Trabout	Portugal	Zerahia	Italia Shalom
Tsadik	Ashkenaz		
Vaena	*see* Baena		
Valensi	Yehia		

Source: Michael Molho "Les Synagogues de Salonique" in Carasso, *Les Juifs de Salonique, 1492–1943.* Reproduced with permission of Elie Carasso (publisher).

Glossary

Adafina. Meal cooked over a slow fire by Sephardic Jews for the Sabbath. To keep the meal warm throughout the Sabbath, when fires could not be lit, Jewish cooks sometimes buried the cooking food under hot rocks (from the Arabic *dafina*, meaning *bury*).

Al Andalus. Arab name for the western states, Spain.

Alboracos. Name given to baptized Jews. This ironic term refers to the baptized Jews who seemed otherwise unchanged; like Mohammad's magical steed, Alborak, which was neither horse nor mule, baptized Jews were neither Jewish nor Christian.

Aljama. Community, Jewish or Moslem; from the Arabic *jama*, gather or gathering.

Aljamiado. Spanish language written in Hebrew script.

Andalusia. Moslem Spain, essentially the southern half of Spain. (*see Al Andalus*).

Anusim. Jews forced to convert to another religion (Hebrew language).

Arian Christianity. Followers of Arius reasoned that Jesus could not logically co-exist with God and, therefore, must be subservient to him. Because Arian Christians did not accept the Trinity concept of God as Father, Son, and Holy Spirit, the Catholic Church considered Arianism to be heresy.

Ashkenazic. (Hebrew *German*). Jew of European origin.

Auto-da-fe. Literally, *act of faith*. Ceremony during which Inquisition officials meted out public punishment.

B.C.E. Before Common Era. Equivalent to B.C. *See* C.E.

Bled el siba. Land of dissidence. Part of Morocco not under control of the king of Morocco. *See* Makhzen.

C.E. Common Era. Equivalent to A.D. *See* B.C.E.

Crypto-Jews. Converts who kept the Jewish faith secretly.

Defter. Turkish register.

Geniza. (plural, *genizot*). A place where sacred Jewish documents and books to be disposed of are buried to obey the admonishment not to knowingly destroy pages that might include the name of God.

Ghetto. Jewish quarter, named after first one in Venice.

Gibraltar. Derived from *Jebel al Tariq* (mountain of Tariq), allegedly named after the Moor Tariq ibn Ziyad, who led the forces that invaded the peninsula.

Grana. Spanish-Portuguese community of Tunis. From the Arabic word for Leghorn. *See* Tuansa.

Hakham. Title of Sephardic rabbi. From Hebrew meaning *wise*.

Hara. Jewish quarter in Tunisia. From Arabic meaning *lane*.
Harat al barabra. Ashkenazic Jewish quarter in Cairo. From Arabic, *foreigners' quarter*.
Harat al yahud. Jewish quarter in Cairo. From Arabic, *Jewish lane*.
Hidalgo. Spanish nobleman.
Judaize. To observe or retain Jewish traditions.
Juderia. Jewish quarter, in Spanish. *Juderia*, used more frequently in Spanish-speaking Christian northern Spain, usually denoted quarters within a Spanish town. *Aljama*, more frequently used in Andalusia, Arabic-speaking southern Spain, usually referred to separate Jewish entities or villages.
Karaites. Ancient Jewish sect that base their Judaism on the five books of Moses and reject subsequent rabbinical interpretations.
Kehillah Kedoshah. Jewish community.
Ketubah (plural, *ketubot*). Jewish marriage certificate.
Limpieza de sangre. Purity of blood (Spanish).
Limpeza de sangue. Purity of blood (Portuguese).
Makhzen. (*bled el makhzen*). Part of Morocco under control of the king of Morocco. From Arabic for *treasury*. See bled el siba.
Marranos. Pejorative term for crypto-Jews; allegedly means *pigs*.
Mellah. Walled Jewish quarter in Moroccan towns. The first *mellah* was in Fez, allegedly so named because it was built on a salty plain (*mellah* means salt in Arabic).
Moor. Inhabitant of western North Africa, from Latin *maurus*.
Morisco. Moor who converted to Christianity.
Mozarab. Christian who adopted the Arabic culture in Spain.
Pinkas (plural *pinkassim*). Jewish registers.
Reconciliado. Heretic reconciled to the Catholic Church. The *reconciliado's* property was confiscated. Usually a *sanbenito* was to be worn in public.
Relajado. Heretic released to the state by the Inquisition to be burned at the stake.
Responsa. Written rabbinical answers to religious queries.
Romaniot. Jews who lived in the Byzantine Empire. Also known as Greek Jews.
Sanbenito. "Holy sack" was the punishment garment worn by individuals condemned of a non-capital crime by Inquisition officials.
Sancak. Turkish subprovince.
Sefarad. Hebrew term for *Spain*.
Stato civile. Vital records in Italy.
Sofer. Jewish scribe.
Talmud. Rabbinical commentaries on Jewish law (Torah).
Torah. Jewish law or scriptures; five Books of Moses.
Tuansa. Local Jewish community of Tunis—as compared to *grana*.
Vileyet. Turkish province. *See* sancak.
Visigoths. Western Goths. Germanic tribes that invaded the Roman Empire and established kingdoms in France and Spain.

BIBLIOGRAPHY

Note: Although many books listed here are out of print and perhaps difficult to find, they may possibly be located in university or synagogue libraries or from out-of-print book dealers. Also consider using inter-library loan services through many public and most university libraries.

The publications listed in chapter 17, Periodicals are not necessarily included in the bibliography.

Abecassis, Jose Maria. *Genealogia Hebraica: Portugal e Gibraltar, Secs. XVII a XX* (Jewish genealogy: Portugal and Gibraltar, 17th to 20th centuries). 5 vols. Lisbon: Author, 1990. Distributor: Lisbon, Livraria Ferin.

Abensur, Philip. "*Archives du Ministere des Affaires Etrangeres*" (Archives of the Ministry of Foreign Affairs). *Revue du Cercle de Genealogie Juive* 34 (Summer 1993): 10–11.

———. "Sephardic Genealogical Research in Morocco." *Avotaynu* 3, no. 10 (Fall 1994): 40.

———. "*Releve de tombes des anciens cimitieres juifs d'Alger*" (Recordings of tombs in the ancient cemeteries of Algiers). *Etsi* 1, no. 3 (1998): 5.

———. "*Les élèves de l'école de l'Alliance de Baghdad entre 1865 et 1879*" (Students of the Baghdad Alliance School between 1865 and 1879) *Etsi* 5, no. 16 (March 2002): 10–17.

Abensur Hazan, Laurence. *Les Pontremoli: Deux dynasties rabbiniques en Turquie et en Italie: Sources et documents* (The Pontremoli: Two rabbinic dynasties in Turkey and Italy: Sources and documents). Paris: Author, 1997.

Abitbol, M., ed. *Communautes Juives des marges sahariennes du Maghreb* (Jewish communities from the borders of the Sahara in the Maghreb). Jerusalem: Ben Zvi Institute, 1982.

Aciman, Andre. *Out of Egypt.* New York: Farrar Straus Giroux, 1994.

Adler, Elkan Nathan. *Jewish Travellers in the Middle Ages.* New York: Dover Publishers, 1987.

Alexi, Trudi. *The Mezuzah in the Madonna's Foot: Marranos and Other Secret Jews.* New York: Simon & Schuster, 1993.

Alhadeff, Gini. *The Sun at Midday: Tales of a Mediterranean Family.* New York: Pantheon Books, 1997.

Alhadeff, Vittorio. *La Cita en Buenos Aires: Saga de una gran familia Sefaradi* (Appointment in Buenos Aires: Saga of a grand Sephardic Family). Buenos Aires: Grupo Editor Latinoamericano, 1996.

Amador de los Rios, Jose. *Historia Social, Politica y Religiosa de los Judios de Espana y Portugal* (Social, Political and Religious History of the Jews of Spain and Portugal) Madrid: Ediciones Turner, 1984

Angel, Marc D. *The Jews of Rhodes: The History of a Sephardic Community.* New York: Sepher-Hermon Press, 1978.

———. *La America: The Sephardic experience in the United States.* Philadelphia: Jewish Publication Society of America, 1982.

Anglo-Jewish Association. "Historical Notes on the Jews of Gibraltar." *The Seventh Annual Report of the Anglo-Jewish Association.* London, 1878.

Aranov, Saul I. *A Descriptive Catalogue of the Bension Collection of Sephardic Manuscripts and Texts.* Winnipeg, Canada: University of Alberta Press, 1979.

Arbell, Mordechai. " *'La Nacion': Los Judios Hispano-Portugueses del Caribe*" ("The Nation": Spanish-Portuguese Jews of the Caribbean). *Sephardica* 1, no. 1 (March 1984): 85–94. Jewish communities established in the Caribbean by Marranos after their expulsion from Brazil.

———. *Portuguese Jews of Jamaica.* Kingston, Jamaica: Canoe Press, University of West Indies, 2000.

Arditti, Benjamin. *Yehudei Bulgaria bishnot hamishtar hanatsi, 1940-1944* (Bulgarian Jews during the years of the Nazi regime, 1940-1944). Tel Aviv: Author, 1962.

A. Ubieto Arteta. *"Procesos de la Inquisición de Aragon"* (Trials of the Inquisition of Aragon). *Rev. Archivos, Bibliotecas y Museos,* 67 no. 2 (1959): 549-99.

Ashton, Eliyahu. *The Jews of Moslem Spain.* Philadelphia: Jewish Publication Society, 1993.

Assis, Y.T. *The Jews of Santa Coloma de Queralt: An Economic and Demographic Case Study of a Community at the End of the Thirteenth Century.* Jerusalem: Magnes Press, 1988.

———. *Jews in the Crown of Aragon, 1213-1327.* Jerusalem: Central Archives History of the Jewish People, 1995.

———. *Jews in the Crown of Aragon, 1328-1493: Regesta of the Cartas Reales in Archivio de la Corona de Aragon.* Jerusalem: Central Archives History of the Jewish People, 1995.

———. *Jewish Economy in the Medieval Crown of Aragon, 1213-1327.* Leiden, The Netherlands: E.J. Brill, 1997.

Attal, Robert. *Les Juifs de Grece de l'expulsion d'Espagne a nos jours: Bibliographie* (Jews of Greece from the expulsion from Spain to our days: Bilbiography). Jerusalem: Ben Zvi Institute and Hebrew University, 1984.

———. *Les Juifs de Grece de l'expulsion d'Espagne a nos jours: Bibliographie: Additifs a la premiere edition* (Jews of Greece from the Spanish expulsion to our days: Bibliography: Additions to the first edition). Jerusalem: Ben Zvi Institute and Hebrew University, 1984.

Attal, Robert, and Joseph Avivi. *Registres Matrimoniaux de la Communaute Juive Portugaise de Tunis, XVIII-XIX siecles* (Marriage records of the Portuguese Jewish community of Tunis, 18th and 19th centuries). Oriens Judaicus. Jerusalem: Ben Zvi Institute, 1989.

———. *Registres Matrimoniaux de la Communaute Juive Portugaise de Tunis, 1843-1854* (Marriage records of the Portuguese Jewish community of Tunis, 1843-1854). Oriens Judaicus. Jerusalem: Ben Zvi Institute, 2000.

Avrahami, Hannah. "The Jews of Livorno and their Relations with Tunis in the 17th and 18th centuries" (in Hebrew). Thesis, Ramat Gan University, 1979.

Barnett, Lionel D., ed. *Bevis Marks Records Being Contributions to the History of the Spanish and Portuguese Congregation of London: Illustrated by Facsimiles of Documents.* 6 vols. Oxford: Oxford University Press, 1940-97.

    Vol. 3: Abstracts of *ketubot* and civil marriage registers of the Spanish and Portuguese Jews Congregation, 1837-1901.

    Vol. 4: Circumcision register of Isaac and Abraham de Paiba, 1715-75.

    Vol. 5: Birth register (1767-1881) of the Spanish and Portuguese Jews' Congregation, London, including Jewish births (1707-63); register books of the College of Arms

    Vol. 6: Burial register (1733-1918) of the new cemetery of the Spanish Portuguese Jews' Congregation (with some later entries).

Barnett, R.D., and P. Wright. *The Jews of Jamaica: Tombstone Inscriptions 1663-1880.* Jerusalem: Ben Zvi Institute, 1997.

Baer, Yitzhak. *History of the Jews in Christian Spain*. Philadelphia: Jewish Publication Society, 1993.
Beinart, Haim. *Records of the Trials of the Spanish Inquisition in Ciudad Real*. Jerusalem: Israel National Academy of Sciences and Humanities, 1974–81.
———. *Conversos on Trial: The Inquisition in Ciudad Real*. Jerusalem: Magnes Press, Hebrew University, 1981.
———. *The Expulsion of the Jews from Spain* (English trans. of *Gerush Sefarad*). Portland, Ore.: Littman Library of Jewish Civilization, 2002.
Beinart, Haim, ed. "The Great Conversion and the Converso Problem." *The Sephardi Legacy*. Jerusalem: Magnes Press, 1992.
———. "The Jews in Castile." *The Sephardi Legacy*. Jerusalem: Magnes Press, 1992.
———. *The Sephardi Legacy*. Jerusalem: Magnes Press, 1992.
Beinin, Joel. *The Dispersion of Egyptian Jewry: Culture, Politics, and the Formation of a Modern Diaspora*. Los Angeles: University of California Press, 1998.
Bejarano, Margalit. *La Comunidad Hebrea de Cuba: La memoria y la historia* (Hebrew community of Cuba: Memory and history). Jerusalem: Hebrew University, 1996.
Ben Brith, Joseph. "*Die Odyssee der Henrique-Familie.*" In Kieler Werkstücke, ed. *Reihe A, Beiträge zur schleswig-holsteinischen und skandinavischen Geschichte*, Frankfurt am Main: Peter Lang, 2001.
Benbassa, Esther, and Aron Rodriguez. *A Sephardi Life in Southeastern Europe: The Autobiography and Journal of Gabriel Arie, 1863–1939*. Seattle: University of Washington Press, 1998.
———. *Sephardi Jewry: A History of the Judeo-Spanish Community, 14–20th Centuries*. Berkeley: University of California Press, 2000.
Ben Naim, Yosef. *Malkhei rabanan* (Prominent Rabbis [of Morocco]). Jerusalem: 1931.
Bennett, Ralph. "The Jewish of Exotic Surinam and their History," *Avotaynu* 8 (1992): 2, 16.
———. "History of the Jews of the Caribbean." *Los Muestros* (1993): 11.
———. "History of the Jews of Egypt." *Avotaynu* 10, no. 1, (1994): 30.
Benoliel, Jose. *Dialecto judeo-hispano-marroqui o hakitia* (Morrocan Judeo-Spanish Dialect or Hakitia). Madrid: Author, 1977.
Bensimon, Agnes. *Hassan II et les Juifs: Histoire d'une Emigration Secrete* (Hassan II and the Jews: History of a Secret Emigration). Paris: Seuil, 1991.
Bentes, Abraham Ramiro. *Primeiros immigrantes hebreus na Amazonia: Instillacao da primeira communidade israelite brasiliera* (First Jewish immigrants in the Amazon: Installation of the first Brazilian Jewish community). Rio de Janeiro: Gráficos Borsoi, 1987.
———. *Das Ruinas de Jerusalem a Verdajante Amazonia* (Ruins of Jerusalem in the Green Amazon). Rio de Janeiro: Edicoes Bloch, 1987.
Benoliel, Jose. *Dialecto judeo-hispano-marroqui o hakitia*. Madrid, 1977.
Bensoussan, David and Asher Knafu. *Ketoubbot de Mogador* (Ketubot of Magador). Montreal: Éditions Du Lys, 2002.
Bernstein, Baruch. *The Chuettas of Majorca*. New York: Ktav, 1972.
Bierbrier, Morris. "Tracing Ancestors in Italy and Turkey." *Syllabus: 21st International Conference on Jewish Genealogy*. London, 2001.
Birmingham, Stephen. *The Grandees: America's Sephardic Elite*. New York: Harper & Row, 1971.
Birnbaum, Solomon A. *The Hebrew Scripts*. 2 vols. London: Paleographica, 1956, 1971.

Blazquez Miguel, Juan. *La Inquisición en Castilla-La Mancha* (Inquisition in Castile-La Mancha). Cordoba, Spain: Universidad de Cordoba, 1986.

———. *Catálogo de los procesos inquisitoriales del Tribunal de Santo Oficio de Murcia* (Catalog of the Inquisition Trials of the Murcia Tribunal). Murgetana, 74, (1987): 7–109.

———. *Ciudad Real y la Inquisición, 1483–1820* (Ciudad Real and the Inquisition). Ciudad Real, Spain: Comision Municipal de Cultura, 1987.

———. *La Inquisición* (The Inquisition). Madrid: Ediciones Penthalon, 1988.

———. *Toledot: Historia del Toledo judio* (Generations: History of Jewish Toledo). Toledo, Spain: Editorial Arcano, 1989.

———. *La Inquisición en Cataluña: El tribunal del Santo Oficio de Barcelona, 1487–1820* (Inquisition in Catalonia: Holy Office tribunal of Barcelona, 1487-1820). Toledo, Spain: Editorial Arcano, 1990.

———. *Madrid-judios, herejes y brujas: El Tribunal de Corte (1650–1820)* (Jews of Madrid, heretics, and witches: The Royal Tribunal (1650-1820). Toledo, Spain: Editorial Arcano, 1990.

Bohm, Gunter. "The First Sephardic Synagogues in South America and in the Caribbean Area." *Studio Rosenthaliana* 22, no. 1 (Spring 1988): 1–14.

Bonnin, Pere. *Sangre judia: Espagnoles de ascendencia hebrea y antisemitismo cristiano* (Jewish blood: Spaniards of Jewish ancestry and Christian anti-Semitism), 2d ed. Barcelona: Flor del Viento Ediciones, 1998.

Boyd-Bowman, Peter. *Indice geobiografico de 56 mil pobladores de America* (Geobiographical index of 56,000 American villagers). 2 vols. Mexico City: Fondo de Cultura Economica, 1985.

Brody, Robert. *The Geonim of Babylonia and the Shaping of Medieval Jewish Culture*. New Haven: Yale University Press, 1998.

Bruckmayer, Daniel. *Dizionario degli ebrei* (Dictionary of the Jews). Rome: Ed. Carucci, 1985.

Bruno, Louis, and Elie Malka. *Receuil de textes Judeo-Arabes de Fes* (Collection of Judeo-Arabic texts from Fez). Rabat, Morocco: Hautes Etudes Marocaines, 1939.

Bunis, David M. "The History of Judezmo Orthography." Working papers in Yiddish and East European Jewish Studies. Max Weinreich Center for Advanced Studies, *YIVO* 2 (1974): 1–55.

Cahen, "*Les Juifs de Martinique*" (Jews of Martinique). *Revue des etudes juives* 31, 102–114.

Carasso, Elie, ed. *L'Echelle de Jacob: Une famille Sefarade de Salonique* (Jacob's ladder: A Sephardic family of Salonica). Tarascon, France: Cousins de Salonique, 1993.

———. *Les Juifs de Salonique, 1492–1943* (Jews of Salonica, 1492–1943). Tarascon, France: Cousins de Salonique, 1993.

Carmack, Sharon DeBartolo. *Organizing Your Family History Research*. (Cincinnati: Betterway Books, 1999).

Caro, Yosef. *Shulchan Aruch.*

Caselli, Paola. *Italia judaica: Gli ebrei in Sicilia sino all'espulsione del 1492* (Jews in Sicily after the 1492 expulsion). *[in Atti del V convegno internazionale, Palermo 15–19 giugno 1992]* Rome: Ministero per i beni culturali e ambientali, Ufficio centrale per i beni archivistici, 1995.

de Castries, Henry. *Les Sources inedites de l'histoire du Maroc: Archives et bibliotheques d'Angleterre, de la France, de l'Espagne, du Portugal, des Bas Pays* (Unpublished sources of the History of Morocco: Archives and libraries of England, France, Spain, Portugal, and The Netherlands). 27 vols. Paris: Ernst Leroux, 1918.

Catálogo de las causas contra la fe seguidas ante el Tribunal del Santo Oficial de la Inquisición de Toledo y de las informationes genealógicas de los pretendientes a oficios del mismo. Madrid: Tip. de la Revista de archivos, bibliotecas y museos, 1903.

Cercle de Genealogie Juive. Comite Algerien d'Etudes Sociales: Le livre d'or du Judaisme Algerien (1914-1918), 1er fascicule, Septembre 1919 (Algerian committee for social studies: The golden book of Algerian Judaism 1914–1918). Reprint Paris: Cercle de Genealogie Juive, 2000.

Cevdet, Ahmet. *Tezakir* (Reminiscences). Ankara: Türk Tarih Kurumu Basimevi, 1953–1967.

Chary, Frederick B. *The Bulgarian Jews and the Final Solution 1940–1944.* Pittsburgh: University of Pittsburgh Press, 1972.

Chouraqui, André N. *Between East and West: A History of the Jews of North Africa.* Philadelphia: Jewish Publication Society, 1968.

Cohen, Benyamin Rafael. *Malkhei Tarshish* (Prominent Rabbis of Tarshish [Tunisian Rabbis]). Jerusalem: 1986.

Cohen, Judith. Personal communication.

Cohen, M.A., and A.J. Peck, eds. *Sephardim in the Americas: Studies in Culture and History.* Tuscaloosa and London: University of Alabama Press, 1993.

Cohen, Mark R. *Under Crescent and Cross: The Jews in the Middle Ages.* Princeton, N.J.: Princeton University Press, 1994.

Cole, Trafford R. *Italian Genealogical Records: How to Use Italian Civil, Ecclesiastical, and Other Records in Family History Research.* Salt Lake City: Ancestry, 1995.

Colletta, John Philip. *Finding Italian Roots: The Complete Guide for Americans.* Baltimore: Genealogical Publishing Co., 1996.

Corcos, David. *Studies in the History of the Jews of Morocco* (in English and Hebrew). Jerusalem: Rubin Mass, 1976.

Cortes i Cortes, Gabriel. *Historia de los Judios Mallorquines y sus descendientes cristianos* (History of the Majorcan Jews and their Christian descendants). 2 vols. Palma de Mallorca: Imagen, 1985.

Culi, Jacob. *Meam Loez.* 1730.

*Deca Na Lomaci Rata u Neza Visnoj Drza vi Hrvatskoj 1941–45 Jasenovac (*Children killed in the Jasenovac concentration camp. Washington, D.C.: United States Holocause Memorial Museum.

Deshen, Shlomo. *The Mellah Society.* Chicago: University of Chicago Press, 1989.

Donate Sebastia, J., and J.R. Magdalena Nom de Deu. *Jewish Communities in Valencia.* Jerusalem: Magnes Press, 1990.

———. *Three Jewish Communities in Medieval Valencia: Castellon de la Plana, Burriana, Villareal.* Jerusalem: Magnes Press, Hebrew University, 1990.

Editions du Scribe. *Juifs d'Egypte: Images et Textes* (Jews of Egypt: Images and texts), 2d ed. Paris: Author, 1984.

Eisenbeth, Maurice. *Les Juifs de l'Afrique du Nord: Démographie et onomastique* (Jews of North Africa: Demographics and onomastics). Algiers: Imprimerie du Lycée, 1936.

Elazar, Daniel J. *The Balkan Jewish Communities: Yugoslavia, Bulgaria, Greece and Turkey.* Lanham, Maryland: University Press of America, 1984.

———. *The Other Jews: The Sephardim Today.* New York: Basic Books, 1992.

Elnecave, Nissim. *Los Hijos de Ibero-Franconia* (Sons of Iberia-Franconia). Buenos Aires: Ediciones La Luz, 1981.

Emmanuel, Isaac Samuel. *Gedole Salonica le doratam* (Great Jews of Salonica). Tel-Aiv: Defus A. Strod, 1936.

———. *Histoire des Israelites de Salonique* (History of the Jews of Salonica), Paris: Thonon, 1936.

———. *Precious Stones of the Jews of Curaçao, 1656–1956*. New York: Bloch Publishing, 1957.

———. *Marsevoth Saloniki* (Salonican tombstones), Jerusalem: Ben Zvi Institute, 1963.

Emmanuel, Isaac S., and Suzanne A. Emmanuel. *History of the Jews of the Netherlands Antilles*. 2 vols. Cincinnati and Curaçao: American Jewish Archives, 1970.

Encyclopaedia Judaica. 17 vols. Jerusalem: Encyclopaedia Judaica-Ketav, 1971.

Entsiklopedyah shel galuyot (Encyclopedia of the Jewish diaspora), c.f. Bulgaria.

Epstein, Ellen Robinson, and Jane Lewit. *Record and remember : tracing your roots through oral history*. Lanham, Md.: Scarborough House, 1994.

Epstein, Isidore. *The Responsa of Rabbi Simon ben Zemah Duran as a Source of the History of the Jews in North Africa*. London: Oxford University Press, 1930.

Errera, Milantia Bourla. *Moïse Levy, un rabbin au Congo - 1937–1991* (Moise Levy: A rabbi in the Congo - 1937–1991). Brussels: La Longue Vue and Consistoire Central Israélite de Belgique, 2000.

Fargeon, Maurice, ed. *Les Juifs en Egypte: Depuis les origines jusqu'a ce jour* (Jews in Egypt: From the origins to today). Cairo: Imprimerie Paul Barbey, 1938.

———. *Annuaire des Juifs d'Egypte et du proche orient* (Yearbook of the Jews of Egypt and the Near East). Cairo: La Societe des Editions Historiques Juives d'Egypte, 1942, 1943.

Farhi, Gentille. "*La situation linguistique du sephardite a Istanbul*" (Linguistic situation of Judeo-Spanish in Istanbul). *Hispanic Review* 5 (1937), 151–58.

Feldman, Larry. *Anglo-Americans in Spanish Archives: Lists of Anglo-American Settlers in the Spanish Colonies of America, A Finding Aid*. Baltimore Maryland: Genealogical Publishing Co., 1991.

Fidanque. *Kol Shearith Israel: Cien años de vida judía en Panamá, 1876–1976* (Kol Shearith Israel: A hundred years of Jewish life in Panama, 1876–1976). Panama: Igmar, 1977.

Filippini, Jean-Pierre. "*La Comunita israelitica di Livorno durante il periodico napoleonico*" (Jewish Community of Leghorn during the Napoleonic period). *Rivista Italiana di Studi Napoleonici* 19 (1982): 77–113.

———. *Livorno e gli Ebrei dell' Africa del Nord nel settecento* (Livorno and the Jews of North Africa during the 1700s). Florence: Ed. Olschski, 1990.

———. "*Le Port de Livourne et la Toscane, 1676–1814*" (Port of Livorno and Tuscany, 1676–1814). Doct. thesis, University of Paris, 1990.

Flamand, Pierre. *Les communautes israelites du Sud-Marocain: Essai de description et d'analyse de la vie juive en milieu berbere* (Jewish communities of southern Morocco: Descriptive essay and analysis of Jewish life among the Berbers). Casablanca, Morocco: Imprimeries reunies, 1959. (Part of series *Diaspora en terre d'Islam*).

———. *Quelques manifestations de l'esprit populaire dans les juiveries du Sud-Marocain* (Some manifestations of the popular spirit in the Jewish communities of southern Morocco). Casablanca: Imprimeries reunies, 1959. (Part of series *Diaspora en terre d'Islam*).

Franco, Hezkia. *Les martyrs juifs de Rhodes et de Cos.* (Jewish Martyrs of Rhodes and Cos). Elizabethville, Congo: Author, 1952.

Franco, Moise. *Essai sur l'histoire des Israelites de l'Empire Ottoman depuis les origines jusqu'a nos jours* (Essay on the history of the Jews of the Ottoman Empire from its origins to our days). Paris: Dularcher, 1897.

Frattarelli Fisher, Lucia. "*Portoghesi, ebrei ponentini ed ebrei levantini nella Toscana dei Medici (1549–1737)*." In *Le migrazioni internazionali dal medioevo all'età contemporanea: Il caso italiano, Roma 11–12 gennaio 1990.* Rome, 1990.

Frayman, Erdal. *Yuksekkaldirim'da Yuz Yillik bir Sinagog/Askenazlar* (A hundred-year-old synagogue in Yuksekkaldirim/Ashkenazic Jews). Istanbul: 2000.

Freedman-Morris, Mona. *Scattered Seeds: A Guide to Jewish Genealogy.* Boca Raton, Fla.: RJ Press, 1998.

Freidenreich, Harriet Pass. *The Jews of Yugoslavia: A Quest for Community.* Philadelphia: Jewish Publication Society, 1979.

Fromer, Rebecca Camhi. *The House by the Sea: A Portrait of the Holocaust in Greece.* San Francisco: Mercury House, 1998.

Frumkin, A. *Toldot Khakhmei Yerushalayim* (Generations of Jerusalem rabbis). Jerusalem, 1872.

Galante, Avram. *Histoire des Juifs d'Istanbul* (History of the Jews of Istanbul). 2 vols. Istanbul: Husnutabiat, 1941, 1942.

———. *Histoire des Juifs de Turquie* (History of the Jews of Turkey). Istanbul: Editions ISIS, 1985.

Gaon, Moshe David. *Yehudei haMizrah beEretz Yisrael* (Oriental Jews in Eretz Yisrael). Jerusalem: 1928.

Gaon, Solomon and Mitchell M. Serels, eds. *Del fuego: Sephardim and the Holocaust.* New York: Sepher-Hermon Press, 1995.

Garbayo, N.Moreno. *Catalogo de alegaciones fiscales* (Catalog of fiscal allegations). Madrid 1977.

Garces, Jorge A. *Paleografia espanola y sus peculiaridades en America* (Spanish Paleography and its peculiarities in America). Quito, Ecuador: 1949.

Gerber, Jane. *Jewish Society in Fez 1450–1700: Studies in Communal and Economic life.* Leiden, The Netherlands: E.J. Brill, 1980.

———. *The Jews of Spain: A History of the Sephardic Experience.* New York: Free Press Macmillan, 1992.

Gilbert, Martin. *The Jews of Arab Lands: Their History In Maps.* London: Board of Deputies of British Jews, 1976.

Ginio, Alisa. *Jews, Christians, and Muslims in the Mediterranean world after 1492.* Portland, Ore.: Frank Cass, 1992.

Goitein, S.D. *Letters of Medieval Traders.* Princeton, N.J.: Princeton University Press, 1973.

Goitein S.D. ed. *Jews and Arabs*, New York: Schocken Books, 1974.

Goldberg, Harvey. *Jewish Life in Muslim Libya.* Chicago: University of Chicago Press, 1990.

Goldberg, Harvey E. ed. *Sephardi and Middle Eastern Jewries: History and Culture.* New York: Jewish Theological Seminary, 1996.

Goldemberg, Isaac, ed. *El gran libro de la America judia* (Great book of Jewish America). San Juan: Editorial de la Universidad de Puerto Rico, 1998.

Goldenberg, Andre, ed. *Juifs du Maroc: Images et Textes* (Jews of Morocco: Images and texts). Paris: Les Editions du Scribe, 1992.

Graetz, H. *History of the Jews.* Philadelphia: Jewish Publication Society of America, 1891–98.

Greenleaf, Richard. *The Mexican Inquisition of the Sixteenth Century.* Albuquerque: University of New Mexico Press.

Haddad, Heskel M. *Jews of Arab and Islamic Countries.* New York: Shengold, 1984.

Harris, Tracy. "The Prognosis for Judeo-Spanish: Its Description, Present Status, Survival and Decline, with Implications for the Study of Language Death in General." Ph.D. diss., Georgetown University, 1979.

Hartog, Johannes. *The Jews and St. Eustatius: The Eighteenth Century Jewish Congregation Honen Dalim, and Description of the Old Cemetery.* St. Maarten, Netherlands Antilles: T.M. Pandt, 1976.

Hernàndez, Frances "The Secret Jews of the Southwest" in Cohen, M. A., and Peck, A. J., ed. *Sephardim in the Americas: Studies in Culture and History.* Tuscaloosa and London: University of Alabama Press, 1993. (History and names of converso families).

Hilfman, P.A. "Notes on the History of the Jews of Surinam." *Publications of the American Jewish Historical Society* 18: 179 ff.

Hinojosa Montalvo, Jose. *The Jews of the Kingdom of Valencia: From Persecution to Expulsion, 1391–1492.* Jerusalem: Magnes Press, Hebrew University, 1993.

Hirschberg, H.Z. (J.W.). *A History of the Jews of North Africa.* 2 vols. Leiden: E.J. Brill, 1974.

Hyamson, Albert Montefiore. *The Sephardim of England: A History of the Spanish and Portuguese Jewish Community, 1492–1951.* London: Methuen, 1951.

Hyman, Mavis. *Jews of the Raj.* London: Hyman Publishers, 1995.

Immanuel, Yizchak Shmuel. *Great Jews of Saloniki according to their Generations: 500 Epitaphs from the Jewish Cemetery of Saloniki 1500–1660.* Tel Aviv: A. Strod & Sons, 1936.

Isaacs, Abraham Lionel. *The Jews of Majorca.* London: Methuen, 1936.

Jerusalmi, Isaac. *From Ottoman Turkish to Ladino.* Cincinnati, Oh.: Ladino Books, 1990.

Jews in Macedonia during the Second World War 1941–45. Washington D.C.: United States Holocaust Memorial Museum.

Juhasz, Esther, ed., *Sephardi Jews of the Ottoman Empire: Aspects of Material Culture.* Jerusalem: Israel Museum and Jerusalem Publishing House, 1990.

Katz, J. Encyclopedia Judaica, c.f. Ladino.

Kerem, Yitzhak. "Sources on Greek Jewry in the Special Archives in Moscow" *Sharsheret Hadorot*, no. 2 (April 1993).

Kramer, Gudrun. *The Jews in Modern Egypt, 1914–1952.* Seattle: Univ of Washington Press, 1989.

Krasner-Khait, Barbara. *Discovering Your Jewish Ancestors.* Bountiful, Utah: Heritage Quest, 2001.

Kurzweil. Arthur. *From Generation to Generation: How to Trace Your Jewish Genealogy and Family History.* Northvale, N.J.: Jason Aronson, 1994.

Lacave, Jose Luis. "Material Remains." In Haim Beinart, ed. *The Sephardi Legacy.* Jerusalem: Magnes Press, 1992.

Lackey, Richard S. *A Manual for Documenting Family Histories and Genealogical Records.* New Orleans: Polyanthos, 1980.

Laredo, Abraham. *Les Noms des Juifs du Maroc* (Names of the Jews of Morocco). Madrid: Institut Montano, 1978.

Laskier, Michael M. *The Alliance Israelite and the Jewish Communities of Morocco 1862–1962.* Albany: State University of New York Press, 1983.

———. *The Jews of Egypt, 1920–1970.* New York: New York University Press, 1992.

Latapie, Roger. *"Etat actuel des cimitieres juifs d'Algerie"* (Present State of Algerian Jewish Cemeteries). *Etsi*, no. 3 (1998): 3–4.

Lazar, Moshe. *The Sephardic Tradition: Ladino and Spanish Jewish Literature.* New York: Norton, 1972.

Lea, Charles Henry. *The Inquisition in the Spanish Dependencies.* London: Macmillan, 1992.

Leon Tello, Pilar. *Judios de Toledo* (Jews of Toledo). Madrid: Institut Arias Montano, 1979.

Leroy, Beatrice. *The Jews of Navarre in the Late Middle Ages.* Jerusalem: Magnes Press, Hebrew University, 1985.

Levine, Robert. *Tropical Diaspora: The Jewish Experience in Cuba.* Gainesville: University Press of Florida, 1993.

Levi (Lavi), Habib. *Comprehensive History of the Jews of Iran: The Outset of the Diaspora.* George W. Maschke, trans. Costa Mesa, Calif.: Mazda Publisher, Cultural Foundation of Habib Levi, 1999.

Levy, Avigdor. *Jews of the Ottoman Empire.* Washington, D.C.: Darwin Press, 1994.

Levy, Lionel. *La Nation Juive Portuguaise: Livourne, Amsterdam, Tunis 1591-1951* (The Portuguese Jewish Nation: Livorno, Amsterdam, Tunis 1591-1951). Paris: L'Harmattan, 1999.

Levy, Rebecca Amato. *I Remember Rhodes.* New York: Sepher-Hermon Press, 1987.

Lewis, Bernard. *The Jews of Islam.* Princeton, N.J.: Princeton University Press, 1984.

———. *What Went Wrong: Western Impact and Middle Eastern Response.* Oxford: Oxford University, 2002.

Lida, Dinah. "Language of the Sephardim in Anglo-America." In *Sephardim in the Americas: Studies in Culture and History,"* Martin Cohen and Abraham J. Peck, eds. Tuscaloosa: American Jewish Archives and University of Alabama Press, 1993.

Liebman, Seymour B. *The Inquisitors and the Jews in the New World.* Miami: University of Miami Press, 1975.

Littman, David. *Jews under Muslim Rule: The Case of Persia. Wiener Library Bulletin* 34, nos. 49-50 (1979).

Loeb, L.B. "*Dhimmi* Status and Jewish Rules in Iranian Society." In *Jews among Muslims,* Deshen and Zenner, eds. New York: New York University Press, 1996.

Luzzatto, Aldo. *Biblioteca Italo-Evraica* (Italian-Jewish library). Milan: Franco Angeli Libri, 1989.

———. *Ebrei di Livorno tra due censimenti (1841-1938): Memoria familiare et identita* (Jews of Livorno through two censuses [1841-1938]: Family memoires and identity). Livorno: Commune di Livorno Belforte, 1990.

———. *La communita ebraica di Venezia e il suo antico cimitero* (Jewish community of Venice and its ancient cemetery). 2 vols. Milan: Il Polifilo, 2000.

Mack Smith, Dennis. *Italy: A Modern History.* Ann Arbor: University of Michigan, 1969.

Malinowski, Arlene. "Aspects of Contemporary Judeo-Spanish in Israel Based on Oral and Written Sources." Ph.D. diss., University of Michigan, 1979.

Malka, Eli. *Jacob's Children in the Land of the Mahdi: Jews of the Sudan.* Syracuse, N.Y.: Syracuse University Press, 1997.

Margolis, Max L., and Alexander Marx. *A History of the Jewish People.* New York: Athenaeum, 1927.

Margolinsky. *299 epitaphs on the Jewish cemetery in St. Thomas, W.I. 1837–1916. Compiled from records in the archives of the Jewish Community in Copenhagen.* Copenhagen, 1965.

Martsiano, Eliyahu Rafael. *Histoire et généalogie des Juifs de Debdou, Maroc: La généalogie de la communauté juive de Debdou et l'ascendance de toutes les familles qui la composent, à la lumière de sources et de documents inédits* (History and genealogy of the Jews of Debdou,

Morocco: Genealogy of the Jewish community of Debdou and the ancestry of all the families that make it up, in the light of unpublished sources and documents). Montreal: Éditions Élysée, 2000.

———. *Malkhei Yeshurun* (Prominent Algerian Rabbis). Jerusalem: Mekhon ha-Rasham, 2000.

Matkovski, Alexander. *A History of the Jews in Macedonia*. Skopje, Yugoslavia: Macedonian Review Editions, 1982.

Medina, Jose Toribio. *Historia del tribunal de la Inquisicion de Lima, 1569–1820* (History of the Inquisition tribunal of Lima, 1569–1820). Santiago de Chile: Fondo Historico y Bibliografico J.T. Medina, 1956.

Melammed, Renee Levine. "Some Death and Mourning customs of Castilian Conversas." In *Exile and Diaspora*. Jerusalem: Ben-Zvi Institute, 1991.

Menton, Arthur F. *The Book of Destiny: Toledot Charlap*. Cold Spring Harbor, New York: King David, 1996.

———. *Ancilla to Toledot Charlap*. Cold Spring Harbor, New York: King David, 1999.

Metz, Allen "Those of the Hebrew Nation...: The Sephardic Experience in Colonial Latin America" in Cohen, M. A., and Peck, A. J., ed. *Sephardim in the Americas: Studies in Culture and History*. Tuscaloosa and London: University of Alabama Press, 1993.

Mezan, Saul. *Les Juifs Espagnols en Bulgarie* (Spanish Jews in Bulgaria). Sofia, Bulgaria: Amichpat, 1925.

Mitchell, T.F. *Writing Arabic: A Practical Introduction to the Ruq'ah Script*. Oxford: Oxford University Press, 1990.

Modiano, Mario. *Hamehune Modilliano: The Genealogical Story of the Modiano Family from ~1570 to our days*. Athens: Author, 2000.

Moissis, Asher. *Les noms des juifs de Grece* (Names of Jews from Greece). Gordo, France: Carasso, 1991.

Mokotoff, Gary and Warren Blatt. *Getting Started in Jewish Genealogy*. Bergenfield, N.J.: Avotaynu, 1999.

Molho, Michael. *Literatura sefardita de Oriente* (Sephardic literature of the Orient). Madrid: Instituto Arias Montano, 1960.

———. *Tombstones of the Jewish Cemetery of Salonica*. Tel Aviv: Machon Leheker Yahadut Saloniki, 1974.

———. "Les Synagogues de Salonique" (Synagogues of Salonica). In Carasso, *Les Juifs de Salonique, 1492–1943* (Jews of Salonica, 1492–1943). Tarascon, France: Cousins de Salonique, 1993.

de Molina, Rafael, Conde y Delgado. *La Expulsion de Los Judios de la Corona de Aragon* (Expulsion of the Jews of the Aragon Crown). Zaragoza, Spain: Institucion Fernando el Catolico, 1991.

Moscona, Isaac M. "Zaproizkhoda na familnite imena na bulgarskite evrei" (Origins of Family Names of Bulgarian Jews). *Godishnik* 2: 111–137, 1967.

Mostyn, Trevor. *Egypt's Belle Epoque: Cairo 1865–1952*. London and New York: Quartet Books, 1989.

Nahoum, Henri. *Les Juifs de Smyrne, 19ieme et 20ieme siecle* (Jews of Smyrna, 19th and 20th centuries). Paris: Editions Aubier-Histoires, 1997.

Nehama, Joseph. "Le dialecte Judeo-espagnol et le Ladino" (Judeo-Spanish dialect and Ladino). *Tresoro de los judios sefardies* 6 (1964): 57–64.

———. *Histoire des Juifs de Salonique* (History of the Jews of Salonica). 7 vols. Thessalonica, Greece: Author, 1935–78.

Nelson, Lynn. *A Genealogist's Guide to Discovering Your Italian Ancestors*. Cincinnati, Oh.: Betterway Books, 1997.

Nemoy, Leon. *Karaite Anthology*. New Haven, Conn.: Yale University Press, 1952, 1980.

Netanyahu, Benzion. *The Origins of the Inquisition in XIV Century Spain*. New York: Random House, 1995.

———. *The Marranos of Spain: From the Late 14th to the Early 16th Century according to Contemporary Sources*. Ithaca, N.Y.: Cornell University Press, 1999.

Netzer, Amnon ed. *Padyavand*. 3 vols. Costa Mesa, Calif.: Mazda Publishers, 1997 and 1998. In English and Farsi.

Nidel, David S. *Modern Descendants of Conversos in New Mexico*. Western States Jewish Historical Quarterly, Vol. XVI, No. 3: 194–292.

Novinsky, Anita. *Cristãos novos na Bahia: história* (New Christians of Bahia: History). Sãn Paulo: Editôra Perspectiva, 1972.

Obejas, Achy. *Days of Awe*. New York: Ballantine, 2001.

O'Callaghan, Joseph F. *A History of Medieval Spain*. Ithaca, N.Y.: Cornell University Press, 1975.

Oelman, Timothy. *Marrano Poets: An Anthology*. Portland, Ore.: Littman Library of Jewish Civilization, 1985.

Ortiz, Dominguez. *Judeoconversos en la espana y America* (Jewish *conversos* in Spain and America). Madrid: Ediciones Istmo, 1971.

———. *Judeoconversos en la espana moderna* (Jewish *conversos* in modern Spain). Madrid: Editorial Mapfre, Paseo de Ricoletos, 1992.

Ovadia, David. *Fez ve hakhameha* (Fez and its rabbis). Jerusalem: 1979.

Pardo, Oscar. "Argentina." *Avotaynu* 2, 1986.

Pardo, Oscar. "Argentina" *Avotaynu* 3, Summer 1987, 18–23.

Paris, Erna. *The End of Days*. Amherst, N.Y.: Promethius Books, 1995.

Patai, Raphael. *The Vanished Worlds of Jewry*. New York: Macmillan, 1981.

———. *Jadid al Islam: The Jewish "New Muslims" of Meshed*. Detroit: Wayne State University Press, 1997.

Pavoncello, Nello. *Antiche famiglie ebraiche italiane* (Ancient Jewish Italian families). Rome: Carucci editore, 1982.

Pennell, C.R. *Morocco since 1830: A History*. New York: New York University Press, 2000.

Perera, Victor. *The Cross and the Pear Tree: A Sephardic Journey*. New York: Knopf, 1995.

Perez Ramirez, Dimas. *Catalogo del Archivo de la Inquisición de Cuenca* (Catalog of the Cuenca Inquisition Archive). Madrid: Fundación Universitaria Española, 1982.

Pflaum, H. "*Une ancienne satire espagnole contre les marranes*" (An ancient Spanish satire against the marranos). *Revue des Etudes Juives* 86 (1928): 131–150.

Pimienta, S. *Indice del Libro de Actas de la Communidad Hebrea de Tanger, 1860–1875* (Index to the first Book of Acts of the Jewish community of Tangier, 1860–1875). Paris: 1992.

de la Plaza Bores, Angel. *Guia del Investigador* (Researcher's Guide). Madrid: Ministerio de Cultura, 1992.

Porter, Stephen. *Jamaican Records*. Contact author at stephen.porter@virgin.net.

Postal, Bernard, and Malcolm H. Stern. *Tourist's Guide to Jewish History in the Caribbean*. New York: American Airlines, 1975.

Rahmani, Moise. *Shalom Bwana: La saga des Juifs du Congo* (Shalom Bwana: Saga of the Jews of the Congo). Paris: Romillat, 2002.

Ramirez, D. Perez. *Catalogo del Archivo de la Inquisición de Cuenca* (Catalogue of the Archive of the Inquisition of Cuenca). Madrid. 1982.

Raphael, Chaim. *The Road from Babylon: The Story of Sephardi and Oriental Jews*. New York: Harper & Row, 1985.

Raphael, David. *The Expulsion 1492 Chronicles*. North Hollywood, Calif.: Carmi House Press; New York: Sephardic House.

Recanati, David, ed. *Zichron Saloniki, Gedulata Vehurvata Shel Yerushalayim Debalkan*. Tel Aviv: Havaad Lehotsaat Sefer Kehilat Saloniki, 1972.

Regne, Jean. *History of the Jews in Aragon: Collection of Regesta and Court Documents 1213-1327*. Jerusalem: Magnes Press, 1978.

Rejwan, Nissim. *The Jews of Iraq: 3000 Years of History and Culture*. Boulder, Colo.: Westview Press, 1985.

Renan, Ernest. *Histoire generale des langues semitiques* (General history of Semitic languages), 4th ed. Paris: Michel Levy Freres, 1863.

Ricard, Robert. "*Notes sur l'immigration des Israelites marocains en Amerique espagnole et au Bresil*" (Notes on the immigration of Moroccan Jews in Spanish America and in Brazil). *Revue Africaine*, 1944.

de los Rios, Don Jose Amador. *Historia social, politica y religiosa de los Judios de Espana y Portugal* (Social, political and religious history of the Jews of Spain and Portugal). Madrid: Imprenta de T. Fortanet, 1875.

Rivlin, Bracha, ed. *Encyclopaedia of Jewish Communities from their Foundation till after the Holocaust: Greece* (in Hebrew). Jerusalem: Yad Vashem, 1998.

Rocco, Benedetto. "*Le tre lingue usate dagli ebrei in Sicilia dal sec. XII al sec. XV*" (Three languages used by Jews in Sicily of the 12th to 15th centuries). In *Italia judaica: Gli ebrei in, Sicilia sino all'espulsione del 1492: atti del convegno internazionale, Palermo, 15-19 guigno 1992*. Rome: Ministero per I beni culturali e ambientali, Ufficio centrale per I beni archivisti, 1995.

Rodriguez Fernandez, Justiniano. *La Juderia de la Ciudad de Leon* (Jewish quarter of the city of Leon). Leon, Spain: Centro de estudios e investigacion "San Isidro," Archivo Historico Diocesano, 1969.

Rodriguez Galindo, A. "*El Museo Canario: Catalogo y extractos de la Inquisición de Canarias*" (Canaries Museum: Catalog and extracts from the Inquisition of the Canaries). Museo Canario, nos. 89–103 (1966–69): 129–243; and vols. 31–32, (1970–71): 135–68.

Roffe, Sarina. "The Term Sephardic Jew." Accessed at www.jewishgen.org/sefardsig/sephardic_roffe.htm.

Romanelli, Samuel. *Travail in an Arab Land*. Tuscaloosa: University of Alabama Press, 1989.

Romano, David. "The Jews' contribution to Medicine and General Learning". In Beinart, Haim, ed. *The Sephardi Legacy*. Jerusalem: Magnes Press, 1992.

Rosenzweig. "*Judios en la Amazonia Peruana, 1870–1949*" (Jews in the Peruvian Amazon, 1870–1949). *Majshavot: Pensiamentos* 4, nos. 1–2. (1967): 19–30.

Roth, Cecil. *The House of Nasi: 1. Dona Gracia*. Philadelphia: Jewish Publication Society of America, 1948.

———. *The House of Nasi: 2. The Duke of Naxos*. Philadelphia: Jewish Publication Society of America, 1948.

———. *A History of the Marranos*, 4th ed. New York: Hermon Press, 1974.

———. *The Spanish Inquisition*. New York: W.W. Norton & Company, 1996.

Roth, Leon. *The Guide for the Perplexed: Moses Maimonides.* London: Gainsborough Press, 1948.

Roth, Norman. *Conversos, Inquisition, and the Expulsion of the Jews from Spain.* Madison: University of Wisconsin Press, 1995.

Rozen, Mina. "Jewish Cemeteries in Turkey." In Esther Juhasz, ed., *Sephardi Jews of the Ottoman Empire: Aspects of Material Culture.* Jerusalem: Israel Museum and Jerusalem Publishing House, 1990.

Rozanes, Shlomo Avraham. *Korot Hayehudim Beturkia Vebeartzot Hakedem: Divrei Yemai Yisrael Betogarma Al-Pi Mekorot Rishonoim* (History of the Jews of Turkey and of the Middle East). 6 vols. Vol. I, Tel Aviv: 1930; Vol II-V, Sofia, Bulgaria: 1934–8; Vol. VI, Jerusalem: 1948.

Ryskamp, George, R. *Finding your Hispanic Roots.*, Inc, Baltimore: Genealogical Publishing, 1997.

Sacerdoti, Annie. *Guida alla'Italia Ebraica* (Guide to Jewish Italy). Casale Monferrato, Italy: Casa Editrice Marietti, 1986.

———. *Guide to Jewish Italy.* Brooklyn, N.Y.: Israelowitz, 1989.

Sachar, H.M. *Farewell Espana: The World of the Sephardim Remembered* New York: Vintage Books, 1995.

Sack, Sallyann Amdur. *Guide to Jewish Genealogy in Israel.* Teaneck, N.J.: Avotaynu, 1995.

Sack, Sallyann Amdur and Gary Mokotoff, eds. *Avotaynu Guide to Jewish Genealogy* Bergenfield, New Jersey: Avotaynu, in press.

Salafranca Ortega, J.F. *Historia de la poblacion judia de Melilla desde su reconquista por espana hasda 1936* (History of the Jewish population of Melilla from its Spanish reconquest to 1936). Málaga, Spain: Editorial Algazara, 1995.

Salom, Margot F. *In Sure Dwellings: A Journey from Expulsion to Assimilation.* Australia: Seaview Press, 1998.

Sarchar, Houman, ed. *Esther's Children.* Philadelphia: Jewish Publication Society, 2002.

Sassoon, David Solomon. *A History of the Jews in Baghdad.* New York: AMS Press, 1982.

Schaert, Samuele. *I Cognome degli Ebrai d'Italia* (Surnames of the Jews of Italy). Florence: Casa Editrice Israel, 1925.

Schwarzfuchs, Simon. "The Sicilian Jewish Communities in the Ottoman Empire (in Italian)." *Italia judaica: Gli ebrei in Sicilia sino all'espulsione del 1492: atti del convegno internazionale, Palermo, 15–19 guigno 1992* (Jewish Italy: Sicilian Jews after the 1492 expulsion: Acts of the International Convention, Palermo, 15-19 June 1992). Rome: Ministero per I beni culturali e ambientali, Ufficio centrale per I beni archivisti, 1995.

Sealtiel, Robert. *Genealogical Research in Holland.* Paper presented at the 19th Annual Conference on Jewish Genealogy, New York, 1999.

Sealtiel-Olsen, Vibeke. "Aliases in Amsterdam." *Etsi* 4, no. 12 (March 2001): 3–7.

———. "Sephardic Genealogical Investigations in Amsterdam." *Etsi* 2, no. 6 (October 1999): 10–13.

———. "Sephardic Family Names in Amsterdam, 1598–2000" *Etsi* 3, no. 10 (October 2000): 8–14.

Segal, Ariel. *Jews of the Amazon: Self-Exile in Earthly Paradise.* Philadelphia: Jewish Publication Society, 1999.

Serels, Mitchell M. *A History of the Jews of Tangier in the Nineteenth and Twentieth Centuries.* New York: Sepher-Hermon Press, 1991.

Serfaty, A.B.M. *The Jews of Gibraltar under British Rule.* Gibraltar, 1933.

Shaw, Stanford J. *History of the Ottoman Empire and Modern Turkey.* 2 vols. Cambridge and New York: Cambridge University Press, 1976.

———. *Jews of the Ottoman Empire and Turkish Republic.* New York: New York University Press, 1991.

Simonsohn, Shlomo. *Bibliografia per la storia degli Ebrei in Italia, 1986–1995* (Bibliography of the history of the Jews of Italy, 1986–1995) (in Italian & Hebrew). *Biblioteca Italo-ebraica.* Rome and Tel Aviv: Menorah University, 1997.

Singerman, Robert. *The Jews in Spain and Portugal.* New York: Garland Publishing, 1975.

Stern, Malcolm H. *First American Jewish Families: 600 Genealogies 1654–1988,* 3d ed. Baltimore: Ottenheimer Publishers, 1991.

———."Portuguese Sephardim in the Americas." Cohen, M. A., and Peck, A. J., eds., *Sephardim in the Americas: Studies in Culture and History.* Tuscaloosa and London: University of Alabama Press, 1993.

———. "A Successful Caribbean Restoration: The Nevis Story" *Publication of the American Jewish Historical Society*, September 1971, Vol. LXI, No. 1. Contains tombstone inscriptions.

Stillman, Norman A. *The Jews of Arab Lands: A History and Source Book.* Philadelphia: Jewish Publication Society of America, 1979.

Studemund-Halevy, Michael. *Biographisches lexikon der hamburger sefarden: die Grabinschriften des Portugiesenfriedhofs an der Königstrasse in Hamburg-Altona* (Biographical lexicon of Hamburg Sephardim: on the epitaphs from the Portuguese Cemetery in Koenig Street in Hambug/Altona). Hamburg, Germany: Christians and Institute fur die Geschichte der deutschen Juden, 2000.

Sutton, Joseph A.D. *Magic Carpet: Aleppo-in-Flatbush: The Story of a Unique Ethnic Jewish Community.* New York: Thayer-Jacoby, 1979.

Tagger, Mathilde. *Index to Malkhei Tarshish* (in Hebrew). Jerusalem: Ben Zvi Institute, 1994.

———. *Juifs Marocains au Bresil* (Paris: Revue du Cercle Généalogie Juive, no 38, summer, 1994).

———. "Bulgarian Jewish names in the Second World War Period" *Sharsheret Hadorot*, Vol. 10, No. 1, April 1996.

———. "Sefarad: Une etymologie." *Etsi* 1, no. 1 (1998): 3.

Talbi, Mohamed. "*Un nouveau fragment de l'histoire de l'Occident musulman*" (A new fragment of the history of the Moslem West), *Cahiers de Tunisie* 19, nos. 73–74 (1971): 19-52.

Tamir, Vicky. *Bulgaria and Her Jews: The History of a Dubious Symbiosis.* New York: Sepher-Hermon Press for Yeshiva University Press, 1979.

Tanakh: A New Translation of the Holy Scriptures according to the Traditional Hebrew Text. Philadelphia and Jerusalem: Jewish Publication Society, 1985.

Tanugi, Y. *Toldot Hakhamei Tunis* (Generations of Tunis rabbis). Jerusalem: Bnei Brak, 1988.

Taranto, Roland. "Les noms de famille juifs à Smyrne" (Jewish Surnames in Smyrna) *Etsi*, Vol. 5 No 16, March 2002.

Toaff, Renzo. *La Nazione ebrea a Livorno e a Pisa, 1591–1700* (Hebrew Nation in Livorno and Pisa). Florence: Ed. Olschski, 1990.

Toledano, Joseph. *La Saga des Familles: Les Juifs du Maroc et leurs noms* (Family sagas: Jews of Morocco and their names). Tel Aviv: Stavit, 1983.

———. *Une histoire des familles: Les noms de famille Juifs d'Afrique du Nord* (Family history: Family names of the Jews of North Africa). Jerusalem: Author, 1999. (Obtain from author, P.O. Box 26308, 91262 Jerusalem, Israel).

Toledano, Moise Jacob. *Neer Hamaarab* (Light of the west). Jerusalem, 1911.

Vajda, Georges. *Juda ben Nissim ibn Malka: Philosophe Juif Marocain.* Paris: Institut des Hautes Etudes Marocaines and Larose, 1954.

Weinstein, Barbara. *The Amazon Rubber Boom, 1850–1920.* Stanford, Cal.: Stanford University Press, 1983.

Wiznitzer, Arnold. *The Records of the Earliest Jewish Community in the New World.* New York: American Jewish Historical Society, 1954.

———. *Jews in Colonial Brazil.* New York: Columbia University Press, 1960.

Wolff, Egon, and Frieda Wolff. *Sepulturas de Israelitas* (Jewish tombstones). 4 vols. Sao Paolo: Centro de Estudos Judaicos, 1976–1989.

———. *Dicionário biográfico* (Biographical Dictionary). Rio de Janeiro: Author, 1986.

———. *Guia histórico da comunidade judaica de São Paulo* (Historical Guide for the Jewish Community of Sao Paulo). São Paulo: Editora B'nei B'rith, 1988.

———. "Sephardic Jews in Northern Brazil in the 19th Century." *Avotaynu* 9, no. 4 (1993).

Yerushalmi, Yosef Hayim. *From Spanish Court to Italian Ghetto: Isaac Cardoso: A Study in Seventeenth-Century Marranism and Jewish Apologetics.* New York: Columbia University Press, 1971, 1981.

Yogev, Gedalia. *Diamonds and Coral: Anglo–Dutch Jews and 18th Century Trade.* New York: Leicester University Press, 1978.

Zack, Joel A. *The synagogues of Morocco : an architectural and preservation survey.* New York: World Monuments Fund, 1993.

Zafrani, Haim. *Juifs d'Andalousie et du Maghreb* (Jews of Andalusia and the Maghreb). Paris: Maisonneuve & Larose, 1996.

Zimler, Richard. *The Last Kabbalist of Lisbon.* Woodstock, N.Y.: Overlook Press, 1998.

Zimmels, H.J. *Ashkenazim and Sephardim.* Farnborough, England: Gregg International Publishers, 1969.

Zugic, Tomislav. *Jugoslevni u Koncentracion Legoru Ausvic 1941–45* (Yugoslavs deported to Auschwitz). United States Holocaust Memorial Museum.

ibn Zur, Jacob ben Rubin. *Et Sofer.* 16th century.

SURNAME INDEX

Aalamani, 291
Aaron, 291
Aba, 291
Abadi, 291
Abas, 291
Abastado, 309
Abazardiel, 291
Abboudi, 289
Abdala, 290
Abdalah, 291
Abdalla, 289
Abdallah, 288
Abdias, 273, 295
Abeasis, 287
Abecassis, 51, 287, 288, 292, 307
Abehsera, 288
Abejdid, 51
Aben Cadoc, 275
Aben Sur, Jacob, 30
Abenatar, 270
Abendana, 291
Abendanno, 271
Abengeld, 291
Abenhateus, 291
Abenrey, 269
Abensour, 269, 288
Abensur, 51, 57, 269, 287, 291
Abenvenisti, 270
Abergel, 288
Abetan, 288
Abikhzer, 288
Abilash, 290
Abimelekh, 273
Abira, 291
Abisror, 288
Abitbol, 269, 287, 288
Abitboul, 269
Abizmil, 288
Aboab, 48, 269, 287, 288, 291
Aboab-Mualim, 291
Aboaf, 264
Aboav, 291, 309
Aboav DaFonseca, 291
Abocara, Reine, 160
Aboccara, 295
Abod, 291
Abohbot, 287

Abotbol, 291
Abou, 288
Abouaf, 269
Aboucaya, 295
Aboudraham, 288
Aboulafia, 288, 309
Aboulker, 291
Abourbia, 288
Abourmad, 288
Abrabanel, 5, 12, 70, 102, 203, 269, 288, 291
   Isaac, 70, 203
   Samuel, 48
Abraham, 291
Abrahamdebalmes, 291
Abraham-Fonseca, 291
Abramico, 291
Abravalla, 291
Abravanel, 269, 291, 309
Abravanel-Dormido, 291
Abrebaya, Elie, 305
Absidid, 287
Abu Hassira, rabbi, 307
Abudaraahan, 291
Abudarham, 287
Abudarraham, 291
Abuhab, 269
Abuhana, 273
Abuhenna, 273
Abulafia, 269, 291
Abulker, 291
Abulner, 291
Acday, 272
Acencadoque, 275
Acher, 290
Achour, 295
Acouni, 309
Acris, 287
Adadi, 291
Adahan, 295
Adas, 291
Adato, 291
Adatto, 291
Ades, 289
Adi, 288, 295
Adjiman, 291
Adrehi, 287

Adret, 291
Adroki, 290
Adron, 291
Adrotiel, 288
Adroxi, 290
Adut, 291
Aeleon, 289
Aelion, 291, 309
Afias, 309
Aflalo, 287, 288
Aflalos, 291
Afriat, 31, 288
Aghion, 289
Aghmati, 291
Agialmo, Vitali, 307
Agostari, 309
Aguado, 291
Aguiar, 243
Aguilar, 290, 291
Aguilar, Rabbi Moses Rafael de, 243
Aharon, 290, 291, 309
Aharoni, 289
Ahim, 291
Aisha, 78
Aji, 309
Akawa, 291
Akin, 291
Akiva, 309
Aknin, 269, 291
Akoka, 288
Akrich, 288
al Fasi. *See also* Alfasi, Fasi
Al Fasi, 37, 38
Al Frangi, 76
Alabalah, 290
Aladjem, 290
Alafia, 269
Alalouf, 291
Alamanni, 291
Alami, 291
Alashkar, 291
Alashkaz, 291
Alaskar, 291
Alatar, 270
Alatino, 291
Albaili, 295

334 • *Sephardic Genealogy: Discovering Your Sephardic Ancestors and Their World*

Albala, 291
Albala DeLevy, 291
Albalah, 290
Albalia, 291
Alban, 295
Albaranes, 288
Albas, 290
Albasa, 290
Albaz, 269
Albert, Sara Marie, 305
Albo, 287, 288, 291
Albuhayre, 290
Alburzhi, 291
Alcabets, 291
Alcaforada, 291
Alcalay, 290, 291, 309
Alcheh, 309
Alcheikh, 288
Alchekh, 291
Alcoforado, 291
AlCorsi, 291
AlDahari, 291
AlDamari, 291
Alegre, 291
Aleman, 309
Alemano, 291
Alfacar, 291
AlFakharmeir, 291
Alfandari, 290, 291, 309
AlFaradzh, 291
Alfasi, 270, 271, 291, 294. *See also* Al Fasi, Fasi
Alfasi, rabbi Isaac, 6, 38
AlFayumi, 291
Alfon, 272
Alfonso, 291
Alfonta, 288
Algava, 309
Algazi, 291
Alhadef, 264, 309
Alhadeff, 270
Alhades, 309
Alhadyb, 270
Alhaik, 291
AlHak, 291
Alhakim, 272
Alhalel, 290
Alhanati, 309
AlHarizi, 291

Ali, 291
Aljadef, 291
Aljanati, 291
AlJarizi, 291
Al-Jirizi, 291
Alkabes, 290
Alkabets, 291
AlKabisi, 291
Alkaim, 287
Alkalai, 290
Alkalay, 291
Alkhadif, 270
Alkolukbre, 290
Allalouf, 309
Allemano, 291
Alloro, 295
Alloul, 288
Almaalem, 288
Almaizi, 295
Almalech, 290
Almaleh, 290, 291
Almalki, 273
Almalqui, 273
Almarilyo, 310
Almosnino, 291, 309
Almoznino, 290, 291
Alon, 289
Alroi, 291
Alsheij, 291
Alsheikh, 291
Alshij, 291
AlTaban, 291
Altaras, 291, 309
Altaras, Aron, 306
Altaraz, 288
Altauso, 291
Altia, 288
Altit, 288
AlTusari, 291
Aluch, 291
Alvarenga, 291
Alvares, 291
Alvo, 309
AlYamani, 291
Alzafrani, 275
Amada, 290
Amadia, 291
Amar, 287, 288, 291, 295, 309
Amaradji, 310

Amghar, 288
Amiel, 288, 310
Amir, 310
Amiras, 310
Amon, 310
AmonYaari, 291
Amor, 288, 291
Amorborgo, 295
Amozeg, 288
Amram, 287, 291, 310
Amselem, 287, 288
Amsili, 288
Amzalag, 291
Amzalak, 264, 287
Amzallag, 288
Anahory, 287
Anakas, 295
Anashiksan, 291
Anatoli, 291
Anavi, 290
Anconina, 288
Andalusi/Fasi/Sikili, 291
Anenturiel, 291
Anfaoni, 291
Anfaoui, 288
Angel, 291, 310
Angel, Rabbi Marc, 4
Ani, 289
Anidjar, 288
Ankri, 288
Annaquab, 288
Anonios, 270
Antebi, 291
Anzancot, 291
Anzhel, 290
Apsheh, 290
Aqnine, 269
Aragon, 270
Arajel, 288
Arama, 288, 290, 310
Arama, Shemouel, 305
Arapis, 270
Arari, 310
Araujo, Juan, 235
Arav, 290
Arbib, 295
Archivolti, 291
Arditi, 264, 270
Arditti, 290, 310

Surname Index • 335

Ardutiel, 291
Arenus, 291
Arie, 290
Arikas, 295
Arnaldes, 310
Arneti, 291
Aroio, 291
Arokas, 310
Aron, 310
Arotchas, 310
Arouh, 310
Arous, 295
Aroyo, 290
Arragel, 291
Arrouas, 288
Artemion, 291
Artom, 291
Artona, 295
Arucheti, 290
Arueste, 291
Arughetti, 307
Aruguet, 291
Aruj, 291
Arye, 290
Arzt, 305
Asael, 290
Asayol, 287
Asbili, 288
Ascarelli, 291
Ascoli, 295
Aseo, 291
Asher, 291, 310
Ashkenazi, 5, 179, 270, 280, 291, 295, 310
Askari, 291
Askenazi, 287
Aslan, 290
Assa, 290, 291
Assabagh, 274
Assabti, 288
Assael, 310
Assafar, 295
Assaraf, 288
Assayac, 51
Assayag, 51, 287
Asseo, 290, 310
Asser, 291
Assfar, 295
Assor, 288

Assouline, 280, 288
Assuied, 295
Assusi, 291
Astrik, 290
Astrologo, 295
Astruc, 291
Astrug, 290
Astuk, 290
Asulin, 270
Ata, 291
Atar, 291
Atataros, 291
Atazouri, 295
Athias, 51, 287, 291
Atias, 290, 291
Atrani, 291
Atrutel, 287
Attal, 270, 291, 295
Attar, 288, 291
Attia, 295
Attias, 51, 291, 295, 310
Attie, 264, 265
Attiias, 291
Atturki, 275
Atunes-Rois, 291
Auday, 51, 287, 288
Avayou, 310
Avenreyna, 269
Aviad, 291
Avigador, 291
Avigdor, 290
Avishay, 290
Aviz, 291
Avlas, 310
Avraham, 291, 310
Awad, 291
Ayash, 291, 310
Azan, 272
Azancot, 51, 287
Azar, 288, 291
Azareff, 291
Azaria, 291, 310
Azavey, 287
Azday, 272
Azencot, 288
Azerad, 287, 288
Azeroual, 288
Azevedo, 47
Azirad, Moshe, 308

Aziz, 291
Aziza, 288
Azogui, 288
Azoulay, 288, 295
Azouz, 310
Azran, 288
Azriel, 290, 310
Azubid, 291
Azuelos, 287, 288
Azulay, 51, 243, 270, 287, 291
Baal Shem Tov, 7
Bachi, 291
Baena, 310
Bagrat, 291
Bahloul, 288
Bahtit, 288
Bais, 295
Bais, Solomon, 160
Bakish, 290
Bakrat YKhalas, 291
Bakri, 291
Balam, 291
Baldomir, 291
Bale, 291
Balenci, 275
Balensi, 287
Banco, 291
Banin, 291
Banon, 287, 288
Baquis, 287
Baraja, 310
Barajel, 291
Barani, Rachel Hermine, 305
BarAvraham, 310
Barazani, 291
Barcessat, 51
Barchillon, 291
Barchilom, 287
Barchilon, 270, 288
Barcilon, 270
Barcilon, Louna, 308
BarDavid, 310
Barel, 291
BarElazar, 310
Bargansa, 295
Bargas, 295
Bargeloni, 270
Barmalil, 270
BarNatan, 291

Barnathan, 290
Barnes, 295
Baron, 291, 295
Baros, 291
Barouhiel, 310
Baroukh, 288, 289, 307, 310
Barrios (Holland), 46
Barrocas, 264
Barsheshet, 288
BarSion, 310
Baruch, 290, 295
Baruel, 287
Baruh, 290
Baruj, 291
Baruk, 288
Barun, 291
Barzilai, 70, 291
Barzilay, 310
Basan, 290, 291
Basilea, 291
Basivi, 295
Basola, 291
Bassan, 290, 291, 295
Bassani, 291
Bassiouni, 289
Basso, 310
Basto, 291
Basula, 291
Battan, 289, 295
Battat, 291
Bauri, 291
BautistaPeres, 291
Bazilay-Bargueloni, 291
Becheton, 51
Bedersi, 291
Behar, 289, 290, 291
Behmoaram, 290
Behmoaras, 290
Beirav, 291
Beja, 310
Bejar, 291
Belahdeb, 288
Belahsen, 288
Belasco, 291
Belforte, 291
Belhassen, 295
Belicha, 288
Belilos, 289
Bellaiche, 295

Bellenstein, 289
Bembaron, 295
Ben Aderet, 30
ben Aknine, 269
Ben Ashurqui, 273
Ben Atar, 310
Ben David, 310
Ben Djoya, 310
Ben Ezra, 310
ben Ezra, Moses, 36
Ben Mayor, 310
ben Melekh, 269, 273
ben Nahman, 273
Ben Nahmias, 310
Ben Rey, 269
Ben Santchi, 310
Ben Sarah, 310
Ben Senor, 274
Ben Sushan, 57, 270
ben Sussan, 270
Ben Yaesh, 310
Ben Zion, 310
Benabu, 287
BenAdi, 295
Benadiba, 288
Benadon, 310
BenAdriat, 291
Benady, 287
Benaim, 287, 288, 289
Benaksas, 288
Benamara, 288
Benamor, 51, 287
Benamram, 288
Benamu, 291
Benardout, 310
Benaroch, 288
Benaroy, 290
Benaroya, 290
Benarroch, 51
Benarus, 287
Benas, 291
Benasuly, 270
Benatar, 270, 287
BenAtar, 291
Benatar, Abraham G., 307
Benatov, 290
Benaudis, 288
Benayon, 51
BenAyon, 291

Benazeraf, 288
Benazeref, 291
BenBaron, 295
Benbasat, 290
Benbassa, 289
Benbassat, 291
Benbunan, 287
Benchaya, 287
Bencheton, 51
Benchetrit, 287
Benchimol, 51, 243, 287, 291
Benchimon, 51
Benchlmol, 288
Bendahan, 287
Bendana, 295
Bendavid, 288
BenDavid, 289
Bendelac, 291
Bendelack, 287
Bendelak, 51, 288
Bendelek, 51
Benderly, Rebecca, 305
Bendran, 287
Bendrao, 288
BenEfraim, 293
Benelbaz, 51
Benelisha, 287
Beneluz, 287
Benelzra, 288
Benezra, 288
BenEzra, 289
Benforado, 310
Benghouzi, 288
Bengio, 288, 291
Benhaim, 288
Benhamu, 291
Benhayon, 287
Benibgui, 288
Beniciki, 288
Beniesh, 290
Benin, 289
Beniso, 287
BenIsrael, 291
Beniste, 275
Benisty, 288
Benitah, 287
Benjamim, 287
Benjamin, 291
Benjeresh, 291

Surname Index • 337

Benjo, 51, 287
Benkemoun, 288
BenKikis, 291
BenLassin, 289
Benlolo, 288
Benmaimon, 288
BenMalka, 289
Benmayor, 290
Benmergui, 287
Benmiyara, 287
Benmozegh, 291
Benmuyal, 287
BenNatan, 310
Bennou, 289
Benoalid, 287
Benoasat, 290
Benoliel, 51, 243, 287, 291
Benou, 289
Benouziglio, 311
Benouziyo, 311
Benrimoj, 287
Benron, 311
Benros, 287
Benroubi, 311
BenRubi, 289
Bensabat, 287, 291
Bensadon, 287
Bensaloha, 287
Bensantchi, 291
Bensaude, 264, 287, 288
Benselum, 287
Benshabat, 288
Bensheton, 287
BenShoham, 310
Bensid, 291
Bensihum, Elisa, 307
BenSimeon, 295
Bensimon, 51, 287, 288
BenSion, 289
Bensiti, 270
Bensliman, 287
BenSoussan, 310
Bensultan, 275
Bensusan, 287
Bentata, 287
Bentes, 51
Bentolila, 288
Bentubo, 287
Bentura, 290

Benudis, 287
Benvalia, 291
Benvenist, 270
Benveniste, 264, 270, 275, 291, 311
BenVeniste, 291
Benvenisti, 290
Benvenisti, Simon, 307
BenWaish, 288
Benwalid, 288
Benyaech, 290
BenYaiche, 295
Benyair, 288
BenYosef, 291
Benyozef, 290
Benyuli, 287
Benyunes, 287
Benzacar, 287
Benzakein, 308
Benzaquen, 51, 243, 287, 288, 291
Benzaquin, 51
Benzecry, 51, 287
BenZeev, 291
Benzenou, 288
Benzimra, 287
Benzion, 311
Berab, 291
Beraha, 290, 291
Beraja, 291
Berajia, 291
Berakha, 311
Berchmann, 289
Berda, 295
Berdugo, 76, 264, 275, 287, 288, 291. *See also* Verdugo. *also* Fig 14
Berechia, 291
Berejia, 291
Beressi, 311
Beretvas, 291
Berez, 291
Bergel, 287
Bergmann, 289
Beriro, 288
Berkowitz, 289
Berlenstein, 289
Berlilo, 287
Bernardete, 291

Bernays, 291
Bernstein, 289
Berouchel, Stella, 308
Bertinore, 291
Bertinoro, 291
Berujim, 291
Bessantchi, 311
Bessis, 291, 295
Betache, 274
Betito, 288, 295
Betitou, Joseph, 306
Beton, 270
Betoun, 270
Betsalel, 291
Bettach, 288
Betzalel, 290
Bezalel, 291
Bezes, 311
Bibas, 287, 288, 291
Bidzherano, 290
Bienvenida, 78
Bienvenido, 311
Bigio, 264, 265
Bigo, 289
Bijaoui, 295
Biniamin, 311
Bises, 295
Bismuth, 295
Bitales, 275
Bitran, 311
Bitton, 270, 288, 291
Bivas, 291, 311
Biyla, 290
Biziz, 295
Blanca, 291
Blau, 289
Bloch, 289
Blum, 287
Blumenthal, Lucy, 307
Boccara, 295
Bodoch, 288
Bofill, 76
Boghachadji, 291
Bohana, 273
Bohbot, 288
Bohudana, 287
Boiro, 295
Bonacosa, 291
Bonafos, 291

Bonan, 291, 295
Bonanasco, 291
Bonano, 311
Bonastruc, 291
Bonaventura, Enfo, 280
Bonchara, 291
Bondabi, 291
Bondavin, 291
Bondi, 295
Bondia, 76
Bondion, 76
Bonenfant, 76
BonetSarfati, 291
Bonfia, 295
Bonfiglioli, Giuliu, 280
Bonfil, 291
Bonfils, 76, 291
Bonhom, 76
Bonjorn, 291
Bonjuhes, 291
Bonsenyor, 274
Bonsignour, 274
Borcatsa, 295
Bordzhel, 291
Borgel, 295
Bossidan, 289
Botbol, 264, 269, 270, 288
Botton, 291, 308
Bouaziz, 288
Boublil, 295
Boucarra, 295
Boucfti, 288
Bouganim, 288
Bouhadana, 288
Boujenah, 295
Boukhobza, 295
Boulafia, 269
Bourla, 311
Bouskila, 288
Boussidan, 288
Boutbol, 270
Bouzaglo, 288
Bragadini, 291
Brambir, Adela, 307
Brami, 295
Braunschweig, 289
Braunstein, 289
Braunstein, Bellina, 305
Bravo, 291

Brigham, 287
Brito, 291
Broudo, 311
Brudo, 287
Btesh, 289
Bueno, 291, 295, 311
Bueno-DeMesquita, 291
BulFaradzh, 291
Burla, 290
Busach, 291
Busal, 291
Busnach, 291
Buzaglo, 287
Bytton, 287
Caba, 274
Cabalero, 270
Cabaliero, 270
Caballero, 270
Cabalo, 271
Cabay, 272
Cabelli, 311
Cabessa, 288
Cabra, 291
Cabral-DaGama, 291
Caceres, 291
Cadeau, 291
Cadoche, 291
Cagi, 287
Calderon, 290
Calef, 290
Calo, 295
Calorras, 311
Calson, 291
Calvo, 291, 295
Camhi, 290
Camio, 295
Cammondo, 180
Camondo, 203
Campano, 311
Campeyas, 311
Campus, 295
Candero, 288
Candiote, 291
Candioti, 291
Canetti, 290
Canias, 291
Cansino, 287, 291
Cantarini, 291
Capon, 291, 311

Capoua, 295
Capouano, 311
Capsali, 291
Caraco, 291
Carasso, 290
Carasso (Levi), 311
Caravallio, 295
Carcassona, 291
Cardoso, 287, 291
Cardoza, 270
Cardozo, 264, 270, 288, 291, 295
Cariglio, 295
Cario, 290
Carmi, 270, 295
Carmona, 289, 291
Caro, 271, 288, 291, 295
Rabbi Yosef, 4
Carseni, 287
Carsinet, 291
Cartoso, 270
Cartozo, 295
Carvajal, 291
Carvalho, 271, 291
Carvallo, 291
Cases, 291
Caslari, 292
Cassin, 291
Cassorla (website), 264
Cassuto, 291, 295, 305, 311
Cassuto (website), 264
Castel, 287
Castelnuevo, 295
CastelNuevo, 291
Castiel, 288
Castiglioni, 291
Castorianos, 271
Castro, 271, 289, 291, 295, 311
Castyright, 291
Catalano, 291
Catalini, 291Catan, 311
Cataui, 291
Cattan, 295
Cattaoui, 289
Cattaui, 264, 291
Cavaliero, 289
Cavalleria, 291
Cavallio, 295
Cazes, 264, 287, 288, 291, 293, 307, 311

Surname Index • 339

Cazes (website), 265
Cemah, 290
Cerf, 265
Cesana, 295
Chababo, Rahel, 308
Chaltiel, 274
Chaprut, 291
Charbit, 271, 288
Chasan, 272
Chasdai, 272
Chaufan, 291
Cheba, Ezra Tou, 307
Chehebar, 291
Chelebi, 311
Chelibon, 311
Chemla, 295
Chenio, 311
Chetrit, 288
Chico, 311
Chimino, 311
Chiriki, 291
Chkeiran, 288
Chlouch, 288
Choukroun, 288
Chriqui, 288
Chumaceiro, 291
Cicurel, 291
Cillalongo, 291
Cimhi, 311
Cittanova, 295
Coen, Mayer, 305
Cohen, 48, 51, 73, 235, 243, 271, 287, 288, 289, 290, 291, 295, 306, 307, 308, 311
Cohen Benardout, 311
Cohenbenoliel, 291
Cohen-deLara, 295
Cohen-Hadria, 264
CohenHemsi, 290
CohenScali, 288
Cohen-Scali, 264, 271
Cohen-Solal, 295
Cohen-Tanougi, 295
Colon, 291
Colorini, 291
Colorni, 291
Combriso, 291
Comprado, 311
Comtino, 292

Cona, 292
Conambriel, 292
Conforte, 290, 311
Conorte, 290
Conqui, 288
Conquy, 287
Constantine, 295
Constantino, 292
Corcos, 271, 280, 288, 292, 295
Cordovero, 292, 311
Coriat, 287, 288, 292
Coronel, 295
Corsino, 292
Cortissos, Antonio Hidalgo, 48
Coscas, 295
Coshti, 289
Costa, 295
Costantini, 292
Coune, 311
Counio, 311
Coutiel, 311
Coutilo, 311
Covo, 311
Crasto, Miguel de, 48
Cremieux, 292
Cremieux-Moie, 292
Crescas, 76, 292
Crespin, 271, 290, 292, 311
Crimas, 295
Crimisi, 295
Crispin, 271
Crudcoriat, 292
Cubi, 287
Cuenca, 311
Culi, 292
Curiel, 280, 292, 295
da Costa, 48, 265
Da Silva, 271
Dabah, 292
Dabbah, 292
Dabela, 51, 288
Dabella, 292
Daca, 290
daCosta, 292
Dacosta, 7
Dades, 288
Dadia, 288
Dadoun, 288
Dadoune, 295

Dafan, 311
Dafret, 290
Dahan, 51, 243, 288, 289, 292, 295
Daian, 295
Dall'arpa, 292
Dalven, 271
Dalyan, 271
daMercado, 292
Dana, 292
Danan, 287, 288, 292
Dangoor, 292
Dangor, Tifaha, 307
Dangour, 307
Dangour, 307
Daniel, 292, 311
Danino, 288
Dannon, 289
Danon, 271, 288, 290, 292
Daoud, 289
daPeschera, 292
Dapiera, 292
daPisa, 292
Dardour, 295
Dari, 292
Darman, 292
Darmon, 295
Darmouni, 295
Darnim, 292
daRosa, 292
daSilva, 292
Dasilva, 292
Dassa, 311
Dato, 292
Daud, 292
Davan, 233
David, 289, 290, 292, 295, 312
Daviddepomis, 292
Davis, 287
Davitchon, 290
Dayan, 271, 288, 289, 292
De Acco, Shemuel, 294
De Aragon, 270, 271
de Barrios, 292. *See also* Barrios
De Fez, 271
de LaRosa, 292
De Levante, 273
de Loyola yHaro, 292
de Madeiros, 48

De Medina, 273
De Picciotto, 280
de Pina, 48
De Pinto, 274
De Silva, 271
De Sola, 280
de SolaPool, 292
De Vries, 280
deAcevedo, 292
deArmiento, 292
deAvila, 292
DeBarros, 291
deBetinoro, 292
deCamondo, 292
Decaro, 290
deCastro, 292
Decastro, 271
deCouto, 292
deEstrella, 292
Defaz, 270
deFulda, 292
deHerat, 292
deJorena, 292
deJorjena, 292
Dekalo, 290
Del Medico, 274
Del Vecchio, 280
deLara, 292
Delareya, 290
deLattes, 292
deLavega, 292
Delblanco, 280
Delbourgo, David R., 307
deLemon, 292
deLeon, 292
Delgado, 292
deLis, 292
DellaTorre, 292
Delmar, 51, 287, 288, 292
Delmedigo, 292
DelMedigo, 292
Delonga, 292
Delouya, 295
Deloya, 288
deLuna, 292
Demaestre, 292
deMercado, 292
deMierbeave, 292
deModena, 292

deMontalto, 292
deOliveira, 292
deOria, 292
deOya, 292
dePablo, 292
dePalermo, Moses, 293
DePas, 295
dePina, 292
dePisa, 292
dePomi, 292
deRoma, 292
deRossi, 292
Dery, 288
deSale, 292
deSamuel, 292
deSequeyra, 292
deSilva, 292
DeSilva, 293
deSola, 292
deSousa, 292
deSymons, 292
deTarso, 292
deToledo, 292
deTolosa, 292
deTorres, 292
deTudela, 292
deVictorio, 292
Devir, 292
deVoltera, 292
deVolterra, 292
Dias, 292
DiasPalma, 295
Dias-Santiago, 292
Diaz, 48, 75
diCapua, 292
Dicunia, 295
Diena, 292
Dina, 292
diNigarelli, 292
Diouani, 295
diSegni, 292
Disegni, 292
Ditrani, 292
Divekar, 292
Diwan, 288
Djahon, 312
Djain, 290
Djaldeti, 290
Djiba, 290

Djilletes, 312
Djirassi, 312
Djivany, 290
Dolmodou, Mordekhai, 308
Dondon, 271
Donna, 290
Donnolo, 292
Dosa, 292
Douali, 295
Douek, 289
doVale, 292
D'pomi, 292
Drago, 292
Drago deLemos, 292
Drigg, 289
Drihem, 288
D'rossi, 292
Dunash, Jacob bar, 38
Dunash, Jacob ben, 6
Dunio, 292
Duran, 292
Durant, 292
Duwayk, 292
D'vecchi, 292
Dwek, 289
Dzhalil, 292
Dzhama, 292
Dzhamil, 292
Dzherasi, 290
Dzhian, 292
Dzian, 292
Ebbo, Moche, 305
Ebreo, 292
Ecija, 292
Edery, 51
Edni, 292
Efendi, 292
Effendi, 292
Efrati, 292
Eini, 289
Ejica, 292
El Fasi, 6
El Turqui, 275
Elahmi, 295
Elajim, 295
Elalouf, 288
Elaluf, 51
El-Ankawa, 292
Elazar, 264, 290, 312

Surname Index • 341

Elbaz, 269, 288, 292
Eleazar, 292
ElEini, 289
Elfassi, 270, 288, 295
Elgrabli, 288
Elhadad, 288
Elhaik, 295
Elhakim, 272
Elharar, 288
Elhyani, 288
Eli, 290
Elia, 292
Eliah, 292
Eliahou, 312
Eliakim, 292, 312
Elias, 226, 280, 290, 292
Elie, 292
Eliezer, 290, 292, 312
Elimelekh, 312
Elisha, 312
Elkabas, 288
Elkana, 295
Elkayim, 288
Elkeslassy, 288
Elkouby, 288
Elkrief, 288
Elmaleh, 287, 288, 292
Elmalih, 295
Elmekies, 288
Elmoznino, 288
Elnecave, 292
Elportogues, 295
Elpronti, 295
Elvas, 269
Elyashar, 292
Emasllen, 292
Eminenti, 295
Emsani, 292
Enajar, 295
Encaona, 292
Encaoua, 288
Enriques, 160, 295. *See also* Henriques
Ephraim, 292
Erera, 292, 312
Ereza, 292
Ergas, 292, 312
Errera, 295
Esaguy, 287

Escaloni, 312
Escapa, 292, 312
Escayo, 312
Escobar, 292
Esformes, 312
Eshkanazi, 270
Eshkenazi, 290, 292
Eshkol, 292
Eskenazi, 307, 312
Eskinazi, 270
Eskouri, 288
Esnaty, 287
Espinoza, 292, 295
Essebagh, 274
Esther, 57
Estrougano, 312
Estrougo, 312
Estroumsa, 312
Etazer, 295
Etedgui, 288
Etouil, 295
Eturki, 275
Evans, 292
Ezafrani, 275
Ezberro, 295
Ezdra, 290
Ezdras, 292
Ezekiel, 292
Ezequias, 292
Ezerzer, 288
Ezobi, 292
Ezra, 226, 289, 292
Ezrati, 312
Faba, 292
Faisevi, 312
Falanca, Albert Joseph, 305
Falaquera, 292
Falcon, 292, 312
Fano, 292
Faquimi, 292
Farache, 51, 287
Faradji, 312
Faraggi, 290
Farfara, Daoud, 307
Farhi, 232, 264, 271, 289, 290, 292
Farisol, 292
Farissol, 292
Farji, 292

Farrar, 292
Farrisol, 292
Faruy, 290
Fasi, 270
Favela, 292
Fayumi, 292
Fedida, 288
Feinstein, 289
Fellous, 295
Ferares, 271, 287
Fermi, 292
Fernandes, 292
Fernandes-Brandao, 292
Fernandez, 292
Fernandez-Carvajal, 292
Ferrera, 312
Ferreres, 271
Fhima, 288
Figo, 292
Finaro, 295
Finia, 295
Finiro, 295
Finsi, 287, 295
Fintzi, 290
Finzi, 292, 295
Fiorentino, 292, 295
Fisso, 312
Fisson, Heneina, 307
Fitoussi, 295
Flah, 295
Florentin, 290, 292, 312
Foinquincs, 51
Foinquinos, 271, 287
Follinquinos, 271
Fonquinos, 51
Fonseca, 291, 292, 293
Fonseca, Rabbi Isaac Aboab da (Amsterdam), 243
Formiggini, 292
Forrester, 264
Forti, 289, 295
Fortunee, 290
Fougi, 295
Fouinquinos, 288
Foyinquinos, 271
Foz, 292
Franca, 272
Frances, 76, 292, 312
Franchetti, 295

Franco, 20, 48, 51, 243, 272, 289, 292, 295, 312
Franses, 292
Fransiz, 290
Fredman, Abraham, 306
Freoa, 295
Fresco, 287, 292
Funaro, 295
Furtado, 292
Gabai, 272, 295
Gabail, 292
Gabari, 292
Gabay, 287, 288, 292, 295
Gabbai, 51, 57, 289, 308
website, 264
Gabbay, 51, 243, 272
Gabirol, 292
Gabison, 295
Gabizon, 287, 292
Gabra, 289
Gabriel, 289
Gabriol, 292
Gabriol, Solomon ibn, 16
Gadol, 292
Gagin, 29, 272
Gaguin, 272, 292, 312
Gagurn, 288
Galanos, 272
Galante, 292
Galea, 312
Galicchi, 292
Galico, 292
Galidi, 312
Galimidi, 292
Galipapa, 292
Gallego, 312
Gallico, 292
Gamaliel, 292
Gambach, 292, 293
Gandus, 295
Gaon, 48, 173, 289, 292
Gaon, Sherira, 54
Garci, 295
Garcia, 264, 292
Garji, 292
Garsin, 295
Garson, 287, 295
Garti, 290
Garzon, 288, 292

Gatanio, 292
Gattegno, 312
Gavios, 312
Gavison, 288, 292
Gavriel, 312
Gedalia, 312
Gedelicia, 292
Gegate, 292
Gelfand, 265
Gerondi, 292
Gershan, 292
Gershom, 292
Gershon, 289, 290, 312
Gerson, 290
Ghalula, 295
Ghanem, 295
Ghozlan, 288, 295
Gidilia, 295
Gilbert, 292
Gimsi, 295
Girondi, 292
Gitakila, 292
Godefroi, 292
Goldenberg, 289, 306
Goldring, 289
Gomez, 74, 264, 269, 292
Gonzales, 295
Gordji, 312
Gormezano, 312
Gozaglo, 292
Gozlan, 292
Gracia, 292
Gracian, 292
Gradis, 292
Granata, 292
Graziani, 292
Greenberg, 289
Grego, 295
Grotas, 312
Grunberg, 307
Guadella, 272
Guedalha, 272
Guedalia, 272, 288, 292, 295
Guenun, 292
Gueron, 290
Guershom, 292
Guetta, 295
Guez, 295
Guigui, 288

Guiguiati, 295
Gurdzhi, 292
Guttieres, 295
Guttman, Bernard, 306
Gwertzman, 289
Ha Levi, 6, 16, 38
Ha Rofe, 274
Haam, 292
haBabli, 292
Hababou, 295
haBargueloni, 292
haBavli, 292
Habib, 271, 292, 295, 312
Hacco, Seva Yehouda, 307
Haco, 288
haCohen, 292
Hacohen, 295
Hacohen ha Guer, 312
haDani, 292
Hadani, 292
haDarshan, 292
Hadayo, 312
Haddad, 295
Hadida, 287, 288, 292, 295
Hafarhi, 271
Hagege, 292, 295
Hagiz, 292
Hagouel, 312
Haguiz, 292
haHaver, 292
haHazan, 292
Ha-Hazan, 272
Haim, 289, 290, 292, 312
Haimov, 290
Hakashlari, 292
Hakhmon, 292
Hakim, 264, 272, 289, 292
haKohen, 292
Hakohen, Chemouel, 306
Hakouk, 295
Hakoun, 295
Halac, 292
Halega, 312
Halevi, 292, 306
Ha-Levi, 292
Halevtrani, 292
Halevy, 36, 272, 292, 295, 312
Halevy deAlbaili, 295
Halevy-deLeon, 295

Halevy-Sonsine, 295
Haley, 292
Halfon, 272, 292, 308, 312
Halimi, 295
Haliwa, 288
Halpen, 272
HaMaravi, 292
Hamizrachi, 179
Hammou, 272
Hamon, 292, 312
Hamou, 288
Hamron, 288
Hamu, 272
Hamuy, 272
Hana, 292
HaNaguid, 292
HaNakdan, 292
Hananel, 290, 292, 312
Hanania, 292, 312
haNasi, 292
Hanasi, 292
HaNasi, 292
Handali, 312
Hanen, 312
Haness, 292
Hanoh, 312
Hanoka, 312
Hanouna, 295
HaPaytan, 292Harari, 233, 289, 292
Harboun, 288
Harizi, 292
Harlorki, Joshua (Jeronimo de la Santa Fe), 18
Haroma, 292
Haroun, Aziza abu, 308
Harun, 292
Hasda, 295
Hasdai, 57, 272
Hasday, 272, 292, 312
ha-Sefard, 292
HaSoffer, 275
Hassan, 51, 287, 288, 308
Hasserfaty, 274
Hassid, 295, 312
Hassine, 288
Hasson, 292, 312
Hasson, Behor R., 306
Hassoun, 306

Hatchuel, 287, 292
Hatchwel, 288
Hatshmil, 292
Hattab, 295
Hatwil, 292
Haver, 312
Havivai, 292
Hayat, 292
Hayatt, 312
HaYishari, 292
Hayon, 289, 292
Hayon, Ishak, 308
Hayoun, 295
Hays, 264
Hayuj, Yehuda, 37
Hayyim, 76, 78, 275
Hayyuj, 6
Hazaken, 295
Hazan, 272, 288, 289, 290, 292, 312
Ha-Zarfatti, 274
Hazday, 290
Haziza, 288
Hazot, 288
Heber, 289
Heiman, 289
Heimani, 289
Hekmat, 292
Hemmo, 289
Hemmo, Shlomo, 308
Hemou, 289
Hemsi, 292
Henri, 290
Henrique, 280
Henriques, 7, 48, 280. *See also* Enriques
Henriquez, 74, 269, 292
Henriquez-Gomez, 292
Henriquez-Senior, 292
Herman, 289
Herrera, 292
Heskouni, 295
Hezkiya, 290
Hibat, 292
Hilel, 292
Himi, 288
Hin, 292
Hina, 292
Hindi, 289

Hirida, 312
Hiskouni, 295
Hiya, 292
Hizkiya, 313
Hkim, 272
Hodara, 265
Hornstein, 289
Hoshama, 292
Houdras, 313
Houli, 313
Houri, 295
Houta, 288
Houyomdji, 290
Hoyada, 292
Huino, 292
Hushiel, 292
Ibenrey, 275. *See also* ibn Rey
ibn Attar, 270
Ibn Danan, 29
Ibn Daoud, 12
ibn Ezra, 42, 73, 75
  Abraham, poet, 70
  Moses, poet, 16
ibn Gabirol, 42, 72
ibn Pakuda, 61, 62
ibn Rey, 269, 273
Ibn Zur, 57
IbnEzra, 292
Ichay, 292
Ifergan, 288
Iflah, 288, 295
Ifrah, 288
Ilel, 290
Illouz, 288
Imach, 292
Immanuel, 313
Imola, 292
Inglizi, 289
Isaac, 292, 295
Isaaki, 295
Isak, 290
Iscini, 288
Ishag, 289
Ishaq, 289
Ishkinazi, 289
Iskandari, 292
Israel, 48, 51, 243, 287, 288, 289, 292, 295, 307, 313
Israel-Enriques, 295

Israeli, 292
Issaev, 292
Isserles, 292
Itah, 288
Izrael, 290
Jabes, 265
Jacob, 290, 293
Jacobs, 293
Jacobson, 290
Jagel, 293
Jagiz, 293
Jaim, 293
Jaion, 293
Jais, 293
Jakun, 293
Jalfon, 272, 293
Jalshush, 293
Jami, 295
Jamtsi, 293
Jamuy, 293
Janah, Abulwalid Merwan Ibn, 6, 37
Janan, 293
Jano, 295
Janoj, 293
Jaquete, 293
Jardon, 293
Jarmon, 295
Jasday, 293
Jasid, 293
Javilla, 293
Jay, 293
Jayudzh, 293
Jazan, 293
Jazo, 295
Jerafa, 295
Jezkia, 293
Jida, 293
Jinin, 293
Josefo, 293
Joseph, 290, 293
Josfe, 293
Josue, 295
Journo, 295
Joury, Ibrahim Jacob, 306
Juda, 293
Judah, 293
Juejati, 293
Jushiel, 293

Juzin, 293
Kadoch, 288
Kadoorie, 293
Kadoshi, 287
Kafa, 293
Kafih, 293
Kafusi, 293
Kagig, 293
Kahani, 293
Kakon, 288
Kakona, Yehouda, 306
Kalay, 313
Kalderon, 290
Kalev, 290
Kali, 295
Kalli, 313
Kalmoun, Baroukh ben, 306
Kalonimus, 293
Kamaniel, 293
Kamhi, 290
Kaminski, 289
Kamniel, 293
Kampanaris, 272
Kanarek, 289
Kane, 289
Kanian, 293
Kantzer, 289
Kanzer, 289
Kaplan, 290
Kapo, 290
Kapon, 290
Karakash, 290
Karmi, 270
Karsenti, 288
Kashifi, 293
Kastoria, 293
Katalan, 290
Katan, 288
Katarivas, 290
Katsin, 293
Katzan, 287
Katzuni, 290
Kayra, 293
Kazaz, 293
Kazes, 264
Kazez, 265
Kehimkar, 293
Kemalov, 290
Kessous, 288

Khalaf, 295
Khalas, 293
Khalfon, 272, 288, 293, 295
Khalifa, 288
Khaski, 289
Khayat, 295
Khoshkhash, 295
Khrief, 295
Kiki, 293
Kimhi, 293, 313
Kimji, 293
Klein, 289
Knafo, 288, 293
Koffler, 290
Kokachoeli, 290
Kokkinos, 272
Konein, 289
Konfino, 290
Konforti, 290
Konorti, 290
Kordova, 290
Koren, 290
Koresh, 295
Kouyumdjulu, 290
Kovo, 290
Koyen, 290
Kramer, 289
Krieger, Marcello Abramo, 306
Krusrin, 290
Ksabi, 295
Ktorza, 295
Kudsi, 289
Kuraish, 293
Labadon, 293
Labatt, 293
Labos, 287
Labrat, 293
Labrat, ben Dunash, 6
Labrat, Dunash ben, 37
Laguna, 293
Lahmi, 295
Lahmy, 288
Laluff, 287
Lampronti, 295
Lanaido, 293
Lancry, 51
Laniado, 233
Lapas, 313
Lara, 295

Surname Index • 345

Laredo, 51, 272, 287, 288, 293
Laski, 293
Lasry, 287, 288
Latimi, 293
Lattes, 293
Lavi, 293
Lazarus, 293
Lazimi, 288
Lea, 313
Leal, 313
Lealtad, 293
Leao, 293
Lebe, 295
Leeser, 293
Leilibh, 289
Leja, 313
Lengui, 287
Leon, 293, 295, 313
Leotagi, 295
Lernopranti, 293
Lev, 293
Levi, 51, 73, 287, 290, 293, 295
Levi-Bacrat, 293
Levita, 272, 293
Levitin, 289
LeviValensi, 293
Levy, 51, 243, 272, 288, 289, 290, 293, 295, 308, 313
Levy deAlbaili, 295
Levy deLeon, 295
Levy-BenYuli, 288
Levy-Yuly, Moses, 293
Leznover, Marguerite, 307
Liberman, Moise, 306
Libhar, Maimoun, 308
Librati, 288
Lichtenthal, Rose, 307
Lidzhi, 290
Lieberman, 289
Ligier, 293
Litchi, 313
Lodriguez, 295
Lodriguez-Dicunia, 295
Lodriguez-Enriques, 295
Lodriguez-Silvera, 295
Loeb, 288
Loez-Fonseca, 293
Lombroso, 272, 293
Lopes, 293

Lopes-Dubec, 293
Lopes-Perrera, 295
Lopes-Simoes, 293
Lopez, 48, 75, 293
Lopez-Laguna, 293
Lossia, 290
Loubaton, 288
Lougassy, 288
Louizada, 295
Louk, 288
Louniel, 295
Loupo, 289
Lousky, 288
Louvil, 313
Louzada, 293
Lugashi, 273
Lugasi, 273
Lumbroso, 293, 295
Lumbroso, rabbi Itzhak, 159
Luna, 290
Lunel, 295
Lupo, 290
Luria, 293
Luria, Rabbi Isaac, (ARI), 7
Lusitanus, 293
Lussato, 295
Luzada, 293
Luzzato, 293
Maarabi, Marco, 308
Maarek, 295
Machorro, 313
Madiordo, 313
Madjar family, 5
Madjari, 314
Madmun, 293
Madriaga, 293
Maduro, 293
Madzhani, 293
Madzhar, 290
Mafinfeker, 289
Magangaki, 293
Maggar, 290
Maggiar, 307
Maggioro, 313
Maghrabi, Samuel al, 36
Maghribi, Yehuda ben Samuel ibn Abbas el, 38
Magrilo, 290
Magriso, 293, 313

Mahalalel, 313
Mahfoda, 288
Maimi, 293
Maimon, 265, 273, 293
Maimonides, 33, 42, 62, 273
  Egypt, 162
  genealogy, 72
  website, 265
Maimran, 288
Mair, 313
Majzir, 293
Malabar, 295
Malaki, 273
Malca, 287
Maldonado, 293
Maleha, 293
Maleque, 273
Mali, 293
Malka, 57, 160, 269, 273, 275, 288, 289, 293, 295
  Judah ben Nissim ibn, 37, 38
  Nissim ibn, 37, 38
  Rabbi Jacob ben, 142
  Rabbi Shlomo, 173, 174
  website, 265
Malki, 273
Mallah, 293, 313
Malqui, 273
Maltzan, 293
Mamad, 290
Maman, 287, 293
Mamane, 288
Mamon, 290
Manases, 293
Manass-Israel, 293
Mandel, 313
Mandes-Seixas, 293
Mandil, 273, 290
Mandolino, 293
Mani, 289
Mannifker, 289
Mano, 313
Manoach, 290
Manoah, 290
Manoel, 293
Mansano, 288, 313
Mansour, Yaacob, 306
Mantin, 293
Mantino, 293

Maquin, 288
Maracha, 293
Marache, 288
Maradji, 313
Marciano, 273, 288
Marcos, 273, 289, 313
Marcovitch, 289
Marcus, 273
Mareli, 288
Margalit, 295
Mari, 293
Marini, 293, 295
Markezano, 313
Marnignone, 289
Marouani, 295
Marour, 293
Marques, 287
Marrache, 287
Mars, Daniel, 308
Martassi, 295
Martins, 287
Martziano, 273
Marzouk, 295
Marzuk, 293
Masajaway, 293
Masasini, 289
Mascaran, 293
Mashi, 289
Mashiah, 289, 290
Mashiyah, 290
Massarani, 293
Massarano, 313
Massarini, 293
Masseri, 313
Massias, 287
Massoud, 289
Masud, 293
Matalon, 265, 293, 313
Matana, 287
Mataraso, 293
Matarasso, 313
Matita, 293
Matsliah, 313
Maya, 265
Mayissa, 313
Maymeran, 293
Maymi, 265
Maymo, 273
Mayques, 293

Mazaltov, 290
Mazliah, 313
Mazliah, Ezra Moche, 306
Mazliaj, 293
Mazlou, 313
Mazuki, 289
Medina, 273, 295, 313
Medioni, 288
Medola, 293
Megueres, 287
Meiggs, 293
Meimoun, 295
Meir, 293, 313
Meiri, 293
Mejzir, 293
Meknes, 293
Melal, 51
Melamed, 290
Meldola, 293
Melili, 293
Melkitsedek, 293
Melli, 293
Melloul, 295
Meloul, 288
Melul, 287
Memmi, 293
Menahem, 313
Menajem, 293
Menasce, 289
Menasche, 293
Menashe, 290, 293, 313
Menasse, 289
Mendel, 289
Mendes, 48, 293, 295
  Beatriz de Luna (Dona Gracia), 179
Mendes da Costa, 265
MendesFrance, 293
Mendes-Ossona, 295
Mendez, 269, 293
Mendoza, 293, 295
Menovitch, 289
Meran, 288
Mergui, 288
Merida, 313
Merkado, 290
Merman, 293
Merzan, 289
Mesa, 293

Meshal, 293
Meshoulam, 313
Meshoullam, Moise, 308
Meshulam, 293
Mesquita, David, 47
Messas, 288
Messica, 295
Messina, 295
Mesulam, 290
Metzger, 289
Mevorah, 290, 313
Mevorakh, 293
Mezan, 290, 293
Michaali, Moshe, 307
Michael, 313
Migash, 293
Mihael, 290
Mijan, 313
Miledi, 293
Milhau, 293
Milo, 313
Mimon, 273
Miranda, 313
Mirriam, 11
Mishan, 293
Misrahi, 314
Mitchi, 314
Mitrani, 290
Mizrahi, 273, 275, 289, 290, 293, 295, 314
Mizraim, 293
Mizraji, 293
Moati, 295
Moatti, 293
Modena, 293
Modiano, 314
Modigliani, 293
Modigliano, 293
Modiliano, 295
Modon, 293, 295
Moha, 293
Moise, 293
Moises, 293
Mokata, 314
Molco, 295
Molho, 290, 293, 295, 314
Molhov, 290
Molina, 295
Moljo, 293

Monina, 314
Monsano, 293
Monsanto, 293
Monsino, 293
Monsonego, 288
Montagnana, 293
Montagu, 293
Montalto, 293
Montefiore, 203, 273, 293, 295
Montefioree, 293
Montefiori, 293
Montekio, 314
Montillia, 295
Morais, 293
Morban, 293
Mordechai, 57, 314
Mordejay, 293
Mordoh, 314
Morea, 314
Moreira, 287
Moreno, 273, 288, 295
Moresco, 293
Morillo, Miguel de, 127
MorJose, 287
Moron, 293, 295
Morpourgo, 295
Morpugo, 295
Morpurgo, 293
Mortara, 293
Morteira, 293
Moryoussef, 288
Moscati, 280
Moscato, 293
Moscona, 290
Mosconi, 293
Moses, 293
Moshe, 289, 290, 293, 314
Moshe, Daoud, 308
Moshon, 314
Moskoni, 293
Mosseri, 203, 289
Most, Salomon, 306
Mourad, 289
Mousky, 289
Moussa, 289, 314
Moyal, 288, 293
Mozesh, 293
Mreien, 288
Mrezhen, 293

Muatti, 293
Mucznik, 287
Muginstein, 287
Muiz, 293
Muller, 287
Munk, 293
Munoz, 293
Murad, 293
Murcian, 51
Musa, 293
Musafia, 293
Musafia, Aron, 48
Mustchi, Nico, 306
Myara, 288
Myers, 264, 265
Naar, Salomon, 48
Nabaro, 273
Naccache, 295
Nadjara, 293
Nadler, 289
Nadzbran, 293
Nadzhar, 293
Nadzhara, 293
Nafusi, 293
Nagrela
 Joseph, 42
 Samuel ben Josepf Halevi ibn, 42
Nahama, 293
Nahman, 265, 273, 293, 314
Nahmany, 288
Nahmias, 48, 51, 288, 289, 314
Nahnias, 290
Nahon, 51, 273, 287, 288, 293, 295
Nahori, 288
Nahoum, 314
Nahoum Effendi, 293
Nahum, 289, 293, 295
Nahum Hamarabi, 37
Najar, 295
Najmuli, 293
Nakawa-Elnacave, 293
Naki, 314
Namias, 287, 295
Naphtali, Abraham, 308
Nar/Naar, 314
Narboni, 295
Nardeya, 290

Narro, 293
Nasi, 293
Nassi, 292
Nassi, Nessim, 307
Nata, 293
Nataf, 295
Natan, 290, 293
Nathan, 287
Navaro, 273
Navarra, 293
Navarro, 293, 314
Navon, 290, 293
Nayas, 293
Nedebo, 293
Nedivot, 293
Nefoussi, 314
Negrin, 314
Nehama, 314
Nehemias, 293
Nehemias, Josue, 48
Neria, 293
Netanel, 293
Netira, 293
Nezri, 288
Nicanor, 293
Nicholas, 293
Nidam, 288
Niego, 290
Nieto, 293
Nifoci, 293
Nimir, 293
Ninio, 290
Ninyo, 290
Nissim, 293, 314
Noah, 293
Nono, 293
Noraim, 293
Nounil, 295
Novecks, 289
Nunes, 48, 295
Nunes (de Pina), 48
Nunes De Mattos, 293
Nunes Wais, 293
Nunes-Vais, 295
Nunez, 293
Nunez De Silva, 293
Nunez-Cardoso, 293
Nunez-Carvalho, 293
Obadia, 51, 243, 287, 288, 295

Obadiah, 70, 273
Obadya, 273
Obana, 295
Ohana, 287, 288
O'Hana, 273
Ohanna, 273, 289
Ohayon, 274, 288
Ohnouna, 288
Oiknine, 274, 275
Oliel, 288
Olivares, 314
Oliveira, 287
Oliver, 290
Olmo, 293
Omar, 293
Omara, Sultan, 308
Orabuena, 293
Oreja, 314
Orsani, 293
Ortasse, 289
Orvieto, 293
Ossona, 295
Ossuna, 293
Ottolenghi, 265, 293
Ouaiche, 295
Ouaknin, 274
Ouaknine, 289
Ouakrat, 289
Ouanounou, 289
Ouazana, 289
Ouri, 314
Ouriel, 314
Outmezguin, 289
Ouyoussef, 288
Ouziel, 275, 289, 314
Ovadia, 273, 293, 314
Ovadia De Bertinoro, 293
Ovadia, prophet, 3
Ovadya, 290
Oz, 293
Oziel, 275
Ozmo, 293
Pachariel, 314
Pacheco, 293
Pacifico, 287, 293
Padilla, 293
Pakuda, 293
Palache, 293
Paladino, 314

Palaggi, 293
Palatgi, 295
Paligi, 295
Pallache, 287, 289
Palma, 295
Palombo, 289
Paltero, 295
Paltigi, 295
Pambuk, 292
Pandjuro, 290
Panigel, 290, 293
Panizhel, 290
Pansir, 295
Pansiri, 295
Paparo, 290
Paparrabalos, 293Papo, 290
Papouchado, 314
Pardo, 290, 293, 314
Pardov, 290
Paredes, 293
Parente, 314
Pariente, 287, 289, 293, 295
Parienti, 295
Pas, 295
Pas, Antonio Sanches de, 48
Pasanno, 295
Passi, 314
Patish, 274
Pavoncello, 295
Pejiel, 293
Pelossof, 314
Penhas, 290
Penso, 293
Penso Mendes, 293
Perahia, 293, 314
Pereira, 293, 314
Pereira family, Holland, 46
Perera, 75, 290. *See also* Perriera
Peres, 295
Perets, 295
Peretz, 290
Perez, 34, 51, 70, 75, 274, 289, 293, 314
Perfet, 293
Pergola, 293
Perreira, 274. *See also* Perera
Pessah, 314
Pesso, 314
Pezaro, Salomon, 307

Piade, 293
Piatelli, 293
Picciotto, 280
Pichi, 314
Pichon, 293
Picotta, 233
Pidzhi, 290
Pignero, 295
Pilo, 314
Pilosof, 290
Pimienta, 287, 289
Pincherele, 293
Pinctzu, 290
Pinehas, 293
Pinhas, 314
Pinheiro, 295
Pinheiros, 265
Pinkas, 290
Pinto, 46, 51, 52, 274, 280, 287, 289, 293, 295, 307, 314
Pipano, 314
Piperno, 295
Pirosa, 295
Pisa, 274
Piyade, 290
Piza, 293
Planes, 293
Platero, 295
Polako, 295
Policar, 290, 314
Polikar, 290
Polon, 289
Pontremoli, 289, 293
Porfeta, 314
Portaleone, 293
Porto, 293
Pougi, 295
Prato, 289, 293
Presente, 290
Prezente, 290
Primo, 290, 293
Proops, 293
Pynto, 274
Pyrrhus, 293
Qattawi, 289
Querido, 294
Querub, 287
Quraysh, Yehuda ibn, 37
Raban, 294

Surname Index • 349

Rabi, 274
Rachel, 290, 294
Ragon, 271
Rahabi, 294
Rahamim, 290, 314
Rahaminov, 290
Rajpurkar, 294
Raka, 294
Ramirez, 294
Raphael, 78, 290, 314
Ratsbashi, 294
Ratshabi, 294
Ravena, 294
Ravenna, 294
Razon, 315
Rebibo, 289
Recanati, 294, 315
Refetov, 290
Reggio, 294
Reich, 289
Reino, 273
Remos, 294
Reouven, 315
Reuven, 294
Reuveni, 294
Revah, 289, 315
Reyno, 269
Ribbi, 274
Ribeiro, 294
Riboh, 289
Ricardo, 294
Ricchi, 294
Rieti, 294
Rignano, 295
Rimokh, 289
Risenfeld, 289
Rivca, 290
Roa, 295
Robles, 294
Rodrig, 290
Rodrigues, 294
Rodrigues-Mendes, 294
Rodrigues-Pereire, 294
Rodriguez, 7, 74, 75, 130, 269, 289, 294, 295, 331
Rodriguez-Sanches, 294
Rodriques, 295
Rofe, 274
Roffe, 51, 274, 287

Rogelio, 294
Roha, 315
Romanelli, 294
Romano, 294, 315
Romi, 179
Romy, 289
Ronko, 290
Rophe, 274
Rosales, 274, 315
Rosanes, 290, 294
Rosenfeld, 306, 307
Rosilio, 289
Rossi, 294
Rouach, 289
Rouah, 289
Roubissa, 315
Rousso, 315
Rouvio, 315
Rovigo, 294
Rozales, 274
Ruah, 287
Rubin, 289, 294
Rubio, 294
Rudiac, 290
Ruimy, 289
Russo, 5, 179
Ruti, 289
Rygor, 287
Saada, 289, 295
Saadi, 294, 315
Saadia, 294
Saadiya (*gaon*), 60, 62, 162
Saadoun, 295
Saayas, 315
Saba, 289
Sabag, 274
Sabah, 274, 289
Saban, Yaacoub, 308
Sabath, 287
Sabba, 51
Sabban, 295
Sabban, Esther, 308
Sabor, 294
Sacchetto, 294
Sacerdoti, 274, 294
Sacouto, 295
Sada, 294
Sadaga, 294
Sad-Aldawla, 294

Sadicario, 315
Sadoc, 275
Sadok, 315
Sadoun, 289
Sadox, 275
Safadi, 289
Safadia, 289
Safan, 315
Safir, 294
Safra, 289
Sagdoun, 295
Sagrani, 289
Saguiz, 294
Saieg, 294
Saimen, 294
Sakri, 294
Sala, 294, 295
Salama, 287
Salamias, 315
Salamon, 294
Salamon De Trani, 294
Salamons, 294
Salas, 294
Saleh, 289
Salem, 289, 294, 315
Salgado, 51
Salih, 294
Salmon, 315
Salmona, 306, 315
Salom, 294, 295
Salomon, 294, 307
    website, 265
Saloum, 315
Saltiel, 274, 315. *See also* Sealtiel
Saltillana, 295
Saltoun, 289
Salvador, 294
Salvator, 289
Samama, 294, 295
Samaya, 294
Samlaich, 294
Samokovlio, 294
Samoura, 315
Samson, 294
Samuel, 294
San Martin, Juan de, 127
Sananes, 287, 289
Santa Fe, 18
Santaliana, 295

Santiago, 294
Santob, 76, 274
Santon, 76
Sanu, 294
Saoul, 315
Sapir, 294
Saporta, 289, 315
Saportas, 294
Saraga, 289
Saragga, 287
Saragosti, 294
Saragoussi, 315
Saraval, 294
Sarbia, 295
Sardas, 294
Sarfati, 5, 48, 274, 289, 290, 291, 294, 295, 315
Sarfatti, 292
Sarmad, 294
Sarok, 294
Sarraf, 51
Sarrano, 315
Saruk, 294
Sas Portas, 294
Sason, 290, 294
Sasoon, 294
Sasporta, 294
Sasportas, 294
Sasportas, Isaac, 47
Sasson, 57, 73, 274, 289, 294, 315
Sassoon, 226, 274, 294
Saul, 294
Sayag, 289
Sberro, 295
Scares, 51
Schechter, 289
Schlesinger, 289
Schnur, 290
Schocron, 287
Sciaki, 315
Sciaky, 294
Sealtiel, 280
Sebag, 274, 287, 289
Seban, 289
Sebbag, 264, 265
Sedacca, 294
Sedbon, 295
Sedequias, 294

Sefaradi, 294
Sefas-Alfasi, 294
Sefata, 294
Segal, 287
Segoura, 315
Seliktar, 290
Seloaf, 294
Selouk, 289
Semach, 290
Semach, Jacob, 48
Semah, 295
Semaha, 295
Semaj, 294
Senior, 274, 294
Senor, 274, 315
Senoriu, 294
Senouf, 295
Sento, 274
Sentob, 274
Senyor, 294
Sephiha, 315
Sequerra, 287, 294
Sereni, 294
Sereno, 294
Serequi, 287
Serer, 315
Serero, 274, 289, 315
Serfati, 76, 274, 294
Serfaty, 51, 287
Seror, 294
Seroussi, 289
Serrafe, 287
Serrerosarfaty, 294
Serrulha, 243
Serruya, 51, 243
Seruya, 265, 287
Servadio, 295
Servi, 295
Setbon, 295
Setroug, 295
Settouna, 295
Sevi, 294
Sevilia, 315
Seviliya, 290
Sevillano, 274
Sevy, 294
Sfez, 295
Sforno, 294
Shaban, 315

Shabato, 315
Shabazi, 294
Shabetay, 290, 294, 315
Shabrabak, 294
Shagi, 294
Shahun, 294
Shaki, 315
Shakra, 289
Shakri, 294
Shalajar, 295
Shalazar, 295
Shalom, 47, 275, 294, 295, 315
Shalom-Kujayl, 294
Shaltiel, 12, 48, 70, 102, 274, 294. *See also* Sealtiel
website, 265
Shama, 289, 294
Shami, 315
Shamli, 290
Shaoul, 289, 315
Shapiro, 289
Shaprut, 78
Shaprut, Hasdai ibn, 6, 16, 72
Sharabi, 294, 295
Sharabia, 295
Sharabig, 295
Sharbit, 271
Shaul, 294
Shaulov, 290
Shebokh, 295
Shelemo, 294
Shelomo, 315
Shelush, 294
Shemama, 295
Shemaria, 294
Shemouel, 315
Shemtob, 76, 274
Shenouda, 289
Sherira, 294
Sheshet, 294
Shevah, 315
Shibi, 315
Shimjon, 294
Shimon, 315
Shimoni, 294
Shimshi, 315
Shindook, 294
Shitouvi, 315
Shivilio, 315

Surname Index • 351

Shoel, 316
Shofet, 294
Shoshan, 294
Shoua, 289
Shoulam, 316
Shounina, 316
Shouraqui, 275
Shoushana, 289
Shuraqui, 273, 275
Shushan, 294
Siboani, 289
Siboni, 289, 292, 294
Sicso, 295
Sicsu, 51, 287
Sid, 294
Sides, 316
Sidi, 290, 294
Sidis, 289
Sidun, 294
Sieff, 294
Siesu, 294
Sigmar, 294
Signia, 295
Siksu, 289
Siliera, 294
Silvera, 233, 289, 295
Simaha, 316
Simeon, 294, 295
Simon, 294
Simone-Simha, 294
Simoni, 289
Sinai, 289
Sinauer, 289
Sion, 295, 316
Sira, 295
Sirioti, 316
Siscu, 243
Sisso, 289
Sitri, 295
Slama, 295
Slelatt, 294
Smaja, 295
Smouha, 289
Soberano, 269, 273, 275
Sodicky, 294
Soeira, Manuel Diaz, 48
Sofat, 294
Sofer, 275
Soffer, 275

Soiano, 294
Sokolov, 289
Solal, 295
Solas, 295
Solima, 295
Soliman, 294
Solomon, David, 294
Somej, 294
Somekh, 294
Soncino, 294
Sonino, 295
Sonsine, 295
Sopher, 275
Soref, 290
Soria, 295
Soriano, 179, 275, 289, 294, 306
Sorrulha, 51
Sorruya, 51
Sosportos, 294
Soto, 7, 271, 275, 316
Soudry, 289
Soulam, 294, 316
Soulema, 316
Souraqi, 275
Sousa, Samuel de, 48
Soussan, 289
Soustiel, 316
Souzine, 295
Spinadel, 290
Spinoza, 294, 295
Spinoza, Baruch, 45
Spizzichino, 295
Steinhart, 289
Stora, 294
Strologo, 295
Stulmacher, 289
Suares, 295
Suied, 295
Suissa, 289
Suleiman, 289
Sullam, 294
Sultan, 275, 289
Sunbal, 289, 294
Sussan, 294
Svevo, 294
Tabiana, 294
Tabib, 295
Tabit, 294
Taboh, 316

Tabul, 294
Tadjer, 294
Tadzhes, 290
Tagger, 290
Tagjer, 290
Tagliocozzo, 294
Taieb, 295
Taigan, 295
Taitashak, 294
Talbi, 316
Talvi, 290
Tam, 294
Tamim, 294
Tamim, Dunash ben, 6, 38
Tammam, 289
Tammam, Shalom, 308
Tamman, 289
Tammin, Dunash ben, 158
Tandjir, 275
Tangi, 287
Tangier, 275
Tangui, 289
Tanjir, 275
Tanougi, 295
Tanzir, 275
Tapia, 295
Tapia, Moses, 160
Tapiero, 287, 289
Taragano, 316
Taranto, 275, 290. *See also* Toranto
Taregano, 287
Tarfon, 316
Tartas, 294
Taurel, 287, 294
Tawa, 294
Tawil, 289
Tayb, 294
Tayeb, 294
Tazartes, 316
Tchitchek, 290
Tebol, 270
Teboul, 294
Tedeschi, 295
Tedesco, 5
Tedesqui, 287
Teixeira, 294
Teixeira-Pinto, 294
Templo, 294

Temstet, 289
Termin, 316
Terracini, 294
Terrasina, 294
Testa, 294
Teubal, 294
Tevah, 316
Teveth, 316
Tiano, 316
Tibbon, 294
Tiboli, 294
Timsit, 295
Tisignia, 295
Tito, 295
Tivoli, 294, 295
Tob Elam, 76
Tobali, 289
Tobelem, 287
Tobelom, 51
Tobi, 289
Tobias, 265
Toblem, 289
Toboul, 269
Toledano, 7, 47, 75, 275, 287, 289, 294, 307, 316
website, 265
Toledo, 294
Tolicciano, 295
Tomas, 294
Toranto, 275. *See also* Taranto
Tores, 294
Torjman, 289
Torres, 294, 316
Torres, David, 47
Toubiana, 295
Touro, 264, 265, 294
Touvi, 316
Trabout, 316
Trani, 294
Treves, 294
Trounga, Sultana, 308
Tsadik, 316
Tsahalon, 294
Tsalaj, 294
Tsarefati, 294
Tsemaj, 294
Tsevi, 294
Tsova, 294
Tuati, 287

Tudela, Benjamin of, 16, 70, 165
Tueta, 289
Turetsky, 289
Turqui, 275
Tuval, 289
Uaknin, 275
Ukba, 294
Ulhoa, 294
Urbini, Jacques, 307
Uriah, 294
Usque, 294
Uzan, 294, 295
Uziel, 275, 287, 290, 294
Uzziel, 275
Vadzhar, 294
Vaena, 316
Vaez, 294
Vago, 289
Vais, 295
Valensi, 275, 295, 316
Varicas, 287
Varsano, 290, 316
Vas Dias, 280
Venezia, 290, 316
Veniste, 275
Ventoura, 316
Ventura, 294, 295
Verdugo, 275. *See also* Berdugo
Verga, 294
Vetura, 294
Veyissid, 316
Victoria, 292
Vida, 78
Vidal, 275, 289
Vidas, 76
Vidash, 294
Viegas, 294
Vilariali, 295
Vital, 76, 275, 294, 316
Vitale, 280
Vitalis, 275
Viton, 275
Voltera, 295
Volterra, 294
Vosnali, 316
Wahba, 289
Wahnish, 289
Wahnon, 287

Wais, 289
Wakar, 294
Wakasa, 294
Waknin, 274, 275, 287
Weill, 290
Weinberg, 289
Weinstein, 290
Wizgan, 289
Wizman, 289
Wolf, 289
Wolfinsohn, 287
Yaakov, 294
Yacar, 316
Yacob, 294
Yacoel, 316
Yacoub, 289
Yacum, Esterina, 306
Yafe, 294
Yahia, 294
Yahiani, 316
Yahuda, 294
Yahudi, 294
Yaiche, 295
Yaish, 294
Yajya, 294
Yakar, 294
Yakhia, 295
Yakub, 294
Yana, 294
Yanez, 294
Yarhi, 290
Yatah, 294
Yayez, 294
Yedidia, 294
Yeheskel, 316
Yehia, 295
Yehiel, 294, 316
Yehoshoua, 316
Yehoshua, 294
Yehouda, 316
Yehouda Shelomo, 316
Yehouroun, 316
Yehuda, 294
Yehuda, Shlomo ben, 38
Yejiel, 294
Yekutiel, 294
Yekutiel-Kohen, 294
Yeni, 316
Yermia, 316

Surname Index • 353

Yeroham, 290
Yerouham, 316
Yerushalmi, 290, 294
Yesha, 294
Yeshua, 290
Yetah, 289
Yettah, 289
Yeuda, 294
Yijah, 294
Yishag, 294
Yisjak, 294
Yitsaki, 294
Yitshak, 316
Yitsjak, 294
Yitzak, 294
Ymar, 289
Yoel, 316
Yojay, 294
Yom Tob, 76
Yom Tov, 294
Yomtov, 290, 316
Yona, 289, 290, 294, 316
Yosef, 294
Yoseph, 294, 316
Younes, 295
Youssef Sijilmassi, Judah ben, 37
Yuazari, 290
Yuda, 294

Yuda-Roussillon, 294
Yulzari, 290
Yusef, 294
Zabaro, 289
Zacout, 295
Zacouto, 295
Zacut, 294
Zacuto, 294
Zacutus-Lusitanos, 294
Zadoc, 275
Zadoq, 275
Zafaran, 316
Zafrana, 295
Zafrani, 275, 289
Zafrany, 287
Zaga, Youssef Youda, 308
Zagury, 51, 287, 289
Zahariya, 290
Zahit, 294
Zahula, 294
Zaibi, 295
Zakar, 294, 316
Zakay, 294, 316
Zaken, 294, 295
Zakine, 265
Zaky, 294
Zamero, 289
Zammam, Shalom, 308
Zaoui, 289

Zaraya, 316
Zarefati, 294
Zarfati, 274, 280
Zarka, 295
Zazo, 295
Zazon, 289
Zazoun, 295
Zeevi, 294
Zegbib, 295
Zeghel, Nessim Levy, 308
Zeitoun, 295
Zekri, 289
Zelvi, 294
Zemat, 294
Zennah, 76
Zequi, 294
Zerah, 295
Zerahia, 316
Zerbib, 294
Zhuli, 294
Ziki, 295
Zimra, 289, 294
Zini, 289
Znati, 289
Zonana, 290
Zrihen, 289
Zuta, 294

INDEX

Abraham, patriarch, 12, 38
  meaning of name, 70
  name change, 77
  start of biblical genealogy, 70
adafina, 317
ahl al kitab, 41
al Andalus, 6, 13, 317
Alba, Duke of, 45, 46
alboracos, 18, 317
Albuquerque, Francisco de, 22
Alcaraz, Inquisitional tribunal of, 304
Alfonso VI of Castille, 17
Algeria
  Algerian Jews in Holland, 47
  Alliance Israelite Universelle, 141
  Almohad and Masmuda tribes, 36
  Avotaynu articles on, 113
  Berber population, 35
  changes in place names, 155
  civil records, 152
  France, Jewish records in, 141, 153
  France, Jews who died fighting for, 157
  French citizenship of Jews, 152
  genealogical resources, 152–57
  Jewish cemeteries, 154
  Jewish surnames, 157
  Spanish exiles migration to, 25, 26, 30
aljama, 317
aljamiado, 317
Alliance Israelite Universelle, 50, 153, 189, 290
  Morocco, 35, 50
  North Africa, 67
  Turkey, 66, 67
Almohad, 36, 37, 42
Amsterdam
  Bibliotheca Rosenthaliana, 222

civil registrations, 219
Jewish burials in, 223
municipal archives, *Gemeentearchief*, 220
New Christians in, 28
Sephardim, 46, 47, 64
Spanish exiles flight to, 27
Andalusia
  Christian Andalusia, 26, 33
  common universe with the Maghreb, 29–38, 65
  culture, 16
  Inquisition, 127
  Jewish population, 43
  Jewish trades in, 16
  language, 60, 61
  massacres of Jews, 36
Anshei Sphard, 7
Antwerp
  conversos, 44
  Sephardim, 64
  Spanish exiles flight to, 27
anusim, 18, 25, 64
  descendants, 102
  glossary, 317
  newslist, 102
appelido, 70–80
Arabic, 60–62, 61
  alphabet, 278
  and Hebrew, 16, 29, 42, 68
  Christian Spain, 61
  Egyptian Jews and, 163
  Jewish names, 6, 75, 94
  Maimonides writings in, 60
  months in Arabic script, 108
  Morocco, 34, 35
  Moslem Andalusia, 15
  Moslem Spain, 29, 42, 60, 61
  North Africa, 62
  numbers, 15
  poetry and Hebrew, 6, 15, 37
  scripts, 58, 62, 182
  Spanish exiles, 64, 65
  Spanish words of Arabic origin, 62
  Valencia, 61

Aracena, Inquisitional tribunal of, 304
Aragon, kingdom of, 19, 134
  and Sicily, 203
  archives, 130
  Inquisition, 127
archives
  Alliance Israelite Universelle (Paris), 141
  Archives Diplomatiques de Nantes, 140
  Archivio Centrale dello Stato, Rome, 206
  Archivo de La Real Audiencia de Zaragoza (Spain), 130
  Archivo Diocesano de Cuenca (Spain), 129
  Archivo General de Indias, 132–33
  Archivo General de la Nacion (Mexico City), 131
  Archivo General deSimancas (Spain), 129
  Holland, 219–23
  Italy, 204
  Macedonian State Archives, 196
  Spain, Church archives, 134
  Spain, Ministerio de Cultura ID card, 134
  Spain, Notarial records, 133
  Turkish Imperial Archives, 180, 196
Argentina, 241–42
  cemeteries, 241
  civil records *Registro Civil*, 242
ARI. *See* Luria
Arian Christianity, 317
Aristotle, 15
Arzilla (Morocco), 30
Asfalou (Morocco), 30
Ashkenazim, 194
  absorbed into Sephardim, 5, 6
  definition, 5, 317
  Egypt, 164, 165

Surname Index • 355

genealogy, xv
Holland, 46, 221
names, 75, 77, 92, 93
percentage of Jewish
    population, 12
Sephardic elements in
    Hassidism, 7
Turkey, 5, 178, 179, 182, 184
auto-da-fe, 19, 317
Averroes, 15
Avila, Inquisitional tribunal of,
    304
B.C.E.. *See also* C.E.
B.C.E., definition, 317
Babylonia, 53-57, 54, 72, 228
    Cyrus, conquest by, 78
    geonim *responsa*, 54
    Jewish exilarch, 55
    Jewish power structures, 55
    Judah, Benjamin and Levy
        tribes, 70
    return of Jewish exiles from,
        31, 71
    Sherira (gaon), 57
    Talmudic academies, 38, 53-
        57, 72
Badis, king of Granada, 42
Baghdad, 14, 15
    Abbassid caliphate, 55, 228
    Jewish governors, 229
    Jewish merchants, 55
    street of booksellers, 61
    talmudic academies, 55
Balaguer, Inquisitional tribunal
    of, 304
Balearic islands, 21
Barcelona
    archives, 130
    Inquisitional tribunal of, 304
    Jews, 25
    takkanot (rabbinic
        ordinances), 30
Bayonne (France), *conversos*, 44
Beinart, 27
Belalcazar, Inquisitional tribunal
    of, 304
Belem (Amazon), 50, 51
Ben Veniste. *See also* Benveniste
Ben Zvi Institute, Jerusalem,
    159, 182
Benjamin of Tudela, 193

Ben-Malka. *See also* Malka
Berbers, 37, 68
    and Jews, 35
    dialects, 35, 68
    ibn Khaldun's writings
        about, 35
    invading Spain, 13
    Jewish trade with, 68
    judaized, 35
    legends about Jews, 32
    Libya, 35
    Marinid tribe, 37
    Morocco, 35
    names among Jews, 76
    Philistines, 30
    Sanhaja tribe, 36
    south Morocco, 34, 35
    tribal struggles, 36
    Tunisia, 35
    Zenata tribe, 37
Beth Hatefutsoth Museum (Tel
    Aviv), 189
Beth Hatefutsoth Museum, Tel
    Aviv, 192, 223
Bevis Marks synagogue, 47
bled el makhzen, 149, 318
bled el siba, 149, 317
B'nai B'rith
    Egypt, 162, 164, 165, 167
    Sudan, 173
Boniface XIII, pope, 18
Bordeaux (France), *conversos*, 44
Brazil, 242-44
    congregation Ben Zur, 242
    congregation Magen
        Abraham (Mauricia), 242
    conversos in, 51
    Moroccan Jews, 243
    Pernambuco, 242
Brussels, *conversos*, 44
Bulgaria, 187-98
    American Sephardic
        Federation holdings, 189
    anti-Semitism, 188
    Jewish archives, 189
    names of Jews, 188
    Peshev, 188
    Soviet occupation, 188
    Suggested Reading, 197
Burgos, Inquisitional tribunal of,
    304

Byzantium, 32
C.E.. *See also* B.C.E.
C.E., definition, 317
Calahorra, Inquisitional tribunal
    of, 304
Calatayud, Inquisitional
    tribunal of, 304
calendars, 107-10
    conversion tools, 109-10
    Egypt, 109
    Gregorian, 108
    Hijra (Moslem), 108
    Islamic civil, 109
    Jewish, 108
    Julian, 107
    Ottoman civil, 108
    Turkey, 181
Caribbean, 235-40
    Suggested Reading. *See*
Caro, Rabbi Yosef, 4
Carthaginians, 35
Casa de la Contratacion, Seville,
    133
Casablanca (Morocco), 51, 139
Castile, kingdom of, 19
    Inquisition, 127
    Jews flight from, 25
    language, 63
Catalunya, 25
Catholicism
    descendants of Jews in
        Amazon, 51
    Jewish conversion to, 7, 13,
        27, 43, 45, 93
    Jews contaminating, 20
    names of Sephardic
        converts, 75
    Visigoths, 13
cemeteries
    Alexandria (Egypt), 168
    Algeria, 155
    Amazon, Peruvian, 240
    Argentina, 241
    Belem (Amazonia), 50
    Curaçao, 235, 236, 239, 258
    Egypt, 162, 168, 305, 306, 307
    England, 321
    Holland, 220, 223, 260
    Iquitos (Peru), 51
    Iran, 231
    Jerusalem, 175

356 • *Sephardic Genealogy: Discovering Your Sephardic Ancestors and Their World*

Karaite, 168
Khartoum (Sudan), 175
Morocco, 121, 122, 144, 150
Nevis, 115, 259
Persia, 231
Rhodes, 258
Salonica (Greece), 326
Sophia (Bulgaria), 290
Turkey, 184
Venice, 328
census
  Holland, 220
  Italy, 206
  Izmir, 183
  Leghorn (Livorno), 207, 209
  Martinique, 239
  Montefiore (Egypt), 169
  Palestine (Ottoman), 297
  Turkey, 184
  United States, 249, 264
Central Archives for the History of the Jewish People (Jerusalem), 139, 152, 160, 183, 196, 224, 242, 261
Ceuta (Morocco), 29, 142
Church of Jesus Christ of Latter-day Saints, 135, 153, 154, 190, 204, 206, 237, 249, 263
Ciudad Real, Inquisitional tribunal of, 304
Columbus, 20, 22, 61
  possible crypto-Jew, 20
Constantinople, 26, 178, 179, 180. *See also* Istanbul
conversos, 34, 64, 134, 202, 235
  Brazil, 51
  descendants of, 102
  Holland, 45
  Inquisition, 34
  judaizing, 20
  limpieza de sangre, 21
  names of, 74, 75
  New World, 20, 21, 22
  Portugal, 28, 44
  pre-expulsion flight, 25
  records, 93
  satired as *alboracos*, 18
  Spain, 18, 19, 27, 28
  Spanish nobility, 19
Cordoba
  and Fez, 29

Inquisition, 26, 128, 304
Jewish flight to the caliphate, 25
library, 15
Council of Toledo, 29, 32
Cromwell, 45
crypto-Jews, 18, 21, 27, 44, 317.
  See also conversos
  Argentina, 44
  Brazil, 44
  Colombia, 44
  descendants of, 102
  New World, 22
  southwestern United States, 44
Cuenca, Inquisitional tribunal of, 304
Curaçao, 47, 235
  and other Sephardic communities, 236
  cemetery, 235
  Mikve Israel synagogue, 235
  Neve Shalom synagogue, 235
Damanhour (Egypt), cemetery, 307
Damascus, 14
Danon. *was* Dondon-Danon
darb el harb, 40
darb el Islam, 40
darb el salah, 40
David, king. *See* King David
de Fonseca. *See also* Fonseca
Debdou (Morocco), 30
defter (Turkish register), 317
dhimmis (protected people), 41, 42, 179, 230
diaspora, Spanish, 25–28
Djidio. *See* Judeo-Spanish
Dominicans, 19
Durango, Inquisitional tribunal of, 304
Dutch East India Company, 47
Dutch West India Company, 47, 246
East India Company. *See* Dutch East India Company
Eastern Europe, 5
  Spanish exiles flight to, 27
Egypt, 71, 162–72
  Alliance Israelite Universelle, 141

and Kairouan, 158
and Sudan, 173
Ashkenazim in, 164
B'nai B'rith, 162, 164, 165
calendar, 109
cemeteries, 168, 305–17
chief rabbinates, 165
civil records, 169
Egyptian Jewish diaspora, 169
foreign citizenship of Jews, 163
historical society, 102
Iberian exiles to, 163
Jewish communities, 163, 167
Jewish migration to Spain, 6, 16
Jewish records, 166
Karaites, 164
Maimonides, 33
migration from the Ottoman Empire, 163
Montefiore census, 169
Ottoman archives, 297
Sicilian Jews, 203
suggested reading, 170
tombstone inscriptions, 305
vital records, 166
vital records outside Egypt, 170
El Cid, Rodrigo Diaz de Vivar, 17
El Fasi. *See also* Alfasi
el Moro. See Tariq ibn Ziyad
England, 108, 142, 203
  Moroccan Jews, 50
  Sephardim, 45, 48, 64, 70
  Sudan Jews, 173
Esnoga synagogue, Amsterdam, 47
Estella, Inquisitional tribunal of, 304
Expulsion Edict, 20, 25, 26, 43
Expulsion from Portugal, 21
Ferarra Bible, 63
Ferdinand di Medici, 159
Ferdinand of Aragon, 19, 21, 33
  Inquisition, 127
Ferrer, 18

Index • 357

Fez (Morocco), 24, 30, 33, 37, 38, 39, 139
  and Cordoba, 29
France, 30
  Algerian records, 152
  antisemitism, 17, 68
  Hebrew, 59
  Inquisition, 126
  Moroccan Jews, 141, 142
  Spanish exiles, 20, 30, 43, 44
  Tunisian Jews, 159
Frankfurt, Spanish exiles flight to, 27
French (language), 67–68
Gaon, Talmudic Academy, 56
Genealogical research
  and history, xviii, 89
  calendars and conversion tools, 107–10
  computers and the Internet, 100–103, 253–66
  country resources. *See* individual countries
  differences between Ashkenazic and Sephardic, 91–95
  documenting sources, 97
  ethics, 90
  newslists, 101
  onomastics (names), 70–80, 269–75. *See also* Index of Persons
  periodicals, 111–24
  software, 104
  websites, 253–66. *See* individual countries
geniza, 14, 16, 32, 54, 317
  Cairo, 53, 54, 57, 165
  definition of, 32
geonim
  Saadiya, 62, 162
Geonim, 53–57
Germany, 5
Gerona
  Inquisitional tribunal of, 304
  Jewish population, 25
ghetto, 317
Gibraltar, 13, 33, 49, 317
Golden Age of Sephardic Jews, 14

Maghreb connection, 6, 29, 37
  names and language, 6
Granada, 29
  Badis, king of, 42
  Catholic conquest of, 43
  conquest of, 19, 20
  Garnatat al Yahud, 42
  Inquisition, 127, 128, 304
  library, 61
  Moroccan Jews, 29, 36
  Spanish Jews flight to, 25
Greece, 64, 65
  ancient philosophers, 15, 42, 58
  Jewish translations of Greek classics, 15
  Levanic Hebrew, 59
  Romaniot Jews, 5
  websites, 257
Gregory IX, pope, 127
Gregory VII, pope, 17
Guadalupe, Inquisitional tribunal of, 304
hakham, 317
Hakitia, 34, 63, 65. *See* Judeo-Spanish
haradj tax on dhimmis, 41
harat al barabra, 318
harat al yahud, 318
Harun al Rashid, 225
Hebrew, 58–60
  calendar, 108
  grammar, 16, 37
  Jewish names, 6
  Moors, 15
  poetry, 6, 15, 37
  pronounciations, 7
  scripts, 59
  similarities to Arabic, 62
  translations from Greek and Arabic documents, 62
hidalgo, 318
Hispania, 13
Holland
  alias names, 48
  Amsterdam rabbinical school archives, 221
  Amsterdam Sephardic congregation names, 221
  archives, 219–23

Ashkenazim, 46
Ashkenazim in, 47
Beth Haim Cemetery, 223
Bibliotheca Rosenthaliana, 220, 222, 223
Centraal Bureau voor Genealogie (Central Bureau of Genealogy), 219, 221, 222
conversos, 44, 45
Curaçao, 235
Dutch East India company, 222
Dutch West India company, 222
Gemeentearchief (city archives), 219, 220
genealogical records, 92
gezinskaarten (family record cards), 219
Hebrew printing press, 223
Holocaust, 91
Institute of War Documentation, 220, 222
Jewish records, 220
Jewish restrictions in, 46
language of Sephardim, 6
Napoleon and, 46, 47
Nazis in, 48
Ouderkerk cemetery, 220, 223
persoonskaarten (personal record cards), 219
Protestants, 46
rabbinate, 45
Royal Dutch Society for Genealogy and Heraldry, 222
Sephardim, 22, 43–48, 44, 47, 64, 219–24
  trading decline, 47
Trouwen in Mokum, 221
Tunisian Jews, 161
Iberia
  arrival of Jews, 11
  flight of Jews, 63
  Moors, 13, 14
  myths about Sephardic history, 25, 178
  North African trade, 25
  pre-expulsion exiles from, 65
  Visigoths, 13

ibn Khaldun, historian, 35, 36
Ifrane (Morocco), 30, 31, 32
   cemetery in, 32
Imazigh. See Berber
India, Iraqi and Syrian Jews, 226
Inquisition, 19, 20, 21, 126, 127, 129
   Americas, 44
   Andalusia, 127
   Aragon, 127
   Cartagena, 132
   Castille, 127
   Ciudad Real, 127
   Cordoba, 127, 128
   Cuenca, 128
   Dominicans, 126
   France, 126
   Granada, 127, 128
   Jewish family trees, 48
   Llerena, 128
   Logorno, 128
   Murcia, 129
   New Granada, 131
   New World, 131
   records, 90, 93, 128
   Rome, 126
   Santiago, 128
   Seville, 127, 128
   Spain, 34, 128
   Toledo, 127, 128, 129
   Torquemada, Grand Inquisitor, 127
   tribunals in Spain, 304
   tribunals in the New World, 131
   Valencia, 128
   Valladolid, 128
   Zaragoza, 128
Iran. *See* Persia
Iraq
   bedel-il-askar tax, 227
   Harun al Rashid, 225
   Jews, 225–27
   settlements in India, 226
   zionism, 225
Isabella, queen of Spain, 19, 20, 21
Islam's view of the world, 40
   ahl al kitab (people of the book), 41

darb el harb (sphere of war), 40
darb el Islam (sphere of Islam), 40
darb el salah (sphere of peace), 40
dhimmis (protected people), 41
haradj tax on Jews, 41
jiziya tax on Jews, 41
Pact of Omar, 41
Ismailia (Egypt)
   cemetery, 306
Istanbul, 26, 64, 141, 177, 178, 179, 184
   Jewish records, 183
   Sicilian Jews, 203
Italy, 68, 202–18
   ancestral towns, 205
   archives, 204
   archivi communale, 204, 205
   archivi di stato, 204
   Ashkenazim and the Palestinian tradition, 7, 53
   census, 206
   ghetto, 202
   Jewish cemeteries, 207
   Jewish communities in Rome, 202
   Jewish records, 207
   Maghreb Jews, 142, 203
   Napoleon Bonaparte, 205
   notarial records, 207
   Papal States, 202
   regions and provinces, 206, 211, 212
   Research strategies, 204
   Sephardim and Ashkenazim, 74, 203
   Sicily, 60, 203
   Spanish exiles flight to, 21, 26, 27, 34, 43, 44
   stato civile, 204, 205, 208
   Venice, 202
   vital records, 206
Jaen, Inquisitional tribunal of, 304
Jaketia. *See* Haketia
Jamaica, 236–38
   synagogue records, 236
   tombstone inscriptions, 237

Jerez, Inquisitional tribunal of, 304
Jeronimo de la Santa Fe (Joshua Harlorki), 18
Jerusalem, 6, 11, 26, 70, 242, 325
   destruction of first Temple, 72
jiziya tax on dhimmis, 41
Joao II, king of Portugal, 20
judaizing, 19, 318
Judeo-Arabic
   and Hebrew, 59
   definition, 62
   Morocco, 35
   North Africa, 59, 62
   replaced by French, 67
Judeo-Berber, 68
Judeo-Spanish, 4, 62–67, 63. *See also* Ladino
   Ladino, 63
   replaced by French, 67
   website, 257
   written in Hebrew script, 59
juderia, 318
Kafr El Zayat (Egypt), cemetery, 308
Kairouan, 6, 158
Kamen, 27
Karaites, 55, 164, 229, 329
   Egypt, 164
   Poland, 164
ketubah, 84, 88, 93, 122, 123, 143, 144, 145, 159, 160, 165, 166, 174, 182, 256, 281, 295, 318
Khaldun. *See* Ibn Khaldun
King David, 30, 55, 70, 77
   descent from, 12, 55, 76
Koran, 15, 41
Ladino, 34, 62, 64, 65, 67, 68, 112. *See also* Judeo-Spanish. *See also* Judeo-Spanish
   Judeo-Spanish, 63
languages
   Arabic, 60–62
   French, 67
   Judeo-Berber, 68
   Judeo-Spanish, 62–67
   Ladino, 62
Larrache (Morocco), 30
Las Palmas, Inquisitional tribunal of, 304

Index • 359

Leghorn (Livorno) Sephardic community, 159
Leon, Inquisitional tribunal of, 304
Lerida, Inquisitional tribunal of, 304
limpeza de sangue, 318
limpieza de sangre, 21, 133, 318
Lisbon, 21, 26
   forced conversions of Jews, 44
Llerena, Inquisitional tribunal of, 304
Logroño, Inquisitional tribunal of, 304
London, 33, 167, 331
Lucena (Spain), 29, 36
Luria, rabbi Isaac, 7
Machivelli's Prince, 19
Madrid, Inquisitional tribunal of, 304
Maghreb
   Berbers, 35
   common cultural universe with Andalusia, 65
   conversos, 34
   early Jewish settlement, 30
   maaravic Hebrew script, 59
   Spanish exiles, 6
Maimonides, 15, 16, 25, 33, 163
   Guide to the perplexed, 15
   Letter on Apostasy, 33, 40
   Mishneh Torah, 29
   writing in Arabic, 29, 60
Majorca, 22, 25, 30, 130, 155
Malca. *See also* Malka
Manaus (Amazon), 51
Manuel I, king of Portugal, 21
Marco Polo, 16
marranos, 318. See conversos
Massa (Morocco), 30
Mauritania, 31
Medina Campo, Inquisitional tribunal of, 304
Meknes (Morocco), 30, 139, 144
Melilla (Morocco), 142
mellah, 318
millet, 34, 66, 67, 177
minhag sepharad, 7
Mishneh Torah, 29, 33
Mogador (Morocco), 51, 139

Mohammad, prophet, 18, 39, 41, 108
Monzon, Inquisitional tribunal of, 304
Moors, 13, 14, 15, 16, 17, 19, 29, 33, 42
   definition, 318
   Granada, 43
   Jews in army that invaded Spain, 13, 29
   Moslem Spain, 6
morisco, 318
Morocco, 31, 32, 36
   Alfasi, rabbi Isaac, 38
   Alliance Israelite Universelle, 141
   Amazon, 51
   Amazon, migration to, 22, 49-51
   and Spain, 14, 25, 37
   Andalusia, common culture, 29-38
   Archives Diplomatiques de Nantes, 140
   Atlas mountains, 30, 31, 32, 34
   Jews, 35, 36
   Berber dialects, 68
   Berber population, 35
   Casablanca Beth Din resources, 143
   cemeteries, 144
   civil registrations, 143
   collection of ancient manuscripts, 142
   economy, 50
   et sofer, 147
   foreign consulates, 142
   French citizenship, 141
   genealogical records, 139-51
   hakitia, 64, 65
   Holland, 47
   Jewish kingdoms, 31
   Jewish migration patterns, 49
   Jewish migration to Spain, 6, 16
   Jewish names, 146
   Jews, 30, 31, 36, 37, 49, 70, 139, 142

   Jews emmigrating to Algeria, 152
   linguistic groups, 34
   notarial records (France), 141
   population exchanges with Spain, 32
   Saadian Sharifs, 37
   scholars and Spain, 16
   Spanish enclave, 34
   Spanish exiles, 13, 25, 26, 30, 33, 43, 65
   Spanish traditions, 66
   Tangier, 6
   Tetuan, 6
   tribe of Ephraim in, 31
Moslem Spain, 61, 63, 64
mozarab, 15, 318
Murcia, Inquisitional tribunal of, 304
names. *See also* Sephardim, names
   Bulgaria, 188
   Christian, or babtismal, 73
   converso, 74
   descriptive, 73
   patronymics, 75
   Roman, 73
   Spanish, 74
Napoleon
   adoption of surnames, 73
   emancipation of Jews, 39, 68
   Holland, 46
   Italy, 205
Nazis, 26, 67, 219
   and Karaites, 164
Nebuchadnezzar, 31, 55, 72, 225, 228
Netanyahu, 27
Netherlands. *See* Holland
Netherlands, Spanish, 45
New Christians, 25, 27, 28
New World
   Columbus and *conversos*, 20
   conversos, 22
   Inquisition, 132
   Moroccan Jews, 50, 51
   Spanish exiles flight to, 27
Newport, 47
niño santo, 20
nombre, 70-80

North Africa
  Alliance Israelite
    Universelle, 67, 154
  French language, 68
  Hebrew script, 59
  Italian ancestry, 203, 204
  Majorcan Jews, 30
  population exchanges with
    Spain, 6, 11, 43
  Sephardim, 4, 44
  Spanish enclaves, 142
  Spanish exiles, 6, 20, 21, 25,
    26, 43, 44, 65
  Talmudic academies, 53
Osma, Inquisitional tribunal of,
  304
Osmanlica, 58, 61, 181, 182
Ottoman Empire
  Ashkenazim, 6
  decline, 179
  Jewish haven, 177
  legislation, 176
  organization, 177
  Osmanli dynasty, 176
  Romaniot Jews, 178
  Sephardim, 44, 178, 179
  Spanish exiles, 21, 26, 27, 43,
    62
Pact of Omar, 41, 42, 229
Palencia, Inquisitional tribunal
  of, 304
Palestine, Spanish exiles to, 43
Palma, Inquisitional tribunal of,
  304
Pamplona, Inquisitional
  tribunal of, 304
Papal states, 27
paper-making, 15
Paris
  conversos, 44
  Department of Foreign
    Affairs archives, 140
passenger lists
  Argentina, 241, 242
  England, 115
  New York, 92, 263
  Seville, 126, 132-33
  United States, 91
Perez family of Morocco, 34
Periodicals, 111
Persia, 228-31

Alliance Israelite
  Universelle in, 230
archives, 231
cemeteries, 231
Cyrus II, 228
genealogical resources, 231
Jewish oppression, 229
Jews of Babylonia, 228
Persian calendar, 109, 182
Persian Jews, 230
Shiites, 229
Shiraz, 229
suggested reading, 231
Umayyad caliphate, 228
Philistines, 30
Phoenicians, 31, 62, 158
plague, black, 17
Plasencia, Inquisitional tribunal
  of, 304
Plato, 15
Poland, 5, 16
  Spanish exiles flight to, 27
Port Said (Egypt), cemetery, 305
Portugal, 47, 68, 183
  Brazil, 44
  conversos, 22, 28, 44, 46
  exploration journeys, 22
  expulsion of Jews, 21, 30
  forced conversions, 18, 21
  Hebrew script, 59
  Inquisition, 21, 27
  Jewish history, 11-25
  Jewish population, 43
  Jewish ship navigators, 22
  migration to Italy, 202
  Moroccan Jews, 142
  Sephardim in, 45
  Spanish exiles, 20, 26, 43
Querido. *See also* Habib
Rabat (Morocco), 30, 51
Rashi script, 174
Reccared, 13
reconciliado, 318
relajado, 318
relapsos, 45
Renaissance, European
  sources in Moslem Spain,
  15, 58
responsa, 318

Rhodes, 64, 113, 122, 124, 171,
  178. *See also* bibliography
  section
  cemetery, 258
  Internet, 257
Rodrigo, 13, 14
romancero, 34
Romaniot (Greek) Jews, 5, 318
Romaniot Jews, 6, 34, 119, 178,
  179, 187
Romans, *rumi*, 109
Rome, Sephardim, 27
Romniot Jews, 194
Safed, 27
Safi (Morocco), 30, 141, 144
Salamanca, Inquisitional
  tribunal of, 304
Sale (Morocco), 30, 144
Salonica, 26, 64, 176, 178, 193-98
  Genealogical resources, 196-
    97
  Holocaust, 91
  Jewish communities, 193
  Macedonian State Archives,
    196
  Sicilian Jews, 203
  Suggested Reading, 197
  Synagogues, 194-95
  Turkish Imperial Archives,
    196
San Tome, 26
sanbenito, 20, 318
sancak, 318
Santiago, Inquisitional tribunal
  of, 304
scripts
  Arabic, 62
  Ashkenazi Hebrew cursive,
    59
  Italian, 208
  Itallik Hebrew, 59
  Levanic Hebrew, 59
  Maaravic Hebrew, 59
  mashait Hebrew, 60
  Parsic Hebrew, 59
  Rashi script, 59
  Sephardic Hebrew, 59, 69
  Zarfatic Hebrew, 59, 60
sefarad, 3, 318
sefer toledot, 71, 76
sefer yohasin, 71, 76

Sefrou (Morocco), 139
Segovia, Inquisitional tribunal of, 304
Sephardim, 26, 47, 68, 269
   absorption of non-Sephardim, 5
   aliases of Dutch Sephardim, 48
   Amazon, 49-51
   American Sephardic Federation, 4
   articles from periodicals, 111
   Babylonian roots, 53
   Bension collection of documents, 142
   communities in exile, 43
   cursive Hebrew script, 59
   definition, 3, 4
   documents, 58
   evolution of Sephardic names, 70-80
   exiles, 178
   family websites, 264
   geonim, 56
   Golden Age in Spain, 29
   Hebrew Immigrant Aid Society records, 250
   Hebrew script, 69
   Holland, 22, 45
   Italian Jews, 203
   ketubot, 93
   languages, 58-69
      aljamiado in Aguilar de Campóo, 59
      Arabic, 60-62
      French, 67-68
      Hebrew, 58-60
      Judeo-Spanish, 62-67
      Ladino, 62-67
   migration to Holland, 44
   migration to United States, 91
   names, 5, 46, 70-80, 70, 76, 78, 92, 269-75, 278-79, 278-79
   names of Babylonian origin, 57
   naming conventions, 77, 93
   naming patterns, 76
   percentage of Jewish population, 12
   Persia, 41
   religious differences with Ashkenazim, 7
   Rome, 27
   the Ottoman Empire, 42
   the United States, 65
   Turkey, 42
   under Islamic rule, 39-42, 39-42
   websites, 255
   World Sephardic Federation, 173
   writers, 67
Sepher Yohasin, 72
Seville, 18, 19, 26, 33, 70
   ArchivoGeneral de Indias, 93
   Inquisitional tribunal of, 304
Sfard, 7
Shulchan Arukh, 4, 7
Sicily, Jewish languages in, 60
Siguenza, Inquisitional tribunal of, 304
sofer, 318
Solitreo, 59, 64, 183
South America
   Spanish exiles, 44
Spain
   and the Maghreb, 29-38
   archives for Aragon, 126
   archives for Barcelona, 126
   archives for Castille, 126
   Archivio General de Indias in Seville, 126
   Christian, 6, 16
   genealogical records, 126-38
   Jewish history, 11-25
   Jewish population, 43
   Jews in pre-Muslim Spain, 13
   Moslem Granada, 42
   Moslem Spain, 38, 41, 42, 126
Spaniol. See Judeo-Spanish
Spaniolit. See Judeo-Spanish
Spinoza, 27
St. Eustatatia, 236
St. Martin, 235
stato civile, 318
Sudan
   Jewish archives of, 174
   Jews in, 173-75
Suez (Egypt), cemetery, 306
synagogues
   Amazon, 50
   Bevis Marks, London, 47
   Bulgaria, 187
   Caribbean, 322
   Curaçao, 47, 235
   Egypt, 162, 164, 165, 167, 168, 173
   Eschel Abraham, 50
   Esnoga in Amsterdam, 47, 260
   geniza, 54
   Jamaica, 236
   Karaite, 164
   Morocco, 144
   N.Y.C., 4, 251
   records, 91, 143
   Romaniot in Turkey, 178
   Salonica, 194-95
   South America, 322
   Spain, 20
   Sudan, 173
   Touro, Newport, Rhode Island, 47, 246
   Tunisia, 158
   Turkey, 182
   Virgin Islands, U.S., 237
Syria
   Aleppo, Jews in, 232, 233
   Archives Diplomatiques de Nantes, 233
   Damascus, Jews in, 203, 233
   Farhi family, 232
   genealogical resources, 232
   history, 232
   Jews in, 232-34
   Kamishli, 233
   Suggested Reading, 233
Tafilalt, 31
Talmud, 318
Talmudic academy
   Andalusia, 53
   Babylonia, 53, 55
   North Africa, 53
   Pumbadita, 53, 55, 56, 72
   Sura, 53, 55, 56, 72
Tamgrout (Morocco), 31

Tangier (Morocco), 6, 51, 144
Tantah (Egypt), cemetery, 308
Tariq ibn Ziyad, 13, 14, 32
Tarragona, Inquisitional
  tribunal of, 304
Tarshish, 12
Tazzarine (Morocco), 30
Telouet, 31
Teruel, Inquisitional tribunal of, 304
Tetuan (Morocco), 6, 29, 30, 33, 34, 49, 51, 141, 143, 144
Toledo, 13, 17, 29, 32, 134, 144, 160
  Inquisition, 128, 304
Torah, 318
Torquemada, 19, 127
toshabim, 33, 34
tuansa, 318
Tudela
  Benjamin of, 16
  Inquisitional tribunal of, 304
Tunisia, 26, 141, 158–61
  Berber population, 35
  Grana community, 34, 68, 158, 159, 295, 317
  and Italy, 159
  Jews and foreign protection, 160
  notarial records (France), 141
  Spanish Jews flight to, 30
  Tuansa community, 158, 159, 318
  and France, 159
Turkey, 3, 4, 5, 16, 65, 66, 108, 141, 176–98, 177, 180
  Alliance Israelite Universelle, 67
  Ataturk reforms, 67
  calendar, 181
  Cammondo family, 180
  devlet, vileyet, caza, sancak, 177
  government, 176
  hakham bashi, 177
  Istanbul Jewish records, 183
  Italian ancestry, 204
  Italian Jews, 203
  janissaries, 179, 180
  Jewish records, 182
  Latin alphabet adoption, 181
  Naxos, Duke of, 179
  osmanlica, 181
  research requirements, 180
  Sephardic culture, 179
  Spanish exiles to, 43
  tombstones, 184
  Turkish Imperial Archives, 180
Ummayad, 14
United States
  census records, 249
  Dutch West India company, 246
  genealogical resources, 247–51
  Jewish records, 250
  Jews in, 246–51
  Ladino newspapers, 247
  naturalization records, 248
  New Amsterdam, 246
  Newport, 246
  passenger lists, 249
  Rhode Island, 246
  Sephardic brotherhood organizations, 250
Uthman, Sultan, 176
Valencia, 17, 18, 25, 61
  Inquisition, 128, 304
Valladolid, Inquisitional tribunal of, 304
Venice
  origins of North African and Turkish Jews, 203
  Spanish exiles flight to, 27
vileyet, 318
Virgin Islands, United States, 237–40
Visigoths, 13, 318
  and the Jews, 32
  Catholicism, 13
  conquest of Iberia, 13
  defeat by Moors, 13
  Jews, 14
  name evolution, 73
vital records
  Algeria (in France), 152
  Argentina, 242
  Egypt, 166, 169
  Holland, 220
  Italy, 204–7
  Morocco, 143
  Tunisia, 160
  Turkey, 184
  United States, 247
Volubilis Roman ruins, Morocco, 31
West India Company. *See* Dutch West India Company
Western Europe, 6, 34
William of Orange, 45, 46
Yugoslavia, 190–98
  American Jewish Archives, 193
  Diaspora Museum archives, 192
  Genealogical Resources, 191
  Holocaust, 190
  Jewish Historical Museum of Belgrade, 191
  Ottoman archives, 191
  Red Army Nazi archives (Osobyi), 192, 196
  Suggested Reading, 197
  United States Holocaust Museum archives, 192, 196
  Yad Vashem archives, 191
Zagora (Morocco), 30, 31
Zamosc, Poland, Spanish exiles flight to, 27
Zaragoza, Inquisitional tribunal of, 304

HOUSTON PUBLIC LIBRARY

R01242 77991

```
         ICLAY   GEN
                 929.1
                 08924
                 M251
                 USA
MALKA, JEFFREY S.
    SEPHARDIC GENE-
ALOGY : DISCOVERING
YOUR SEPHARDIC
```